SPORTSMEN
AND
GAMESMEN

SPORTSMEN AND GAMESMEN

JOHN DIZIKES

HOUGHTON MIFFLIN COMPANY BOSTON

1981

Library of Congress Cataloging in Publication Data
Dizikes, John, date
Sportsmen and gamesmen.
Includes bibliographical references and index.
1. Sports — United States — History.   2. Sports —
United States — Biography.   I. Title.
GV583.D59   796.0973   80-17238

ISBN 0-395-27776-0

Printed in the United States of America

S 10 9 8 7 6 5 4 3 2 1

An earlier version of chapter 10 appeared in *The Yale Review,*
Spring 1978. Copyright © 1978 by Yale University.

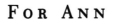

FOR ANN

The true state of every nation
is the state of common life.

Acknowledgments

IN THE NOTES at the end of this volume I have indicated some of the books and newspapers I have used, but there are many more, unnamed and unremembered, that I am obligated to. I am also indebted to the staffs of numerous institutions, of which I can name only a few here: the University Library, Cambridge, England; the Library of Congress; the New Jersey Historical Society; the New York Historical Society; the New York Public Library; the Bancroft Library of the University of California at Berkeley; and the McHenry Library of the University of California at Santa Cruz. I am grateful to the New Jersey Historical Society and to the New York Historical Society for permission to use manuscript materials in their possession. Some of my research was supported by faculty research funds granted by the University of California, Santa Cruz.

A few words of thanks are very little to give in return for the encouragement so generously given me by many students at Santa Cruz, especially by the students of Cowell College. I hope that the text will somehow communicate a sense of my gratitude for their help and pleasure in their company. I owe an extra note of thanks to Bruce Cantz, Jim Currin, Robert Goff, Phyllis Halpin, Charles Natanson, Donald Nicholl, Richard Randolph, Forrest Robinson, Jasper Rose, Charles Selberg, and Ron Yerxa. Special thanks are due to Joan Hodgson, of the McHenry Library, who indefatigably secured indispensable books and microfilm, and to Louise and Todd Newberry, Paul Schoellhamer, Margaret Sowers, Lee and Byron Stookey, and Mary Takayanagi. Helen and Christopher Morris read part of the text in an early form, and Walter Dubler read it all, most helpfully, at a later stage. Charlotte Cassidy typed many different versions many times. Helen Morris and Helen Dizikes did the index. Above all, I want to thank Eloise and Page Smith, who, over the years, have made everything possible.

Contents

Illustrations

PART I

CITY AND COUNTRY

ANDREW JACKSON

1

The Sportsman
and the Hermitage

COUNTRY GAMES, like country ways, change very slowly. In the days of Andrew Jackson the outdoor sports of American country people — hunting and fishing and horse racing — remained very much what they had been since time immemorial; and the principal forms of country play — wrestling and jumping, running and throwing — would have been immediately recognizable to Ulysses. The tenacity of this tradition of sportive amusement was, for many Americans, a source of considerable consolation, reassuring them about the continuity of a part of their lives older than the English language, older than the Christian Bible, older even than the philosophies of the Greeks.

For many other people, however, the persistence of this propensity for pleasures that were pointless and transitory was a cause of dismay. Such a one was Francis Asbury, the indomitable Methodist bishop who, reflecting on his many journeys through the western and southern American frontier in the 1790s, described the white inhabitants from that point of view: "Worldly people, intolerably ignorant of God: playing, dancing, swearing, racing; these are their common practices and pursuits." This led him to conclude, rather grimly, "There is little genuine religion in the world." Bishop Asbury was struck by the greater piety of the black people, many of whom spoke "lovingly of the goodness of God."[1] In his journal he failed to mention their amusements, but then life under slavery wasn't very amusing. Still, the bishop's observations unmistakably bore out the old aphorism: "Some of the virtues may be modern, but all the vices are ancient."[2]

Even so, changes were taking place. These ancient sports and games existed in America in a new environment in which the abundance of natural life, the profusion of new species, and the availability of land all shaped new sporting forms, new attitudes. In such an environment, English games and sports, immigrants like the people themselves, altered their names and rules and social associations. Much remained familiar, but even the familiar became different. The Revolution and independence speeded the process by adding the dynamic element of nationalism. In the years that followed, this combined with the rapid growth of cities, the spread of industry, and the invention of new forms of communication and transportation. By Andrew Jackson's day the most powerful element of all — democracy — came into full play. Many forms of sport had traditionally been exclusive, the monopoly of the few. Now Americans contemplated the possibility of sports and games for the many. Early in the nineteenth century a visiting Frenchman made this point forcefully.

> Democracy is too new a comer upon the earth to have been able as yet to organize its pleasures and amusements. In Europe, our pleasures are essentially exclusive, they are aristocratic like Europe itself. In this matter, then, as in politics, the American democracy has yet to create everything fresh.[3]

The gradual transformation of the aristocratic sporting tradition into a popular one is the theme of this book. And where better to explore some of the details of this process than in the sporting life and career of that personification of democracy, Andrew Jackson?

*

We begin with the words of a woman who had known Andrew Jackson as a young man in Salisbury, North Carolina, from 1785 to 1787 and then, forty years later, heard the news that he was a nominee for the presidency:

> What! Jackson up for President? *Jackson.* Andrew Jackson? Why, when he was here he was such a rake that my husband would not bring him into the house! It is true he *might* have taken him out to the stable to weigh horses for a race, and might drink a glass of whiskey with him *there.* Well, if Andrew Jackson can be President, anybody can![4]

From the stables to the presidency — the very symbol of democratic achievement. What applied to politics applied to sport. In just the same way one might say, if Andrew Jackson could be a sportsman, then anybody could.

But what about the private citizen as opposed to the public hero? Where did the American sportsman go when he left the stables? In Andrew Jackson's case, it was to the Hermitage, a handsome house that, with its pillared portico and curving carriage way, its spacious grounds and many cultivated acres spreading beyond, its stables and servants and field workers, represented a very old and familiar symbol of power, wealth, and privilege.

That an American sportsman, even in the brave new dawn of democracy, should end up in a house like that was not surprising; it was testimony to the extraordinary spell the past cast over the present. For most Americans the Hermitage represented the traditional British culture of which they were still very much a part, despite the Revolution. Traditions were not like clothes to be put on and off at will; they were less a matter of choice than most people imagined. The complex cluster of traditions the Hermitage represented for Americans was, like their language and their law, their names and their sports and games, something inherited.

Was this an inescapable inheritance? If so, what happened to that American determination to elude the specter of the past? To create their own architecture, their own literature, their own sports? Change had already taken place. The Hermitage was not one fixed and final entity. It represented a tradition of becoming, not a tradition of being. Four different houses were built on the same site in the space of thirty years. The great country houses of England had also changed, of course, with one architectural style giving way to another — a more leisurely pace of change measured in centuries. In America change seemed much faster: "Ten years in America is almost equal to a century in the old continent," said one traveler; and another remarked: "In this country fifteen years is an age."[5] But the speed of change was less puzzling than the uncertainty of its direction. The first Hermitage was made of logs. Each succeeding version was grander than the one before and each prompted the same question. If every log cabin wished to become the White House, then what became of the onward march of American equality?

Anyway, architecture alone could be very misleading. The Hermitage implied a very different society from the one that actually surrounded it. Its classical columns gave no hint that its farm laborers were slaves and that all around it was frontier wilderness. In the same way, it supplied uncertain clues as to the emerging sporting style of its occupant. In the early years of the nineteenth century, that sporting style was divided in its aspirations and confused in its practice because it was identified with the past even while it looked to the future. History had finished the sportsman of the Hermitage even less than it had finished his house. The American sportsman was in the making and on the make. His story doesn't really end with the Hermitage. It begins there.

*

The evolution of an American sporting style involved Andrew Jackson in some lively contradictions. The old style, after all, represented two of the things he most particularly despised: Englishness and aristocracy. The mere possibility that Napoleon was about to invade England provoked him to write to a friend in 1798:

> Do not then be surprised if my next letter should announce a revolution in England. Should Bonaparte make a landing on the English shore, tyranny will be humbled, a throne crushed, and republic will spring from the wreck, and millions of distressed people restored to the rights of man by the conquering arm of Bonaparte.[6]

In Jackson's mind it was the old England of George III, whose army he crushed at New Orleans. Many Americans shared his views, which helps explain the emotional power of that victory.

Therefore indigenous American traditions had to be encouraged, within which a native sporting culture could grow up. As a delegate to the constitutional convention for the Tennessee territory in 1795, Jackson strongly opposed the proposal that the forthcoming state be named Franklin or Washington. Such an idea reeked of colonial mentality. Rather, Jackson admired what the people of Kentucky had done in choosing a name native to the region (he personally preferred the Indian pronunciation of Kain-tuck-ee), and he urged upon his fellow delegates the Indian name of the Great Crooked River — Tennessee, a word which, he said, "had as sweet a flavor on the tongue as hot corncakes and honey."[7] He wanted American manners, American pronunciation; so he named his horses for American heroes, American places.

Jackson's republicanism was equally ardent. His early letters to Thomas Jefferson were addressed to "citizen Jefferson." He subscribed to the view that the United States must be an example of a simpler, more virtuous way of life. All taint of aristocracy and monarchy must be scrubbed out, in sport as in everything else. This was already happening. When a visiting Frenchman, Baron Quenet, saw members of the Richmond, Virginia, Quoits Club — doctors, lawyers, and judges (among them John Marshall) — playing with their coats off, he expressed astonishment that "the dignitaries of the land could thus intermix with private citizens," and added that "he had never before seen the real beauty of republicanism."[8]

Very well. But the Hermitage didn't suggest men bowling with their coats off. It exemplified a horse-racing culture, and nothing represented the old ideal of aristocratic privilege more than that. What place did the sport of kings have in a republic where, as Jackson once wrote to Thomas Jefferson, "merit alone should lead to preferment"?[9] The more one thought about such questions, the more confusing they seemed. Almost forty years later, near the end of his life, Andrew Jackson was still puzzling over them. He had given his old friend Francis P. Blair a filly named Emuckfau, along with a summary of her ancestry. In his letter of thanks, Blair promised that Emuckfau's "proud ancestry" would never be "tarnished by a low connection," but Blair also insisted that such blood pride was not a betrayal of American ideals. On the contrary, he wrote, Americans had a duty to try to defeat the Europeans in the very things in which they took such arrogant pride. And in what more than in horse racing?

> I think it worthy of the ambition of a Republican to ride "booted and spurred," what the nobility abroad value almost as much as their own blood, and I hope I shall have many descendants from *Emuckfau* . . . which will set them above the Great abroad, in a particular in which they pride themselves most, and without violating any of the doctrines of our Democracy.[10]

That was the way out of the dilemma. Let there be a contest of cultures. Some day, American sportsmen might carry their challenge across the Atlantic. As in the arts and in letters, in commerce and in technology, so too in sports: American success would testify to the validity of democracy.

Many people remained skeptical. What if, instead of democratizing or Americanizing sports and games, Americans found themselves succumbing to foreign values and customs? It was a horse, after all, that toppled Troy. Despite Francis Blair's sophistry, wasn't talk of bloodlines and breeding and ancestry deeply suspect in republicans? Maybe Josh Billings, the popular humorist, put it best when, with the irreverence of frontier satire, he mentioned his admiration for the mosquito, "which had some of the best blood in the country."

The attempt to find answers to such questions bound together the fraternity of American sportsmen in the years from 1800 to the Civil War. In style, spirit, and values Andrew Jackson best symbolized their efforts. Other sportsmen had larger resources, greater successes, longer sporting careers. But no other American sportsman combined public and private values so forcefully; no one else balanced so evenly a respect for traditions of the past with an eagerness to create new ones for the future. Andrew Jackson came into his own as a sportsman just as the nineteenth century began. He played an important sporting role in its first quarter and lived through four and a half decades of it. Many sportsmen of the Age of Jackson did not admire him uncritically or share all his values. But they all played in his shadow.[11]

*

No one would have guessed this from the circumstances of Andrew Jackson's birth and upbringing. He was born of Anglo-Irish stock in 1767, in the area of North Carolina called the Waxhaws. His father died before he was born; his mother and both his brothers were dead by the time he was fourteen. His life was not all deprivation and loss, however; in his early years there was also play, the spontaneous, improvised play of youth as well as the collective, if loosely organized, sport of country boys — wrestling, foot races, and riding. The chief residue of all this was a desire to excel and the harsh sense, which never left him, that life was a fight for survival.

At fifteen Jackson went to Charleston, South Carolina, where he inherited a very small legacy. He promptly used it to cavort with the sons of wealthy and prominent families in most of the common sports and games of the time: cockfighting, card playing, horse racing. The money didn't last long. In later years he commented ruefully: "I was a raw lad then, but I did my best."[12] He was learning about life. On his way to Charleston he had got into a game of "rattle and snap" and, short of cash, bet everything he then owned — his horse — on one throw of the dice. He won $200. But he was nobody's fool and didn't push his luck too far. He never threw dice again.

In Charleston there was amusement for Jackson but no future, and he believed exceedingly in the future. He moved to Salisbury, North Carolina, to study law. His Salisbury activities, so vividly remembered by the woman with whose words we began, were succinctly summed up to the same general effect by someone else:

He did not trouble the law-books much.
He was more in the stable than in the office.
He was the head of all the rowdies hereabouts.[13]

Rowdiness and the stables! The association of these two was familiar enough. Equally familiar was the association of country sport with bloodshed. This was reflected in Andrew Jackson's passion for one of the common sports of the time, cockfighting.[14] It was everywhere in the southern and middle states and, although very much frowned on, in New England too. In the Carolinas and Tennessee, rival church parishes put up cocks to fight; the cockpits were often in the town square, and the crowds there were large and vocal. Eventually, cockfighting was overshadowed by horse racing as a popular sport. The growing disapproval of respectable opinion finally made it illegal, even in the South and West. But it remained very popular throughout the nineteenth century and was impossible to eradicate (as it still is), especially among those people who didn't care about respectability. People cling to their amusements as tenaciously as to a creed, language, or idea; for many, especially the poorer and more inarticulate, support for cockfighting, and later for prize fighting, was a form of social and political dissent.

Such ideas were very far from the thoughts of a young boy whose heart was given to cockfighting. Among the papers and letters collected after Jackson's death is a scrap of paper dated 1779, the earliest of his personal papers that can be dated with reasonable accuracy. It is entitled "A Memorandum how to Feed a Cock before you him Fight."

> Take and give him some Pickle Beef Cut fine 3 times a day and give him sweet Milk instead of water to Drink give him Dry Indien Corn that hase been Dryn up in smoke give him Lighte wheat Bread Soked in sweet Milk feed him as Much as he Can Eat for Eaight Days.[15]

Years later, when he had grown up, his interest was as strong as ever — witness this description of him calling out praise and encouragement for two of his cocks in the cockpit in the public square in Nashville:

> Hurrah! My Dominica! Ten dollars on my Bernadotte! Twenty dollars on my Bernadotte! Who'll take me up? Well done, My Bernadotte! My Bernadotte for ever![16]

Jackson named one of his prize cocks for Napoleon's Marshall Bernadotte, because cockfighting's bloodiness was emblematic of animal courage, as was war itself. Jackson paid one of his gamecocks the ultimate tribute of which he was capable by comparing it to the greatest military hero of the age: "There is no greater emblem of bravery on earth," Jackson said; "Bonaparte is not braver."[17] Sporting prowess was physical prowess.

Physical prowess was exemplified by horsemanship. In his own time, and down to ours, the most memorable popular images of Andrew Jackson were those of the Man on Horseback — General Jackson, mounted on Old Duke, "riding the whirlwind's wing, and pouring the storm of death on the invaders of this land of freedom";[18] the popular hero, riding alone down Pennsylvania Avenue on the way to the White House after his first inauguration as President. For some people, the Man on Horseback was a traditional image of fear — the would-be dictator, riding roughshod over all opposition.

At the same time, there was a very different image of the man on horseback. It was an image of cunning and skill: the horse trader. Democracy meant bargaining for votes, not commanding obedience: Andy Jackson, horse trading. Candidate Jackson sought men's votes and earned their loyalty. It was this prudent and canny Jackson whom Nathaniel Hawthorne saw in 1833, when, in his second term as President, his enemies scattered and confounded but neither murdered nor imprisoned, the old man of almost seventy rode unostentatiously into Salem, on horseback, in the dusk of evening.

> Surely he was a great man, and his native strength as well of intellect as of character, compelled every man to be his tool that came within his reach; and the more cunning the individual might be, it served only to make him the sharper tool.[19]

Everything changed, but neither vicissitude nor victory changed *him*. People clung to him as a symbol of continuity, of unchanging values. And he was, in many ways, still the same boy of fifteen whose first known autograph appeared on a piece of paper on which he appraised the value of a horse. Which kind of horseman was he, then? The European conqueror or the American democrat? Both. The aristocrat of the Hermitage blended with the cunning frontiersman. Political leadership in a democracy united both: "I do not pretend to know much, but I do know men and horses."[20]

*

In 1788, upon completing his legal studies and apprenticeship in Salisbury, Andrew Jackson mounted his horse and rode off into the wilderness of the Tennessee territory. He became a typical entrepreneur of the time: restless, energetic. He shared in the ravenous land hunger, accumulating title to all the acres he could lay his hands on. Payment for many transactions was in kind, and a lawyer's fee, for a case of no great importance, might well be a "six-forty," a section of land of 640 acres. By 1791 Jackson was able to buy his first large farm, Hunter's Hill, and begin farming it. He had already received enough cattle and horses, as fees, to stock it. By 1798 he owned title to an estimated 50,000 acres of land. Had it all been combined into one tract, it would have been equivalent in size to an entire county.

So far so good. As master of Hunter's Hill, Jackson had gained the chief source of wealth and the primary symbol of status — land. Sporting aristocracies had always been rooted in the land. In Europe, holdings such as his brought wealth and security. Jackson should have felt secure, but he didn't, and his position was in fact much less settled than it seemed. Ownership of all those acres didn't bring any certain income. Much of Jackson's land was forested; most of it was land without laborers or tenants or towns. Nor did ownership necessarily confer a fixed social position. Jackson had not been limited to any one role in seeking his fortune; he began as a debt collector and in the 1790s went on to other things — congressman, senator, judge, planter, merchant, and general, some of these activities performed simultaneously. But this mobility resulted in continuing social ambiguity. The land Jackson bought had no social or historical heritage. Land was a commodity, a counter in a highly speculative game still being played; its payoff lay mostly in the future. Jackson's situation was both familiar and puzzling: he was land-poor.

In 1798 Jackson resigned his seat in the United States Senate in order to devote all his energies to his many different business enterprises, the chief of which was importing goods from the East. This soon plunged him into deep trouble. The Philadelphia middleman with whom he dealt went bankrupt, and Jackson came to the brink of ruin. The next six years were in some ways the severest test of Jackson's life, and during this time many of his social, economic, and political attitudes became fixed. He economized and finally paid back every penny of principal and interest. Forever after he hated reckless extravagance and was deeply skeptical of heedless impetuosity. Above all, he hated "paper" money and believed whole-heartedly in hard cash and in the moral validity of contracts.

But he hadn't abandoned his willingness to take a chance. By 1805 he had begun to get straight, and promptly expanded his enterprises once again. All through the previous decade he had been buying and selling horses and racing in a modest way. Now horse racing was one of several interests he developed. He sold Hunter's Hill and bought two new places. One was the log house called the Hermitage. The other, which he bought with the aid of two partners, was a plot of land called Clover Bottom, about four miles from the Hermitage and seven miles from Nashville. In these two places Andrew Jackson's sporting, social, and business lives were intimately joined, in the style and form that would increasingly characterize all American sporting life in the years ahead — a middle class, commercial, popular style, not an "aristocratic" one.

Clover Bottom was a beautiful meadow on Stone's River. The partners set up a store there and had many other irons in the fire. They imported goods from the East, which they sold directly to customers in the store or bartered for other commodities — whiskey and slaves — which they then sent down the river to Natchez and New Orleans by flatboat. They built their own keelboat yard at Clover Bottom. For a time they had branch stores at Lebanon and at Gallatin, Tennessee. All the while, Jackson managed the Hermitage, supervised his slaves, raised corn, wheat, horses, cows, and mules, and repaired his own equipment, including his cotton gin and his 125-gallon still.

The meadow at Clover Bottom was large enough for a one-mile race course, with room left over for spectators and their vehicles. The construction of a race course had been begun by the previous owners. Jackson and Company took over a two-thirds interest and enlarged and improved the track. They built booths for hucksters, a tavern, and stables. For the next few years Jackson was a commuting businessman-sportsman, riding in every day from the Hermitage to Clover Bottom, overseeing the course and the semiannual meetings, checking on the many commercial operations, and working in the store. He waited on customers during the day and rode home at night, with the regularity of a clerk in a counting house.

None of his contemporaries thought this peculiar, but it was certainly different from the life of the English gentry of the time. For Jackson — landed gentleman, commercial adventurer, sporting entrepreneur — all these roles were perfectly compatible. There was

no snobbishness about trade. As a businessman Jackson had a reputation for being decisive, prompt, and completely honest. Debts
were a question of honor, no more and no less than anything else.

Jackson combined aristocratic impulse with bourgeois prudence.
There was a willingness to speculate but also a desire to live within
one's means; a hatred of debt vied with an awareness of great rewards for chance-taking. Jackson would have mightily disapproved
of Lord Alvanley's great maxim for the improvident: "There is no
reason that because you have no money you should not have anything else." Lord Alvanley had gone through his own fortune and
had helped several other people go through theirs. Peers in Britain
were at this time still personally invulnerable to their creditors, but
there was no such legal protection for American sportsmen who
went broke.

Jackson was a generous host. The contrast between such open-
handedness and the proverbial Yankee penny-pinching was one of
the bases for the much-loved picture of the feckless and reckless
southern aristocracy. Of course some planters were improvident.
Potential wealth seemed dazzlingly, temptingly near at hand. But
the actual means available to American sportsmen were very modest, even meager. Wade Hampton, the leading sportsman of South
Carolina, was in very much the same position as Jackson. "I am
vastly partial to your elegant seat and fine tract of land," Hampton
wrote to Jackson after having visited the Hermitage. Hampton had
gone on to New Orleans to buy some horses, but, chronically short
of cash, like everyone else, he had had to give up that idea. "My face
is turned the wrong course for purchases," he wrote to Jackson, and
then concluded on a slightly more dashing note: "I must come and
give you all a lesson or shall lose my credit as a sportsman."[21] Wade
Hampton needn't have worried. They were all sportsmen on credit.

Breeding and selling horses was the most important source of income for Jackson, and the most dependable. He made more money
from Truxton, his best horse, than from any other single piece of
property he owned. Jackson established a reputation as the best
horse breeder in the region. Other breeders came from all over to
buy from him. And in horse breeding, buying, and trading, in which
dishonesty was a byword, Jackson's businesslike methods and well-
attested integrity were important assets. His knowledge of horses
was extensive, by the standards of his time; and despite all his scorn
for book learning, he had the standard medical and genealogical
books in his library. He also practiced as a veterinary physician and

surgeon in his own stables and for his neighbors and friends.

The other important source of income during this time was betting. Wagering was widespread. Since cash was always scarce, people bet anything and everything: clothes, watches, jewelry, land, slaves, barrels of whiskey, and carriages. This being so, the modest size of wagers in America, as compared with those in Britain at the same time, indicates how much the Americans had to improvise. Jackson's stepson reported to him the case of a man who had lost $4,000 and who, to recoup his losses, offered to bet him $6,000 in land certificates, but the stepson prudently refused such "dashing." The heirs had to be prudent too. By midcentury, conditions were changing, as we shall see in the lives of John Stevens and Richard Ten Broeck. Then, after the Civil War, American sportsmen with enormous fortunes came onto the scene. The Jeromes, Keenes, and Whitneys could afford "any dashing." That lay six decades in the future — a long while as Americans reckoned time, but not a very long period compared with the century and a half of horse-racing history that had preceded Andrew Jackson's birth.

*

The first white settlers coming to Virginia brought horses with them, for the horse was essential to civilized life as Europeans knew it. Horses multiplied so rapidly that they were soon running wild; catching them in the woods became an early sport. In 1724 Hugh Jones wrote: "They are such Lovers of Riding, that almost every ordinary Person keeps a Horse."[22] American farmers originally preferred oxen for farm labor, but as horses were so much more plentiful they became the chief work animals, and persistent efforts were made to improve their quality. As early as 1640 Massachusetts had enough surplus horses to begin shipping them to the Caribbean. By 1700, stimulated especially by demand from the West Indies, horse trading and selling formed an intricate business network throughout all the colonies, the center of which was Rhode Island, whose horse plantations became famous. The implications of this were far-reaching: an exclusive privilege had become commonly available.

Horses have always been raced for sport, and Americans were no exception: races took place wherever and whenever men met on horseback and the spirit of rivalry and competition and play moved them — in the open spaces, or along paths cleared through the woods. In this informal and unorganized form of play, horse racing was common to all sections of the country, whatever the law or prevailing moral code might be. This is especially worth remembering in regard to New England, which was notorious for its reputed hostility to play.

Seventeenth-century horse racing was very much alike everywhere. Sectional differences began to develop with the beginning of formal organization of horse racing as a spectator sport. This began in the middle of the seventeenth century in New York, where, in 1664, the first English governor established a race course called New Market, on Hempstead Plains, Long Island, offering prizes for the fastest entrants — a way of introducing the Dutch population to English ways. The strategy worked. New Yorkers became, and remained, passionate horsemen. Formal racing in the South dates from 1688, when a race meet was held at Malvern Hill, Virginia, though earlier meets may well have been held but not recorded. In any event, in both North and South such efforts were sporadic; nothing long-lasting was established.

The random and largely improvised form of horse racing began to change in the middle of the eighteenth century, from which time we can begin to think of it as the precursor of our contemporary sport. More formal preparations were made for racing matches and meets. Groups of men got together to form jockey clubs and to set out rules and regulations. The first notices appeared in newsbills and newspapers. All this was modeled on English practice, of course. At this time, English horse racing entered a period of unprecedented growth. The Newmarket Jockey Club began to assume central control and regulation to match its historical and social preeminence. Nothing remotely like it could be established in the primitive conditions of decentralized American colonial racing, but its influence did have an important consequence: it fixed even more powerfully in the American mind the already considerable prestige of Newmarket as the model of what proper racing really was.

The first regular American race meeting dates from the 1760s, when the first "permanent" race course also came into being. This was built by an immigrant Yorkshireman named Thomas Nightingale and was called — what else? — Newmarket. Other "permanent" courses were laid out in the middle and late eighteenth century in Maryland and in South Carolina, both states in which horse racing was as enthusiastically pursued as anywhere. In these same years three race courses were established in or near Manhattan, and several in New Jersey and Pennsylvania. It was at this point that a very different pattern developed in New England, where formal horse racing remained interdicted until well into the nineteenth century. It was not horse racing that the Yankee Puritans loathed; it was the gambling that invariably came with it.

These race courses were permanent in the intentions and hopes of their builders, but, with the rarest exception, they were as short-lived as everything that had gone before. (The important exception was the race course at Charleston, South Carolina, which lasted from the 1780s to the Civil War.) Anyway, the facilities were crude enough. Courses weren't enclosed, and no admission was charged. There were no stands. People stood, or they sat on horseback or in coaches pulled up alongside the running track. Someone was designated as starter, and someone else verified the winning horse, if the result was close. Procedures and rules were rather vague, so countless disagreements arose. As there was no central authority to decide these disputes, arguments about bets not infrequently ended up in court. The courts generally upheld the obligation to pay gambling debts, even where such gambling was illegal. A racing meet consisted of one or two races, with very few horses entered. Most meets lasted one day, occasionally two. One English custom continued in America although it was just at this time going out of fashion in England: races were made up of heats, the winner taking two out of three or sometimes up to three out of five; and Americans clung to the English practice of long races of two to four miles.

The starting marker was a line scratched across the turf, or a stick or pole thrust into the ground; the same sort of thing marked the finish line. Labor to clear land solely for racing was scarce; to expend it on something used only a handful of days each year was out of the question. As a result, race courses in America were most often laid out on land that had already been cleared for cultivation but had been abandoned, allowing the native grass to grow back. The resulting turf was very rough, an appropriate symbol for the style of racing as a whole.

Even so, horse racing flourished in the years just before the Revolutionary War. The war seriously disturbed this increasingly popular sport. The two armies took whatever horses they could get their hands on; there was extensive damage to property, and some prominent horsemen and breeders on the Loyalist side had their possessions confiscated. Horse racing's growth was only temporarily disturbed, however, for it had slowly but surely established itself in popular affection.

The greatest effect of the war was on the historical understanding of subsequent generations. The war came to be viewed as a cataclysm that had destroyed a golden age of racing; the sport had supposedly been in the hands of a high-minded aristocracy, which raced horses to improve the breed rather than to gain vulgar commercial profit. In this view, even worse conditions followed the war, for peace brought with it a period of crass commercialism in which new men with coarser values set horse racing's tone.[23]

Such a view was greatly exaggerated. The Revolutionary War didn't destroy a sporting aristocracy. A few sportsmen belonged to families of acknowledged preeminence, and quite a remarkable number of perfectly ordinary sportsmen insisted on seeing themselves as members of a social elite. But there really was no sporting aristocracy, in the English sense, to destroy. The war didn't introduce commercialism into horse racing; American horse racing had always been a part of colonial commercial life. Equally important, the war didn't allow new men to enter the sport for the first time; new men had been entering it, as they had been entering American society in general, all through the preceding decades. In the seventeenth century the same thing had been going on, as it always goes on in any society. For example, in 1674 a tailor in Virginia was fined by the county court for

> having made a race for his mare to runn with a horse belonging to Mr. Matthew Slader for two thousand pounds of tobacco and cask, it being contrary to law for a Labourer to make a race, being a sport for Gentlemen.[24]

The law the would-be sportsman encountered was evidence of the unquestioned determination of North American Englishmen to establish a conventionally ordered society in which many activities, sport among them, were the privilege of a few — an aristocracy or a modest number of landed gentlemen. But that determination could not be realized, or could be realized only partially and with increasing difficulty. People tried desperately to keep sports and games exclusive, but they failed; they went on trying and failing. By the beginning of the nineteenth century such laws had become dead letters or had been removed from the books. Andrew Jackson knew he could be a sportsman, because he knew he was as much a gentleman as anyone else.

The anonymous woman's words about Jackson, which we set out earlier, should now be somewhat clearer, in the context of the historical developments we have discussed. For her, the discrepancy between the traditional social order, which she still accepted whole-heartedly as an ideal, and the reality of an American social world in which a man like Andrew Jackson might become head of state was as surprising as it was grotesque. Subsequent generations of people who shared her social views saw the Revolution as a kind of barrier that separated the upstarts and interlopers from the real aristocracy. What the woman didn't understand, and what has remained un-clear, is a final and remarkable irony: inside, and not too far beneath the surface, these new Jacksonian democratic sportsmen had pow-erful doubts about their own authenticity.

*

One group of newcomers did enter horse racing immediately before, during, and after the war. These were the numerous Anglo-Irish emigrants, who had developed new ideas about business entrepre-neurship, which they applied to the raising and racing of horses. The Jacksons were among them. Their ideas had to do with the changed function of horse breeding and the altered status of the breeder. In pre-Revolutionary times the breeding services of stal-lions were exclusively for the servicing of the owner's mares, or of those of his friends or acquaintances. Now this changed. Growing demand made it more efficient and remunerative to make breeding services available for public sale; and to organize this, there emerged a new phenomenon, the professional importers and stal-lioneers who arranged for horse breeding for the market and who made such services available to anyone who had the money to pay for them.

This wasn't entirely new. The importation of saddle-horse stock from England, as we have seen, had always been an important com-mercial enterprise; but it had been largely a personal and private one. Now it was impersonally thrown open to the market. And it caught hold quickly. By Jackson's day, the breeding business was an important and familiar part of the sporting business. Nor were all of these men entirely "new." Some of the stallioneer importers were older, well-established horsemen, both sportsmen and merchants. If new men were an old story, then American sport as business was equally old.

This, then, was the background of an almost legendary event — the importation to America of four stallions, from whom all sub-sequent "thoroughbred" pedigrees are supposedly derived: Medley, in 1783/84; Shark and Messenger, in 1788; and Diomed, in 1798. Sporting events and personalities, human or otherwise, being deeply embedded in popular culture, readily become sources for folklore, as the charming story of Messenger shows. According to the legend, Messenger, having escaped from the oppressive monarchical atmosphere of Great Britain, was so exhilarated by sniffing the air of a free country, while being led down the ship's gangplank in Philadelphia, that he broke away from his handlers and charged wildly through the streets of the city. The land of the fast and free!

Messenger and the three other well-known stallions were part of the process by which the race horse, in America, became more sharply differentiated from the ordinary workhorse. From the 1780s on, a much greater emphasis was put on scientific breeding. Before this, although people tried to improve their stock, their resources were limited and their objectives haphazard. Now these professional breeders tried to breed for specific qualities, above all, speed. In the half-century after the Revolution, a horse's pedigree became more significant and valuable than it had been before; hence the increasing talk about bloodlines. No wonder Jacksonian democrats were disturbed.

And yet, the significance of Messenger goes much deeper than that, and in an opposite direction from what worried democrats. The Messenger story is actually a symbol of human aspirations for equality. In America in the 1780s and 1790s, pedigrees were discovered in no time at all for an astonishingly large number of horses. Common sense suggests that the descendants of those four English immigrants did not suddenly drive all unpedigreed horses from the field of competition; but this was a matter with which common sense had little to do. Well might an American sportsman write scathingly about the "dunghill blood" in American stables.[25] Many an ordinary nag quickly rose on the thoroughbred social scale. The adulteration of thoroughbred blood was like that which was taking place in American society as a whole — a society in which distinctions of superiority were dissolved, and lowly creatures made themselves the equal of supposedly superior ones.

At a less exalted level, the actual business of pedigrees was a hopeless tangle of greed, ignorance, hoax, and simple deceit. The sporting newspapers of later years were filled with examples of contradictory claims, allegations of forged documents, spurious records, and owners' mysterious lapses of memory. As we shall see in chapter 3, William Porter founded his sporting paper largely to try to introduce some semblance of order and honesty into the proceedings. But he had little power, and his labors had only a modest effect. The whole business was a field day for con men and tricksters. In the memorably understated words of an American turf historian, "In no other department of human knowledge has there been such a universal and persistent habit of misrepresenting the truth of history as in matters relating to the horse."[26]

The disorder and dishonesty involving pedigrees was only part of the entirely unregulated expansion of horse racing in the 1790s. Its growth was marked by unrestrained gambling and flagrant dishonesty of all sorts. A revulsion in public feeling took place, perhaps not unconnected with the intense religious revivals that erupted at this time, especially in northern towns and cities. Led by New York, which assumed the uncharacteristic role of repentant sinner and moral reformer, the middle states prohibited public racing for stakes or purses and closed down the race courses.

Only the South effectively resisted. Of course in practice there was considerable violation of this prohibition in the North, and clandestine racing did take place; but from 1802 until about 1820 all formal legal horse racing was southern. This period, and not a supposed earlier golden age, marked the most significant period of southern racing, and its most brilliant phase. And, with the Carolinas taking the lead, there was another development of great importance at this time. Southern racing, formerly limited to the states along the Atlantic seaboard, expanded westward. As the new nation exploded beyond its Atlantic margins, the traditions of racing that were carried into the new states of Tennessee and Kentucky and Louisiana were southern ones, so that American racing in these areas was partly southern and partly western, an uncertain mixture of Old England and the new frontier. And this development, in turn, laid the basis for the brief-lived but colorful racing in and around New Orleans half a century later.

Which brings us to the nineteenth century's very uncertain sporting dawn and that moment when Andrew Jackson set out from Salisbury, North Carolina, to Tennessee, carrying all his worldly goods in his saddlebags and on the packhorse that trailed behind. In every way he was the symbol of the new sportsman, beginning again, in conditions of unusual change and fluidity. Much more important than the material goods Andrew Jackson took with him were the ideas he carried in his head; the ideas of the old English

The Hermitage

sporting life, at once bewitching and repellent, jostling uneasily alongside new values and aspirations. The old ideas achieved their expression in that historical memory called the Hermitage. The new ones, less clear-cut and coherent, began to be worked out at Clover Bottom.

2

The General
and the Colonel

THE GREATEST MOMENTS in Andrew Jackson's sporting career involved Truxton; and the history of that horse was the kind of story much loved by sporting fans everywhere, one whose familiarity never dulled its appeal. Replete with elements of suspense and risk-taking, it was the story of a champion arising from humble beginnings. Very like Jackson's own story, of course. It began at a race meet in the spring of 1805. There Jackson watched his horse lose to a horse named Greyhound. But it wasn't the winner that caught Jackson's eye; it was Truxton, the other horse in the three-horse field. Jackson had seen a special quality in that horse not immediately apparent to anyone else. He was convinced that Truxton lost only because he was not in proper running condition. And Jackson knew what to do about that.

So Jackson bought Truxton from the Virginia stable that owned him, although it was a very inconvenient time to spend the money, and put him through a severe training program. His methods, even for the time, were harsh ones. He believed in working a horse to the limit of its endurance, or beyond, believing that by such means a "will to win" could be implanted in the mind and spirit of the animal. If not, then the horse was not worth bothering about. Jackson was neither sentimental about horses nor reluctant to run them, even if they were physically unfit, when it suited his purposes. He was eager to justify his intuition and his investment. By the fall of 1805 Truxton was ready.

First there was a rematch against Greyhound, for a side bet of $5,000, which produced considerable excitement in the surrounding area and heavy betting on both sides. Hundreds of horses and numerous 640-acre tracts were staked, and Jackson accepted wagers worth $1,500 in wearing apparel. One of Jackson's friends bet all his own money, the horse on which he rode to the race, and fifteen horses belonging to his unsuspecting friends. Truxton won, replenishing the finances (and wardrobes) of Jackson and his friends.

During the next year, 1806, came the most famous event of Jackson's racing career, and one of the earliest memorable races of American turf history. It attracted one of the largest crowds ever to have watched a sporting event and showed that horse racing had come of age in Tennessee. The race was between Truxton and Plowboy, a horse owned by one of Jackson's chief political rivals. Feelings between the two stables were more than usually strained. The tempers of Plowboy's supporters were not improved by the fact that an earlier match race had been cancelled because Plowboy was injured, forcing his backers to pay a forfeit.

Two days before the race, Truxton suffered an injury to one of his thighs, which caused severe swelling. Jackson's friends advised him to forfeit, not least because they were disinclined to cover bets when their horse had little chance of winning. Jackson examined Truxton carefully. When he spoke to a horse, he looked it directly in the eyes, just as he looked at men when he spoke to them. He took a good long look and decided Truxton was fit to run.[1]

And run he did. The match was two heats out of three, two miles each; Truxton, a six-year-old, carried 124 pounds, while Plowboy, an eight-year-old, carried 130. Truxton ran the race of his life and won the first heat with surprising ease. But at the finish he was limping very badly. Jackson insisted on running him in the second heat, which took place in a pelting rainstorm. By now nothing could stop Truxton, who, despite lameness and rain, won by about sixty yards. It was a glorious triumph. Only one thing tainted the victory for Jackson, an unrelenting hater who didn't believe in half measures. The injury to Truxton had undoubtedly reduced the amount of money bet. Otherwise, his opponents might have been wiped out. As he put it, with a nice classical touch: "Carthage would have been ruined."[2]

Truxton, Jackson's greatest horse, didn't lose often and was never beaten at two miles. He was also unusually successful in stud; in the years that followed, more than 400 of his offspring ran in races all over the country. No wonder Jackson visited his stable the last thing every night before retiring. For his part, though of an unruly and ill-tempered disposition, Truxton was fond of his master, who could control him when no one else could. Or so at least local folklore had it: Andrew Jackson, tamer of horses — and of men.

*

In these years Tennessee solidified its position as one of the horse-racing centers of the country, although leadership gradually shifted to Kentucky. During Jackson's racing years, racing there was on a modest scale. Kentucky had no large cities, and its courses couldn't offer large sums. Anyway, it wasn't racing that made Kentucky famous. It was the breeding, raising, and selling of horses. In this regard, Kentucky was in the oldest of American sporting traditions, the horse business. Kentuckians were formidably competitive and aggressive businessmen; with them, the commercial angle was uppermost and undisguised. The syrupy sentiment came later. Other horse breeders found Kentuckians so tough in bargaining that some of them got laws passed in their home states forbidding the importation of Kentucky stock.

Andrew Jackson's withdrawal from racing, in the 1820s, to devote himself to national politics coincided with the shift of horse-racing predominance from Tennessee to Kentucky and with the return of legal racing to the middle states. The development of American horse racing in the 1820s ran counter to the growing trend toward sectional political animosity. For the first time, a sense of a national sporting fraternity among horsemen was developing, a fragile sentiment without any central direction. Like any other fraternity, it depended on shared values, those values that Jackson had put into practice at Clover Bottom, values he represented for all American sportsmen. What values were they?

Staying power — *"bottom," as it was called.* Americans wanted long-distance runners, so they ran their horses three or four miles, two or three (or more) times a day. Speed didn't count for much. It was bottom that distinguished the thoroughbred from the ill-bred quarter horse and the plodding workhorse. Human nature revealed itself most clearly over the long haul. Early success shouldn't go to the head of a real sportsman, nor should early failure keep a good man down. Look at Truxton. A schoolmate used to say that as a boy, when he wrestled with the slender Jackson, "I could throw him three times out of four but he would never stay throwed."[3]

A realistic understanding of human nature. "You are entering into life," wrote Jackson to his stepson in 1834, "unacquainted with the world and the duplicity of mankind."[4] Closer acquaintance revealed mankind as harsh and selfish. Where better to learn this than on the race course, where the prizes were tempting, the restraints few, and the springs of human conduct most exposed to view. Clover Bottom was Vanity Fair.

Willingness to take a risk. This was everywhere; not everyone bet, but almost everyone gambled in some way. The overheated atmosphere of the race course was an ideal place to learn to be cool, to calculate the odds, to avoid the cardinal sporting error — self-deception. But having done so, if the odds seemed right, better to take a chance than risk being left at the post. One might begin in the Waxhaws and end up in the Hermitage. A letter written when Jackson was sixty-five reveals how fiercely the competitive fires still flared. Asked by his nephew for advice about whether to run Polly Baker in a race, Jackson replied with some practical advice: make sure the filly is fit; run her against the best horses in the stable, because actual competition, not running against the clock, is the best test. He then concluded with a recommendation that summed up a lifetime of chance-taking in a sentence: "You must risque to win."[5]

Risk-taking was rooted in a basic optimism about life's opportunities. Skepticism about human nature was balanced against the sense of material possibility and natural abundance. Jackson persuaded himself that many of his horses were potential winners. His letters were filled with confidence. Of Bolivar: "I am of the belief, that by nature, if his breathing has not been injured, he is one of the first runners owned in America." Of Citizen: "the best brood horse now in America, and if his colts perform pretty well on the turf his blood will sell him for ten thousand dollars."[6]

Sometimes Jackson raised his expectations too high. One of his trainers, tired of always being told how promising the new crop of colts was — with the clear implication that it was *his* fault if they didn't do well — finally set his chief straight with true Jacksonian bluntness:

> My own opinion is that not one of them will doe to compeet with first-reight harses and when they are brought on the Turf if they are not entered with Judgement you will have them disgrasd.[7]

Jackson admired straight talk and wanted the truth. But there were limits. He retained his expectations. And fired the trainer.

Determination to win — at almost any cost. Here was an oddity. Materialistic and matter-of-fact, Jackson and his contemporaries believed that the quality which ultimately determined success was an intangible one: the will to win. Will power began with self-discipline. "People who stood close to him when he was foaming and champing and pawing," a close observer wrote of Jackson, "could see there was a patent curb in his bridle which the rider had a quiet but firm hold of."[8] Self-mastery led to mastery of others, a determination and capacity to bend events, rivals, even chance to one's own advantage. When fundamental interests were at stake Jackson did what had to be done, and his opponents and critics admired this quality almost as much as his supporters did. Wrote George Templeton Strong, no friend or supporter of Jackson's:

> The "Old Hero" is dead . . . Well, with all the man's transgressions, it should also be borne in mind that he was at least thoroughly in earnest in all he did. There was neither hesitation nor humbug in his composition, and what his hand found to do, he did with such might as was in him . . .[9]

Of the many stories about Jackson that reveal this quality, a less familiar one comes from those early Tennessee days when his sporting values were being shaped and he had resolved to "try conclusions with the world." Judge Jackson was holding court in a shanty in a tiny village when a large man, armed with a pistol and a bowie knife, began parading about outside, cursing judge and jury alike. Jackson asked the sheriff to arrest the man for contempt of court, but the sheriff was reluctant even to organize a posse to subdue the troublemaker. Jackson, as judge, ordered him to do so. "Mr. Sheriff, ince you cannot obey my order, summon me; yes, sir, summon me!"

The sheriff did as he was told. Jackson, pistols in hand, walked up to the bully, who was by now defiantly strutting about in the center of the village. Without saying a word, Jackson raised one of his pistols. The bully eyed Jackson for a long moment, then meekly surrendered, much to the surprise of the bystanders. He was later asked why, after his earlier truculence, he had yielded so docilely to Jackson:

> Why, when he came up, I looked him in the eye, and I saw shoot, and there wasn't shoot in nary other eye in the crowd; and so I says to myself, says I, hoss, it's about time to sing small, and so I did.[10]

*

Hercules, however, also played the role of Hamlet. At least if he wished to combine his private sporting life with a public one. Until the middle of the 1820s, Jackson's image had emphasized the fearless-frontiersman side of his character. In the last twenty years of his life, the other side was emphasized, and he was associated more with the exercise of caution than with the display of prowess. Jackson feared no person, but he was very sensitive to one thing — social disapproval. And he shrewdly understood that as American sporting culture became more democratic, the American sportsman increasingly had to recognize one master at least: public opinion.

Equally important for those who sought positions of public power and leadership, the definition of public behavior was enlarged (or the definition of what was private was narrowed). Jackson went to considerable lengths to show that he had put disreputable habits behind him. He wrote a memorandum, dated about 1824, which stated: "It is a positive falsehood that Genl. Jackson had been either at a cock fight or sports of a similar nature for the last thirteen years."[11] And although it is not entirely clear how far he was pre- pared to go in actual practice, Jackson didn't wish to be associated publicly with horse racing, or even with breeding horses for sale. He wrote to his stepson to rebuke him for not immediately sending some colts from the Hermitage to be trained elsewhere, and ordered him to go further: "Have the turf closed, plowed up and permit not a horse to be galloped on it," he wrote. Later he expressed pleasure that his instructions had been carried out so that no one "might have construed that I was encouraging racing."[12]

Jackson had not changed his private views about racing, nor had he surrendered to hypocrisy because of the need to win votes. He had yielded to, even anticipated, public opinion, because his own sporting values and style were a compromise between the newer middle-class values and the older aristocratic ones. He was cautious because he was genuinely uncertain about the precise relationship between his public and his private life. Above all, he acted as he did because by the 1820s the implications of a crucial fact of American social history were becoming clear: in the governing class, political power was separate from a supportive tradition of confident social leadership.

Two brief comparisons with England are in order. In nothing were American sportsmen more inhibited publicly than in avoiding any hint of sexual impropriety. Contrast this with the behavior of Augustus Henry Fitzroy, third duke of Grafton. Like Jackson, Grafton was a politician and a keen sportsman. His horses won the Derby three times. In the politics of the 1770s and 1780s, where personal qualities mattered a good deal, Grafton was timid and uncertain. But socially the reverse was true. In society, individual conduct, however odd, could usually be absorbed within the collective protection of a class that was in an unassailable position of superiority. The public could be more than damned: it could be ignored. So Grafton appeared in public, at the opera and at Newmarket, with Mrs. Horton, a woman notorious for the number of her lovers: "The Duke of Grafton's Mrs. Horton, the Duke of Somerset's Mrs. Horton, everybody's Mrs. Horton," wrote Horace Walpole, who continued: "In his Grace's view, the world should be postponed to a whore and a horserace."[13]

True, the duke, a generation older than Jackson, was part of an eighteenth-century culture that even in England was beginning to be challenged in its manners and morals as the nineteenth century began. But nothing like that tradition of aristocratic disregard for public opinion had ever existed in America, where the prevailing attitude in the eighteenth century, even in its early years, can be characterized by the words of Benjamin Franklin.

> In order to secure my credit and character as a tradesman, I took care not only to be in reality industrious and frugal, but to avoid all appearance to the contrary. I drest plainly; I was seen at no places of idle diversion. I never went out a fishing or shooting.[14]

Faint echoes of something like aristocratic disdain can be discerned in the lives and public careers of Alexander Hamilton, Gouverneur Morris, Aaron Burr, and a few southerners. A trace of it can be found, in Jacksonian times, in the frontier swashbuckling of Henry Clay. Mrs. Clay, when asked by a Washington busybody if she were not distressed by her husband's gambling, replied with great spirit: "Sometimes, yes, but really he almost always wins."[15]

A different, seemingly trivial, example leads to our second revealing comparison. In the late 1830s Martin Van Buren, Jackson's political heir, was bitterly attacked for his personal depravity in having a billiard table in the White House! Here the wickedness inhered in Van Buren's supposed frivolity; it was an example of the feeling that, even when not depraved or licentious, sports and games were not serious, not useful, not productive. Why was Van Buren *playing,* especially when, in the midst of an economic depression, business was so bad? The way out, for the American sportsman, was to be as serious about his sport as about his business; and it was better still to prove the seriousness of the sport by making it *into* a business. No bourgeois ever thought money wasn't serious.

In the meantime, the American sportsman had to be wary and prudent in public. And this was precisely what Edward George Geoffrey Smith Stanley, fourteenth earl of Derby, never had to be. Jackson was a generation older than Stanley, but in many personal respects they were similar: they had the same offhand manner in masculine company, the same personal aloofness, the same impression of personal force. "Stanley speaks like a man who never knew what fear or even modesty was," said Macaulay. The first half of that sentence could most emphatically be applied to Jackson, while the second half most emphatically could not. By comparison, Jackson's public style was prim, almost courtly. Stanley could go anywhere, do anything. Here is a well-known description of him in a betting room:

> In the midst of a crowd of blacklegs, betting men, and loose characters of every description, in uproarious spirits, chaffing, rowing, and shouting with laughter, and joking . . . It really was a sight and a wonder to see any man playing such different parts, and I don't suppose there is any other man who could act so naturally, and obey all his impulses in such a way, utterly regardless of appearance, and not care what anybody might think of the Minister, and the statesman, so long as he could have his fun.[16]

Stanley *was* an exceptional individual, but so was Jackson. The great difference between them was in the social traditions available to each. There weren't such betting rooms in Washington, and if there had been, Jackson couldn't, and wouldn't, have frequented them.

*

Jackson had to be on his guard, and he most anticipated the American sportsman of the future when he was on guard. Washington was as dangerous as the frontier; maybe *more* dangerous. Eternal anxiety was the price of social ambiguity. Stony-faced, poker-faced, the Jacksonian sportsman usually didn't lose control, even when he exploded in a terrible rage; and he was capable of the most terrible rage. Don't get mad, get even. Think of what happened to the Indians.

Everything Americans inherited from Europe was subtly transformed. Americans took up that vestige of European aristocratic culture, the duel. They made it into something different, even though it looked like the same old thing and they often thought it was the same old thing. American duels were marked by a desire to gain revenge as much as by the need to redeem one's honor, and they were fought with a savage desire to kill. Armistead Thomas Mason, former senator from Virginia, was killed in a duel in which muskets were used — at six paces! Jackson's persistent reputation for frontier savagery derived more from his notoriety as a duelist than from anything else. He had killed a man in a duel fought in that spirit.[17]

Some of the sportsman's rage may have been an unconscious response to the legacy of confining, irksome, and burdensome European culture. Eternally seduced by the splendors of the Hermitage, the Jacksonian sportsman found he had built himself a prison. There are glimpses in Jackson's life and career of that quality D. H. Lawrence discerned in the frontiersman: "hard, isolate, and a killer."[18] This was the quality of cold-blooded calculation, of violence that was dreadfully emotionless, matter-of-fact. It went with the poker face developed to contain and conceal the surging emotions inside. Of course that is how Jacksonians viewed the American Indian, that first and noblest of New World sportsmen, whose image remained deeply attractive, not least because he didn't have to bother about Europe.

Jackson's old friend Sam Houston liked to strip off conventional garb and dress up like an Indian, and there was something of the Indian in Jackson too. It was said that, from force of habit learned in his Indian campaigns, Old Hickory always slept with one eye open. Jackson the Indian-fighter was actually the reverse side of Jackson the Indian. Maybe, instead of being made over into something new, the American sportsman really wanted to be something native, old, and free: free to roam, free to play, free from the past.

II

As Andrew Jackson's sporting career came to a close in the 1820s, William R. Johnson of Virginia emerged as the leading national figure on the American turf. Now wholly forgotten, Colonel Johnson was in his day thought so resourceful and all-conquering that his admiring contemporaries paid the mightiest compliment of which they were capable by calling him "the Napoleon of the turf." What was it about him they found so remarkable?

*

William Ransom Johnson was born in 1782 in Warren County, North Carolina, not far from Andrew Jackson's birthplace, in an area famous for its horses and horsemanship. Even by the demanding standards of the area, William Johnson as a young man showed unusual skill in training and racing horses; breeding them seems never to have interested him much. In 1803 he married the daughter of the master of Oakland, a plantation near Petersburg, in Chesterfield County, Virginia. Although he continued living in North Carolina, Johnson established a racing stable at Oakland and pursued his racing career from there. He was remarkably successful from the start. Between 1807 and 1810 he won a considerable number of races, established his reputation, and developed one of the best-known horses of the time, Sir Archy. In 1816 Johnson moved his residence to Virginia and undertook a "mercantile venture" in Petersburg. Within a few more years, presumably upon the death of his father-in-law, he became established as the master of Oakland.[19]

There, in the heart of the Virginia horse-racing country, Colonel Johnson was perfectly situated to live the life of the traditional southern sporting gentleman. He served in the North Carolina House of Representatives and, after the move to Virginia, represented Chesterfield County in the Virginia House and Senate, retiring from politics in 1837. He was the classic cavalier sportsman: a generous host, unfailingly polite, imperturbably affable. As he grew older he became a splendid figure, with a flowing mane of white hair and the kind of large head always described as "leonine."

In public affairs Colonel Johnson carried little weight. This was partly a matter of individual personality, but it had more to do with the type of sporting figure he was. Something about him verged on caricature, and he was in fact a kind of caricature of the older Jacksonian type of sportsman. After the Civil War, Johnson's type reappeared in that charming but powerless version of the southern gentleman, the Kentucky colonel; and there was always something funny about the colonels of Kentucky. The sense of caricature grew out of the contrast with the older Jacksonian type, whose style was one of power. By contrast, Colonel Johnson's energies seemed directed toward horse racing as a business in itself, a business that called for qualities other than power. It called more for cleverness, for psychological subtlety. We can see this in the new development in American horse racing in the 1820s, which established Colonel Johnson's national reputation — the North-versus-South match races.

*

In November of 1822, American Eclipse, owned by Cornelius W. Van Ranst of New York, easily defeated a highly regarded Virginia horse on the Washington Course in Charleston, South Carolina. That night, at a dinner for northern guests, Colonel Johnson challenged the North, offering to produce a southern horse for a rematch, at $20,000 a side, a staggeringly large sum of money for the time. One of the northerners present, a young New York sportsman named John Cox Stevens, accepted the southern challenge, not without considerable inward trepidation at the amount of money involved. (And of course the amount may have been intended by the wily colonel as a bluff to cow the northerners.) Arrangements were soon worked out. The new Union Course, on Long Island, a few miles outside Brooklyn, was chosen as the site for the race, and the date was set for May 27, 1823.

Colonel Johnson was in charge of selecting the southern horse, and, after various mishaps and difficulties, he picked Sir Henry. The novelty of this race, coming as it did soon after the lifting of the ban on horse racing in New York, produced enormous interest. On the day of the race, the roads leading to the Union Course were crowded with people. Some observers guessed that 60,000 made it to the course, and, although that was probably a considerable overestimate, the crowd must have been the largest ever assembled up to that point for an American sporting event, and one of the largest that had been brought together for any occasion in the history of the United States. People jammed into the small stands, perched on any available vantage point, and swarmed all over the course. A new form of excitement had been introduced into American sports: the excitement of the crowd itself.

Everyone was there — everyone but Colonel Johnson, who, for the only time in his long racing career, didn't come up to scratch. He lay disconsolately in his New York City hotel room, a victim of the red wine and celebrations of the night before. It was tactfully announced that he had eaten some lobster that didn't agree with him. American Eclipse, a nine-year-old, sported crimson colors and carried 126 pounds. Sir Henry, with colors of sky blue, was a four-year-old and carried 108 pounds. Eclipse was familiar with the course, having raced and won there in 1821 and 1822, but to offset this slight advantage there was trouble about Eclipse's jockey. Sam Purdy, one of the leading riders of the day, was supposed to ride him, but he had a disagreement with Eclipse's managers and refused to ride; he was replaced by William Crafts. As the time for the race approached, there was another difficulty — that of clearing the course of people. But this was finally accomplished. The betting was tremendous, right up to the time when the two horses approached the starting line for their walking start. Henry went off the strong favorite.

The first heat was very close. Henry led all the way and won by a length. Southerners were exultant that their judgment had been vindicated. Eclipse's managers attributed his defeat not to his rival's superiority but to the fact that William Crafts found it difficult to control the big horse. In the half-hour interval before the next heat, drastic remedies were decided upon. Sam Purdy was somehow prevailed upon to change his mind and come down out of the stands to ride Eclipse. Once again the horses were off, and for over two miles Henry held a very narrow lead. At intervals Eclipse tried to pass, but Henry held him off each time. At two and a half miles, Eclipse once again tried to get by. Among the notables present was John Randolph, whose high-pitched voice pierced through the roar of the crowd: "You can't do it, Mr. Purdy! You can't do it, Mr. Purdy! You can't do it, Mr. Purdy!"[20] But Mr. Purdy did do it. Eclipse took the lead and held on to win by one length, in a pounding finish.

There was another half-hour interval before the deciding heat. Now the southerners made a change. The boy who had been on Henry was replaced by Arthur Taylor, a famous trainer who handled Colonel Johnson's horses. Once again the horses walked up, and then they were off, for the last time. This time Eclipse took the lead. Horses rarely ran hard from the start, their riders preferring to pace them at a slower rate, to save something for a hard finish. But Sam Purdy pushed Eclipse hard from the first: "It was risk all, for all, he did not hesitate." The two horses matched stride for stride for the first mile, and for the second, and then the third, while the crowd shouted in a frenzy of excitement and astonishment. In the fourth mile, with both riders whipping and spurring, Henry made his move. The two horses ran the next half mile so close together that they were indistinguishable. But when they came to the last furlong it was Henry who fell back. Eclipse sustained the relentless pace and led by two lengths at the finish.

It was an unforgettable sporting contest, highlighted by the two-hour duration, the varying fortunes, the changes of riders and tactics, the excitement of the crowd, and, above all, the closeness of each of the heats. For many Americans who knew little or nothing of the dim colonial decades or of the scattered local events of those early years, modern American horse racing began with that race, at that place, on that date. This was also the occasion of the first recorded alibi in American sporting history. John Randolph explained the northern victory to disbelieving and shocked southerners by saying: "It was not Eclipse but the lobsters that beat Henry."[21]

Eclipse and Henry inaugurated a series of North–South races, which were a feature of American horse racing for the next twenty years. Individual owners made their own terms and arrangements, and a number of men were involved, but John Stevens of New York and Commodore Robert Stockton and William Gibbons of New Jersey played important roles for the North, while Colonel Johnson dominated the southern scene and emerged as the master arranger and organizer. There were more than forty of these races, of different kinds and at different places, during the next two decades. Most of them — and the most celebrated ones — took place on the Union Course. The rivalry was practically even throughout, with the South having a slight edge in victories and in stakes won.

The Eclipse–Henry race was a portent of things to come. Match races had long been common between towns or sections of a state, or between states, but this first race drew a good deal of its emotional significance from the bitter controversy between the North and South that had resulted in the Missouri Compromise of only two years before. As a perceptive historian of early American sport wrote long ago: "Except for the Missouri debates, this was the first great contest between the two sections."[22] By the middle of the 1840s, sectional rivalry pervaded everything. The exceptionally exciting match race between Peytona and Fashion in 1845 was accompanied by frenzied sectional fervor. Such feelings were too bitter to be contained by anything as peaceful as a horse race. The Mexican War brought an end to such contests and introduced fifteen years of conflict, culminating in civil war. Meanwhile, the great days of horse racing on the Atlantic seaboard were coming to an end, and the colonel's career was drawing to a close. In the 1850s, the center of horse-racing interest shifted to the newer South and to New Orleans.

*

Colonel Johnson's career involved him in forms of business organization that were familiar in their separate aspects but new in their combined form. Match races no longer emerged spontaneously out of personal rivalry or accidental opportunity, as they had always done in the past. The colonel bought and sold horses, and trained and raced them, with one consistent objective — to make matches. The colonel's matches were different in another respect as well. They were run for the betting that accompanied them, not for the purses. No regular meeting gave Johnson the opportunity to bring together the necessary combination of horses, owners, backers, and money. The betting was the chief adventure.[23]

Johnson was the first national racing figure whose fame depended entirely upon his racing career; and his travels were nationwide, from Canada to New Orleans and from New York through the middle states to the deep South. He didn't travel randomly: he established a kind of circuit. And he didn't travel because of personal whim; he had little choice in the matter. He traveled because his sporting and gambling life couldn't be supported by a local culture affording only local resources. For most Jacksonian horsemen, racing was local in its scope, or, at most, regional, as it had been at Clover Bottom. A race might occasionally draw people from miles away, but for the most part spectators and horses came from nearby. Local audiences and wagers were insufficient for the colonel's purposes, although he had to depend on race meetings of that sort for his day-to-day operations. In general he went where the money was, and the money was in or near cities. The Union Course was neither convenient nor neutral for southerners. The races were held there because the largest crowds, the largest purses, and the liveliest betting were attracted there.

By the late eighteenth century, the situation in Britain was already significantly different. A number of celebrated races had been established — the St. Leger, and Oaks, and of course the Derby — that were truly national events; they were regularly scheduled and attracted crowds of people of all classes, from near and far. Many race courses were near towns and cities. Ascot had been established by Queen Anne precisely so that a course would be convenient to her in London. But British horse racing was predominantly a country sport, in the social as well as geographic sense of the word. Its national existence depended on the support of a gentry and aristocracy whose culture was that of the country and the country house.[24] In America, the absence of such a clearly defined and nationally cohesive class structure gave sporting life a different character. The prosperity of American horse racing was already more dependent on promotion and publicity, or on special match races. The audience for American racing was not established but potential, something to be created, not to be taken for granted.

Colonel Johnson was famous for his shrewdness as a judge of horses. Richard Ten Broeck, his youthful partner and eventual successor, a man not given to perfunctory flattery, thought him "the best judge of horses I have ever known,"[25] and he was continually described as a "magician with horse flesh." Yet he delegated the actual training of his horses to Arthur Taylor. People were impressed by Johnson's mastery of timing, his ability to bring a horse up to prime condition for a precise date, often scheduled long before. And what most impressed people about that was not that he won, because his winning and losing record in the match races was not exceptional, but how much money he won, and how often he won when he was expected to lose.

In short, the timing that impressed everyone involved Johnson's skill as a bettor. In November of 1837, four horses were involved in a remarkable match, and his Lady Clifden overcame great odds to win. This race was probably the high point of the colonel's turf career: it revealed, to onlookers, the full extent of his cunning as a tactician, for Lady Clifden had been beaten only the week before, at Camden, New Jersey, by one of the same horses entered in this race at the Union Course. The colonel was aiming for the bigger, later race, and he won it. As one writer put it: "Never was a race more palpably won out of the fire." And never were the colonel's "profound judgment, experience and surpassing tact so signally displayed." For tact, read "crafty gambler's coolness."[26]

These complex betting ventures required special arrangements. Johnson sometimes owned the horse he matched, or a share of it, and sometimes he did not; the name given as the owner's was not always that of the actual owner. To handle the bets made, partnerships were formed, often involving several persons; these partners might then make their own arrangements to share profits and losses. Johnson was by no means a free agent; racing was crowded with knowledgeable men of strong, even obstinate, opinions. The colonel had to be persuasive as well as decisive, more wily than powerful. As his reputation grew, he probably found that people increasingly deferred to him, and that it was easier to get his own way. But that way could not have been simple. Fifty years later, he would have been an independent manager and promoter. In his own time, he remained within the older tradition of regional partisanship.

He always had to be managing and moving pieces about, as though he were at a chessboard and not on the race course. The chess metaphor is an important one in American sports history; we shall encounter it directly in chapter 7, in our discussion of Paul Morphy, and indirectly on other occasions. It is at the heart of Colonel Johnson's contribution to the development of an American sporting style, and the reason he deserves to be ranked with Andrew Jackson as a sporting figure. Johnson represents the gamesman of the future, just as Jackson, in this regard, represents the English sportsman of the past.

*

What was implied by the term *gamesman?* It was not by any means a type unique to American sporting culture. Gamesmen were to be found in other cultures and at other times. Indeed the relationship between the gamesman and the sportsman goes back to the archetypal basis of play as a human activity. Nor is there any simple or clear distinction to be made between the sportsman and the gamesman: the differences are a matter of emphasis and temperament. But those differences are important and interesting. Let's examine some of them.[27]

The gamesman fundamentally differed from the sportsman in his attitude toward rules. Whereas the sportsman accepted both the explicit rules of the game and the unwritten code of conduct that went with them, the gamesman acknowledged the rules but refused to recognize the existence of any code of conduct. The gamesman didn't violate the rules directly. That was important. The gamesman was not a cheater. (The type has deteriorated in the twentieth century!) For one thing, the gamesman knew that in the long run the cheater would be found out and prohibited from playing in games he wished to take part in, with people whose company he desired. (The gamesman had a hankering for respectability.) Even more important, the rules were part of the game the gamesman was playing. He acknowledged the rules in order to circumvent them when it suited him. Getting around, bending, or undermining the rules, without clearly breaking them, was, for the gamesman, a fundamental part of the game. (Some professions furnished better material for gamesmanship than did sports; law and politics are classic examples, and it is not surprising that they have been so closely identified in American history.) An early example of the sporting gamesman was Captain William J. Minor, a leading Mississippi turfman, very bold and greedy, whose leading characteristic the sporting *Spirit of the Times* described very frankly:

> We who happen to know Captain Minor, know that he has acquired some celebrity for making and unmaking rules as they would happen best to suit him at the times.[28]

This aspect of the game was often the most interesting for the gamesman. But never the most important. The gamesman wanted to win: all his efforts were directed toward winning.

There were other shades of emphasis that distinguished the gamesman from the sportsman. The gamesman aspired to complete objectivity; he hoped to calculate the odds of a situation in their entirety, so that even his own consciousness was only one more objective fact to be calculated. The accomplished gamesman exhibited a degree of detachment so extraordinary that, at his most exalted, there was something almost heroic about him. One can see why this style appealed so powerfully to nineteenth-century Americans: the gamesman's attitude seemed "scientific."

The gamesman was amoral about implicit values and codes. He felt no shame whatsoever in violating the sportsman's code of conduct. Games, sports, and competition of all kinds were not honorific or moral contests at all for him; they were matters of technical skill. This meant that the gamesman emphasized psychological means and states of mind, not physical strength or force. Gamesmanship, in its origins, was in some ways a substitute for physical prowess. The gamesman worked circuitously, by indirection. He especially counted on being able to disconcert his opponent or rival. He was a calculator, and the use of surprise was one of his prime strategies. The gamesman thrived on situations of ambiguity and uncertainty. He always wanted to complicate, not to simplify. He was therefore most in his element in any sport or game associated with betting. All the calculations led to that. If the gamesman won the pot, it didn't matter to him if he didn't win anything else. And if he didn't win it, then all else was vanity.[29]

The sportsman had in him elements of the gamesman, just as the gamesman was also a good sport in many respects. Andrew Jackson, a sportsman through and through, knew very well that at certain moments one must dissemble or conceal one's true feelings in order to achieve a goal. A friend said of him: "No man knew better when to get into a passion and when not."[30] But little of that quality carried over into his conception of himself as a sportsman — one of the things that marks him as a figure from the past. The tradition of good sportsmanship was one of the few aspects of British culture he found admirable.

We come back again, as we have so often, to the American desire to create a new and distinctive sporting culture. For Jackson and many contemporaries his own age, the gentlemanly code of sporting behavior inherited from England was not something that needed changing. In the 1820s Jackson's views began to differ in this respect from those of many Jacksonians. For the younger generation, that code of honorable behavior seemed increasingly irrelevant, perhaps wholly un-American. It was unwritten, like the British constitution, and notoriously difficult to define. It was based on implicit values the English didn't need to spell out; but American sportsmen, even as they developed a fragile sense of sporting fraternity, were conscious of how diverse they were, and of how little they could take for granted. They looked for something explicit, for uniform rules — their rules, not someone else's. And as they did that, they also did the opposite: they began to break free from any rules that bound too tightly. Inherited rules should be suspect. Rules should always be changing, like America itself. Otherwise, inherited rules might be used as a kind of trick to keep new men out of the game; they might be a form of protection for the weaker or less able. In this respect, these younger Jacksonians were truer to the new spirit of their times than the Old Man, for they wanted to free themselves from the dead rules of the past.

This is the historical and social origin of what was to become distinctive about the gamesman's role in American sports and in American culture as a whole. While the cruder forms of the gamesman — the trickster and the con man — were common everywhere, they were always marginal figures despised by respectable classes. In America, the gamesman came to be the dominant sporting and cultural type as the nineteenth century wore on; his style influenced the style and values of other professions and other activities. Although the American people formally continued to pay lip service to the sportsman and his code of honor, the gamesman possessed the qualities that were most likely to gain victory and that, as a result, gained their deepest respect. The ambiguity of the gamesman's view of the game clearly reflected the ambiguities of American culture. However, so powerful was the old English tradition of good sportsmanship — the idea that there was something more important than winning — that even hard-boiled gamesmen felt a bit ashamed to admit that they didn't believe in it. But only a bit. And not for long.

There are many types of the gamesman, and the most important of these in the history of American sports was the gamesman as manager, as controlling genius. This type was only in its rudimentary stage of development in Jacksonian America, because material means were not sufficiently abundant to give the manager enough to play with. But his time was coming, and he would rise triumphantly into his own in the twentieth century. Colonel Johnson was this type. He was not just wily in the ways a frontiersman was wily. He was also far-seeing. He was a strategist with a plan, one might even say a game plan. In his great victory with Lady Clifden in 1837, Johnson knew precisely what needed to be done, and his only difficulty was in finding the proper means to carry it out. "The slightest deviation from his orders," wrote a journalist with breathless admiration, "would have lost a race so nicely balanced that good management was to decide it."[31] Colonel Johnson was the first of the great managers in American sporting life, a brilliant analytical mind, on the sidelines or in the stands, who saw several moves ahead of his opponents. He was the general in command, the detached and unemotional chess master moving men and pieces according to a preordained plan.

*

Colonel Johnson typified the emerging American gamesman in another very interesting way. Early on he assumed, in his sporting and in his public life, the American sporting face — the poker face. This was one of the ways in which sport most influenced other aspects of American culture; the poker face of sporting events eventually became the face for all public occasions.

Where did it come from? From Rome, and from the Stoics' composure in the face of triumph and disaster. A more immediate source was Great Britain, where nonchalance had long been an integral part of aristocratic style. Added to this was the growing prevalence, in the middle classes, of maintaining a stiff upper lip, perhaps as a reaction to the histrionics of romanticism. Sport and diplomacy formed a double influence. British jockeys, widely recognized as the premier riders in the world, were distinguished by their "imperturbability of countenance"; no matter what riding difficulties they might find themselves in, "their faces were no indexes to their troubles." International diplomacy evolved a public style very much like this: that of the diplomat wary in the presence of other diplomats. It was said of Talleyrand that even "a kick on his hind parts would produce no change whatever in the expression of his face."

What were its American sources? The frontiersman, with an ear cocked for sounds of danger; his antagonist, the redskin, betraying not a flicker of emotion; the Yankee, giving nothing away. But of course the poker face was associated most of all with gamblers and gambling. It came up from New Orleans, along with poker itself, up the Mississippi, through the land of con men and bunko artists and taletellers, carried and diffused by the riverboat men. Poker steadily gained in popularity in the United States through the 1820s and 1830s, until, by the 1840s, it was played in respectable places as well as raffish card rooms; and by that time it was being cited as the game that revealed the most about a man's nerves and character under pressure. The poker face was a means of establishing mastery; the nerveless self-control evinced by it was described in countless stories, one of which concerned Sam Bugg, the famous Nashville gambler.

One day Sam was watching a card game in which a well-known cardsharp was taking the other players for all they were worth by using a stacked deck. Sam got into the game and prepared his countermove: he stacked a fresh deck so as to give the cardsharp four kings, while giving another member of the party four aces. But how was he to get the stacked deck into the game?

Sam managed in the following way. He brushed an imaginary spider from the gambler's collar, diverting his attention for only an instant, but long enough to introduce the new deck of cards. Sam Bugg's cards soon did their work. Realizing in a flash what had been done to him, "without a change of muscle," the gambler drawled to Sam: "Mr. Bugg, the next time you see a spider biting me, let him bite on." [32]

Colonel Johnson, too, was always in poker-faced control of the situation. After the great match race of 1842, in which Fashion, owned by William Gibbons of New Jersey, beat his Boston, the colonel was on his way home. At some point he became aware that a pickpocket was trying to rob him. Without betraying any emotion at all, the colonel seized the pickpocket's hand and said in his cool and quiet way: "My man, you are mistaken. Mr. Gibbons won the purse, not I."[33]

With this in mind, the popularity of match races, which had faded out in England, is more easily explained. One reason Americans clung to this kind of racing was because there often were not enough horses in a locality to fill up a racing card for a number of consecutive races. Numerous heats filled the bill and stimulated wagering. But the match race had a special appeal for Jacksonians. They saw it as a form of duel between individuals. The emphasis was shifted from the horses to their owners and managers. That was what made Colonel Johnson's mastery of the form so impressive to his contemporaries. In his control of this kind of duel he seemed most Napoleonic.

So we return to that title, applied universally to anyone who towered over his peers in the scope of his ambition and power. But the figure of Napoleon also represented something newer than martial glory. In *Representative Men,* one of the major books of the Jacksonian period, Ralph Waldo Emerson put his finger on the new phenomenon that Bonaparte signified — the career open to talents, the breaking up of the old structure of aristocratic privilege. Napoleon represented

> the antagonism between the Conservative and the democratic classes; between those who have made their fortunes, and the young and the poor who have fortunes to make.

In describing this second class of men, Emerson could equally well have been writing of Jacksonian sportsmen: "bold, self-relying, desiring to keep open every avenue to the competition of all, and to multiply avenues."[34]

Unlike his great prototype, however, Colonel Johnson's end came neither in exile nor as anticlimax. He was on one of his ceaseless campaigns, this time in the new Southwest of Alabama and Mississippi, lured there by the glitter of more luxuriant opportunities. Although his own days of greatness had passed, the colonel more than held his own in that extraordinary milieu of con men, gamblers, and tricksters, until, on February 9, 1849, in Mobile, he collapsed suddenly and died.

American sporting life was increasingly open to new talents, and it was equally open to new and unorthodox games. William Ransom Johnson might not have been very pleased to be remembered as the first great American gamesman, but so he was. And although his ancestors on his mother's side had been in America since the middle of the seventeenth century, he was also in this Napoleonic sense a new man. But then, in the United States, new men and new games were a very old story.

WILLIAM T. PORTER

3

William T. Porter and
the *Spirit of the Times*

WILLIAM TROTTER PORTER was born in Newbury, Vermont, on December 24, 1809, of a family that had been in America for eight generations. His paternal grandfather, Asa Porter, mixed roles and occupations in a distinctively American manner. An English traveler had noted this phenomenon in describing a man who was "a farmer, a merchant, and a parson, all these occupations though seemingly so different, he carries on with the greatest regularity and without confusion."[1] And so Asa Porter managed to be an archconservative in his social views, a Tory in politics, and also a merchant and inveterate speculator whose eye was always on the future. Yet he lived, as nearly as he could, in the style of an eighteenth-century English country gentleman, with a large house, extensive grounds, fine horses, a family coat of arms, and the title of colonel.

The colonel's situation exemplified the complex relationship in American society between the appearance and the reality of social position. Asa Porter's social position was based more on his wealth than on his ancestry, which wasn't, after all, very different from that of most of his neighbors. But his wealth was much less firmly established than it seemed. Much of his estate consisted of unproductive acres without tenants, who, when secured, were not easily managed. Even more troubling, the legal title to land was often shaky. In addition, the colonel's stiff-necked loyalty to the crown during the Revolutionary War didn't help any. So tangled did the colonel's affairs become in the 1780s and 1790s that one of his sons, Benjamin, who was a lawyer, gave up his law practice in order to handle his father's affairs, which were by that time a hopeless snarl of conflicting claims of tenants, squatters, and the proprietor.

Benjamin Porter had a family of five sons and one daughter, William Trotter being his fourth son. Benjamin enjoyed outdoor sports and taught them to all his children. He was especially fond of riding and spent much of every day in the saddle, traveling on business from New York to Canada. The Porters were a gregarious and lively family, and Benjamin Porter was a most attractive social companion. William inherited his father's sociable temperament.[2]

This comfortable, expansive life came to a sudden end in 1817, when, at age forty-six, Benjamin Porter found he had heart disease. Desperately he attempted to put his father's and his own affairs in some semblance of order. Years later, his son's biographer wrote that "if five more years of active life had been vouchsafed him," Benjamin Porter would surely have converted that property of vast potential into actual wealth, for he was involved in "various enterprises of pith and high promise."[3] Ah! those myriad acres, those various enterprises, that golden promise! A familiar motif, this glittering thread of potential but often illusory wealth, running through these early decades of American sporting history. One recalls Andrew Jackson's extensive landholdings, high hopes, and near bankruptcy and thinks also of Mr. Hawkins, in Mark Twain's *The Gilded Age,* who, on his deathbed, begged his family to hang on to their Tennessee acres:

> I am leaving you in cruel poverty, I have been — so foolish — so short-sighted. But courage! A better day is coming. Never lose sight of the Tennessee land. Be wary. There is wealth stored up for you there — wealth that is boundless.

Benjamin Porter died within a year after finding he had heart disease, and the old colonel died three months later. The estate, when finally settled among many heirs, had dwindled to almost nothing. Benjamin's widow moved to Hanover, New Hampshire, where one son enrolled in Dartmouth College and the younger children entered Moore's Charity School, whose headmaster, Archilaus F. Putnam, was a Yankee type hallowed in American literature and folklore — the Yankee schoolmaster, firm but fair, and devoted to letters. In John Greenleaf Whittier's *Snow-Bound,* that classic statement of the American country past, the schoolmaster played and sang along with his pupils. So much for folklore and poetry. The actual Archilaus Putnam was a harsh, flogging, implacable-eyed pedant, determined to cram a classical education into his pupils and root out of them any trace of frivolity or fun. The Porter children all hated the school and did everything they could to escape it. "Old Put's" floggings, along with declining economic opportunities in the New England countryside, began the dispersal of the Porter family.

In these early decades of the nineteenth century the Porters, restless, ambitious, and energetic, were typical of countless other New England men and women. They wandered south and west and everywhere over the seas; they began new businesses and entered new occupations. And during this time they moved steadily from the countryside to towns and cities. They excelled in trade, inventions, and journalism. Publishing and printing attracted them, because they had a long tradition of literacy and concern with language. This inventiveness, business skill, and literacy would soon be applied to American games and sports.

William Porter had shown some promise as a scholar, but he doesn't seem to have enjoyed reading about the Greeks and Romans and was likely to be found with Walton's *Compleat Angler* hidden inside his Vergil. He liked action-filled contemporary stories. He persuaded his mother to allow him to leave school and take up printing, "suggested by the life of Dr. Franklin, which he was then reading for the fiftieth time." So he was sent to an establishment in Massachusetts that was acceptable to his mother because it printed Bibles and religious tracts.

In 1825 Mrs. Porter died, and within a few weeks the Porters were "all cut adrift from the home anchorage forever." William continued working in the printing office, and life soon began to reveal new possibilities far removed from religious tracts and scholarship. He added a taste for urban amusements to the love of country sports that had originated in his childhood, inspired by the example of his father's riding and fishing. He also gained his first experience of big-city life, going with a friend to Boston, where, among other delights, he saw his first circus.

William Porter decided on a career as a journalist. He moved from job to job, slowly working his way south. His progress was more than geographic. He was also moving steadily away from the conventional beliefs of his New England forebears, and toward something more cosmopolitan. New Englanders were being transformed from Puritans into Yankees.[4] His father had loosened the bonds by softening the old antagonism toward amusement. The Porter sons, with William Trotter leading the way, would go much further and make amusement their careers. Not surprisingly, then, William Porter, "with a light heart and lighter purse," gravitated to that mecca of amusement, New York City.[5]

*

William Porter's arrival in New York City, at the beginning of the 1830s, coincided with an important cultural development — the birth of the popular press in the United States. Many elements were involved in this: the new technology that made possible steam-driven presses capable of rapidly printing thousands of copies; reduced costs, so that papers could sell for a penny; and an improved postal system that spread the word more quickly to an increasingly literate public. William Porter was in exactly the best place at the right time.

It didn't take much to start a paper in those days: "One could start a paper on faith and a hundred dollar bill," a contemporary journal reported. This wasn't much of an exaggeration. In 1841 Horace Greeley began the *Tribune* with $3,000. Papers sprang up like mushrooms, to meet the apparently insatiable demand; "and then there comes a frost, a killing frost, in the form of bills due and debts unpaid."[6] Historians can only guess at the number of magazines and newspapers that emerged, for even the names of most of these are now lost; but in this frenzied process, New York City became the nation's publishing capital.

Publishing was a young man's life. William Porter, twenty-two, took a job in a printing office. The city's journalistic fraternity was crowded with young New Englanders of backgrounds very like Porter's, a few of whom eventually became famous: Henry Raymond, age twenty-one, from Vermont; Horace Greeley (who worked in the same printing office, and, briefly, on Porter's first paper), age twenty, from New Hampshire; Benjamin Day, also twenty, from Massachusetts; and Nathaniel Currier, age twenty-one, from the same state. Many aspiring journalists, if they were not New Englanders, were English: James Gordon Bennett, James Parton, and E. L. Godkin, for instance.

Determined, like all the rest, to make a name for himself by editing his own paper, William Porter was very unlike them in the kind of paper he wanted; it was his "cherished purpose" to publish a weekly sporting paper. On December 10, 1831, Porter and a friend brought out the first issue of the *Spirit of the Times*. Little is known about this paper in its earliest form, because its circulation was not large enough to keep it going. Porter combined it with another paper and then took on the editing of two other ephemeral sheets. Nothing helped. The *Spirit* failed, and Porter had to sell. But he continued working as a journalist and didn't give up his idea. In a few years he bought back the copyright to the title he wanted, and in January, 1835, the *Spirit of the Times* began again.[7] There would be many ups and downs ahead, but at last he was off and running.

*

The cultural spirit of the times was increasingly urban. It craved amusement, which Porter was determined to supply — especially the amusement of the race course. But he could not go too far too fast.[8] He was acutely aware that many people, otherwise favorably disposed to sport and to sporting amusement, retained a "morbid apprehension of the ruinous and indefinite mischiefs" associated with "the very name race course."[9] When even Andrew Jackson had to move warily in the face of such opinion, it is no wonder William Porter was cautious.

Hesitantly and gradually, Porter worked out his editorial strategy for combating such views. His approach was two-pronged. His first argument emphasized the practical usefulness of sport. The agricultural, horse-breeding, and horse-raising interests in the United States were economically important. Shrewdly Porter spotted the chink in the armor of the Puritan Party, which regarded all amusements and pastimes as "frivolous, at the least," and, presumably at the worst, as "unprofitable." Porter emphasized a point all ambitious Americans could appreciate. Sport was potentially an important business. If it were made more businesslike, more businessmen could be sportsmen.[10]

Porter's second approach was geographic. Taking for granted that there was a "kindly feeling for the turf" in the middle states and in the old South, Porter directed his attention to the southwest of the 1820s and 1830s — Mississippi, Alabama, Arkansas, and Louisiana, the boisterous and rapidly expanding cotton lands of the new South. As he later described it:

> Trammelled by circumstances, retarded by inexperience, we groped our way slowly into those Southern and Western regions of our country, where the sports we advocate were more generally appreciated and more liberally encouraged.[11]

To stimulate circulation and make contacts, William Porter made a lengthy visit to the South and West in the autumn of 1838, return-

ing "with enlarged and enlightened views of the character and condition of the agricultural districts."[12]

The agricultural districts. That was the group his paper had to
come to terms with. What kind of sportsmen would these farmers
be? (They were farmers; there was nothing else to call them.) William Porter wrestled with that question for two decades but never
made up his mind firmly as to what the proper answer was. He assumed that these farmers would be molded in the tradition of English country sporting life, with people like himself as the leading
lights. And so the general social tone of the early *Spirit of the Times*
was a trifle superior, with a muted but unmistakable English accent. Yet he recognized (or suspected) that these farmers didn't live
in a firmly established sporting culture. Frontiersmen did not become aristocrats by building a Hermitage, and farmers did not
become squires by reading the *Spirit*. Besides, from fairly early on,
William Porter was attracted to these sportsmen-in-the-making, because they were already different from any other type and would
remain so. He was something of a renegade from his own Puritan
culture and sympathized with the uncouth and marginal characters
he glimpsed in his expedition of 1838.

There was another contradiction to be faced. The paper's aim was
to make itself useful to farmers; this it did by stressing the importance of animal stock to national prosperity and by giving encouragement to the increasingly popular movement for county fairs,
livestock shows, and displays of agricultural implements. So Porter
offered his services, at a moderate commission, to buy things for
people in remote areas — cattle, horses, machinery, books, fighting
cocks, and carriages. But he charged for services rendered and
didn't see farming as a sacred way of life. His family had been professional and commercial for generations. The values of these early
days of American popular journalism are important, for they reveal
the urban entrepreneurial spirit William Porter took for granted.

To some extent Porter resolved these contradictions by seeing the
Spirit as a mediating instrument, a means of bringing these diverse
groups, classes, and interests together. He organized meetings of
northern, southern, and western horsemen; he made the offices of
the *Spirit* a neutral meeting ground for everyone. He hoped that out
of this interplay the backwoods and backwaters would be tied
together and the American sportsman would evolve on his own, in
his own way. But difficulties remained.

*

The first years of the journal were predictably precarious. The chief problem, always — the lack of ready cash to conduct affairs — resulted from the inability or unwillingness of subscribers to pay their bills. The panic of 1837, and the protracted depression that followed it, hit especially hard, aggravating the problem many times over. Subscription rates were raised, partly to weed out undependable subscribers and uncollectible accounts, but this reduced circulation and only raised again the question, about which William Porter wavered, as to whether the *Spirit* should be an exclusive or a popular journal.

Hard times weren't the only source of trouble. Business management wasn't William Porter's strong point. There were too many demands on his time; he was attempting to edit and write and conduct business trips almost alone. On the business side he was much too lenient. One of his older brothers, George, was a lawyer who lived in New York City and wrote occasional sporting pieces for the paper. In the late 1830s George gave up his law practice to devote himself to managing the paper's legal and business affairs, just as his father had done for his grandfather years before.

Unfortunately, the results were also similar. The Porters attempted to solidify the paper's shaky position by expanding its operation, buying out their chief rival, the *American Turf Register;* but that only postponed the day of reckoning, which came in 1842, when the *Spirit* was about to go under. A printer named John Richards bought the paper and took business management into his own hands, keeping William Porter as editor.

William Porter was now free to concentrate his energies on a project dear to his sporting heart — the reform of horse racing. In the spring of 1839 he organized a meeting of northern sportsmen to consider ways to reinvigorate horse racing in New York and New Jersey, where it had fallen into one of its periodic states of disrepute. Porter received strong support from John Cox Stevens, and the result was the reformation of the New York Jockey Club.

This was only the first step along the road to proper reform, however. Porter argued that horse racing was potentially a very profitable business enterprise and that its ills were mainly due to the absence of farsighted and honest business leadership. But horse racing wouldn't attract such leaders until the scale of its operations was enlarged. Then local failings and petty rivalries could be overcome, the general public would gain confidence in what it was invited to patronize, and the size of the interested general public would vastly increase. This meant that horse racing must become much more nationally systematic and uniform, and this, in turn, would require some kind of central regulating body with real power. Without it the turf would continue to merit at least some of the criticism constantly hurled at it.

Here Porter, like other of the sportsmen in these pages, came face to face with the powerful reality of American sectional feeling. What he wanted was direction from the center, "a tribunal of some sort, to which the various Jockey Clubs, as well as individuals, could resort for the adjustment of controverted questions."[13] In short, something like the Newmarket Jockey Club in England, which, at this same time, under the aggressive leadership of Admiral Rous and Lord George Bentinck, faced similar problems and resolved them by establishing its position of predominant authority.[14] But how was one to go about establishing such a body in the United States?

Porter turned to a venerable American political device. He issued a call for a national turf convention, and then used all his powers of editorial persuasion and personal influence to bring this convention into being. There was a good deal of discussion of his proposal. Nothing came of it. A few local centers of racing authority already existed, of course, in New York, Baltimore, and Charleston, as well as many local jockey clubs; but such groups were not about to give up any of their authority to a central body, even if there was a central body to relinquish it to. States rights and local control were old traditions in the United States, strongly entwined in every aspect of political, social, and cultural life.[15] One wonders if William Porter, usually so practical and realistic in his views, really understood how fantastic it was to imagine that South Carolinians, for example, would, in the 1840s, sympathize with such a notion (and a northern notion at that).

It was not just a matter of geography. The problem Porter faced was more complex still. Localism and regionalism existed in England too; but the problem in the United States had also to do with the absence of available means for overcoming local particularism. In England, as in the United States, most sportsmen vehemently insisted on keeping sports entirely outside the control of any government agency. But in England in these years there was a private alternative. The Newmarket Jockey Club reformed and regulated racing. Couldn't Newmarket be reproduced in America as the governing body for American horsemen?

The answer, Porter found, was "no." And this was essentially because of the same condition that had rendered Andrew Jackson so vulnerable in resisting public opinion: the absence of a homogeneous upper class. Admiral Rous and Lord George Bentinck gradually extended and expanded the power of Newmarket because Newmarket had behind it the intangible but potent authority of one hundred and fifty years of existence; because Newmarket was connected, as well, with the prestige of royal patronage; and, above all, because they were able to draw on the support of a small but immensely powerful group of members, whose influence was irresistible because their social standing was undeniable. No such group existed in America, and it was beyond the power of William Porter's persuasiveness and affability to call one into being.

What was the identity of that elusive American sportsman who read (but didn't always pay for) the *Spirit of the Times?* It was still in the process of changing. Had William Porter built a replica of the Newmarket Jockey Club in America, he would have been indulging in a kind of folly. Yet he was trying to reproduce a social institution in conditions that were equally indeterminate. If American institutions and social arrangements were so different from those in England, then what were their proper national embodiments? Or might it be that America was one nation politically but not socially? For a person like William Porter, with a vision of a national sporting community, it was frustrating to live in a federal culture where competition, not cooperation, was the keynote. In this respect, Colonel Johnson was closer to the spirit of American racing life than William Porter. The most appropriate symbol for the spirit of these Jacksonian times was not the convention but the match race.

*

Although the desire to create some kind of formal central authority came to nothing, the *Spirit of the Times* itself became a kind of national sporting center, one of those informal, voluntary associations that, at this time, so impressed Alexis de Tocqueville. It served as a place to send and receive messages, a refuge in foreign parts, a sportsman's home away from home. Subscribers wrote to Porter for answers. They also wrote simply to exchange a few words with a man whom most had never seen or would see but who somehow seemed approachable. The *Spirit's* contributors, almost all unpaid, sent in a flood of reports about many things other than sports and games — reports of the odd happenings, the wonders and curiosities of the still largely uncharted land in which they found themselves — so that the *Spirit*'s office had about it somewhat the same atmosphere as P. T. Barnum's nearby museum, and served the same function: the amusement of strangers.

The paper also did two other things for American sportsmen. It served as a central record-keeping and statistical bureau, week after week feeding the readers' insatiable desire for facts, information, details, and statistics. In almost every issue the editor pleaded with his readers in outlying districts to furnish him with the same data — facts about meetings held, records of races run, and information about breeding pedigrees.

> Many of his decisions and sporting reports will be quoted as authority for generations to come. He possessed a fund of sporting statistics unequalled by any other man in America.[16]

In a culture of change, Porter and his paper were sources of security and stability. Tom Owen, one of the comic writers of the period, referred to "your *Times* which has not changed, while all other times have."[17] By preserving ephemeral moments of a culture of haste and hurry, Porter served the sportsmen of his day as historian.

William Porter also served as an arbiter. Many disputes and questions depended upon interpretation, not facts, for their resolution. His fair-mindedness made him an ideal judge. The deference paid him was exceptional, perhaps a clue to his cultural significance.

> He was received throughout the country as the umpire of all controverted points, not only in matters growing out of the specialties of his paper, but in all questions of friendly argument, which would not take parties into court. During his editorial career, he had probably decided more disputes, involving the award of money, than any judge who ever sat upon a bench; and what is more remarkable in this connection is, that his decisions were always cheerfully acquiesced in, and never were made the subject of appeal.[18]

William Porter saw himself as continuing the English sporting tradition, its rules, procedures, and spirit, at least until something else could take its place. He accepted the idea of a code of sportsmanship and worked to make it effective in the United States. But even as he did so, the tide was moving in another direction. In presiding over a culture that was moving from the country to the city, he was also presiding, at another level, over a sporting culture that was moving from the customary to the prescriptive. Custom was giving way to rules.

*

From the outset, William Porter had wished his paper to deal with other forms of entertainment besides sports. As a result, the *Spirit* had weekly reviews of theater, opera, concerts and recitals, and dance. He gradually broadened its interest and popularized its tone and style by making it more like the penny press of the time.

The tone of the penny press was personal; its news columns sparkled with slangy wit and raciness; it cared much more for liveliness than for dignity. The penny press was not entirely froth and levity, however; it had a bold and unconventional side, dealing in honest terms with crime, business, and politics in ways many readers thought were shockingly coarse.

The desire to dig out and report news also led many New York City papers to establish Washington bureaus and European correspondents. Papers became less parochial. Greeley's *Tribune* in particular had a first-rate book section. In addition, these papers devoted considerable attention, in a somewhat satirical and indiscreet manner, to social life in the city and nation; and out of this developed the society page and the gossip column of a later day. These developments were reflected in the *Spirit,* which had book reviews, business and political news, special reports from foreign correspondents, a column of sporting gossip, and a great deal of space devoted to jokes, puns, and (supposed) witticisms, these latter the bits that make the most tiresome reading today. Still modeled to some extent on English sporting journals, the *Spirit* steadily developed its own tone.

The *Spirit* also published fiction, and out of this came its great contribution to American letters. At first it drew heavily on articles reprinted from English journals, and on original stories by English writers; but more and more Porter printed and supported American writers and writing. He believed that English literary magazines "beat us a long way," and, although he and his colleagues reviewed American and English literature in a remarkably open-minded way — witness the discriminating appreciation of Herman Melville, Fenimore Cooper, Charles Dickens, and the Brontës — Porter didn't think the time was yet ripe for the flowering of a native tradition in the higher forms of literature.

But the time *was* just right for the flowering of a native tradition in popular forms of literature, especially sporting literature. In this genre, Americans more than held their own. England, which had boasted respectable sporting magazines for over a century, was losing its superiority; its sporting literature was exhausted. To give some semblance of life to their shopworn sketches, British writers resorted to locating them in foreign and exotic places — India, Canada, the United States. "It is rare that you open either of the sporting magazines in Britain," Porter wrote, "without finding a bear, a buffalo, or a panther hunt in the United States." Why? Because American scenes were fresher, more colorful.[19]

Andrew Jackson's generation had begun the task of redefining the American relation to European culture but had left that task unfinished: it had fashioned houses like the Hermitage, banks like Greek temples, prisons like Egyptian tombs, and stories that were pale imitations of English ones. Europe still loomed magisterially in the imagination of all Americans. Now, for the generation that came of age in the 1830s, changes were taking place. William Ellery Channing had broken new ground with an earlier but still-influential essay, "Remarks on National Literature"; Washington Irving and James Fenimore Cooper, in stories, novels, and travel accounts, explored native themes as well as old-world ones. And then, to cap the cultural ferment of the Jacksonian era, while William Porter was pondering the condition of American sporting journalism a far greater voice than his delivered a famous manifesto.

In Cambridge, Massachusetts, in August of 1837, Ralph Waldo Emerson defined the American cultural situation in his lecture/essay "The American Scholar," in phrases long-since familiar, so familiar and so often repeated that it is difficult to suggest the excitement with which they were first heard and read and which led Oliver Wendell Holmes to describe them as "a second declaration of independence."

Although his words were unusually fresh and arresting, there was nothing new in Emerson's declaration that Americans must break free from their feeble dependence upon a European past:

> Our day of dependence, our long apprenticeship to the learning of other lands, draws to a close. The millions that around us are rushing into life, cannot always be fed on the sere remains of foreign harvest. Too long have we listened to the Courtly Muses of Europe.

More important was the fact that Emerson turned the relationship between America and Europe upside down. Americans no longer needed to ape European traditions, inherit European learning, and copy European art; Europeans must now begin to learn from America. And what Americans had to teach them about was the culture of the future — a democratic culture that was common, lowly, and popular.

Events, actions, arise, that must be sung, that will sing themselves. I ask not for the great, the remote, the romantic. I embrace the common, I explore and sit at the feet of the familiar, the low. Give me insight into today, and you may have the antique and future worlds.

Emerson's proclamation rang down through succeeding generations because it touched on ideas deeply embedded in American thought since the Revolution: that the true American subjects would be new and popular ones. His influence on other famous figures of American thought is too well known to need repeating, but we shouldn't forget that in every decade in the nineteenth century it was also felt by the insignificant, the obscure, the millions who never wrote down their ideas at all. Emerson's insistence that the ordinary things of life — "the milk in the pan; the ballad in the street; the news of the boat" — were marvelous, deeply moved his ordinary countrymen. Fifty years after "The American Scholar," for example, an obscure historian of a humble aspect of American life, the volunteer fire companies of New York City, expressed Emersonian ideas in Emersonian accents:

I believe in the great common tides of life around us. I believe that I have brushed against and continue to brush against as great heroes on our sidewalks every day as ever Homer sang and puffed. Here are Ajax and Agammemnon and Achilles, and so on, only dear readers, you probably know them under the name of Smith or Brown or Rogers, out in the country. In the furrows or lifting up our axes against the thick trees are just such men, such heroes.[20]

It was in this same spirit that William Porter's imagination was seized by the newest and freshest aspect of American sporting culture, the new Southwest that was leaping into life along the rapidly moving frontier with

an exhaustless supply of material . . . the adventurous life of a frontier settler, incidents of travel over prairies and among mountains hitherto unknown to the white man, the singular variety of manners in different states . . .[21]

Porter had always thought of these people as potential subscribers and supporters, but now, as the first trickle of stories about this new frontier came into his New York office, it slowly dawned on him that he had struck a journalistic gold mine. He sought out authors and encouraged them to write more, attempted to identify unknown talent, and helped the writers get their stories published later in book form. He edited two of the most famous and important collections of such stories, *The Big Bear of Arkansas* (1846) and *The Quarter Horse and Other Tales* (1848). These became the national rage. William Porter thus responded to the Emersonian challenge and helped create a modest but long-lasting American literary tradition. But in view of the history of American sport, we can see that he got far more than he bargained for.

*

What he got was the tall tale. And the tall tale and southwestern humor in general bear an interesting relation to American sporting culture.[22] It is through literature that we know most about a widespread but shadowy historical type, crucial in the history of the American sporting style. This disreputable and remarkable figure came up out of the swamps and forests, floated up and down the rivers, and settled everywhere along the riverbanks, as Huckleberry Finn found when he came ashore.

He was the outsider, the marginal man, the trickster; and he contributed something to the eventual dominance of the gamesman in American culture. The trickster had all the frontiersman's cunning, deviltry, and lack of deference to his supposed betters. He tricked everyone: his parents, his kin, his friends, and total strangers. He was totally unheroic; he alternately whined and snarled. He was occasionally nasty and brutal, especially to anyone weaker than he. But his enormous vitality and almost disarming brazenness compensated for a great deal.

The trickster was an inexhaustible creator of games. He turned everything into a game: camp meetings, wedding nights, burials, horse races. His need to gamble was pathological. His precarious, skimpy, implausible life was a kind of extended game of chance. His chief sport was horse racing, and there he was most in his element. His horse racing had nothing to do with Newmarket, and everything to do with the common life around him. His racehorses were quarter horses, and commoner, more democratic — not to say spavined and scrawny — examples of the species didn't exist. But they served his purpose, which was to use horses to trick people and show them up for fools.

His greatest contribution to American sports, however, was that he made no distinction at all between sport and other aspects of life. The trickster's notions, however much opposed by most respectable people, eventually colored every aspect of the life around him. With some polish and with a generation or two behind him, the trickster became a gamesman; but he never became the traditional sportsman. The things he hated most were authority, individual or traditional, and rules.

This trickster was an element of disorder. His motto was Simon Suggs's: "It pays to be shifty in a new country." And he went on believing that, long after the country ceased to be new, or to be country.

*

The *Spirit* flourished in the late 1840s, its circulation reaching its highest point, something like 40,000 persons per year; and maybe ten persons read it for each one who subscribed. It was said to have the largest foreign circulation of any American paper, of any type, during this time. Porter had succeeded, to some extent, in expanding the enterprise to reach more ordinary people, not just the wealthier, self-proclaimed, sportsmen. In the middle of the decade, he wrote, with justifiable pride:

> The number of gentlemen with interest in the success of the Turf in this country, has more than doubled within the last ten years, and it is daily becoming more and more popular. We have nothing here to do but to go on and prosper, keeping in view this single fact, that if the legitimate ends of the Turf are staunchly maintained, it must become at length universally and eminently popular with all classes of society.[23]

He had staked a good deal on the belief that sporting amusement could be satisfying without becoming trivial and that sporting sociability could be warm without being dissipated. He had won the gamble he took in leaving home, cutting adrift from the old ways, and moving to New York City. Or had he?

Without exception those who knew William Porter loved him. All described him as sweet, generous, almost childlike in his simplicity. He was by common consent an inspired editor. Yet none of these virtues or talents was enough to outweigh the view that his life had been one of wasted effort.

His character was not the type Americans most respected, nor had his editorial career shown the qualities his contemporaries so admired in journalists such as Greeley and Raymond. They were men of influence and power. They were purposeful, single-minded, and controlling. They were managers. And so after Porter's death, when his brother-in-law wrote his biography, he reshaped Porter's career, making it seem more impressive by singling out for praise that indomitable energy which enabled him to carry out from its first and discouraging inception to a successful issue, the fixed, definite, precise, great idea of his youth, the introduction and advancement of a fresh, original and captivating department of letters.[24]

That was the way it should have been. The discovery and emergence of southwestern humor should have been seen as part of a conscious strategy. It is doubtful that William Porter would have recognized the young man who was supposed to have always had that "fixed, definite, precise idea" about what he was going to do. He would surely have recalled instead the uncertainty, the groping, the large role chance played in everything. But then, just as he was old-fashioned in accepting the idea of a code of sportsmanship, he was also out of tune with his time because he thought of sport as play, and of play as a fundamental part of life.

*

For a brief period, sports and journalism reunited the Porter family in New York City. In their collective high spirits and mutual affection they were an appealing group. "That band of brothers," wrote a friend, "united as we never remember to have seen or heard of any other brothers: those five, brave, gallant, good glorious Porters."[25]

The Porter brothers had many gifts, but they never had the gift of good health. Their time together, in the late 1830s, was very brief. Benjamin went into commerce and moved to Mobile, Alabama, where, in December 1840, he died suddenly in his mid-thirties. After the *Spirit* came under John Richards's management, George, closest to William in sympathies and interest, also went south, to New Orleans, where he worked as associate editor of the *New Orleans Picayune*. He made a successful career as a journalist, writing about the city and its racing. But his career was cut short when, in 1849, in his middle forties, he died suddenly of "bilious fever." The oldest brother, T. Olcott, died next, in 1852 in New York, at age forty-nine. No Porter brother had so far lived to be fifty.

Only William and Francis, the youngest, remained. Francis shared the family's "natural taste" for writing and contributed theatrical criticism to the *Spirit*. But he never settled completely on journalism as a career. In 1846 he joined George in New Orleans and worked on the *Picayune*. Soon after George's death, Francis learned that he was suffering from consumption. He visited Europe in the summer and fall of 1854, in the forlorn hope of regaining his health, but it was no use. He returned to New Orleans and died there in February of 1855.

No wonder that after all this William Porter never again "seemed his old self"; part of him had died with his brothers. He lacked zest and buoyancy; even his interest in the *Spirit* diminished, although he slogged away at his editorial duties. It was supposed that Francis's death had crushed him completely. But suddenly, in 1856, he surprised his friends and the American sporting fraternity. He left the *Spirit of the Times* and associated himself with a new sporting publication, called, in his honor, *Porter's Spirit of the Times.*

His enthusiasm revived. The new paper's emphasis was much more sympathetic to urban life than the old *Spirit*'s had been; that former balance in William Porter's mind was now tipped toward the city and the city's amusements. He expressed the same rapturous love for the vitality of a sprawling city that one finds in Walt Whitman. New York, for William Porter, was Babylon: "the home of sells, dodges, bunkum," "this patent, double-spring ever-moving highly elastic city." It was P. T. Barnum's city, the city of the urban trickster, and it was also the city of Mose the B'Hoy, the urban rowdy, whose acquaintance we'll make in chapter 8. *Porter's Spirit* contained more about spectator sports, less about field sports; there was more criticism of rural bigotry, and even more criticism of the respectable classes. It contained less southwestern humor: that stream was running dry. There was also greater sympathy for the crude, rough, and sometimes violent people of the city. William Porter now wrote about prize fighting, which had barely received notice in the old *Spirit* and then only to be roundly condemned. Prize fighting was still much opposed, but "like it or not, pugilism was growing in the U.S." Although William Porter thought it deplorable in many ways, it could not be ignored. Pugilists were "public facts," and prize fighting showed "the spirit of the times." [26]

There were limits beyond which the new paper would not go — limits of social propriety. *Porter's Spirit,* like most Jacksonian sportsmen, was embarrassed by vulgarity. The editor primly promised his new readers that he would not reproduce prize-fight slang in his column. (He had been cautious enough about the tall tales in that respect. In a letter to the publishers of one of his collections of southwestern humor, he warned that "there may be an occasional indelicate expression or allusion that it would be desirable to expunge.") [27]

The emphasis of *Porter's Spirit,* although it did not mark a fundamental change in the editor's views, was an interesting one; but William Porter was no longer able to sustain the effort required for his duties as editor. After the first few weeks Porter wrote less and less. The main thing he had left to give the paper was his name. "Care, disappointment, and that sickness of heart which he concealed from the world, began to tell on face and form and mental activity."[28] Even his most vital impulse, his sociability, began to ebb. He lived more alone, solacing his weary spirits by occasionally going trout fishing in the country.

The middle 1850s were a deeply troubling time for him. As the federal union broke up, the national fraternity of sportsmen also disintegrated. The offices of the *Spirit* had been a haven for strangers, and this had been especially important for southerners. Until William Porter left it, the *Spirit of the Times* had always had close ties with the South, with its literature and its point of view; and the Porter family had strong southern associations. While Porter was editor, the *Spirit* kept up its wide reportage of southern sport, in particular racing in the New Orleans area, where Richard Ten Broeck, the up-and-coming sportsman of the time, was pushing it to new levels of popularity. And the *Spirit*'s correspondence columns still gave southerners an opportunity to communicate with northerners, even as talking began to give way to fighting. But one by one even those ties were breaking. Francis's death ended the direct family connection, and William Porter's new paper was much less sympathetic than the old *Spirit* had been. In 1858 Johnson Jones Hooper wrote:

> Many of us here in the South, have been accustomed to regard the "Old Spirit" as the single remaining link which bound us in kindly feeling and sympathy to New York . . . For the love of the "old times," and for the memory of old friends, let us rally to the aid of the glorious old *Spirit*.[29]

It was too late. In 1861 *Porter's Spirit of the Times* again combined with the old *Spirit,* but by then it was a different world.

William Porter felt that "he had to all intents and purposes about done with life." What he now wrote was primarily retrospective — the obituaries of his old friends. In 1857 he commemorated John Cox Stevens; in 1858, he memorialized Wade Hampton of South Carolina; that same year he recorded, with "painful sorrow," the death of Henry William Herbert, whose sporting sketches the *Spirit* had helped make popular. He was in fact writing the obituary of the Jacksonian sporting world.

In July of 1858 William Trotter Porter caught cold, got congestion of the lungs, and took to his bed to die. As described by his brother-in-law, his last hours made an affecting scene. He asked that the curtains of his room be opened, and, as the sun flooded the room, he murmured, "how beautiful." It was as if at that instant he had "caught sight of the blue hills of Newbury, and the white palings of the cottage where he was born, and heard the far away toll of the village bell, which brought back to his fading memory the objects which surrounded his boyhood. He breathed the names of his father and of his brothers, adding with a last effort, 'I want to go home.' "[30]

Perhaps. But there is no indication that, once he had left Newbury, he ever went back. The American sportsman had abandoned his country home, whether an imposing one like the Hermitage or a small white cottage in the New England hills. Country ways, like country sports, were becoming citified, and William Porter had done his utmost to help that happen. In so doing he had also helped to sever country roots and the country sense of place. Had he done his countrymen a service or a disservice? His reply to this question, had he ever felt impelled to give one, might well have been that many Americans had for years had no home to return to. After all, he hadn't originated the incessant movement of the American people. Long before he was born, his own family's history had been marked by change as well as continuity, and other families were breaking up just as the Porters had. Yes, Americans had once and for all turned away from their country past — sometimes harsh and narrow, sometimes rich and sustaining — and their future lives would be in cities. Once and for all. And yet: even as they moved forward, they looked back, with an unappeasable longing for the fading memories of those objects that had surrounded their childhoods, for those country ways they had left behind forever. In this, as in so many other ways, William Porter and his brothers reflected the spirit of their times.

HENRY WILLIAM HERBERT

4

Henry William Herbert
and Frank Forester

THE CEDARS, a cottage built in the Gothic style made popular in the 1840s by the landscape architect Andrew Jackson Downing, all wooden crenelations and gingerbread decoration, stood in a grove of trees on the banks of the Passaic River in New Jersey. Gothic buildings were supposed to convey something of an air of mystery, and at night, or during days of autumnal overcast or winter's gloom, the Cedars may well have succeeded in doing so. One approached it by way of a path that ran beside a moldering cemetery and then passed under a large fantastic wooden gate and along an even darker stretch, through cedar trees. In addition to its air of romantic mystery, this part of the path was remarkable for being lined with the kennels of watchdogs, most notably Sailor, an immense Newfoundland, whose specialty was to rescue those visitors who, under the influence of drink, Gothic twilight, or the morose hospitality of their eccentric host, from time to time jumped or fell into the Passaic.

Inside, the house was as gloomy as its surroundings. An enormous staircase dominated the entrance, a staircase appropriate for a mansion of baronial proportions but which, in this modest-sized cottage, had the double disadvantage of leading nowhere in particular and leaving little room for anything else. Most of the rest of the house, with the exception of a few heraldic devices carved into the woodwork, was never finished. Its walls remained unpainted, its floors uncarpeted. There were no curtains or blinds, and only a few of the bedrooms had adequate furniture.

The master of the Cedars was Henry William Herbert, writer, sportsman, and gentleman, who, under the pen name Frank Forester, wrote the first enduring American sporting fiction. Although he struck his contemporaries in those days as being even gloomier than his house, this had not always been so. But even in the best of times his spirits had fluctuated wildly; and that kind of oscillation marked everything about him. Henry Herbert's life was marked by doubleness — in his career, his temperament, his culture, even his personal identity.

His melodramatic, self-dramatizing moods were thought of as Byronic; but Henry Herbert was more readily identifiable as a character from a tale of Edgar Allan Poe — one of Poe's stories of buried life, in which there figured a protagonist who wandered about at night through empty echoing halls, whose mind was preyed upon by some dreadful, mysterious secret, and who, solitary and tormented, sought to expiate, through ecstasies of guilt and remorse, some nameless sin.

Some of Herbert's actual guilt and remorse had to do with the memory of his dead wife. For him, the romantic dream of enduring holy love easily became the romantic love of death. To commemorate certain events of their life together, events not always remembered happily, but now known only to himself, Henry Herbert would take out a mahogany jewel box that contained certain precious relics: a bit of bridal veil, satin slippers, a few wisps of white ribbon now faded and yellow. He would fondle these objects, press them to his lips, and shower them with tears. Outbursts of remorse were followed by periods of inaction. Night after night he sat in front of his fireplace, gazing above it at a portrait of his wife, by his late friend Henry Inman, and contemplating the roaring fire.

By day, and out of doors, Henry Herbert was no less bizarre. His sporting style, in its wild mixing of elements, resembled the architecture of his time; it combined aspects of the frontiersman, the European dandy, and the recluse. With a dog trailing behind him, Henry Herbert would appear wearing a shooting jacket of rough material, shot through with a fantastic mixture of bright colors; a vivid cutaway coat and a waistcoat with elaborate buttons; bright pantaloons; hunting brogans; and a frieze cap. Of course this wasn't really Henry Herbert at all, but Frank Forester — Frank Forester in the process of being transformed from a European gentleman sportsman into an American frontier sportsman, still a white man but now also part Indian.

However bizarre he seemed and whatever the nature of his dreadful secrets — and Henry Herbert did possess some secrets gnawing away inside — there were other more mundane explanations for the general oddity of his manner. He was an exile. He was also an immigrant enduring heartbreak and dislocation as he attempted to establish himself in an unfamiliar society in a strange land, making himself over to fit into new surroundings. He saw himself as the personification of British sporting traditions that were to be translated into American ones, with himself as translator. The duality of his life and his fiction was at least partly the result of the meeting of British sporting traditions and American reality.

Given the burden of that division, it isn't surprising that Herbert's life was marked by failure and breakdown. It wasn't marked by those things alone, however. By its end something lasting had been achieved, something that entitles Herbert to an important place in the history of American sport. This was the achievement of Frank Forester, and we shall try to find out more about him and what he accomplished. But before we do that, we must find out who Henry Herbert was and where he came from.

*

Henry William Herbert was born in London on April 7, 1807, a descendant, on both sides of his family, of members of the peerage. His father, a naturalist, man of letters, and Dean of Manchester in the Church of England, himself a younger son, taught his young son to hunt and fish. Educated at Eton and at Caius College, Cambridge, Henry Herbert gained a modest reputation for scholarship and found full scope there for a convivial social life, which he added to his lifelong passion for field sports.

Henry Herbert completed his studies in 1830 and then got into "difficulties," the precise nature of which remains unclear to this day.[1] Given the class to which he belonged and the Regency period in which he grew up, nothing would have been less surprising than spendthrift and licentious ways in a young sporting blood. Whatever Herbert's troubles were, they shaped his subsequent life and preyed on his mind. His family regarded them as serious and took stern measures. A fresh start was insisted upon. In November, 1831, Henry William Herbert emigrated to America.

But not at first to the United States. He landed in New York City (at just the time William Porter was starting his first sporting paper: their paths soon crossed) but went straight to Canada, where "the social manners and tendencies of the British aristocracy were more freely imitated than by the inhabitants of the Atlantic states" and where "gentlemen of limited means but of a determined social position" could find "like spirits."[2] But things didn't work out as Herbert had anticipated; throughout his life things rarely did. He gained some knowledge of Canadian field sports, but he didn't like Canada and returned to New York City.

There his money ran out, and, pushed into a corner, he made his first adjustment to American social values. Although his self-esteem "revolted against the idea of becoming a public tutor," he drew on his Cambridge training and degree to get a job as a teacher of Greek and Latin. However mortifying it was to be salaried, the money allowed him to cultivate the style of a gentleman and to associate with the kind of men whose company was congenial to him.

What style and what kind of men? Henry Herbert discovered that these questions were very difficult to answer. For all their talk of equality and their supposed contempt for titles, many Americans did so love a lord, or the son of a lord, or, failing that, the son of the son of a lord! Canada wasn't the only Western country where British manners were imitated. In these early years Herbert was an attractive figure, slender and supple, mustachioed and rather dashing. He became "recognized as a personage of distinction amid the circle of sportsmen who proved only too glad to emulate his manners and habits." In the lively literary and journalistic worlds of New York City, Herbert found companions who combined sporting interests with literary ones, as he would have expected to find in England. He began to write, submitting essays to several of the leading local weeklies. When these were rejected, as might have been predicted, the egotistical young man showed an irascible side, regarded rejection as a personal affront, and responded in what for New York was also a predictable way: he founded his own journal, the *American Monthly Magazine*.

This effort didn't last long, but it attracted several contributors of note and, in addition, established its editor, who wrote many of the articles himself, as a professional writer; it determined his career. It also increased his acquaintance with more of the young men about town, some of whom were socially well connected and were also avid sportsmen. In their company he explored the woodlands of Orange and Sullivan counties in New York and, beyond them, the untouched wilderness of the Adirondacks.

*

Once settled in the city, Henry Herbert assumed that he would, in the traditional manner, be able to consolidate his interests as gentleman, sportsman, and writer along conventional lines. For him and for those companions who shared his views, those conventional lines meant the English sporting tradition. Most simply put, this tradition had two dominant social principles: it was part of a society in which social standing could be defined with clarity and authority; and the society was one in which social standing was based primarily upon family and the ownership of land. On these matters, Herbert believed there could be no compromise.

This aspect of Herbert's career has about it elements of Jacksonian social comedy and would not have been out of place in one of James Fenimore Cooper's contemporary novels of manners. A large part of the comedy inhered in the way in which Herbert, in a society where adaptability was all and improvisation was a way of life, displayed a mad tenacity in living by his transatlantic social ideals — a tenacity that finally raised his behavior above mere snobbery.

According to Herbert's code, there could be no fudging, even in small matters. Sport must be wholly unconnected with money. So when the English pugilist William Fuller retired from the prize ring and came to Manhattan to set up a gymnasium for young men of the leisured class, Herbert suspected the taint of "professionalism" and would not recommend Fuller to his friends until he was convinced that Fuller no longer fought for money. Even this simple matter actually put Herbert in an odd position, since in England members of his social class often associated with pugilists in any capacity they wished. A majority of respectable Americans were prepared to support Herbert's views, but not for his reasons. American society opposed prize fighting not because it was commercial but because it was immoral. Clearly, translation of English social values into American terms would not be easy.

Herbert would have nothing to do with actors, an attitude still held by many Americans;[3] but in New York City, where theatrical and sporting circles were already much mixed together, this attitude strained the patience of his contemporaries. It must have seemed tiresome to William Porter, whose paper supported the theater. Herbert never allowed cards to be played in his home, because he insisted that a gentleman never played anything for money. Conventional society approved of this, too, but among sportsmen it seemed to be the kind of thin-blooded, tight-lipped puritanism they associated with their enemies and not their friends. And for a man like Colonel Johnson, this attitude would have seemed not tiresome but peculiar. The colonel moved in masculine sporting circles where poker was the game for sportsmen and where sportsmen played everything for money.

In regard to pugilists, actors, and cardplayers, American social usage was still somewhat uncertain, and this lack of clarity was one of the things Herbert found most exasperating. But in one respect his attitude went far beyond what was acceptable. Herbert didn't disguise his feeling that the true sportsman must hold commerce and trade in contempt. On numerous occasions his aversion to merchants and tradesmen kept him from attending dinners, because "he could not conscientiously assume a seat at a convivial table with men, be they whom they may be, he could not respect from a strictly social point of view." In his books, which abound with references to "peddling burghers" and "fat, greasy merchant princes," Herbert insisted that this distinction was fundamental. Where did such views leave him in the bustling bourgeois culture of America, where merchants and tradesmen had achieved social ascendancy years before and where commerce was not just respectable but was a dominant way of life?

Even more important, where did it leave him in a society where there was almost nothing that could be distinguished as a "strictly social point of view"? Family antecedents still mattered in narrow social circles, but such circles were increasingly unable to impose their standards on society as a whole and were even ceasing to try; instead, people withdrew into selective groups they protected vigorously from outside intrusion. Even as his friends talked about the older social ideal that Herbert represented to them, they bowed to the inevitable. With older families rapidly giving way to the new men streaming into cities from all over the country, and with money firmly established as the primary criterion for social standing, the ruling class took the form of a plutocracy consisting of members as diverse as August Belmont and John Jacob Astor, John C. Stevens and William T. Porter. American sportsmen could imitate the old architecture, copy the old sporting language, mimic the manners and ape the stories of the old sporting culture with some success; but without the social and economic structure that made a clearly marked hierarchical society possible in England, Herbert and his friends could imitate the social manners of the British aristocracy till the cows came home, and all to no effect. Where did all this leave Henry Herbert then? Virtually alone.

The "effortless superiority" of the true aristocrat was impossible in such circumstances. Every effect was too self-conscious, too strained; haughtiness ended up as personal rudeness. The irascible side of Herbert's nature came to the fore. He treated publishers "in no over-gracious manner," suitable no doubt for men who were in trade. Worse, his contempt for trade became a form of trickery. Herbert did things that went beyond the acceptable even in an age when dishonesty in the book trade was notorious. No wonder many of his contemporaries eventually decided that any man who talked incessantly about being a gentleman was a bit of a humbug.

*

If the old sporting life was impossible in the American city then perhaps it could be reestablished in the country. This hope, among other things, brought Henry Herbert to the banks of the Passaic. But life in the country didn't work out either. At the Cedars he found that he was not part of an ordered country way of life. This was not due primarily to his personal eccentricities, nor was the newness of the society an important factor, as had been the case in Andrew Jackson's frontier Tennessee. The Cedars stood in country that had been settled for about 200 years. History wasn't lacking. What was lacking was clear social definition. There really was no "country" at all, at least not as Herbert had known it.

Henry James, half a century later, described this peculiarity of the American social landscape as "the absence of the Squire and the Parson."[4] Henry Herbert's experience bore this out. All around him were farmers, and rich ones, but no squires; there were ministers but no parsons; there were houses in the country but there was no country-house culture; there was a countryside but barely a landscape. In New Jersey and upstate New York, Herbert found hunters and fishermen who shared his interests and recognized his sporting skills; but in the company of these people — company he preferred to anything else available to him — he was not among sportsmen as he understood the term.

Herbert couldn't entirely dispense with the city, however much he despised it and its vulgar culture. He had to go there to carry on his work, visit his publishers, and contact various periodicals. On the other hand, he couldn't alternate living in the country and the city; he couldn't be a country sportsman with a place in the city. And this was not just because he was chronically short of money. In England, country and city existed in intimate relation to one another, in a social sense; both had clearly established seasons fixed on the calendar and in customary practice. Both were part of one social tradition; work and play took place in an orderly pattern.

Not so in American sporting society, where routine and season were much more individual and personal. In this way, as in so many others, Henry Herbert's life was divided, and he had to make a continuous, desperate effort to create and maintain order in a world of chronic social indeterminacy. As a commuter he had an unvarying routine organized with almost frantic precision. Twice a week he walked from the Cedars to Newark, did some shopping, and took a train to New York for appointments that were always scheduled for the early afternoon. He then took a train back to Newark, picked up his morning's shopping, and walked back to the Cedars, returning to have dinner at an unvarying hour. Always the same pattern: the same days, the same trains, the same times.

The one comfortable and usable room at the Cedars was the study. Herbert's literary career, so much the product of his imagination, could be best sustained in isolation. His study was equipped with a specially built writing desk, which had innumerable drawers that swung around in circular fashion; in these Herbert put the many different sizes and colors of specially bought paper on which, and only on which, he wrote the different kinds of literature he worked on concurrently. The desk's compartments neatly represented his social, sporting, and literary lives.

Henry Herbert was pulled in opposite directions in another way as well. The overpowering cultural mood of his life was romanticism, a concept difficult to define but impossible to ignore. American sporting history has an interesting and important relationship to it. In Europe, romanticism was equally powerful in social and intellectual terms; there, the gentleman of fashion, letters, and sport could be combined in the figure of the dandy. No comparable role existed for the sportsman in American society. For him (and generally for the American intellectual), romanticism was absorbed within the contemplation of nature. The American sportsman could be transcendent but not eccentric.

American sporting culture was going in the opposite direction from the romantic state of mind; it was more businesslike, more matter of fact. And the new social elements entering it — the frontier rogues and con men like Simon Suggs, and the respectable but uncultured no-nonsense farmer-sportsmen of the Ohio Valley and the Great Plains — were worlds apart from the histrionics of romanticism.

How far from romanticism Jacksonian sporting culture had moved is apparent when one considers the atmosphere surrounding that historical anachronism, the duel, which Henry Herbert persisted in thinking still a necessary feature of the sportsman's style.

The "code duello" in the clear bourgeois light of New Jersey in the 1840s! Impossible to sustain it with a straight face. Henry Herbert certainly couldn't, although he tried desperately. His imbroglios, of which there were many, always descended to farce.

One of Herbert's duels involved a neighbor who was probably insane, and who, after three bungled misfirings, drowned himself in the Passaic. In another, having absurdly chosen a site just over the Canadian border, although it was midwinter, Herbert suffered the public humiliation of getting lost in a snowstorm and arriving on the field of honor long after everyone else had retired in disgust. Later, encountering his antagonist in a New York hotel, another wrangle followed. Herbert drew a pistol, fired, and missed, after which his antagonist knocked him down and threw him out into the street. A third duel was only verbal. A Philadelphian refused to accept Herbert's challenge, so Herbert wrote a pamphlet about the matter — a pamphlet so abusive and ridiculous that certain "indignant southern gentlemen" publicly denounced him for having made an "intentional burlesque" of the whole affair.

The southerners were partly right. It was burlesque. But the opposite of intentional. Aaron Burr's duel with Alexander Hamilton had about it special qualities of drama and tragedy; and Andrew Jackson's duel with John Dickinson exhibited much of the distinctively savage quality of American dueling. But the truth is that even in its early years in America, the duel, like other imported forms of aristocratic honor, verged on self-caricature. Andrew Jackson, for all his personal dignity, was involved in duels that were in some ways quite laughable.

This is only another indication of how unreal the self-conscious southern pretension to aristocratic culture had become. John Randolph, the supposed beau ideal of aristocratic sportsmanship, was as out of date in the 1820s and 1830s as Henry Herbert was in the 1840s and 1850s. There are many interesting parallels between these two, Herbert in New Jersey and Randolph in Virginia: they displayed pretentiousness in their homes, Roanoke and the Cedars, both of which were in reality simply dreary and uncomfortable; they shared the same quality of make-believe; and they revealed the same incipient hysteria bordering on madness.

Colonel Johnson and Henry Herbert overlapped as sportsmen for two decades, and during these years the Jacksonian sportsman, as a figure of brute strength and power, was much altered. The admiration for power remained, and so did the desire to see sporting contests as forms of dueling; but these two would be combined in very different forms in the subsequent history of American sport. In American culture, the savagery of the duel, with most vestiges of aristocratic style stripped away, was incorporated in the ambush and the shoot-out.

*

When he first came to America, Henry Herbert, like many other immigrants, did not know how long he would stay, and he never entirely gave up hope that he might return to England. He didn't become an American citizen, "notwithstanding his expressed desire to be regarded as an American in all other respects and his avowed sympathy with the land in which he was dwelling." But when he decided to be a professional writer, he wished to be recognized as an American one: "an American author of English birth" was how he put it. What did this mean?

One of the publishing fads of the 1830s was the production of giftbooks, elaborate volumes published annually and made up of articles, stories, and engravings (many of these reprints of English work). In 1836 Herbert's "mission of Americanizing himself as an author" took the form of the literary annual *The Magnolia,* which he edited and in which all selections were original work by American writers and artists.[5] Washington Irving, James Fenimore Cooper, and N. P. Willis contributed, and Henry Inman supervised the engravings. Two of these annuals were published, and both sold well. For the rest of his life, one of Herbert's "most striking literary peculiarities was his unbounded affection for American-born authors and artists, to whose productions he invariably gave preference when consulted by publishers."

Giftbooks didn't resolve the question as to the kind of writing he himself should do. He had to make a living, so he tried many things: poetry, biographies of famous military leaders, translations of French history and fiction. More than anything else, he devoted his time to writing historical novels, for it was as a historical novelist that he always believed he would make his reputation. Although some of his novels sold well in England, they failed to sell in the United States. As late as the 1850s he hadn't given up. The enormous success of *Uncle Tom's Cabin* spurred him to one last try, a novel about European slavery. Once again, no luck. He tried his hand at hackwork, writing cheap, lurid historical adventure stories. It was this work that provoked Edgar Allan Poe to say "Herbert has

written more trash than any man living, with the exception of Fay."
But even his trash didn't sell well. Herbert believed his novels were
too historical for American taste, by which he meant that they were
too detailed and scholarly. Whatever the reason, he was separated
from his proper audience, this time by the Atlantic.

One other subject remained for him as a writer: field sports. In
the late 1830s Herbert had begun writing articles about horses and
hunting and fishing, which he contributed to the *American Turf
Register* and the *Spirit of the Times.* These were scholarly pieces,
intended as serious contributions to natural history. Sports fiction,
in the form of light sporting sketches, was another well-established
form; such sketches were a popular staple of all sporting journals.
But American publishers believed there was no audience whatever
for sporting fiction in book form.

One of the members of Herbert's old New York sporting circle
was a lawyer named William P. Haws, who had written sporting
sketches, which Herbert admired, under the pseudonym of J. Cy-
press, Jr. It was an accepted literary convention that such sketches
were too trivial and undignified to appear under an author's real
name. Haws died suddenly in 1841, and Herbert, as an act of com-
memoration and in order to help Haws's widow, determined to edit
these sketches into book form, adding a personal memoir about the
author. No commercial publisher would touch such a book, so it
was put out by a firm of law publishers, appearing in 1842 as *Sporting Scenes and Miscellaneous Writings.* This was the first book of
American sporting fiction.

All through these years Herbert had also been writing sporting
sketches, fictional accounts of the shooting and hunting adventures
of a group of imaginary Anglo-American sportsmen. These appeared
in the *Spirit of the Times,* under the pseudonym Harry Archer, and
proved very popular. George Porter, Herbert's closest friend among
the Porter brothers, encouraged Herbert to write more of these
sketches; at the same time he objected to that particular pseudonym. Harry was too familiar a name, he argued, while Archer suggested obsolete weapons; something more up to date was needed
in go-ahead America, something euphonious, with connotations
of contemporary American woodcraft. And so was born Frank
Forester.

Now, as publishers began to suspect that an audience for sporting
fiction in book form existed in America, the light dawned upon
Henry Herbert. He collected his early sketches, and in 1845 Frank

Forester's first book appeared — *The Warwick Woodlands; or, Things as They Were There Twenty Years Ago.* So great was its success that two more collections soon followed — *My Shooting Box* in 1846 and *The Deerstalkers* in 1849. In the history of American sporting culture, the appearance of Frank Forester makes the year 1845 a date worth remembering.

*

These stories, the adventures of a group of American and English sportsmen, set vaguely in the 1820s and taking place in Orange, Sullivan, and Rockland counties of southeastern New York State, are told by Frank Forester, who is also one of the chief participants. Originating as they did, the stories are not entirely consistent. Unity derives from the appearance and reappearance of the same characters. In spite of this looseness of form, the sketches are part of one extended story, and so it was fitting that they were published in one volume in England, in 1849, as *Frank Forester and His Friends.* Unfortunately, they were never published in that form in the United States.

The main theme of all the stories is the meeting of English and American sporting cultures. This is developed in a number of ways. The characters get involved in various conflicts that entail different national sporting values. The sketches primarily describe a series of hunting and shooting expeditions, and these are the means by which Henry Herbert, speaking through his characters, informed his American audience as to the nature of the English sporting tradition and its transformation in America. His descriptions include a very wide range of detailed aspects: proper techniques of shooting and fishing; dissertations on food and drink; disquisitions on game and equipment; comparisons of the American and English countryside. But he chiefly analyzed the differences and similarities of English and American sport through the examples of the characters themselves. Many of these were in fact drawn from actual English and American sportsmen whom Herbert had encountered over the years, but he presented them not as individuals but as idealized types.

A few brief comments about these characters may show how Henry Herbert turned the messy and confusing reality of his own social life and sporting career into an imaginative picture of clarity and interest, and how the duality, English and American, that so haunted Herbert's life was resolved in his fictional description of national types.

The two most important American sportsmen in Herbert's stories are Commodore A and Tom Draw; they represent the two basic, contrasting American types. The commodore appears infrequently and says little. He is the cultivated American gentleman sportsman, wealthy, well educated, so refined that others are slightly in awe of him and inhibited by his presence. He values intellectual understanding as the hallmark of the highest form of sportsmanship, but he is not an especially skilled sportsman himself. He is the only city dweller in the group, and he represents what the aristocratic type would have been like in America had it been more common. But the fact that he plays a minor role in the stories is significant. In America there are very few like the commodore.

Tom Draw's type is more prevalent. The only major character who is a member of the lower class, he is the American sportsman as natural man. A Falstaffian creature, five feet six inches tall and weighing at least 250 pounds, "a mass of beef and brandy," all natural impulse and appetite, he lives in the country, runs a tavern, and leads hunting expeditions. At the level of natural instinct he surpasses everyone else: he is always drinking, but never drunk; obese, but light on his feet; a crack shot; and a master woodsman.

Tom Draw is one of nature's gentlemen, "full of mirth, of shrewdness, of keen mother wit, of hard horse sense, and last, not least, of the most genuine milk of human kindness." Tom Draw's virtues are country virtues, virtues enough, says Harry Archer pointedly, "to make five hundred men, as men go now-a-days in cities!" Tom is a man with "a heart and soul that would do honor to a prince," and Frank Forester's friends are enraged to find that citified would-be sportsmen sneer at him and snub him because he is not a gentleman.

> Tom Draw not a gentleman! Heaven save the mark! For he has all those points which mark the true gentleman: a kind heart and open hand; unwillingness to hurt the feelings of the humblest; respect for everything that is honorable, great, and noble; and contempt for everything that is not so, however well it may be gilded; promptness to fight for himself, or for his friend, when aggrieved; unblemished courage and undaunted courage; the strength of a lion, added to the stomach of a man.[6]

Tom Draw's chief limitation is that he sports only at an intuitive level; he lacks intellectual understanding. Significantly, Tom Draw and the commodore have nothing to do with each other.

Frank Forester is an upper-class Englishman who has traveled and hunted all around the world and finally settles in the United

States, quickly learning American sporting ways. He is an excellent shot and has considerable physical endurance. He is an acute observer and understands American ways. But there is no future for him in America. He is a figure from the sporting past. Why?

Frank Forester is the sportsman as artist, the sportsman as dandy. He dresses exotically, appearing at one point in a blaze of color: the full-dress blue coat of his old royal regiment, with gold buttons and black velvet cuffs; a lace-trimmed shirt fastened with enamel studs of Venetian gold; a crimson waistcoat; tight-fitting trousers; black silk stockings, and patent-leather pumps. No wonder Tom Draw stares wildly at this display: he has never seen anything like it before. We recognize what is going on; it is Henry Herbert astonishing his Newark neighbors.

This display shows the European dandy's contempt for conventional bourgeois opinion. Advised to wear sober garb in America, Frank Forester perversely insists that deer are actually attracted by gay colors. Despite such foppery, his friends know he is a formidable sportsman, entirely masculine. But such dandyism is also his great limitation; it is what keeps him from being a superlative sportsman. He is playful; he is not fully serious. Frank Forester doesn't have complete control of himself and so cannot be a manager of men. He is not a calculator; it is this that makes him a foreign type, and an old-fashioned one as well.

One of Henry Herbert's shrewdest insights into the American sporting scene of his own time was that he saw the American sporting ideal moving relentlessly in the direction of practical, efficient seriousness. Frank Forester was essentially playful; as the American sportsman became more of a gamesman, he increasingly valued qualities of control, discipline, and self-denial — qualities Frank Forester, and Henry Herbert, lacked. For in this aspect of Frank Forester, Henry Herbert undoubtedly saw much of himself, and saw too that there was no future for him in America.

Harry Archer is also an Englishman now living in the United States, but his relationship to his new home is different from Frank Forester's. Although he has lived a much shorter time in America and knows less about the country in some ways, he has also adapted to it in a way that is impossible for Forester. He has begun transforming himself into an American sportsman — not a sportsman of the type of either the commodore or Tom Draw but one combining the best of their qualities and the best of England's as well.

Harry Archer unites sport and science; he is the sporting type of the future. He is fascinated by problems and interested in their analysis. The commodore at one point defends Harry Archer against the charge that he carries this analytic interest too far.

> There is nothing on earth that makes so great a difference in sports-manship as the observation of small things. I don't call him a sportsman who can walk stoutly, and kill well, unless he can give causes for effects . . . unless he can give a why for every wherefore![7]

His sporting style is distinguished by its functionalism. Every piece of his equipment is perfectly adapted to its specific use, and every part is subordinated to a general effect. Wearing buckskins and moccasins, carrying his buckhorn-handled hunting knife and buffalo-horn powder flask, dressed in browns and greens that blend in with the copper beeches and buckeyes all about, and moving silently through the woods, Harry Archer, by some mysterious proc-ess of cultural assimilation, has already become an American sportsman of the original native type — the Indian.

He is distinguished from the Indian by his capacity for rational analysis and reflection. It is his scientific mentality that raises him above the level of native intuition. He lives in nature and kills in it, and in some ways he is instinctively natural; all animals and all simpler, more natural men and women feel that he is somehow one of them. But though he dresses and hunts like a native, he has not gone native. Harry Archer combines the qualities of Tom Draw and the commodore and adds to them a sense of the old-world tradition from which he derives. This is what makes him the perfect sports-man.

In the figure of Harry Archer, Henry Herbert was also imagina-tively able to transcend the social limitations of the old-world sports-man. Harry Archer is always accompanied by a symbol of the old class-bound order, his English manservant, Timothy Matlock, who bows and scrapes and pulls his forelock in the presence of supe-riors. But Herbert had observed and been deeply attracted by an-other kind of social figure, the man of the frontier — crude, wild, reckless, and sometimes degraded. Himself a kind of exile and social outcast, Henry Herbert found the frontiersman's freedom from convention deeply attractive. Harry Archer can deal with these men; he finds in them a trace of that "sentiment of honor" that marks them as true sportsmen of a sort. "These men," says Harry Archer,

independent yeomen, wild free foresters, living a life of continual excitement, incurring constant peril, familiar with the use of arms, their whole
lives from the cradle to the grave one wild and strange romance, these
men, I say, feel wrongs done to their sense of honour as keenly, and
avenge such as ruthlessly, as the red Indian whom they have supplanted
in these hunting-grounds.[8]

These men were not idealized. For Henry Herbert, the frontier
was a deeply disorganizing environment in which men often sank
into a natural state of amorality. Such were the well-known dangers
of breaking old rules and customs, of freeing oneself from the re-
straining hand of the past! But such frontiersmen, flawed and fal-
lible, belonged to the natural order of humanity. And so too did
another marginal group — black people. Their inclusion in the natural order of humanity reveals a remarkable leap of the moral imagination for Henry Herbert, when one considers his background and
the time in which he wrote.

Blacks lived in the background of Frank Forester's stories, never
speaking, flitting in and out of the kitchens and stables of the inns
and taverns where white sportsmen congregated. Tom Draw holds
the common bigoted views of white countrymen of the 1830s and
'40s. When he finds blacks in Old Jake's Tavern, where they mingle
freely with the whites, he snarls: "It's the darned niggers, I guess.
Why there's enough of 'em to make the moonshine dark . . .
blockin' up the fireside, and stinkin' so no white man could come
nearst it." Harry Archer doesn't share these views. He deals with
the blacks as he does with everyone else: on terms of perfect naturalness. So natural are his dealings with blacks that Tom Draw at
one point says disgustedly: "where you sees Archer, there's never
no scarceness of dogs and niggers."[9]

In one other respect Henry Herbert was not divided from, but
shared, one of the deepest aspirations of the culture of his time.
Like the American transcendentalists, who were his contemporaries, he discerned a fundamental harmony between nature and all
creatures living in it. From this transcendent point of view, all social
distinctions seemed trivial. In the United States this harmony was
most perfectly expressed in the magnificent autumn of the year.
"No imagination, unused to the effects of an autumnal forest in
America, can fancy its unrivalled beauty," Herbert wrote; and its
true beauty was in the equipoise, the stillness, that was at its heart.
Vulgar people thought of sport as action. True sport was the opposite of that; it was the cessation of action and the achievement

of reflection. And autumn was the season most conducive to deep reflection.

Harry Archer's preeminence as a sportsman, we recall, rested upon his capacity for reflection, both scientific and philosophical; his mind was "ever alive to thick-coming fancies." The greatest of these fancies was the vision of people forgetting their petty concerns in order to "mark the beautiful sublimity of nature, and learn the love of the Creator from the loveliness of his created things." Since even "those whom the world calls good and wise and great" often forgot this, then the true sportsman must have compassion.

> What wonder, then, that the rude and ignorant and lowly, whose life is one fierce struggle against suffering and sorrow, should dwell among such scenes unconscious, and creep from their cradles to their graves, unsoftened by the influences which move the poet's soul even to tears.[10]

Although Henry Herbert would probably have loathed the popular politics associated with Andrew Jackson's name, in this sense of transcendent equality and compassion he was true to his Jacksonian heritage.

*

Yet there is a pervasive sense of sadness at the heart of all the stories Frank Forester tells. One reason for this melancholy was the social and economic reality of life in Jacksonian America: the growth of population, the spread of cities, the voracious business speculation, the triumph of commercial values, and the despoiling of the sportsman's countryside. As Frank Forester's world rapidly disappeared, Henry Herbert's world grew more intolerable.

Henry Herbert spoke out against the reckless, widespread exploitation, in every way he could make his voice heard — sporting sketches, natural histories, letters to the *Spirit of the Times*. He argued for the responsible conservation of what remained, before it was too late. He pleaded with his readers to accept the spirit of restraint, and fulminated against the indiscriminate destruction of birds and animals. He reasoned and argued, and, when he was ignored or willfully misunderstood, he lost his temper and raged.

Herbert's principal public effort was a memorial to the New York state legislature, in which he implored the legislators to establish limited hunting seasons to protect animals and birds, and urged them to back up those regulated seasons with force. He attacked the notion that it was somehow antidemocratic to establish fixed hunting seasons, and he heaped scorn on the argument, so familiarly Jacksonian, that only aristocrats favored such schemes; that they were un-American because they smacked of privilege.

Nothing came of this in his lifetime. The indiscriminate slaughter and waste went on, even accelerated. Herbert would have agreed with Henry David Thoreau's rueful comment, made at this same time: "There are many Herring Rivers on the Cape; they will be more numerous than the herrings soon."[11] In this respect, as in many others, Henry Herbert died thinking himself a failure.

Contempt for the idea of "progress" suffused all his writing. The idyllic sporting environment Herbert had found on his arrival in America had been threatened from the very beginning. On their first trip to the Warwick Valley, Forester and Archer pass through Paterson, New Jersey, which is already "the filthiest town." They stop at an inn, only to find that the proprietor, "bit by the land mania," has left for the West. A village they pass through is desolate. "Its story is soon told," says Archer; "a speculating, clever New York merchant — a water-power project, a failure, and a consequent desertion of the project." When *The Warwick Woodlands* was published in book form, Herbert added a footnote warning readers not to go to Warwick in search of sport. The book described the area twenty years before the "juggernaut of improvement" had devastated the countryside, sparing nothing. Even the country's natural features had been deformed, "the hillsides all denuded," and the "bright streams dammed by unsightly pools."

The first half of *The Warwick Woodlands* ends with a poignant farewell to Greenwood Lake — which is a kind of Eden of innocent sportiveness — and with an invocation to the spirits of those earliest American sportsmen, who had also been vanquished by progress but whose spirits still haunted the landscape.

> Adieu! fair Greenwood Lake! Long may it be before thy rugged hills be stripped of their green garniture or thy bright waters marred by the unpicturesque improvements of man's avarice! — for truly thou, in this utilitarian age, and at brief distance from America's metropolis, art young, and innocent, and unpolluted, as when the red man drank of thy pure waters, long centuries ere he dreamed of the pale-faced oppressors who have already rooted out his race from half its native continent.[12]

The sadness in Frank Forester's stories was perhaps also due to the fact that Frank Forester, Harry Archer, and the rest are for the most part men without women; and when women are present the men find it very difficult to talk to them. There are only two kinds of women in these stories: upper-class women, who are cold and self-controlled, and lower-class women, who are passionate and unrestrained. Maria D'Arcey represents the former type. Although American-born, she marries an Englishman. She is too fastidious to live in the thinner, more democratic atmosphere of America. She belongs in a traditional sporting world where she can be supported in proper style. Mary Marten, by contrast, represents the other kind of woman, passionate and depraved. Like many male writers, Herbert found the women he disapproved of were the most interesting; but of course his sportsmen really have no future with such women. They are for sexual use but not for marriage.

It is remarkable that Henry Herbert, with his tenuous grip on American social reality, should see so clearly the pattern of sexual relationships that had been established in American sporting culture and that were to be repeated over and over again in the future. The men typically exhibit exaggerated masculinity, intense timidity, and stammering inarticulateness. Frank Forester and his friends spend a great deal of time in depressing banter about their sexual goings-on, accompanied by a vast amount of smirking and winking. Yet almost nothing can be said openly. Has the noble Harry Archer ever been in love? Ever been with a woman? He is said to have been "a sparkin a gal" in New York City, which leads one exasperated character to break out: "I never knowed as you was a gal man." "Thunder," responds Tom Draw, "I'd be pleased to know who is, if Aircher ain't."

So he may be a "gal man," but Harry Archer himself says that he is not a "marrying man." Why not? Frank Forester at one point says to him, "Do you know, Harry, I have often wondered, so much of your time as you pass with them, that you have never — "

"Frank! don't for God's sake! you hurt me," Archer replies, in an altered tone, with an indescribable expression crossing his face, leaving him very pale.[13]

No more is ever said on the subject. Harry Archer's "indescribable expression" brings us back to those unmentionable "difficulties" in England, which propelled Henry Herbert to the New World in the first place, to the oddly mixed fate and double life he found there — the idealized life of Frank Forester and his friends in the Warwick Woodlands, as opposed to the gloomy actuality of the Cedars.

*

Many of Henry Herbert's friends were dead or permanently estranged. By the middle of the 1850s, his fragile connection with the outside world was breaking. In 1855/56 he edited a weekly "Sporting Chronicle" in *Frank Leslies Illustrated Newspaper,* but he then lost that position. Money was short. He was forced to write begging letters to friends and, even more humiliating, to publishers.

> You ought not to be angry with me. You cannot imagine what I have gone through in the last three weeks. I lived three days on bread and tea, with only a few embers to warm me.[14]

He often had no candles to light. He became moodier than ever, more uncurbed in speech, violent in temper, and erratic and impetuous in manner.

But he went on working on his greatest work of nonfiction — *Horses and Horsemanship of the United States.* From childhood he had loved horses; loved riding them, studying them, collecting materials, and ransacking the past for information about them. At a time when everyone thought him finished as a writer, he somehow found the stamina and power of concentration to finish his work and see its two large volumes through the press in 1857. It was well reviewed and received with astonishment. The reviewer in one London sporting magazine assumed that the author was American.

Then, in February of 1858, in his typically impetuous way, Henry Herbert married again. Disaster quickly followed. Little is known of his wife beyond her name and the fact that she had been divorced from an actor! They lived at the Cedars, and within three months she left him. She never told him the truth but made up some story that, for a while, deceived him as to her intentions. Eventually he began to suspect what was up and moved to New York to look for her, hoping that this might restore her to him. But he never saw her again. On May 16, 1858, apparently by chance, he learned, through a newspaper notice, of her intention to divorce him.

He may have been contemplating suicide for some time; death certainly was much on his mind. He had prepared his will, named his executors, provided for his burial, described the headstone he wished placed over his grave. That day he wrote two long letters, to the local coroner and to the local press, explaining his motives and absolving his wife of any responsibility for what he was doing.

The manner of his death dramatized the convivial social sense that was so oddly at war with his other, damaged, antisocial self. He invited several old friends to dinner at his hotel, the Stevens House, very near where he had begun his American life a quarter of a century before. Only one guest showed up. The two of them ate and drank, one wonders how heartily, and then Herbert left the table, determined to "crown the dinner with a harrowing catastrophe." He went into an inner room (in which he had hung his first wife's portrait, brought there from the Cedars). With a perfect sense of the duality that had marked his American life, he stood directly in front of a full-length mirror; and, taking aim from its reflection, shot himself in the heart.

Henry William Herbert was buried in Mt. Pleasant cemetery in Newark. For eighteen years his grave remained unmarked, his relatives in England refusing to send money for that purpose. Finally, in 1876, some admirers of his writings had a headstone set above his grave, exactly as he had specified in his will; on it appeared the single word, *infelicissimus*, "most unhappy."

PART II

THE CHALLENGE TO ENGLAND

JOHN COX STEVENS

5

John Cox Stevens
and America

ONE JULY DAY in 1844, Philip Hone, a former mayor of New York City, keen observer of its life and amusements, and diary-keeper, reported an unusual scene in the splendid amphitheater and crossroads that is New York harbor:

> There is a gay, saucy-looking squadron of schooner yachts lying off the Battery. About a dozen of these handsome little vessels . . . are preparing for a voyage to Newport under the command of that excellent fellow John C. Stevens as commodore, who hoists his broad pennant and makes his signals in the most approved man-of-war style. Crowds of people, especially of the fairer sort, go down to witness this mimic display of maritime glory.[1]

This incident marked the establishment of the New York Yacht Club. It also set in motion a more complex chain of occurrences, which resulted in the first major American sporting challenge to Great Britain.

The leading part in all this was played by one of the foremost sportsmen of Jacksonian America, John Cox Stevens, who was Colonel Johnson's match-race antagonist and a friend of William Porter. He was a member of the remarkable Stevens family of New Jersey and New York, whose history touched American sporting life at many different points.[2]

The history of the Stevens family is a story of continuous movement stretching over a century; a chronicle of sails and steam and horses. They alternated between the sports of the country and the sports of the city, between business as sport and sport as business. Eventually, with John Cox leading the way, they traveled beyond

New York harbor, beyond the Middle Atlantic coastline, and across the Atlantic, thus completing the circle of family fortunes that had begun in England.

*

From the time of the first landings in the New World, Americans had depended upon the sea for most of their travel from colony to colony. Remote though they were in many respects, Americans had remained a part of British culture, while they pushed inland with painful slowness, by means of the Atlantic Ocean — the fierce and formidable Atlantic, which both kept them in touch with Europe and divided them from it. Their maritime traditions, their ships and sailing were thoroughly British; but these, like everything else, were slowly changed in the course of time by new circumstances and conditions.[3]

Large American sailing vessels resembled their British counterparts throughout most of the eighteenth century, but in the development of small craft, American shipbuilders began to deviate from British designs. Small ships were the mainstay of the American coastal trade and the extensive trade with the Caribbean. They were also the chief instruments of a major American colonial business — smuggling. All during the frequent eighteenth-century wars against the French and Spanish, small ships were too insignificant and numerous to be protected by the British fleet. As a result, they depended upon speed and maneuverability for their safety, and these qualities were more valued than freight-carrying capacity.

By the time of the Revolution a sailing vessel had been developed that was distinctively American — the "Virginia built" clipper schooner. (The word *clipper* came from the verb *to clip,* which originally meant to move wings rapidly, to fly — a word first applied to fast horses and only later to sailing ships.) Independence freed Americans from the British government's control but also deprived them of its economic support. Now American merchants were thrust out on their own, forced to break into enclosed systems of trade and gain entry into new markets. In the 1780s and 1790s, with growing audacity, they sailed farther and farther, touching on remote and exotic shores — the Baltic, the far reaches of the Mediterranean, the East Indies, and China.

This precarious trade, often improvised on the spot, rarely flowed in regular and predictable channels; well-known harbors and established docking facilities were not always available. Once again the emphasis had to be upon speed and lightness, rather than upon sturdiness of construction. American ships had long had a dismal reputation in Britain; they were known as shoddy Yankee products notorious for their cheapness, built often of unseasoned, inferior wood. They were "sale-built" ships, the British sneered; and the chanciness of their kind of trade did sometimes require that the ship, as well as the cargo, be sold on the spot. Nor were these admittedly fast-sailing ships at all handsome in detail. They were stark, often undecorated.

The War of 1812 gave an enormous impetus to American consciousness of seamanship and sailing. The conditions of the naval aspect of the war dictated innovation and improvisation. At best, Americans could challenge British control of the seas only intermittently. This meant that, although they built somewhat larger ships than they had ever done before, Americans never directly challenged the battleships of the British line. The American weapon was the privateer, a schooner that was "built to fly rather than to fight and to escape rather than to attack." American builders once again ran risks to gain their objectives; these ships were lightly built, heavily sparred, and neither comfortable nor especially safe. During the war the American public suffered through a series of humiliations, on land, at the hands of the British — Andrew Jackson's forces always excepted — and was therefore astonished and heartened by a series of famous victories on the water. But the sailing, not the fighting, qualities of the privateers were the most important things about them. Without a doubt American ships had proved their ability to compete with the British on their own element — the sea.

The American schooner was a wonderful development, perfectly suited to its intended purpose: "She could double like a hare, slip through fingers, laugh at her pursuers." The Americans never formally set down the capacities of these vessels, neither the lines of the hull nor the dimensions of the spars; everything was improvised, intuitive. British builders could not duplicate them, even when they had captured ships for models. The British denied American superiority in all other phases of sea warfare, but they never disputed the excellence of the schooner. This was little consolation for the Americans, who smarted under what they thought was typical British arrogance — praise for the invention but scorn for the inventors.

Despite British opinion, many people (although not all) thought these vessels were beautiful beyond anything then known in naval construction. One of these Yankee schooners was described in a series of sketches written for a British magazine in the early nineteenth century. "She was a most beautiful little craft . . . that floated on the foam light as a sea-gull. Her long slender wands of masts used to swing about as if there were neither shrouds nor stays to support them."[4] Beauty and speed: the two were inseparable.

The evolution of the Yankee clippers steadily continued in the years after the war. Although these vessels were commonly identified around the world as Yankee ships, the region of the country most responsible for evolving them was not New England but the Chesapeake area of the Middle Atlantic states. The *Ann McKim*, built in Baltimore in 1832, marked an important stage in the development of the type; it was the largest ship of this kind built so far, sacrificing capacity for speed. By the 1830s the Yankee clipper was familiar everywhere. The English foreign secretary, Lord Palmerston — no admirer of American things — asked in annoyance about the handwriting of one of his clerks: "Why does he make all his letters slope backwards like the raking masts of an American schooner?"[5]

The way was now prepared for the full flowering of this form in the 1840s and 1850s. In these years Americans challenged the British on the seas. It was a peaceful challenge, but no less intense for that. In commerce, there were contests between steamships, for domination of the Atlantic passenger trade, and between sailing ships, for control of more distant markets. In sport there was, for the first time ever, a direct contest: one American yacht — American designed, American owned, and American sailed — challenged an entire British squadron. And this brings us back to the Stevens family.

*

The first American John Stevens, the Founder, came to New York City from London in 1699, at age seventeen, as an indentured servant. By 1708, while still a clerk, he had begun various commercial transactions that eventually enabled him to lay claim to an enormous tract of land in upstate New York. He became a full-time land speculator, prospered, and began the long-lived family interest in New Jersey, where he acquired an interest in a ferry and in coaches, leaving at his death a family rich in acres and heirs. The next generation produced soldiers and gentleman farmers; but its dominant figure was the second John Stevens, the Squire.

His investments included land, but he paid more attention to coaches and ships. He had gone to sea as a boy, and although he turned his back on further sea adventures by age twenty-seven, some part of his imagination was always touched with the memory of sea adventure. He mortgaged his lands to finance his ships and coaches; and his business affairs, like those of all the merchants of the time, were conducted in a cloud of promissory notes. While cautious by temperament, he sympathized with the revolutionary cause, and, as a result, his personal fortune suffered a good deal because of the war. When the old Squire died in 1792, he left an estate that extended in many directions, of great but precarious promise.

He was succeeded by another John, the Colonel, born in 1749, who increased the family's involvement in public affairs. An ardent patriot, he was made a colonel in the New Jersey militia during the Revolution and later served his state as treasurer. He concentrated the family's business in transportation, and forever fixed the family's style of life as that of merchant gentry. When the estate of the prominent New Jersey Tory landholder William Bayard was confiscated and put up for public auction, the Colonel bought a magnificent 564-acre tract on what was called Hobuck Heights, overlooking New York harbor, directly across from lower Manhattan. He then did what seemed to many New Yorkers an eccentric thing (moving to New Jersey no doubt always does): he built a large house on his Hoboken site, where the family lived during the summers. He also concentrated the family's business in New Jersey, establishing coach lines within the state, and a ferry service to New York.

In 1804 the Colonel mapped out the new city of Hoboken and began selling lots. Meanwhile, he developed his magnificent shoreline site in Hoboken, building a river walk, planting trees, and developing the meadows into a pleasure garden known for decades as the Elysian Fields. In 1814 Colonel Stevens moved to Hoboken for good and lived there the year round. From his house overlooking the water, he oversaw the growing family interest in steamboats.

*

In his large, comfortable Hoboken house, with its outbuildings, walks, stables, and gardens, the Colonel combined country and city ways. Interested in horses and ships, he taught his sons and daughters to ride, swim, and shoot. In 1782 he had married the lively and witty Rachel Cox of New Jersey. They had thirteen children: the

first two were stillborn, and then, in efficiently organized order, between 1785 and 1806, six sons were born, followed by five daughters. The oldest son, born in 1785, was named John Cox.

All of this was part of a familiar pattern of moving up and getting
ahead. But the Colonel was much less conventional than he
seemed. Although his life was pretty much divided into halves by
the two centuries — he lived until 1838 — he was essentially an
urban, industrial entrepreneur who in spirit belonged much more to
the nineteenth century than to the eighteenth. A practical man of
affairs, he also had in him a powerful imaginative streak, which
found its outlet in mechanical invention and in innovation. He was
always on the lookout for new ways of doing things, for new ways to
improve his coaches and ships. He built a small workshop on his
Hoboken estate, where he and his sons, Robert L. and Edwin A. in
particular, tinkered and built models for new devices. A steamboating pioneer in the days of Thomas Jefferson, John Stevens lived long
enough to have his imagination fired, during Andrew Jackson's
presidency, by the possibilities of steam railways.

In May of 1804, a passerby described a characteristic Stevens
family scene:

> We saw . . . a crowd, running toward the river. On inquiring the cause,
> we were informed that Jack Stevens was going over to Hoboken in a
> queer sort of boat . . . We saw a vessel about the size of a row-boat, in
> which there was an engine *but no visible means of propulsion.* The ves-
> sel was soon underway, my late much-valued friend, Commodore Ste-
> vens, acting as coxswain, and the smutty-looking personage who fulfilled
> the duties of engineer, fireman, and crew, was his more practical-minded
> brother, Robert L. Stevens.[6]

That was the *Little Juliana* (named for the Colonel's first daughter),
whose "hidden means of propulsion" was a single-screw propeller.
This didn't work very well, because it tended to make the boat go
round in circles; so, after further experimentation, a twin-screw
propeller was developed. In 1809 the family built the *Phoenix,* a
side-wheel steamboat which that year became the first American
steamboat to sail on the ocean, traveling from Hoboken to Philadelphia. In 1811 the *Juliana,* a larger version of the original boat, became the first regularly running steam ferry. And it was succeeded
in later years by other boats, each faster than the preceding one.
The Stevens family recognized that it couldn't rest content with
past achievements but had to keep moving.

Interested in all forms of going, the Stevens family believed they should be left free to go. The Colonel wanted his steamboats to carry goods and passengers on the Hudson, his own front yard; but he was blocked by the steamship monopoly given Robert Fulton and Robert Livingston by the New York legislature. For years, competing groups battled in the open and behind the scenes to maintain or to break up such monopolies. For opponents of monopoly, this was an important way to break with that inherited past which took for granted a society based on special privilege. The Colonel was against such special privileges in transportation or in anything else. He thought monopoly "uncongenial and incompatible with the nature and genius of our free government."[7]

Colonel Stevens probably never used the term *laissez faire,* but he looked with profound favor on the notion of free competition. The words he would have used to describe his views most likely would have come from his own considerable sporting knowledge: he would have seen the world as a race, as a test of fitness. Competitors should be freed from unnatural hindrances, and their way cleared of artificial obstacles. The race should be to the most fit, and in the long run the race *would* be. He encouraged his sons in all the active sports fit for gentlemen — riding and shooting, steering a steamboat, and sailing a schooner. And not just his sons; his daughters were avid horsewomen. Many decades later, younger members of the family recalled that their spinster aunts, Esther and Catharine, were crack shots with pistols.

The Stevenses were in the thick of the Jacksonian battles about monopoly, which involved bridges, steamboats, and the Bank of the United States. The controversy over the steamboat monopoly ended up in the courts. The Stevenses deliberately sailed one of their steamboats up the Hudson, to provoke a suit; and that suit, brought in the name of the manager of the Hudson River branch of the Stevens's Union Line, James Gibbons, was carried all the way to the United States Supreme Court. In the famous decision of *Gibbons* v. *Ogden,* in 1824, John Marshall and the Court ruled against the monopoly. No wonder the Stevens family expressed its gratitude by naming one of its steamboats *Chief Justice Marshall.* On a more conciliatory note, the first Union Line steamboat put in service on the Hudson after the Court's decision was named the *Olive Branch.*

In addition to many innovations in ship design, the father and brothers invented other things: a cast-iron plough and a multi-tubular boiler, to name two. Most ambitious of all, they labored for years to build an armored warship, getting a federal government contract and spending much of their own money; but the difficulties involved in this project were too great even for Stevens ingenuity. They were also associated with another technological advance that was to bear fruit. From the 1810s on, the Colonel pondered the application of steam technology to land transport. In 1815 the New Jersey legislature granted him the first charter for the development of a railway. By 1825 his plans and ideas were far enough advanced to enable him to build a small steam locomotive and, on part of the Hoboken estate, a small circular railway, of wood, on which he gave the first demonstration of steam locomotion in America. Robert L., the most inventive of the brothers, aware that wood was impractical for permanent rails, designed the iron t-rail and spike, which was later adopted everywhere for railway tracks. This development had another practical result. In 1830 the Stevenses took part in the financing, building, and managing of the Camden and Amboy Railroad, which in the next thirty years brought the family large profits.

*

John Cox Stevens played an important role in all these enterprises. He also displayed a good organizing sense in his horse-racing operations, as well as a mastery of practical detail in sailing. But his gifts were not in business, engineering, or managing. He had inherited that imaginative strain in his family which found its outlet in sporting speculation, in the esthetics of speed, and in the playful sociability that was his personal hallmark.

Horse racing established John Cox Stevens as a sportsman. As soon as the sport was once again legal he took part in a big way. His stables were in Hoboken, but he raced his horses widely in New York and New Jersey and was one of the few northerners to run his horses in the South. When he accepted the challenge that led to the Eclipse–Sir Henry match in 1823, he made his reputation, in racing circles, with one stroke. For twenty-one consecutive years he served as vice president or president of the New York Jockey Club. Some of his most famous races were against Colonel Johnson. Overall, John Stevens came out about even. His most famous horse was Black Maria, a mare that raced between 1829 and 1835, entering twenty-five races and winning thirteen of them, with total earnings of $14,900 — a large sum for those days. She was famous for her closing burst of speed. At the end of the 1830s, Stevens withdrew from horse racing and sold his stable. Baillie Peyton, an old racing friend of Andrew Jackson's, bought Black Maria, and, after a successful career as a brood mare, she died some years later on his plantation in Tennessee.

Stevens was the patron and promoter of many other sports as well. For a while he took an interest in pedestrianism (footracing) and sponsored a much-publicized race of that kind on the Union Course. He donated an area in the Elysian Fields for a cricket pitch and saw to it that the grounds were properly taken care of. For many years he was popularly given credit for introducing cricket in the United States, but that was of course incorrect, because the game had existed in America from early colonial times. At the same time, to forestall criticism for favoring an English game too much, Stevens laid out the Knickerbocker Baseball Grounds, also in the Elysian Fields; and there, on June 19, 1846, the first baseball game of which there is any record was played. This was commemorated, as were a number of John Stevens's other sporting achievements, by one of Nathaniel Currier's most famous prints.

*

John Stevens married a member of the ubiquitous and socially eminent Livingston clan, thereby augmenting his fortune and moving up a bit on the social scale. The Stevenses first lived in a house called Red Hook, some twenty miles north of Poughkeepsie. Then, in the heyday of John C. Stevens's interest in horse racing, they moved to a farmhouse on Long Island, a few miles outside Brooklyn and only three miles from the Union Course. In 1845 they moved back to New York City. Both horse racing, which Stevens had by then given up, and yachting, which he was then emphasizing, were urban sports; John Cox Stevens represented the type that was becoming dominant in America and that would henceforth remain so — the urban sportsman.

The Stevens houses provide us with yet another set of images of the American sportsman at home. The family house on the Hoboken heights had been a handsome, unpretentious colonial house. When it burned down in the late 1840s it was replaced by "the castle," the building that still stands on the grounds of the Stevens Institute of Technology. Like Henry Herbert's Cedars, the Smithsonian Institution building in Washington, D.C., and many other buildings of the period, which were built in the new Gothic fashion, this exemplified the diminishing influence of the eighteenth century and of classicism. Once having broken the spell, American sportsmen were liable to turn to any kind of architecture. They had not been liberated from the tyranny of European history by finding an American style of their own. They now simply had many more European styles to choose from, and might, if they wished, combine several at once.

The Stevens's Manhattan mansion showed this development in its initial stages. Ithiel Town and Alexander Jackson Davis designed a house based on a Hellenistic monument in Athens.[8] The principal feature of the house's exterior was a circular colonnaded porch, capped with a dome and flanked by a group of vertical Tuscan windows. The drawing room, which had long mirrors and many Corinthian columns, reflected the mansion's showy historicism. The other notable feature of the house's interior was the large amount of floor space for dancing. On one occasion Mrs. Stevens employed a company of soldiers to drill on the waxed floors, in order to perfect them for dancing. Although the days of colossal ostentation still lay ahead, the memory of simple republicanism was fading fast.

American contemporaries seemed to derive pleasure from the fact that America now produced plutocrats who compared with the great magnates of Europe. Philip Hone's description of his own feelings bears repeating:

> The Palais Bourbon in Paris, Buckingham Palace in London, the Sans Souci in Berlin, are little grander than this residence of a simple citizen of our republican city; a steamboat builder and proprietor, but a mighty good fellow.[9]

Surely this was the best of both worlds. Although he was partially hidden by the Corinthian foliage and the dazzle of the ballroom floors, it was reassuring to find that the American sportsman was still a good fellow.

And it was largely true. This was a city mansion, not a palace. The distance between its occupant and his employees, though a wide one, was not impassable: the main difference was that he had more money. At Red Hook, John Stevens's first upstate country house, "when he cultivated his farm he led his men in the harvest, and asked no one to cut more grass than he did himself."[10] All the family took an active day-to-day part in the running of the business. They supervised the coaches and steamboats, and not from a safe distance; they bumped over the rough roads, fretted at the not uncommon delays, kept accurate records of performance, thought constantly of ways to save a few minutes. John Cox kept a celebrated stud book — celebrated in the sense that it was honest. (The stud book, in America, was never far in spirit from the ledger and account book. History could be useful, providing a record of practical facts; and statistics were the most practical of facts.) The daughters rode on the steamboats, to check accommodations, cleanliness, china, and food.

The Stevenses were solid and respectable. They didn't patronize the raffish or disreputable; they avoided prize fights and prize fighters. The nearest they came was in naming one of their steamboats *Corinthia*, "an appelation for a dandy, I believe," wrote one of John Cox's sisters. They liked the theater, and the company of actresses and singers, but their connections with the demimonde were discreet. Robert, who never married, "was not to be lured from Madame Otto," a noted singer, "who remained for so many years the object of his most intense devotion."[11] On the other hand, nowhere in the voluminous family records was there any trace of a feeling that building and making, trade and commerce, were shameful or socially demeaning. How fantastic were Henry Herbert's ideas: refusing to sit down to dine with a merchant, when John Cox Stevens, the first sportsman of New York, would sit down with anybody.

*

In the 1840s two events immensely speeded the development of the clipper ship. The first was the intense Anglo-American rivalry in the China tea trade. In 1845 John Griffeths, a remarkable American-born designer-builder, launched the *Rainbow,* which went to China and back in six months, an unprecedented achievement. American merchants now realized that being able to ship tea with such speed would allow them to challenge British domination of the American market. More important was the second event, the discovery of gold in California in 1848. It was the first great gold strike for centuries, and men and women everywhere caught gold fever and made furious haste for El Dorado. Speed was the desire of the whole world, and Americans were not likely to be left behind in that regard. Of the three possible routes to California — overland, by way of the Isthmus of Panama, or around Cape Horn — the Cape Horn route proved fastest and safest, given the right kind of ship. And although every imaginable sort of vessel was pressed into service, the right kind of ship was the clipper.[12]

Speed in sailing was important, and so was speed in construction. Suddenly clippers were being built everywhere along the Atlantic coast, employing thousands of workers and calling on all the skills available. The greatest clipper-ship designer to emerge from all this activity was Donald McKay, a Scotsman, who emigrated to New York City, worked for a while for John Griffeths, and then moved on to Boston. McKay's first great clipper was *Staghound,* which was built in sixty days and which was characterized by a remarkable increase of length as opposed to breadth and depth. An idea that had been slowly evolving for decades was now pushed to what seemed fantastic extremes; the length of the ships was increased more and more, in proportion to the width and depth, and an immense amount of sail was put up — in some cases as much as 8,000 yards. The result was incredible speed and seaworthiness.

The first ship to reach San Francisco after gold was discovered was *South Carolina,* a conventional sailing ship that had taken thirteen months to go the Cape Horn route. This was approximately the same speed at which Richard Henry Dana had traveled in 1831/1833, when he visited California — a journey he described in *Two Years Before the Mast,* a book that popularized sea journeys to exotic lands and influenced Herman Melville. Now *Memnon,* the first clipper to make the trip, did it in 120 days, knocking ten months off the record. In 1850 there was direct competition between four clippers — *Memnon, Honqua, Samuel Russell,* and *Sea Witch. Samuel Russell* eclipsed the first two by making the trip in 109 days; but *Sea Witch* beat that, and beat it badly: 97 days.

Meanwhile, Donald McKay had produced several splendid ships in addition to *Staghound,* their names redolent of the romance of speed: *Lightning, Westward Ho!, Great Republic, Sovereign of the Seas,* each of which "seemed to carry his determination to sea with them." In 1851, his masterpiece, *Flying Cloud,* made the Cape Horn trip in 89 days, then and still the record for a sailing ship. *Flying Cloud* equaled its own record in 1854, and *Andrew Jackson* matched it in 1860. But by then the great days of California sailing were over.

While these magnificent vessels were pushing sailing speed to what seemed its furthest limits, more modest craft were following parallel lines of development, less exaggerated in their proportions and smaller in size but with speed also very much in mind. All through the 1840s and 1850s Americans took to the water on the countless streams, rivers, and bays that cover the North American continent offering pleasure and providing room for competition. Wealthier people, who had the time and money, took up yachting and organized the clubs, regattas, and social life that went with it. Many others, less affluent, took part in less formal ways, for small craft were cheap to build.

Sailing, in its informality and general accessibility, was still a democratic sport. And it was not only a participant's sport. The New York City harbor, for example, served as a kind of sporting arena for improvised competition. Landlubbers, free of charge, climbed the wharves, docks, and roofs of houses and commercial buildings to watch the sport and spectacle. The line between work and play was not clearly drawn, and the ongoing activity of the city was still more popular as amusement than was professional entertainment.

The arrival of a famous ship became a memorable form of civic ritual in New York, a tumult of noise and massed crowds, a public pageant in a community eager for communal display. In May of 1838 a New Yorker described a familiar scene:

> *Great Western* off today: escorted down the bay by seventeen steamboats, with music, flags, and enormous numbers of people crowded all about wharves, buildings, to see her off . . .[13]

This would be repeated many, many times down almost to our own day. In 1859, when the *Great Eastern* docked, Walt Whitman wrote a poem about it, and 143,744 New Yorkers paid a dollar apiece to go aboard and inspect her. Rowing and sailing races of all kinds were held on these protected inland waters; the crews of visiting foreign ships would not infrequently race against local sailors. It was not until after the Civil War that regattas and other races were moved farther away from cities and their harbors, making them less accessible and more exclusive.

What was true of the bays and harbors was also true of the rivers. The Hudson — "a Queen in a republic of rivers" — was the first important site for water sport in America. Steamboating reached its romantic perfection on the Mississippi in the 1850s, but it began on the Hudson, and its important technical advances were made there. On the Hudson, sport was year-round. In winter there was ice yachting, one of the least known but most beautiful of American sports. With the white sails billowing, the boats traveled at amazing speeds, swooping and tacking like swallows, against the backdrop of the lordly hills and cliffs. An Argentinean visitor's description suggests how much river travel there was:

Its waters are always so literally covered by boats that there are traffic jams, as in the streets of great cities. The steamboats cross each other's paths like shooting stars, and tugboats tow a veritable carnival of barges.[14]

Those steamboats, crossing paths like shooting stars, reflected the general mania for speed. This obsession produced a notorious phenomenon — the informal races between commercial steamboats. The very sight of a rival was enough to set the bells ringing in the engine room. A race inevitably followed: a dramatic, heart-stopping, and frequently disastrous contest; for those shooting stars didn't always avoid each other's paths or the still-plentiful snags in uncharted rivers. "More and more steam!" was the cry. "More and more speed!" No matter what the cost in exploding boilers and incinerated passengers. Currier and Ives recorded many of the most famous accidents for eager, if horrified, audiences. Fire, explosion, collision: the passengers had little choice; they were in the hands of their captains (Oh Captain! my Captain!), and the captains were not deterred from racing by pleas, threats, or admonitions. The *Spirit of the Times* explained why.

> "Go ahead" is the motto of the Yankees. Everybody in the country struggles to be in advance of his neighbor, and whether the "deuce takes the hindmost," or whatever else becomes of them nobody cares. In spite of preaching, people will take the fastest boat and fastest train. It matters not how thin-timbered and rickety the one, or how crazy and holting the road the other runs over. *Beat,* the Yankees must — ship-wrecks, blowups and tear-up, to the contrary notwithstanding. Now and then a disaster happens — a dozen, thirty, fifty lives are lost. The people stop, and scold for a moment — the press thunders — everybody is virtuously indignant — and then things move on as before.[15]

Important as the Hudson was, the Mississippi was the great sporting river. Steamboating on that mighty current achieved a wild efflorescence that influenced all aspects of the life on its banks. But the melodramatic aspects of steamboating obscured the wider influence movement had on an everyday life that, in these Jacksonian decades, was still local and circumscribed: the village cut off from outside, the family farmhouse hemmed in by the elements. Transportation, in such a world, created a daily drama of arrivals and departures. For those towns and villages on the water's edge, the movement of ships and boats was a constant enlargement of horizons and a rearrangement of the scenery.

One of these scenes is among the most memorable moments of the American imagination. Who, having read it, could forget the arrival of the steamboat at Hannibal, Missouri, as Mark Twain described it: the white town drowsing in the sunshine of a summer's morning, two clerks sitting asleep in front of their store, the fragrant town drunk asleep in the shadow of the wharf and

> the great Mississippi, the majestic, the magnificent Mississippi, rolling its mile-wide tide along, shining in the sun. Presently a film of dark smoke appears. Instantly a negro drayman, famous for his quick eye and prodigious voice, lifts up the cry "S-t-e-a-m-boat a-coming!" and the scene changes! The town drunkard stirs, the clerks wake up, a furious clatter of drays follows, every house and store pours out a human contribution, and all in a twinkling the dead town is alive and moving. Drays, carts, men, boys, all go hurrying from many quarters to a common center, the wharf.[16]

Ten minutes and the steamboat is once more underway; ten minutes more "and the town is dead again, and the town drunkard asleep by the skids once more."

*

After he retired from the turf, John Cox Stevens concentrated his energy on his earliest sporting love, sailing. Raised on the water's edge, he had swum and sailed from his youth. At age sixty-five he reminisced about this, recalling that he had been "a yacht owner for more than half a century, commencing in 1802 as builder, captain, cook and all hands on the celebrated yacht *Diver,* nine feet long, three feet wide and three feet deep." The development of his yachts mirrored the growth of his experience and his ambitions. *Diver* of 1802 was followed by *Diver* of 1809, the latter twenty feet long. *Trouble,* built in 1816, was fifty-six feet long and may well have been the first American boat of the nineteenth century that could properly be called a yacht. *Wave,* completed in 1823, was the first American-built yacht capable of navigating the Atlantic. *Onkahye* (the word is Indian for "dancing feather"), 1840, ninety-six feet long, made a cruise to the West Indies. John Cox was raising his sights. *Gimcrack,* 1844, was much smaller than *Onkahye,* but in 1846 John's brother Robert designed for him his largest and fastest yacht, *Maria,* recalling the name of his greatest horse.

John Cox Stevens led the way, but numerous others followed close behind. American yachting's origins were as fragmentary and rudimentary as its nineteenth-century growth was rapid. In England, starting in the seventeenth century, yachting was known only among people at court. It spread to the aristocracy during the eighteenth century. The term *yacht* appeared in America at the end of the seventeenth century, used in its modern sense of "pleasure boat." Americans were frugal and conservative; there was no need for, and little interest in, the development of a specialized type of sailing boat. But by the middle of the eighteenth century a few rich men had small vessels fitted out for pleasure cruises very close to shore, for diversion in the bays and inlets in the South as well as in the North. By the late eighteenth century, yachting was common enough to receive specific recognition in Virginia legislation, which exempted pleasure boats from canal tolls. But yachting clubs didn't exist. One was organized in Boston in 1835 but proved to be premature and disbanded itself in 1837. In July of 1844, John Cox, displaying the family flair for organization, assembled a group of his friends, with their boats, in the harbor. On the afternoon of July 30, in the cabin of *Gimcrack,* eight friends joined him in forming the New York Yacht Club — the scene Philip Hone had observed. John Cox was elected the club's commodore.

The following year he provided a headquarters for the club. We have a description from Philip Hone's diary, for he soon dined there.

> They have a club-house — a handsome Gothic cottage in a pleasant grove in the Elysian fields, presided over by that prince of good fellows, John C. Stevens, who makes the punch, superintends the cooking and presides at the table.[17]

John Cox Stevens also organized competitions in design and sailing. In the first of these, a young boy of sixteen, George Steers, the son of an English shipwright who had emigrated to the United States, won the Commodore Prize with the *Martin Van Buren.* Steer's designs made a real breakthrough: yachts came to be shaped much more like clippers, with raking lines, a longer bow, and a cleaner, less stubby stern. John Cox Stevens had discovered an authentic Yankee genius in his own harbor, and the two of them were to go on to greater and more memorable things.

These greater things involved thinking in transatlantic terms. Who could be a serious sailor, in America, and not do so? For years John Stevens's yachts had been oceangoing, and he had continually urged yachtsmen to broaden their horizons. He used the *Spirit of the Times* to engage in spirited arguments about sailing matters. Although amiable and easygoing, John Stevens was not timid in expressing his views or in backing them up — as Colonel Johnson had found out many years before. William Porter, for his part, was happy to applaud the achievements of his friend the commodore, and he delighted in having such an easy case to make. Sailing was moral, manly, and healthy.

> What amusement is there for which so much can be said? Where is there one more manly, healthful, or useful, or so entirely free from objection, as yachting? And where on the face of the globe can a spot be found better adapted to the display of whatever talent or skill we may possess in the construction and management of our crafts? We may in one hour exchange the smooth surface of the Hudson for the rougher one of the bay — and in another, the bay for the broad Atlantic.[18]

The broad Atlantic! Time was moving on. In 1850 John Stevens was sixty-five. How much longer might he have?

Events were now moving toward the climax of Stevens's sporting life. In the autumn of 1850 a friend received a letter inviting Americans to send one of their New York craft to compete in yachting regattas to be held the next year in Britain, as part of the International Exposition. Someone showed John Stevens the letter. He decided to try. As a large oceangoing ship would be required, he formed a syndicate, made up of himself, his brother Edwin, and three friends, to finance it. George Steers was selected to design the ship and supervise the building. Word got back to England. In February of 1851 the Earl of Wilton, Commodore of the Royal Yacht Squadron, wrote Stevens formally inviting him to come to England. The race was set for late August, yachts of all nations were invited, and it was decided that the course would be around the Isle of Wight. The winner would be presented with a cup, valued at £100.

The new ship was launched in May and given the only name suitable to its mission — *America*. There was considerable excitement about it; the *Spirit of the Times* ran weekly accounts of *America*'s progress. But there never was any question about which ship would represent America. *Maria* was not built to withstand gales at sea and could not be sailed to England. Just how good *was America*? A series of trial runs were arranged between *America, Maria,* and a third ship, *Cornelia*. The results were disconcerting. *Cornelia* was completely out of her league, but *Maria* proved the faster of the two Stevens ships. Another trial run brought the same result. Family stories had it that in one short trial *Maria* sailed three times around *America*. This was fanciful, but there were four or five trials, and in each *Maria* unquestionably proved to be faster. (*Maria* was a phenomenon; in later years she outraced many steamboats.) But there was no choice in the matter. The second best would go.

By late June *America* was ready. Her carvings, gilded interior work, and upholstery were shipped separately, to be installed at Le Havre, where she would stop first. Three owners, John Cox, his brother Edwin, and James Hamilton, son of Alexander, were to sail her in the race, but for the crossing they took a steamship. In stripped-down condition, with a crew of thirteen aboard, *America* sailed out of New York harbor on June 21, and headed for England.

*

What were her chances? Despite their growing confidence and occasional brash boasting about clipper speed, knowledgeable American observers had serious doubts that *America* could win. While she was in mid-Atlantic, the *Spirit of the Times* summed up matters judiciously.

> Her chances of winning, under any circumstances, would seem to us to be doubtful. The English Clubs have had the advantage of fifty years experience, backed by unlimited means. The taste is a *national* one, and pursued from the prince to the man-before-the-mast, with energy and devotion little dreamed of in our country. Still, we have a hope that Yankee aptness and ingenuity may prove a match for greater experience and skill.[19]

This was the same situation that would confront Richard Ten Broeck in five years, Paul Morphy in seven, and John Heenan in nine: old and well-established traditions competing against raw and unrefined newness; history and experience on one side, talent and hope on the other. Of course, historical change is itself a kind of contest.

The British certainly believed it unlikely that a single interloper could offer a serious challenge to the numbers and experience massed against her. The very notion of anyone presuming to sail against them was startling enough for "that vast population which swarms in our southern ports, and firmly believes in 'Rule Britannia' as an article of national faith."[20] From the Royal Cork Yacht Club, founded in 1720, down to the Royal London Yacht Club of 1849, there were seventeen yacht clubs in the United Kingdom; and not one had ever laid eyes on a foreign competitor. Until *America* came over the horizon, even the few English yachtsmen who knew of the New York Yacht Club "did not regard it as of the slightest consequence, or as at all likely to interfere with their monopoly of the glory." In the Yacht List of 1850 there was an assertion which no Englishman doubted: that England "was distinguished preeminently and alone for the perfection of science in handling ships."[21]

For all that, English confidence might be no more than complacency. From the time *America* arrived in Le Havre, where she stayed through most of July to be scraped, painted, and outfitted, the British began to worry a bit. Like any sporting contest, this one was to some extent a question of nerves; and from this point on, nerves jangled on both sides. The Americans were reputed to be fearful of spying and possible foul play. The English, on the other hand, began to pick up disturbing accounts of the Yankee clipper's speed. Most ominous of all were the words of the English pilot who boarded *America* to guide her to Cowes: "a regular flying fish; the fleetest of our yachts will have their work cut out to beat her."[22] But words don't decide sporting contests. *America*'s chances were shrouded in uncertainty.

Appropriately, she arrived at the Isle of Wight, on the evening of July 31, in a thick fog, anchoring a few miles from Cowes itself. The next morning there sped toward *America* one of the newest and fastest English cutters, *Lavrock,* sent out to show her into harbor. Was she also sent out to size her up and perhaps show her up? So John Stevens believed. *Lavrock* stuck peculiarly close to *America,* lying to, tacking about. Word of the American craft's arrival had spread quickly, and people were eager to catch a first glimpse; they crowded onto the vessels in the harbor, gathered on the wharves, and stood in the windows of houses bordering the harbor, to watch "the peculiar trial they saw we could not escape."[23] Somewhat hesitantly, the crew ran up her sails, and *America* moved off in the wake of *Lavrock.*

Here was the first challenge for the Americans. "I have seen and been engaged in many exciting trials at sea and on shore," John Stevens said, giving as the most memorable example the race between Eclipse and Henry. But never had he felt "One hundredth part of the fear and dread I felt at the thought of being beaten by *Lavrock* in this eventful trial." He retained his deadpan expression. The American poker face had returned to one of its sources, the land of superb and effortless understatement. But beneath the seeming indifference Stevens fully realized that the next few minutes would tell a great deal about his chances of beating the British.

During the first five minutes not a sound was heard save the beating of our anxious hearts or the slight ripple of water upon the sword-like stem. The captain [fixed] his stern unaltering gaze upon the vessel ahead. The men were motionless as statues, with their eager eyes fastened upon the *Lavrock* with a fixedness and intensity that seemed almost unnatural. No words can describe it. It could not, and did not, last long.[24]

Quickly *America* moved to windward and out of *Lavrock*'s wake, then pulled abreast of her. They came together into the harbor. Whatever the spectators saw — and the first newspaper reports noted *America*'s "graceful and easy manner" — the most important thing was the contest that had been played out in the minds of *America*'s crew. They had won out over that first moment of self-doubt.

*

Three weeks passed between this first appearance and the race, which was finally set for August 23, with eighteen yachts entered — seventeen British and the *America* — and no allowance for tonnage. The route was a fifty-three-mile circuit around the Isle of Wight, beginning and ending at Cowes Castle. *America* remained quietly at her moorings, the object of eager curiosity. British observers struggled to describe her. Her bow, "sharp as a knife blade," and her "low black hull," with its "extreme rake," were her most obvious points.[25] For some, she was "the beau ideal of what one is accustomed to read about in Cooper's novels." Others disputed this. *America* didn't have the delicate spars with cobweb tracery of sail that marked "the sort of phantom ship that Fenimore Cooper likes to paint." She was "big-boned, rather skeletal," with "thick, stiff-looking masts, like hardy sticks." No phantom, she was "ready for work." But what kind of work? "She sits upon [the water] like a duck, and taken with her clean build and saucy raking masts she evidently looks bent on mischief." "Some gentlemen connected with the clubs," said one commentator, "have a wholesome dread of her, and think we have caught a tartar."[26]

The excitement built up steadily. John Stevens issued a challenge to the commodore of the Royal Yacht Club, offering to let him select one or more British yachts to race against *America,* once round the Isle of Wight, for a stake of £10,000. No one accepted his challenge. This annoyed ordinary British seamen, because the Yankees were thereby "allowed to crow over gentlemen." The seamen were also annoyed at the liberal display of stars and stripes on the American ship. ◉

On the seventeenth, the *America* entered the Ryde Regatta, competing against eighteen British schooners and cutters, the course being from Cowes to Ryde and back. Because of a technicality, *America* was not formally eligible to win the regatta, but she made a shambles of the race itself. She started slowly, then put on a terrific burst of speed and shot by all the British ships. And she came back "bowling along like a seagull," faster than she went out, with scarcely any foam at her bows, the waves falling away under her keel and sides, almost as though the ocean offered no resistance.[27]

For many people, that performance settled the outcome; by the time of the great race there was a growing conviction that *America* would win. Yet one could never be certain, and English yachtsmen, like that new fictional character Mr. Micawber, could hope "that something might turn up." Any sense of anticlimax was swallowed up by the excitement of race day. By rail and steamboat, people had poured into Southampton; many sportsmen had even torn themselves away from the moors where they were shooting, "to set at rest the many thousand conjectures as to whether the Royal Yacht Squadron is still invincible, or whether that honour is henceforth to rest with our transatlantic brethren." Cowes was crammed full, not a bed to be had.

The scene was a most animated one. Upwards of one hundred yachts lay at anchorage in the roadstead, which was alive with smaller craft. Booths had been set up along the quay; flags floated from the beautiful villas studding the wooded coast; pennants of various clubs flickered in the light; and from the sea and shore arose an incessant buzz of voices mingled with the splashing of oars. Toward the morning of the twenty-third, there was a light fall of rain, and the cloudy atmosphere promised a breeze, which duly appeared, clearing off the morning mist.

By 9:00 A.M. the competing yachts were in their places, moored in a double line, with *America* considerably astern. At 9:55 the preparatory gun sounded from the clubhouse battery. The crews ran up the sails. At precisely 10:00 the starting gun boomed, and before its smoke had drifted away the splendid frozen tableau dissolved into motion. The flotilla of boats of all kinds and sizes, which would follow along behind the racers, put itself into motion; the steamer carrying the race committee (and the American Minister, Mr. Abbott Lawrence) set off. Stretching away for miles to the horizon, it was such a sight as had never been seen before in the history of yachting, such a sight "as the Adriatic never beheld in all the pride of Venice."[28]

*

The yachts broke away evenly. For a few moments *America* didn't move, then almost imperceptibly set herself in motion. *Gypsy Queen,* all her canvas set, going easily with the tide, took the lead, with *Beatrice* second and *Volante, Constance,* and *Arrow* closely bunched behind. Soon *America* was moving smoothly and beginning to creep up on the leaders, passing some of the cutters. After a quarter of an hour *Gypsy Queen* held the lead, with *America* fourth. The wind freshened a bit and *America* passed *Constance* and *Beatrice* and moved into second; another puff of wind and *America* darted toward *Gypsy Queen.* But the wind left off, *America* fell back, and "little *Volante* came skimming past her with a stupendous jib, swallowing up all the wind that was blowing." The entire fleet of ships, as it passed Osborne House, made a magnificent picture — the fleet-filled sea framed by the white batteries of Portsmouth and the green hills of Hampshire.

Volante caught *Gypsy Queen* and passed her. So far the race had buoyed British hopes. Now the breeze began to quicken, and that favored *America* and the larger ships. *Volante* and *Gypsy Queen* fought for the lead. At 10:45 the breeze picked up even more, and *Gypsy Queen* moved past *Volante* once again, while *America* moved into third. But she could not seem to catch *Volante* or *Gypsy Queen.* "Brother Jonathan's not going to have it all his own way." As the yachts passed Ryde the excitement on shore was very great; as the Sandheads were rounded at 11:00 it was *Volante, Gypsy Queen,* and *America* in that order. Once more the breeze increased. The sailing was well contested and exciting, with the leaders bunched closely together. *Freak* and *Aurora* made moves out of the pack. As they all passed Norman's Land Buoy, *Volante* led by one minute twenty seconds over *Freak,* which was second by only twenty seconds over *Aurora,* which had fifteen seconds over *Gypsy Queen,* which in turn was fifteen seconds ahead of *America.* Three others trailed *America* but were within reach. The rest staggered far to the rear, and some began to retire from the race.

And now *America* showed her quality. As the breeze took the line of her sails, which remained flat as a drumhead, she seemed to "walk along" past cutters and schooners. Flying like the wind, "leaping over, not against, the water," she took the lead. While the cutters were thrashing through the water, sending spray over their bows, and the schooners were wet up to the foot of their foremasts, *America* was dry as a bone and increasing her lead with every passing instant. "No foam, but rather a water jet, rose from her bows; and the greatest point of resistance — for resistance there must be somewhere — seemed about the beam, or just forward of her mainmast, for the seas flashed off from her sides at that point every time she met them." Yankee clipper! This was her quickest bit of sailing. By the time they reached Brading, *America* had left every rival well behind. Even the steamer with the race committee aboard had all she could do to keep up.

The ships kept their course round the Foreland and by Bembridge, *America* sailing past the white and black buoys at a tremendous rate. But at this point there was some confusion, the source of an eventual claim of foul against *America*. She and most of the other yachts went round the Nab lightship on the inside, while *Arrow, Bacchante, Constance,* and *Gypsy Queen* went on the outside. The latter course was the usual one, but sailing orders given the vessels were unclear on this point, and the foul claim was subsequently disallowed. By 12:00 the ship nearest *America* was a full two miles behind. Her rivals were not as bad off as it seemed, for now the breeze died down and the set of the tide was against *America*. Then, at 12:58, *America*'s jib boom broke off, because of faulty handling, and for a quarter of an hour, while her crew gathered up the wreckage, she was thrown into the wind. Even this made little difference. Most of her pursuers were too far astern, some hull-down on the horizon.

The next three hours were slower, wearier work. Several of the ships gave up and returned to Cowes, but *Aurora, Freak,* and *Volante* remained in a small group several miles behind but still pursuing. Unfortunately, *Volante* was fouled by *Freak,* lost her jib boom, and thereby lost "the small glimpse of fortune which the light winds might have given her." By 5:00 *America* had opened up the greatest distance between her and her remaining rivals; *Aurora,* the nearest, was seven and a half miles behind.

They came to the Needles, immense pillars of chalk and limestone that rose up out of the water. There a group of steamships awaited the racers, among them the royal yacht *Victoria and Albert,* which had the royal ensign at the main and the Lord Admiral's flag at the fore. As *America* passed the steamships, she was cheered — a compliment her crew acknowledged by uncovering their heads and waving their hats. Then it was the turn of the Americans, and as *America* passed *Victoria and Albert,* she was so much in command of the race that the crew lowered her ensign, Commodore Stevens took off his hat, and the crew followed his example, though it was as unusual to recognize the appearance of the queen during the race as it would be for a jockey to pull up and salute while riding. All of them remained uncovered for some minutes, until they had passed the royal yacht — "a mark of respect not the less becoming because it was bestowed by republicans."

It was at the Needles that there may have taken place an exchange that captured the mingled astonishment at, and recognition of, *America*'s superiority. As the first of the yachts appeared, the queen turned to her signal master, who was watching through his spyglass.

"Signal master, which yacht is first?"

"The *America,* Your Majesty."

"Which is second?"

"Your Majesty, there is no second."

As there was no wind, the time required to get across the finish line was considerable; so that though the end of the race was actually quite close, it was an anticlimax. *America* didn't receive the winning flag until 8:37. *Aurora,* coming up very rapidly, taking advantage of her very light tonnage and making the most of the whisper of breeze, crossed at 8:45. *Bacchante* finished at 9:30, *Eclipse* at 9:45, *Brilliant* at 1:20 A.M.; the rest were not timed.

*

America had done it. So had George Steers and the crew, and generations of Yankee sailors; and, capping a lifetime of sailing, so had John Cox Stevens. The next day, in a gesture of good sportsmanship, Queen Victoria visited the victors, chatted on deck, and then went below to inspect. She congratulated the owners and, rubbing a shelf in the galley with her handkerchief without finding any dust, complimented the crew on its cleanliness. That night there was a fireworks display along the esplanade, and a party at the clubhouse. There was a presentation of the silver cup, which was exceedingly ornate and ugly and ever after known as the *America*'s Cup. Fame hangs on slender threads of chance. Had the faster American ship sailed in the race, we would now familiarly write of the *Maria*'s Cup. Minister Lawrence made a short speech, acknowledging the prowess of the American ship and its crew and also gracefully reminding his audience that this was but the child giving lessons to the father.

There wasn't much consolation in that for British sailors. The beginning and the end of the race had been well contested, but there were few who doubted *America*'s superiority. Was this superiority also soon to be America's? It may seem to be making too much of a mere sporting contest to suggest that serious people inferred from it a forthcoming American challenge to British naval superiority. But, in the context of the developments of the previous decade, that was undoubtedly the thought in the minds of many. Any British defeat on the sea, the foundation of England's military and commercial power, sent tremors reverberating widely. Andrew Jackson had understood this many, many years before: "It is a great thing to beat the English on the sea, their favorite element." And however much British sailors had prepared themselves for the result of the race, the actual outcome was a blow. "P'sha, sir," the signal master at the lighthouse was heard to say, "catch her! You might as well set a bulldog to catch a hare!" [29] This was troubling for all bulldogs.

A week later *America* rubbed in the humiliation even more in a match race against Robert Stephenson's schooner *Titania*. A world-famous name and an old business acquaintance of John Stevens (the Stevenses had bought one of his locomotives for the Camden & Amboy), Stephenson had been the only person to step forward to accept Stevens's challenge for a match race. The match took place on August 28, with stakes of a modest £100; the course was twenty miles out and back. *America* won with consummate ease, by fifty-two minutes. No wonder there were reports in the papers that British yachtsmen, now converted to the clipper design, were busily engaged in lengthening their bows; and that George Steers had orders for three yachts.

America never returned in triumph to her homeland. Unsentimentally, John Stevens sold her in England, and her former owners returned home as they had come, by steamship. In New York harbor they were greeted by the firing of cannon. At the Astor House that evening, they were given a dinner of stupendous excess by the New York Yacht Club: fourteen courses with half a dozen kinds of wine — quite enough to sink most men and slow down even *Maria*. Why not? It was a triumphant occasion. Many prominent business and professional men were present, and another commodore, Matthew C. Perry, represented the U.S. Navy. Three years

AMERICA

later he would make a more momentous sailing voyage to Japan.

American newspapers crowed loud and long. Whatever the British thought, the Americans were *certain* that this victory symbolized their rising maritime might, and they delighted in reminding the British that they had been "eclipsed by the stars and flogged by the stripes." George Templeton Strong, New York diarist, was revolted by the stridency of Yankee self-congratulation:

> Newspapers crowing over the victory of Stevens's yacht which has beat everything in the British seas; quite creditable to Yankee ship-building, certainly, but not worthy the intolerable, vainglorious vaporings that make every newspaper I take up now ridiculous. One would think yacht-building were the end of man's existence on earth.[30]

But then Strong was a nonsailing, crabby lawyer. John Stevens remained modest as ever; no spread-eagle oratory for him. Quite the reverse. "Long may the bonds of kindred affection and interest, that bind us together at present, remain unbroken."[31]

*

Eighteen fifty-one, a miraculous year of sailing masterpieces: George Steers's *America* and Donald McKay's *Flying Cloud,* triumphs commensurate with America's capacity for wonder at speed. And utility. The clippers were not designed as works of art; they were useful objects. As such they expressed their culture's aspirations — "sharp in the bows, long in the spars, slender to look at and fast to go," wrote Oliver Wendell Holmes, who accurately described them as a direct response "to the forms which the elements impressed upon their builders."[32] These builders were craftsmen and businessmen, artists and sportsmen, driven by the urge to compete, to excel, to convert some inward vision into an act, a gesture, an object. Their statements were few, their language restrained, quite unlike the overheated romanticism of so many of their contemporaries.

These Yankee shipbuilders satisfied the Jacksonian desire for something distinctive, yet the standard against which many Americans continued to measure their culture's achievements was the great tradition of European high culture, in which there was little place for things as humble as sailing ships and ploughs, trotting wagons and tall tales. It is one of the ironies of transatlantic cultural history that while people like Emerson called for new forms and new things, they actually clung to traditional images of excellence — a country house like the Hermitage; a race course like Newmarket; and the splendor of a royal yacht squadron of old-fashioned ships. Even more ironic is the fact that, disdainful as they were, the British were often the first to identify and appreciate the triumphs of the American vernacular in many of its forms: the poetry of Whitman and Frost; the humor of Mark Twain; the clipper ship; and the trotting wagon. They recognized the new when they saw it, and they realized it was beautiful.

The beauty of the useful. This was what English observers noted when they got their first look at the American trotting horse Tom Thumb, in 1829. In some ways his movements seemed rather rough and uncouth, with none of the delicate movements to which English drivers were accustomed. But in other ways his action was beautiful — "in the utilitarian way in which action was defined as beautiful, that is, the ease of his work, while others labored."[33] This was what the American sculptor Horatio Greenough meant when he praised popular art in which form and function were one:

> The men who have reduced locomotion to its simplest elements, in the trotting wagon and the yacht *America,* are nearer to Athens at this moment than they who would bend the Greek temple to every use. I contend for Greek principles, not Greek things. If a flat sail goes nearest the wind, a bellying sail, though picturesque, must be given up. The slender harness and tall gaunt wheels are not only effective, they are beautiful — for they respect the beauty of a horse, and do not uselessly task him.[34]

Greenough was surely right. But it would be contrary to the modest and unpretending spirit of these things to suggest at the same time that they had the qualities, whatever they are, of transcendent art.

Great flights of the imagination soar beyond the utilitarian, beyond any other category, label, or description. Eighteen fifty-one saw the launching of such a work, a flight of the imagination that, like these others, drew its power from the traditions of its culture and reflected its culture's aspirations, but did so in so superlatively personal and original a way as to baffle many of those who first encountered it. Eighteen fifty-one was the year of *Moby-Dick.* Although Herman Melville thought of his novel as utilitarian, a handbook about whales and whaling, it struck his contemporaries as the reverse; it was romantic where other works were matter of fact; word-intoxicated where they were laconic, luxuriant where they were spare. And so Americans dealt with it as best they could by forgetting about it for three-quarters of a century. For many years

America was better known than the *Pequod,* and *Flying Cloud* was more famous than either. Chance often dictates fame, and chance, more than tradition, accounts for the appearance of genius.

*

No one needed to remind John Stevens of the mutability of human life, the evanescence of sporting life. His wife died in 1855; his brother Robert in 1856. He had no children. He left his city mansion and returned to the country, to New Jersey, where he spent his time winding up his affairs. He left *Maria* and all his racing and sailing trophies to Edwin — all but *America*'s Cup, which he left to the New York Yacht Club, *his* yacht club. John Cox Stevens died at the old family castle in Hoboken, on June 10, 1857.

The oddities and ironies of chance were borne out by American maritime history in the years that followed. For one period, between 1830 and the Civil War, the sea caught the popular fancy and stimulated imaginative shipbuilding with wood; but Americans didn't respond innovatively to shipbuilding with iron. The British did, and as things turned out, they need not have worried about the supposed American challenge to their maritime supremacy. The Age of Jackson, the most glorious epoch of American sailing, marked the beginning of the end of American maritime importance. The American imagination remained continental, not seafaring.

Oddly enough, that curious-looking and otherwise insignificant cup has had a much longer existence than the other and more magnificent objects of the great age of American sailing. One by one the clippers vanished, never to reappear. After Edwin Stevens's death, *Maria* was sold to new owners; in 1869 she disappeared at sea. *America* lasted longer. After her sale in 1851 she cruised in the Mediterranean for a number of years, then turned up in United States waters. She became a blockade runner for the Confederacy, was blockaded and then scuttled. Northerners, recalling her glory, raised her, and, when the war was over, took her to Annapolis to be used for training midshipmen. When the British yacht *Cambria* challenged for *America*'s Cup in 1870, *America* was fitted out by the navy and entered in the race; and even at her venerable age she finished fourth, well ahead of *Cambria.* After that her fortunes varied until 1921, when she was bought by public subscription and taken once more to Annapolis. She was destroyed during World War II.

John Cox Stevens's claim to fame was a modest one; perhaps appropriately, *America*'s name has long outlived his own. His personal talents were modest; his successes as a sportsman were the result more of other men's labors than his own. His was a self-indulgent life, perhaps, in some people's eyes, a trivial one. But he was in the right place at the right time for what he wished to do, and he achieved one thing denied to many men with far greater talent than his: in winning the race at Cowes he did something no American had ever done before.

Anyway, his most striking talent, like William Porter's, was for friendship. "Ill-will to his fellow men was discordant to his nature."[35] He relished moments of sociability, on sea or on land, such as the scene with which we began this chapter, and the one with which we end it. Once, to celebrate the launching of a steamboat, he ferried two hundred people to Hoboken, where, on a hillside dotted with tables, flags, and pennants, the guests strolled about the river walk, ate turtle soup and drank champagne, while members of New York and New Jersey boat clubs, dressed in white jackets and trousers, wearing round chip hats and checkered shirts, filled their glasses, the beautiful gardens echoing to toasts, songs, and laughter, John Cox's spirits as abundant and sparkling as his champagne. He accepted equably the oblivion that awaited him, and his ships, and his houses, and even his river walk, content to have flourished as sailor, sportsman, and prince of good fellows and to have sported, for a brief moment, in the Elysian Fields.

RICHARD TEN BROECK

6

Richard Ten Broeck
and the American Invasion

IN THE HALF CENTURY from Andrew Jackson's glory days at Clover Bottom to the Civil War, American horse racing expanded in a spectacular fashion. This growth in the number of race tracks and spectators, races run and purses given, was as uncontrolled and varied as that of the nation itself. The six million people of 1800, living in sixteen states, had by 1850 become twenty-three million people in thirty-one states, in a land area that was two and a half times as large. Actually, the spread of horse racing was greater than even these statistics suggest, because not only were Americans by 1850 racing in places where, a few years before, they hadn't lived — in California, in Texas, and on the plains — but they were also racing in New England, that old citadel of puritan disapproval. Opposition to horse racing remained powerful; and in the 1850s the ascendance of a dogmatic frame of mind associated with abolitionism and temperance posed a renewed threat. We have seen how the atmosphere of that decade distressed William Porter and decimated the audience of the *Spirit of the Times*. But there was no going back. By midcentury, horse racing, in all its varieties, had become firmly established as a national sport.[1]

It had also become a more American sport, during the course of the Jacksonian half century. It wasn't as purely American in style as some patriots demanded: consider the joke in the *Spirit* about the American sportsman "so republican in his notions that he refuses to go to church because the ministers preach of the kingdom of heaven."[2] But neither was it merely the replica of the English style Anglophiles desired. It was a mixture of past and present, like any historical development, but it was decidedly an *American* mixture.

And it was a popular one. Its rough commonness, in style and atmosphere, was one of its features. Horse racing belonged to no one class and no particular section, and it was too heterogeneous to have any one spokesman — a Noah Webster to write its dictionary of American usage, or an Emerson to call its national genius into being.

Change had come about in random and unforeseen ways often difficult to account for. Take one small instance. Americans ran their horses in a counterclockwise direction. In the late eighteenth century this practice still varied considerably from place to place, but by the middle of the nineteenth century a widespread consensus had emerged. Why? No one person or group of persons decided; few people even bothered to talk about it. A small thing, yet puzzling. It may serve as a warning flag to us when we too glibly presume to explain larger questions when the smaller evade us. It may have been the result, as one observer noted, of a common American attitude as powerful as it was simple: the determination to be different.

> The only reason we can give why, in this country we run to the Left, while in Great Britain they run to the Right, is, as in some other things, our countrymen do not choose to follow the lead of their European brethren.[3]

The interplay of material conditions and ideas produced change, but the nature of that change was complex. The transformation of American horse racing was due partly to the absence, which we have already noted, of certain things in American culture: the ignorance of forms and rules; the absence of surplus wealth; the lack of time to prepare slowly and preserve patiently. But American horse racing was not simply a failed version of something else. Changes in American racing were mainly due to the positive strengths and desires of the people who took part, not to limitations and failings. American horse racing was, as it had been in Jackson's day, in the process of becoming. It was rough and disordered because American culture itself was in many ways rough and disordered. It was also vigorous and innovative because the culture was so. The nation was incomplete, its boundaries were indeterminate, its people were polyglot, its manners were in flux; and American horse racing reflected these things.

However different the physical setting and the society, American sportsmen continued to imitate the English racing tradition as best they could: at Rapides, Louisiana, where the track was in a swamp; at Madison County, Illinois, where the track bordered the Great Plains; at Batesville, Arkansas; Terre Haute, Indiana; Tallahassee, Florida; from Big Lick to Cherokee Pond. The result was similar enough so that any visitor from one country to the other would easily have understood the running of the horses. But beyond that the fun began. Countless details had changed. The tone and atmosphere were different. Some of these differences will be the subject of the next few pages.

*

Americans continued to call their horse racing the sport of the turf. But the American turf was metaphoric. With very few exceptions Americans didn't run their horses on that spongy elastic grass, like a piece of fine green cloth, on which British horses ran. They ran them on dirt. Swaths cleared in meadows or cut through woods, abandoned fields cleared once for other purposes — these had been the original American racing sites, but for almost two centuries Americans had persisted in thinking that racing ought properly to take place on grass. Eventually experience showed them that grass was too difficult and expensive to maintain. Common language reflected this development by describing American racing places as "tracks" and not "courses," although the fancier places retained English usage to describe themselves. The dirt tracks were very rough, and, as they had no drainage, this meant that horses had to run through inches of mud after a rainstorm, or contend, in summer, with clouds of swirling dust. By the time Americans could afford the constant care that turf courses required, they had become accustomed to their dirt tracks and preferred them, because they believed these made for faster racing, at least in good weather.

The shape of the racetrack had also changed. The American track was a simple one-mile oval. In its ideal form it was absolutely flat. The oval shape had developed early on, because the first American tracks were not adaptations to nature but victories over nature, paths hacked out of the landscape under the pressure of necessity. And having begun this way, American horsemen went ahead and designed their tracks to suit their purposes. Intimate reconciliation with nature, preached by transcendental philosophers and organic architects, has never appealed much to American sportsmen. They have not been interested in steeplechasing, for example. Nor, to move away from horses for a moment, did American men and women go in for cross-country running for a very long time. Already in Jackson's time pedestrianism, as foot racing was called, took place on racetracks or on the streets of cities. By 1850 the oval shape for an American racetrack was standard almost everywhere.

By contrast, British courses had been adapted to the contours of the landscape and, like it, varied greatly from place to place. Having been altered and modified over a long period of time, they were irregular in shape, winding around natural and manmade objects, rising and falling, looping and bending, with long straight stretches as well. Foreign visitors found the American shape very odd; they complained that American tracks were uniformly boring. There were no odd, quaint, or accidental features. The great English turfman, Admiral Rous, when invited to go to Chester, notable among English courses then for its narrow ovalness, said: "No, I would as soon see horses run around a tub."[4]

The oval shape of American tracks was not due solely to historical origins; it also reflected the fact that American racing was a form of entertainment dependent upon popular support. The English accepted the dictates of nature and the accidents of history: at Epsom Downs the start was a mile from the main grandstand and largely invisible from it. Newmarket deliberately wished racing not to become popular. So little of the racing there could actually be seen by spectators that the course was described as "hanging about in Suffolk for a race that is run in Cambridgeshire." By contrast the spatial organization of American tracks was much more spectator-oriented. Spectators were closer to the running, and the oval shape, with its enclosed infield, encouraged spectators to think of themselves as being at the center of the scene and drama. Foreign observers agreed in describing American sporting crowds as unusually demonstrative and noisy; it was, for foreigners, part of the Americans' easy vulgarity. But it was more. American sporting crowds believed that their presence made a difference in the event itself, that their shouting and encouragement might influence the outcome.

The crowd's sense of being an active and important part of the occasion helps explain the American obsession (then and later) with the size of the crowds. From the Eclipse–Henry race to our own day, crowd-counting has remained a prominent feature of almost every sporting event. It was almost a game in itself. Why? Because the crowd and the sporting event were thought of as equal parts of a moment in history. Counting the crowd was an affirmation of the hope, disguised as a belief, that what was happening would not be forgotten; even if the event turned out not to matter, the size of the crowd might be "historic." Where society was fluid and the historical sense so uncertain, records and statistics were ways of making history. To be counted was to count.

American racetracks catered to spectators in another way. They were not places reserved only for those with arcane knowledge. Their uniformity was a form of reassurance where so many people were new, were strangers. American racetracks invited the uninitiated. Americans, having been to one racetrack, could feel confident in going to any other. They didn't need to learn each track's peculiarities, the Tattenham corner at Epsom or "the bushes" at Newmarket. (It is the same reassurance American tourists find in staying in one identical hotel after another.)

Being popular, American racetracks' physical arrangements for spectators implied social equality. But in these Jacksonian years the powerful tension in American sporting culture, between the exclusiveness of its British past and the democracy of its American future (as Americans saw it anyway), produced extraordinary muddle and confusion. At many tracks the only stand was a rickety and improvised one; safety was never the prime concern. (Richard Ten Broeck used to tell of how he missed part of the Fashion–Peytona match race because the stand collapsed.) Material conditions were very limiting. It took relatively large amounts of money to build the permanent walls, fences, gates, and other facilities that were required if hierarchical social distinctions were to be given material expression. And money for such things had to be surplus capital, because it lay idle for perhaps fifty weeks of the year.

The middle-class character of American society had broken down most of horse racing's pretensions to aristocratic exclusiveness. The next step was to make horse racing entirely popular by openly basing its social organization and style on money. But many American horsemen were not yet able to go this far. Those with conventional social ambitions drew back in alarm and dismay at the implications of such a move; and newer entrepreneurs, without such ambitions, were not yet powerful enough to carry the day. American racing needed to connect itself still more securely to the growing city populations. It needed longer seasons, many more races, and more competitive horses. It also needed much more effective regulation, and, above all, the sanction of laws that would make betting legal at the track but illegal everywhere else. These things would come eventually, under the leadership of enormously powerful plutocrats, but not until well after the Civil War.

In the meantime, American racetracks were like the homes of the famous sportsmen who patronized them: they were somewhere between a traditional past and a future that had yet to find its architectural expression. Jockey clubs did their best to establish clear social distinctions. There might be a club stand for members of the jockey club and guests, and another stand for the general public; or, more often, there was only one stand, which divided into separate areas. A number of tracks prided themselves on providing a separate stand for women. When possible, there were separate entrances and exits to the stands and to the track itself. Where there were different facilities, admissions varied accordingly.

But such arrangements were continually breaking down, as the incessant chorus of demands for more order showed. It was difficult to control crowds at all, let alone force them to pay attention to reserved areas. Subtler kinds of social distinction — clothes, accent, manner — didn't count for much at American tracks, where deference was in short supply. The basic problem went deeper than the absence of capital to build fences.

The problem was that there was no widely accepted principle of social exclusiveness on which an American jockey club could organize itself. In 1832 the Maryland Jockey Club enrolled 237 original members; by the end of the first year, because of the need for wider support, membership was expanded to 300. This was for one race club that, despite its name, was not the only, or even the major, club in one state. Contrast this with the sixty-two-member Newmarket Jockey Club, which functioned, at this same time, as a national English club. Imagine the stands, stables, and club rooms of Newmarket magically rebuilt in Maryland or New York or Clover Bottom. Newmarket would have been just as ambiguous a symbol as the Hermitage.[5]

In one respect, however, Americans had remained very traditional. They clung to a very old-fashioned form of racing, those three- and four-mile races of several heats that were prized in Jackson's and Johnson's days. Americans had kept their faith in "bottom," stamina being the bottom line of pedigree. They sometimes carried this to brutal lengths, running horses fifteen or even twenty miles in one day. Although recognized as excessive, this allowed Americans to emphasize the power and strength of their animals and, through the 1830s and 1840s, to enjoy the rare pleasure of being able to taunt the English for being too new-fangled.

This was changing. American horsemen were becoming more interested in speed and much more conscious of time as a standard of excellence. The English remained less concerned with speed. Their races were shorter, but their horses carried more weight and their jockeys rode at a more leisurely pace. English horsemen took the traditional view that the race was against the competition and not the clock. This had been Jackson's view, of course, and not even the precedent of Eclipse's third heat against Henry could change it. But now Americans kept more accurate track of speed records, and speed increasingly entered into their betting calculations.

These were a few of the aspects of American horse racing that gave it a distinctive flavor, although it was only a small part of the larger scene. Robust and vigorous, that mid-nineteenth-century horse-racing scene was in important ways different from the staid and idealized version usually described.

*

Its tumultuous disorderliness would strike us first: large numbers of unattended horses roamed the grounds, straying onto the track before a race or breaking away and chasing after the horses that were running. Gigs and carriages, parked any which way, cluttered the margins of the track. True, the completely unfenced openness of earlier years was disappearing, as racetracks built barriers of various kinds so that they could charge admission and establish somewhat more orderly habits among their patrons. But their efforts had little effect.

The people were more disorderly than the horses. Spectators roamed anywhere they wished, swarming out on the track at any time. Some tracks employed private constables to keep order; the Union Course resorted to using pugilists to keep the peace — a sure sign of their desperation. In general, however, little policing was done, and spectators had to protect themselves. It was not until the 1830s that a few track operators began to fence off the racing tracks. Richard Ten Broeck remembered races where the crowd was so rough that jockeys were bumped while riding, and a path had to be cleared through the crowd as the horses came down the homestretch. There were outbreaks of fighting. Drunkenness was common, as almost all foreign travelers noted.[6] Various steps were taken to try to control drinking. The Louisville, Kentucky, jockey

PEYTONA VERSUS FASHION

club prohibited the selling of liquor on the premises, except by its own licensed agents. Racetrack crowds were certainly no worse in this respect than were crowds at militia or election days, and they were not as rowdy as crowds at prize fights; but their size made them seem especially troublesome. The real problem, of course, was the inordinate amount of drinking done by the population as a whole.

Judges and stewards had little prestige or authority. Theirs was a difficult and thankless job, but many of their difficulties were of their own doing. They were timid about applying the rules and notoriously reluctant to declare any change in the order of the finish, for fear of provoking the mob. From their point of view there were good reasons for caution. Stewards were often unable to see the violations themselves, had no mechanical devices to assist them, and had little power to enforce their decisions. As a result, the betting crowd assumed the worst about the judges' intelligence and honesty, and were vociferous in making this known.

Jockeys were another unruly element. They came from the dregs of racing life and were held in very low regard. The word itself had many meanings, all implying recklessness, wildness, and deviousness. It is true that, as one proverb had it, "Give me my jockey and you shall choose your trainer"; but once the days had passed in which gentlemen-owners rode their own horses in races, Americans paid little attention to who rode. English jockeys were unquestionably the supreme riders of their day, admired (on the Continent as well as in America) for their fluid command of their horses and for their scientific riding. A few of them became rich and well-known figures in their own right, although the usual end for English jockeys too was drink and the poorhouse. American jockeys were picked because of their availability rather than their skill. Most of them were exercise boys who hung about stables looking for work and could be employed for virtually nothing.

Many jockeys were blacks, usually slaves, for whom riding was simply another aspect (no doubt a more pleasant one) of their everyday work. One black rider, Abe Hawkins, became well known, but the presence of most blacks at the track was not thought to deserve mention. Sir Henry's first rider, in 1823, was a black boy whose name was not given in accounts of the race. Black jockeys rode on northern tracks even in these years when prejudice against blacks remained very strong in the North. And in the general disorderly state of racetracks, north and south, blacks mingled freely with everyone else in the crowds.

The prime consideration for jockeys was that they be feather-light — about ninety pounds — which meant that one aspect of a jockey's life was familiar: newspaper stories referred to the steam baths, diets, and exercises jockeys endured to keep their weight down. All jockeys, white and black, were called "boys," and many began riding as children; but many of them were not boys at all but grown, even oldish, men. The term indicates the general disdain in which they were held, as well as the childishness of their behavior. One commentator noted that "Boys, as they grow older grow wiser but the devil of it is, they grow heavy faster than they grow wise." Many jockeys still rode with spurs, and they all carried whips and used them freely, being as rough with each other as with horses. "They make a wild time of it," someone said matter-of-factly.[7] Expectations of riding competence were very low. The chief thing looked for was that a jockey have the strength to control a big horse over several miles; his main task was that he get off to a decent start; and the modest hope, that he not make an egregious blunder during the running.

There were signs that this was changing. Skilled riders, men of intelligence and independent judgment, were emerging — men such as Joe Laird (whose father was a well-known trainer), and Gilbert W. Patrick, who traveled to the West and South when most jockeys rode only in local areas, and who was especially sought after to ride in important match races. Common sense indicated that a good jockey would increase a horse's chances of winning, witness Mr. Purdy's contribution in the Eclipse–Sir Henry match of 1823. As the length of races was reduced and speed was emphasized more, the importance of the jockey correspondingly increased, as did the importance of strategy and tactics. But the era of the jockey as star performer lay well in the future.

In this process something else happened as well. The old view that horse racing was a simple sport, in which horses ran against each other, began to be replaced by the process of thinking of horse racing as a more complex kind of entertainment and game.

*

The crowds were unruly, the arrangements rough, the jockeys undisciplined. These were symptoms of a deeper disorderliness in the racing of these days — its dishonesty. "The jurisprudence of the turf is entirely too loose," an observer wrote, with prodigious, miraculous understatement.[8] At all racetracks, in England as well as in America, there were as many forms of dishonesty as there were temptations to it. The age-old reputation racing had for wickedness was thoroughly justified, and, as actually conducted in the United States, its wickedness was brought to new levels of perfection. It was not a matter of occasional abuses. Corruption in racing was chronic; trickery and deceit were inseparable from the conduct of the sport.

One reason was that the management of American racetracks was very confused. An important source of this confusion was the separation of ownership and management. Few jockey clubs or racing associations owned the land on which their tracks were located. This produced not only a chronic sense of impermanence, dramatized by the frequency with which racetracks were sold out from under the horses' hooves, as land-hungry American cities relentlessly spread out and gobbled up the land on which the nearby track was invitingly situated; it also produced difficulty in fixing responsibility. The owner of the land often had no connection with the jockey club, knew nothing of the sport itself, and was likely to regard the racetrack as simply a business venture, judging its success by its profits. On the other hand, if he was a sportsman or a member of the jockey club, his personal influence would predominate over the collective authority of the club, when there was a conflict between their interests.[9]

The actual management of the tracks was even more mischievous in its effects. Jockey clubs leased the land, then leased the management of the track to an independent proprietor. Arrangements between club and proprietor as to length and conditions of the lease varied, but in practice the proprietor had great latitude in running the race meet as he saw fit. The jockey club usually retained supervision of the actual racing and decided any questions associated with it; but this was less important than it seemed, because the general tone of the meeting was already established by the time the racing started.

The proprietor set the racing days, fixed the size of purses and stakes, and attempted to raise the money to make these as attractive as possible. He supervised all aspects of the physical setup, took in admission fees, and ran the food and drink concessions or subleased them to independent operators. If there was an inn or hotel on the track or near it, the proprietor often ran that as well. He was responsible for controlling the crowd and assuring order, according to what his notions of order were. But since much of his profit depended on attracting people to the track, the proprietor was not likely to keep many people away. This is an absolutely central fact.

The popular character of American racing already played a large role in shaping it.

Much depended on the knowledge and experience of the proprietor. This ranged from that of a man like Ten Broeck, who was familiar with every aspect of racing, to that of the more typical proprietor, who was a small-time entrepreneur running a shaky and somewhat disreputable business. Proprietors were rarely men of substantial reputation or independent means. They often moved from one track to another and thus had conflicting loyalties, if loyalty ever entered into the situation.

Even more depended on the character of the proprietor. This also ranged across the spectrum, from men of unquestioned probity down to the fly-by-night con men and crooks who came in to make a quick killing, broke their leases, and skipped out with the purses. Proprietors were guilty of the grossest frauds. Purses were announced and never given; or, when given, sometimes turned out to be counterfeit. Attractions were publicized that never came off. Prices and admission fees were jacked up sharply when there was a popular event, and spectators were gouged for adulterated food and drink. Honest proprietors were driven to make exaggerated public demonstrations of their integrity, for instance by actually hanging the purse for a race on the finish post.

Some of these things were bound to happen whatever the arrangements. What made everything worse was the fundamental encouragement to fraud and deceit, in America, that resulted from the absence of any regulation. The track took no responsibility for the security of the horses. There was no control over what food, drink, or drugs might be given them, with or without their owners' permission. They were sometimes stolen or mutilated on the eve of races. One of the most famous forms of fraud was the substitution of a "ringer" — one horse running in place of another; the absence of clear records and authentic pedigrees made it extremely difficult to establish a horse's true identity. A much commoner form of cheating was to lie about a horse's age; the owner sometimes didn't know how old his horse actually was, and the proverbially famous proof of age, "from the horse's mouth," was often inconclusive and disputed.

As for the jockeys! Interfering with other horses was common, and so were other flagrant abuses: pulling a horse up short of the finish line; getting off to a slow start; riding erratically (there were stories of jockeys riding while drunk); or simply not trying. Disciplinary action was unusual and limited in effectiveness. Jockeys could be fined, but few American tracks suspended them from riding or prohibited their coming back on the track to ride. The English practice of "warning off" jockeys was not widely followed, and even when it was — Abe Hawkins, for example, was suspended at Metairie for "positive, and palpable dishonesty, in plain terms, 'throwing off' a race he had already won by sawing his horse around" [10] — it had little effect because there was no central authority to prevent jockeys from going elsewhere and riding with impunity.

Trainers' cheating was less obvious and sometimes indistinguishable from incompetence; horses often started when entirely unfit to run. Trainers also had their own games to play, perhaps unknown to owners or jockeys; they could concentrate on winning one race but not others, or give jockeys deliberately misleading instructions. Sometimes this involved owners as well as trainers and was due to the "play or pay" system, in which money was put up as forfeit if a specified horse didn't start when promised — an effort by proprietors and jockey clubs to make owners live up to their agreements, the result of which, however, was inevitably to give owner and trainer an incentive to start a horse no matter what its condition, in order to save the forfeit.

The things owners could do to fool the public were most damaging of all and most difficult to prove. In any event, the crucial question — whether an owner really was trying to win a race — wasn't a simple matter. Since horses were best worked into condition in actual racing, many races were in fact tuneups; the owner (and his friends) could calculate their bets accordingly. Even when a horse was in top form, an owner might hold it back in one race, in order to raise the odds in a subsequent one, in which the horse would go all out. The "form" of horses was bewildering enough at best, and for anyone with eyes to see, the wildly erratic performance of some horses from one race to the next left little doubt as to the owner's manipulation.

Much that went on at the racetrack lent itself to manipulation. In such an atmosphere of free-flowing uncertainty there flourished that hallmark of the gamesman's presence, the emphasis on "inside" information that might prove useful in determining what game was really being played, and who was doing what to whom. In this regard the triangular relationship of owner, jockey, and trainer came to be the focus of knowledge: each was to some extent dependent upon, and each was capable of tricking, the others; and each was likely to suspect that he alone was being left out of something. All of which fostered that self-conscious racetrack poker-faced blankness. Never let on. Never let up. Never give anything away.

*

The Age of Jackson marked a time when the idea of reform penetrated nearly every aspect of American life. Yet between Jackson's heyday and the Civil War, no reform in the conditions of American racing took place. Why not?

For one thing, sportsmen were wary of speaking out too explicitly about the problems they faced, for fear of playing into the hands of the considerable element that wanted to abolish horse racing rather than reform it. Then, too, reformers were not agreed upon what should be done. William Porter's efforts were mainly concerned with attempts at national organization. Porter was correct in believing that merely local efforts were inadequate. Yet his own hopes for national reform were also futile. The disorder of American racing as it had evolved, a disorder that went deeper than uncouth behavior and confused organization, was social.

Despite their public insistence that all was well with American racing (especially in the South), and that it was a splendid copy, with only a few imperfections here and there, of the wonderful old English pastime, the class of people who saw themselves as the natural leaders of horse-racing society had no doubt what was wrong: American horse racing was too popular. The way to restore order was to see to it that the right people were in the right places — in charge, at the top.

They couldn't put it that bluntly, and so there was a ritualistic quality to the way in which this idea was expressed. Each of the many jockey clubs that bravely sprang to life in these years announced its determination to set things straight in the future. The racecourse might be new, but it was based on the old tried-and-true principles. The Green Lawn Course (which proposed racing on the turf) characterized itself as "the right sort of material to insure success." The Smithland jockey club modestly described itself as consisting of "gentlemen of such liberal minds, liberal feelings and high-toned honor" that it could be depended upon to prevent "anything which may be calculated to bring racing into disrepute." No matter how small or insignificant, the same yearning was always there; witness the Big Lick Jockey Club: "We hope to make a respectable figure on the turf in a few years."[11]

Even at midcentury this search for order still led back to England

and to comparisons with the old image of classic English racing as an example of true aristocratic order. Of course that image was in many ways inaccurate. The sprawling confusion and vulgar festive tone of Derby Day at Epsom often shocked American visitors who expected (and wanted) something else. But it is proof of the deep-seated irrational power of the American desire for social order that no contradictory evidence broke the spell. Newmarket might come to seem common. Beyond Newmarket there was Ascot, and if even Ascot didn't measure up, as American visitors occasionally hinted, there was Goodwood!

Goodwood Park, located on the site of a Danish camp of 992, the country home and private racecourse of the Duke of Richmond, had all the elements required: antiquity, taste, and peacefulness. Its enclosed park, six miles in circumference, exuded order: "A distinct line of demarcation was secured against the obtrusion of the noisy with the orderly so unpleasantly observable at Epsom, Ascot and other Courses."[12] Goodwood's order no doubt owed something to the considerable number of private constables employed by the duke.

An occasional American racecourse seemed to approach this. At Tree Hill Course, near Richmond, Virginia, the jockey club was made up (naturally) "only of gentlemen of highest respectability and moral worth." It offered substantial guarantees of exclusiveness: the course was surrounded by a ditch, eleven feet wide and six feet deep, "to keep off all vagabond intruders"; and there was only one entryway to the course. Best of all, the members' stand was Tree Hill House itself, which held precisely fifty people. No wonder a visitor reported, "I did not see a beastly drunkard nor an uncivil man on the grounds."[13] There was order! There was exclusiveness!

For many people the lesson of Tree Hill was clear. The fundamental cause of Jacksonian social disorder was something graver than drunkenness and incivility. The cause of disorder was democracy. And that could not be reformed. As a sportsman, Andrew Jackson represented an effort to reconcile contradictory elements: traditional practices and social equality. Now, in the 1850s, a Jacksonian reconciliation was impossible under the old terms: southerners were attacking the idea of democracy, and abolitionists were pushing the idea of equality far beyond what Jackson would have approved of. With the collapse of the Whigs, the great American party of traditional sportsmen, the party of the Porters and the Stevenses, the Jacksonian compromise fell to pieces.

Tree Hill was so exclusive as to be insignificant. It was also ripe with intimations of decay, as William Porter had noticed several years before the Civil War, in pronouncing a funeral elegy for what he saw as a departing way of life:

> Now only the family portrait, the gold headed cane, the shoe buckles and the sleeve-buttons, with some few exceptions, remain to the descendants of the illustrious ancestry. His broad lands and silver plate have long ago been divided and sub-divided and at last have gone to strangers.[14]

The fraternity of sportsmen, in America, was always dissolving into an association of strangers. And any visitor to Tree Hill's countryside — "the fine old mansions now decayed and ruined by the magic wand of equality — which leads down to the abyss of universal suffrage and universal desolation" — could see the cause. No wonder Goodwood was peaceful: it had lots of constables and no democracy.

In the North, there was additional evidence of disorder and corruption. Even the longer-lasting racetracks, like the Union Course, originally founded and controlled by solid and substantial characters, eventually fell into vulgar hands, new people from the marginal ranks of society who had no education, no proper stake in society. They were the riffraff of the democratic city. Once again we see the intimate connection between horse racing and American city life. In both, attempts at reform followed the same pattern. From time to time a group of leading citizens organized a reform party (a new jockey club) and campaigned vigorously to win control of city hall (they rebuilt the racetrack and set it on a sound footing). For a while things would seem to go well. But nothing lasted. The reformers found that corruption didn't disappear. The electorate (the racetrack crowd) didn't wish to be reformed. The reformers soon lost enthusiasm — and the next election. And the operators and con men soon took over the jockey club once more.

*

The truth is that not only was the popular character of American horse racing closely connected with its democratic disorder and its invitation to gamesmanship; it *depended* on these. A quick look will show why.

Racetrack people knew horse racing was filled with tricks and fraud, yet they obstinately rebuffed all efforts to rehabilitate their morals, remaining as unrepentant as Tammany Hall. These stable-hands and jockeys, hucksters and gamblers, lived well beyond the limits of social respectability; they didn't live in stately homes or ape current fashions, but they did form a subculture of remarkable continuity, one into which many of them were born and lived all their lives. They were in fact deeply traditional and conservative; their values were theirs by inheritance and not by acquisition, forming a vivid contrast, in this regard, to their supposed betters — that large number of middle-class Americans, besotted with notions of change and progress, who wished to reform them. Therefore, to the track workers, reform was only meddling by outsiders, meddling directed at some uncertain and highly suspect goal. With a kind of stoic resignation they viewed reform as a game; its proponents were adversaries to be foiled. For them, racing mirrored human nature and was, like human nature, unreformable.

What was true of the racetrack workers was also true of a far larger group — the spectators, who, although they complained bitterly on occasion, accepted racing pretty much as it was. But unlike the stoic traditionalism of the workers, the support of spectators was rooted in the Jacksonian emphasis upon individual free will and competition. For them, play and sport were wholly private matters. Men and women went to the racetrack voluntarily, and if in so doing a few got into trouble or lost their money, only fools or hypocrites complained. It was better for racetracks to be honestly conducted than not to be, but it was not a public responsibility to see to this. People had common sense and native wit to protect them, and if they hadn't, then they could only learn through the sometimes bitter lessons of experience. They saw the racetrack as Andrew Jackson had seen it — as a school of life.

This view was stronger in 1850 than it had been earlier. The laissez-faire attitudes that were still struggling for acceptance in the days of Colonel Stevens had largely triumphed by the middle of the century. At Clover Bottom, Andrew Jackson had supervised every detail of the racing. But his paternalistic suspicion of any kind of roguery had now largely been superseded by the notion of a free-for-all — frontier rough-and-tumble translated into business terms. On every main street in the land, racetrack trickery was common commercial practice. "Never buy cows by candlelight," that archrogue Jay Gould would say, in his drawling, deadpan country-bumpkin way. And at the racetrack, or on Wall Street, even daylight wasn't much help.

The increasing popularity and acceptance of horse racing was connected with something else as well. Horse racing was primarily a form of gambling. It was a beautiful, exciting, and occasionally noble form of gambling; but gambling it was. Surely the prohibitionists who wished to abolish it on that account were near the truth? "Listen, then, to an opinion I have often expressed," wrote Oliver Wendell Holmes, who liked horse racing, much to the scandal of proper Bostonians, but who also liked the truth: "everybody knows that racehorses are kept mainly as gambling implements. All that matter about blood and speed we won't discuss; we understand all that; useful — very — of course."[15]

Of course. Racetracks, in Jackson's time, conducted no betting. Gambling was entirely private. A few tracks attempted to exclude or discourage professional gamblers from coming on the premises, but this was difficult to enforce. A few tracks even prohibited betting on the premises altogether. They didn't last long. In general, betting went on everywhere at the track, as men quoted odds to each other and recorded bets.

In England, soon after 1800, a development of great significance occurred, to which relatively little attention has been paid: the appearance of the bookmaker. Previously, betting had been personal, between men or women who knew each other; now, however, as horse racing became popular with many people who were not at the actual place of the racing, betting became institutionalized. In England, the impersonal bookmaker operated out of a gambling house, but, since these were illegal in America, he was encouraged to operate at the racetrack. Reform was involved in this development too. In the early years of the nineteenth century, public forms of gambling had been common and quite respectable. Lottery tickets were sold at all taverns and inns, and the proceeds were used for countless worthy enterprises — schools, churches, hospitals, and the like. Then in the 1830s and 1840s reformers closed down such legal avenues, and governments began to prohibit gambling, which had up to that point only been frowned upon. These efforts were not wholly successful, but the handwriting was on the stable wall. Horse racing became one of the few legal forms of public wagering.[16]

Gambling, loose conditions, disorder, and trickery — these were among the chief reasons for horse racing's spreading appeal. For many Americans, these were expressions of a native way of doing things — perhaps good, perhaps not, but *their* way. Far from being troubled by trickery, hoaxes, and humbugs, racing's tricks and deceptions were part of the fun, a way in which spectators became to some extent participants. Gamesmen themselves, the crowd admired a sport that had such gamey elements. American sporting life resisted the straitjacket of rules just as American social life resisted the straitjacket of clearly defined roles. It delighted in wildness; in wild-card poker games, for example, in which the rules were changed with each new hand. American sportsmen took the adage of the English bookmaker, "A mug is born every minute of the day, and thank Gawd some of 'em live," and they pushed it to brutal lengths: "Never give a sucker an even break." In America, there were no old-world codes of conduct and good sportsmanship that were exclusive, the inheritance of the few. Here, everyone was treated with equal contempt. No privilege protected suckers. This was harsh, but then the world was harsh. And in its rough way it was democratic.

It is as the heir of such emerging traditions that Richard Ten Broeck should be understood. He absorbed the matchmaking tradition of Colonel Johnson, refined it, and took it abroad, becoming in turn the greatest gambler, promoter, and gamesman in American horse racing in the 1850s.

*

Richard Ten Broeck was born in Albany, New York, in May of 1812, of an old Dutch family. Always reticent about his personal life, the only things he mentioned about his boyhood had to do with education and sport. His school had a "stern Hollander" as principal, and his assistant was a "witty Irishman named O'Shaugnessy," who taught classics and was also "head of the department exclusively devoted to the birch."[17] O'Shaugnessy, much of whose time was given to the latter department, did for Ten Broeck what, at almost the same time, "Old Put" did for the Porter boys: that is, he drove Richard as far from schools and books as he could get. The sporting incidents of Ten Broeck's youth were pleasanter to remember. At age eleven he was taken to see Eclipse race against Henry, and the details of the match were fresh in his memory seventy years later.

His schooling finished, Ten Broeck looked about for a suitable career. His family had a tradition of military service. His grandfathers were Revolutionary War officers on the patriot side. So in 1829 he was enrolled at West Point. In a way this made sense, because military life would allow him time for sporting activity, and army and navy officers, scattered throughout the country in isolated garrisons and frontier posts, formed an active, though tiny, sporting fraternity.

Many of them were among the most loyal contributors to the *Spirit of the Times*. But in actual practice there was little future for him in the military. In these Jacksonian years the American military profession, for an ambitious young American man of respectable background but unsettled prospects, was a dead end and not, as in Britain or Europe, a respectable haven for younger or wayward sons. And for someone of Ten Broeck's temperamental independence, a military career was entirely unsuitable. He lasted one year at West Point. In 1830 he was dismissed. "Unable to repress his wild propensities he left in disgrace," one writer said.[18] It is doubtful that *he* thought his leaving a disgrace.

After West Point, Ten Broeck apparently determined on a racing career. But he didn't do the predictable thing and establish himself in New York or New Jersey sporting circles, or settle in the old South. He was probably too much a loner to take any conventional path, and he may well have been attracted by the newer southeastern states, where things were wide open. For the next twenty-five years his field of operations would essentially be the great gambling river, the Mississippi, from Kentucky to New Orleans. Little is known about Ten Broeck in the 1830s. He was learning the rudiments and subtleties of the extraordinary world of American horse racing, and there is a hint of what he was doing in one of his laconic comments: "I spent several years in the South, where my racing career began in earnest."[19] It was a serious business, learning the tricks of his trade.

Sometime in the 1830s he met Colonel Johnson, and, as he later wrote, "owing to my fondness for racing, and his good opinion of me, Colonel William R. Johnson . . . determined to take me into partnership in his many racing ventures."[20] The best evidence of Ten Broeck's horse sense was that he could impress someone as savvy as the colonel. Together they toured the racetracks of the South and the Middle Atlantic states. Studying with the colonel must have been an exhilarating experience. Rather different from West Point.

If we knew more about those "ventures," we would have an incomparable record of the racing and betting practices of the time. What a partnership! This remarkable and intriguing pair were the greatest gamesmen of their day. The differences between them — the thirty years' gap in their ages, the contrasting northern and southern backgrounds — are much less striking than the powerful bonds of complementary temperament and values: both were intrepidly independent, both were capable of cool but audacious gambles, and both were masterful matchmakers and bettors. Colonel Johnson had found his heir.

*

Whatever the ventures and adventures of the partnership, Richard Ten Broeck also operated on his own. He went a step further than the colonel and chose not to establish a permanent home base from which to work. Inevitably most of his time was spent in the humdrum business of moving from track to track, winning and losing modest amounts in unexciting and undramatic fashion. But occasionally, in fragmentary notes in sporting papers, one catches a glimpse of him venturing further afield, making a bolder move. He went to Canada, where four of his horses won nine races, a feat that, according to an admiring *Spirit of the Times,* "marvelously astonished Queen Victoria's lieges." Ten Broeck's own estimate was rather different. He had gone to Canada, he wrote frankly, "to seek new pastures" — that is, bigger betting. "But there was no opportunity for heavy betting," he went on, "and as the purses were small, this Canadian excursion was far from a financial success though" — and here he added an ironic touch — "as actors say under similar circumstances, it was a great artistic success."[21]

Something of an artist and a good deal of an actor, Ten Broeck was a poker player with horses, and, like any poker player, he had to accept the role dictated by whatever hand was dealt him. But the sportsman's success depended on winning races, whereas for Ten Broeck, the gamesman gambler, winning or losing any single race or even a cluster of races was only a means toward his real objective, which was to win the culminating bet. But to achieve that he had to be where there was a great deal of money. And to find that he would go anywhere.

One of his most imaginative — perhaps desperate — ventures was to take a stable of horses to Havana. This enterprise involved leasing a Havana racetrack, which he did; but the venture was a failure. The Cubans were not much interested in American thoroughbreds. There was scant attendance at the races involving Ten Broeck's horses, and little betting took place. Even his imperturbability was slightly ruffled, for he wrote with an uncharacteristic touch of asperity: "Habañeros would as soon see engines run on a railroad."[22]

He returned to New Orleans. In the late 1840s the tide of events began to carry him on to greater adventures. The rise of anti-gambling and temperance movements in the East in the 1840s drove horsemen elsewhere just when the lower Mississippi was entering its heyday. Men were making a great deal of money in cotton and sugar. This money attracted all sorts of businessmen and speculators, who dreamed of new and more exotic ways to make more money out of it, as well as gamblers, who already knew old and familiar ways to spend it. From up and down the Mississippi they converged in New Orleans, generating a speculative hedonism comparable to the gold-rush fever raging through San Francisco at the same time. Both cities were sporting cultures of extravagance and recklessness. The characteristic product of one city was the clipper ship of boundless speed; the mark of the other was a steamboat culture characterized by flamboyant narcissism — the card-sharp, con-man world of the riverboat.

It was the ideal element for Ten Broeck. He involved himself in a number of enterprises. He managed the Bascombe racetrack in Mobile and became treasurer of the Mobile Jockey Club. But the liveliest things were happening in New Orleans, where new sugar and cotton nabobs were spending money. There, Adam L. Bingaman, a Natchez turfman and politician, and Colonel Yelverton N. Oliver, a promoter who had managed tracks in several cities, opened the Bingaman Course, a new track across the river from New Orleans, advertising it as "the people's track" and promoting it with considerable imagination. They reduced the admission fee from one dollar to fifty cents, admitted ladies free of charge, offered popular entertainments such as bull and bear fights in between races, and added other special events. In 1848 they engaged Ten Broeck to manage the track. This gave him the kind of foothold he needed. But he already had in mind grander enterprises (which was just as well, because the Bingaman Course was sold in 1852, and its land developed as town lots).[23]

In 1851 Ten Broeck formed the Metairie Association, a joint-stock company that bought full control of the Metairie Course in New Orleans. This track had been founded in 1838, and its fortunes, like those of all American racetracks, fluctuated greatly. By 1851 it was the oldest track in New Orleans, in terms of continuous operation (others had come and gone), and, by virtue of its antiquity, was the most fashionable. Under Ten Broeck's management it was for several years the best track in the country. He improved the actual racing track and rebuilt the grandstand, erected new stables, and, by increasing the size of the purses offered (getting local shopkeepers and businessmen to contribute money), he attracted many reputable horsemen from the upper southern states, who brought their horses to compete. He also struggled to raise the general tone, by furnishing the ladies' stand with parlors and "retiring" rooms and by requiring that owners supply their jockeys with racing colors, which was rarely done at other tracks.

The result was a distinctive New Orleans racing style, which combined vulgar dash — the men wore green cutaways with brass buttons and flourished riding whips in the grandstand — and provincial uneasiness. A visiting Englishwoman thought the whole scene "a mockery of Newmarket and Epsom," but other observers disagreed with her.[24] At all times the Porter brothers, in New Orleans and in New York, cheered on Ten Broeck's efforts, in the *Spirit of the Times,* praising his honesty and gentlemanly character.

In New Orleans, as elsewhere, the dramatic pattern of Ten Broeck's life was that of the outsider, alone, pitting his judgment and nerve against everybody else's in duels in which the weapons were horses. Up to this time he was still looking for a challenge that would vault him into prominence. With no warning such a once-in-a-lifetime chance appeared.

*

It arose out of a most humdrum incident. At a race in 1853, Ten Broeck watched a horse finish second despite an intriguing flash of speed. He bought the colt, which had been named Darley because of a supposed resemblance to the venerated English eighteenth-century sire, the Darley Arabian. However, that name didn't suit the plan forming in Ten Broeck's mind. "As I desired him to be distinctly an American horse," he later wrote, "I changed the name to Lexington."[25]

Ten Broeck sent Lexington to New Orleans, where he undertook to bring out the latent speed he had detected. All through the winter the conditioning program went forward. In December of 1853, picking his spots, Ten Broeck matched Lexington against Sally Waters, a well-known but not topflight horse, and Lexington won so handily that Ten Broeck must have begun to realize he had something remarkable on his hands. By spring, Lexington was ready. So were his rivals. On April 1, 1854, on the Metairie Course, Ten Broeck's horse ran against three other horses, a large field in those days. Each horse represented a state — Mississippi, Alabama, Loui-

LEXINGTON

MESSENGER

siana — with Lexington running for Kentucky. A large crowd turned out, including ex-president Millard Fillmore, whose somewhat tarnished prestige adorned the judge's stand. The standout was a horse named Lecomte. It had rained heavily during the night, and the track was very heavy, but Lexington reveled in the goo and won the first heat with comparative ease. In the second heat he was pushed very hard by Lecomte, but he won a seemingly decisive victory.

But this was only the first shot of a duel. Lecomte's owner was not convinced. A week later the two horses met again, at Metairie, and raced in four-mile heats. Although some people didn't think Lexington had come out of the previous race in top form, Ten Broeck let him start, and he went off a very heavy favorite. The first heat was tremendously hard-fought all the way, with Lecomte holding on to win narrowly in 7:26, a record-breaking time for the distance. This was a remarkable reversal of form. Lecomte silenced many doubters by winning the second heat as well, in slightly slower time but by a larger margin. The stunning upset was complete. Kentucky had been put in its place, and Richard Ten Broeck had been humbled.

Now it was Ten Broeck's turn to demand a rematch. He insisted that Lexington lost the first heat only because his jockey had pulled him up after three miles, mistaking that for the finish of the race. Lecomte's owner steadfastly refused Ten Broeck's challenge. For months the dispute went on, punctuated by challenges, refusals, rebukes, and growing acrimony. In the long run, it was difficult for Lecomte's owner to refuse Ten Broeck a rematch, since he had agreed to one after the first race; and as each horse had one victory, it seemed the only sporting way to settle the rival claims to superiority.

After a full year of controversy, Ten Broeck arranged a double climax to the now-heated rivalry. The first part of the event was an audacious piece of bravado. Ten Broeck bet $10,000 that Lexington, racing alone, against the clock, would break Lecomte's record of 7:26. Taking no chances, Ten Broeck brought Gil Patrick down from the North to ride Lexington. In a crescendo of swelling suspense and publicity that would have done Rossini proud, Lexington was put to the test in April, 1855, once again at Metairie. Pushed hard all the way by Patrick, he circled the track four times, amid a frenzy of crowd excitement, and smashed Lecomte's record in the astounding time of 7:19½.

News of this amazing feat sped in all directions on the telegraph, setting up the second half of Ten Broeck's drama of challenge and response. No question now that Lexington was ready for the third and climactic run against Lecomte. And when the race took place later that month, before an enormous crowd, there was no drama. Lecomte was thoroughly beaten in the first heat, with Lexington winning in 7:23¾, which, for any other horse at any other time, would have been sensational. Lecomte was withdrawn from the second heat.

Lexington was the unchallenged king of the American turf, Kentucky was avenged, and Ten Broeck had scored the coup of a lifetime. He made the most of it, taking Lexington back to Kentucky in processional triumph. Crowds turned out to see him along the way. Years later, ancient Kentuckians still regaled their audiences with stories of the fabulous match races of 1855 between Lexington and the clock and between Lexington and Lecomte, and told how they came back from New Orleans with a boatload of money.

This was the stuff of legend and in every way an authentic triumph for the horse and its owner.

> All over the sunny South went the word *Lexington*. Far up into the North, even into parts where the race-horse was unknown, travelled the word *Lexington*. There came a day when any little child of America could have told you the story of *Lexington,* the name synonymous with everything that is greatest in a horse. *Lexington* belonged not alone to the turfmen. He was the heritage of the people, and after him there were merely other horses.[26]

By skillful training and attention to detail, Ten Broeck had turned a good racer into a great one; but other aspects of Ten Broeck's management also deserve attention, for they tell us a good deal about American racing near the end of the Jacksonian age.

Lexington seized the national imagination in a way that had not been possible for Eclipse or Boston or any of the earlier horses. There were now many more sporting newspapers, and much more sporting news appeared in ordinary newspapers. But the chief difference was the telegraph, which could transmit information nationally and overnight. Ten Broeck used this new technology to capitalize on the feeling that more was involved in horse racing than the mere running of a horse. Things never noticed before now became important, which shows how far we have come since Truxton, whose story, after all, was very like Lexington's. For example, Lexington became the first horse whose earnings were common knowledge; people speculated about *his* fortune in the same way they did about those of his contemporaries John Jacob Astor and August Belmont. All told, Lexington won $56,000, an enormous sum for the time. That too was now one of Lexington's records.

Yet all of Lexington's success was achieved with a remarkable economy of means. In his entire career Lexington ran in only seven races. Making allowances for the fact that illness cut short his career, and judging by the standards of a time when horses ran infrequently, this was still a very small number. The timing of each race was deft. Each race counted. The race against the clock was a stroke of genius, but the consummate brilliance was the showmanship of the huge bet staked on breaking the world's record. This wasn't a private bet, it was a public event. It became as much the focus of talk as the horses and their races. Additionally, the race pushed American racing further in the direction of establishing speed as the popular standard of achievement. It was the beginning of the end of "bottom."

Much was also involved in the unprecedented outpouring of public admiration and affection for Lexington. His career was a mixture of clear superiority and a touch of fallibility, a most potent combination for a popular sporting hero. The loss to Lecomte gained him sympathy, by allowing him to battle back from adversity. For one year Lexington was the underdog and thereby avoided the danger of seeming to win with mechanical ease. In dramatic terms, the loss was an even greater advantage. On the day of the second match, as we have seen, observers noted that Lexington seemed somewhat unfit; many thought he shouldn't have run at all. Ten Broeck, with a gambler's talent for building the pot, must have calculated that he was not really risking much. If he won, his owner would have to look for new opponents; but if he lost, a third and payoff meeting would be set up. Ten Broeck might actually gain more by losing. The entire affair had become a public event that was no longer entirely in the hands of the individual owners. The danger that Lecomte's owner would resist the public demand for a third meeting was a bluff Ten Broeck knew how to call. The career of Darley/Lexington touched deep springs of archetypal mythmaking. It was more than just an instance of a rise from rags to riches; it was also a case of the lowly being born again.

*

For two decades there had been talk of the possibility of an American owner taking horses to England — "an object which the Sporting World have been looking forward to with utmost interest for many years."[27] In the pages of the *Spirit of the Times* William Porter campaigned unceasingly for such an event, urging American owners to take the risk and insisting that the challenge would be good for American racing, whatever the result. As early as 1844, when A. T. Kirkman, a leading Alabama horseman, expressed interest, it seemed that something might come of the talk. But Kirkman insisted that he be guaranteed odds of 30–1 against him, covering any horse he chose to send. Tattersalls, the leading English betting syndicate, offered odds of 20–1, provided Kirkman name a specific horse. That was the end of that.

The difficulties involved in such an undertaking were formidable: the time involved, the great expense, the immediate danger of the Atlantic crossing, and the longer-range worry about the horses' health; for thoroughbreds rarely traveled well. None of these considerations hindered the spread-eagle jingoes who wrote to the *Spirit* on the subject:

> Brother Jonathan can do anything that is worth the doing as well and as successfully as John Bull, whether it consists in ordering a horse or a fowl, building a ship and fighting her after she is built, and in fact, anything.[28]

Letters like this only reenforced the prevailing English view that even if American horses had improved over the years, there was no telling how good they were, because Americans boasted wildly about everything. American hopes for success were based on factors well described by a British army officer stationed in Canada:

> I still think that to run long distances with speed and endurance, there is nothing like [American] horses in the world . . . Depend upon it there is not one horse in three hundred in England that can run four miles in anything like the time which your horses make.[29]

True or not, this ignored the fact that, in England, American horses would not be running four miles.

So it was that Richard Ten Broeck, with the experience of those preliminary forays to Canada and Cuba behind him, and with the premier horse of his time as his chief weapon, was ready for his greatest venture and greatest gamble. "An idea grew upon me continually till I carried it out," he wrote, "an ambition to beard the English lion in his den." He had carefully thought out what he needed: two American jockeys (one was Gil Patrick), an American trainer, and a full entourage of American grooms and stable boys, among other things. But to prepare everything took well over a year. At last he was ready. In September of 1856 he sailed for England. The American invasion was underway.

*

Ten Broeck went without Lexington. It was found that the champion was going blind, so he had to be left behind in Kentucky. This must have been a staggering blow to Ten Broeck's chances, but he never complained, never made excuses. He had several other good horses in his stable — Lecomte, which he had bought after the last match race; Pryor; and Prioress. It was probably the strongest stable that in practice could have been put together by one man. Still, without Lexington Ten Broeck was leading a raid, not an invasion.

At first he had no success. He had terrible luck with his horses' health. Lecomte never regained his form, and died. So did Pryor. Transatlantic differences were subtle and tricky. His American jockeys couldn't adapt to English conditions, so Ten Broeck sent them home and brought another American over to take their place; still not satisfied, he finally turned to an English jockey, George Fordham, who suited him splendidly and who thus began a racing career that would later make him famous. Gradually Ten Broeck made the necessary adjustments. Unfortunately, American racing fans back home quickly gave up on him and soured on the performance of his horses, whose failure to sweep every race seemed inexplicable to them. Or suspicious. One newspaper charged that the American horses had been tampered with, and modestly demanded, as compensation, that Britain cede Canada to the United States. Even at a less ridiculous level, the failure to achieve any early, dramatic victories caused many American followers to lose interest and to deny that Ten Broeck's invasion involved national prestige at all; it was "simply the experiment of an individual."[30]

Besides the sour grapes involved, there were a number of reasons why Ten Broeck's adventures ceased to attract much attention. The term *invasion,* lively and attention-getting as journalism, was very misleading. The battles that followed the landing of the invaders were diffuse, spread over many racing courses, over a long period of time. The campaign was difficult to follow, especially at such a distance. Ten Broeck wasn't able to achieve a crushing victory, as John Stevens had done at Cowes. And he didn't do the one thing that would have been most comprehensible back home: he didn't win the Derby.

Ten Broeck reached the lowest point of his fortunes at the end of his first year in England, and decided to return to America. Then, in October, 1857, he won his first important race, one of the most sensational races ever run at Newmarket. Prioress finished in a triple-dead-heat in the Cesarewitch Stakes. A runoff was ordered. The weather had been very threatening, and, guessing that a thunderstorm was coming, Ten Broeck ordered that lard be put on Prioress's hooves, to keep dirt from adhering to them. He had her wrapped warmly in blankets and gave her doses of whiskey as a tonic. The downpour came, and the two English horses awaiting the runoff stood shivering in the rain. Whether the result of the lard and whiskey or not, Prioress won the runoff by half a length in a thrilling finish.

After that things looked up. "Winning the Cesarewitch gave me renewed hope and courage," Ten Broeck later wrote. "The following year I met with considerable success."[31] Even more satisfying victories soon followed. In 1859 he won at Goodwood! He won the Goodwood Stakes, and his prize two-year-old, Umpire, won impressively at that meeting. He bought Starke, recognized in the United States as the leading racer of the year, and had him shipped over, to augment his depleted forces. In 1861, Starke, much underweighted, won one of the greatest English races, the Goodwood Cup, with George Fordham, the "Kid," riding him. Ten Broeck said that winning the Goodwood Cup was the summit of his ambitions. He had never expected that he would be able to win the Derby, but he had made a great effort. In 1860 Umpire ran strongly but finished second.

Ten Broeck won the respect and friendship of some of the most distinguished and discriminating figures on the English turf, Admiral Rous, Lord Glasgow, and the duke of Beaufort. The English thought him "a fine judge of racing and a fine, courageous gambler when he made up his mind about a horse." In the popular mind, he was one of the first examples of a new phenomenon, "the great American millionaire"; he was a modern Croesus, "as prodigal with his money as Timon of Athens"; and some English horsemen criticized him for giving his jockeys presents that were too lavish.[32] Popular opinion was wrong, of course; he was in fact anything but a modern Croesus; and the English aristocrats with whom he bet knew this. Someone put it very well: "He mostly had to fend for his living, and his increment came from the Turf."[33] This only increased the English sportsmen's admiration for his cool audacity. In

England, the decade of the 1860s was a time when the aristocracy wagered fantastic sums, sums Ten Broeck had no hope of matching. But he never lost his nerve or his head.

This was the high point of Ten Broeck's racing life, his magical dream of the turf come true. He wrote at greater length about these English years than about all the rest of his racing life. His introduction to the aristocratic sporting style was at Badminton, the home of the duke of Beaufort, with its beautiful grounds, handsome stables, and splendid house, as well as "such lavish hospitality and kindliness as I had never seen before nor have I seen since." There, standing before a case filled with a century's accumulation of racing trophies, he savored the old tradition at its finest. Ten Broeck came back to the United States occasionally, but stayed in England for the greater part of ten years, by the end of which the one-time invader had himself long since been conquered.

His greatest success was his betting. In this regard, too, he had begun badly. The turning point, as one would expect, was his winning the Cesarewitch with Prioress. The story he told later about this has something of the atmosphere of a tall tale and is worth repeating in his own words. Having determined, at that discouraging point, to send everyone back and admit defeat, he had gone to Newmarket to watch Prioress carry his colors for the last time.

> After settling all my bills I found I had but £10 remaining. Going to the course on horse back, without the least intention of betting, I rode to the ring and inquired of a bookmaker the odds.
> I will bet you £100 to £1, Mr. Ten Broeck.
> I answered, £1,000 to £10.
> Done.
> Immediately several bookmakers said, I will bet you the same, Mr. Ten Broeck. Having no more money, I rode off in disgust.

It was the beginning of a remarkable streak of luck. "Matchmaking has always been a peculiar hobby of mine," he wrote, "and while in England through my acquaintance with many of the racing magnates I was enabled to arrange a considerable number." He was especially successful in betting against the earl of Glasgow, a very rich and eccentric Scottish nobleman remarkable for his pure sporting morals and his incorrigible bad luck. He must have been an easy mark for Ten Broeck, who estimated that in all his wagering in England, and not simply that conducted with the hapless earl, he had won an average of three out of four bets, "which proportion was too good to last."

He knew — who better? — that no one can beat the odds forever. He won a great deal of money on Starke's Goodwood Cup victory, but that was nothing compared to his greatest betting effort, the Derby of 1860. Ten Broeck entered Umpire, and bet heavily on him at long odds. Had Umpire won, Ten Broeck would have collected the largest amount of money ever won on a single race by a single individual in the entire history of British horse racing up to that time: £150,000 or, in American money, about $750,000. That would have been a coup to culminate a lifetime. But it was not to be. The year before, or the year after, Umpire might well have done it; but in 1860 he was up against one of the greatest English horses of the time, and a second-place finish was all that could reasonably have been expected of him.

Ten Broeck's success deserves to rank with that of any of the sportsmen who challenged the English in the 1850s. It is true that he didn't score the clear-cut kind of victory John Cox Stevens did. It was also impossible for anyone in horse racing to make the dramatic impact on the sport that Paul Morphy was to make on chess. But Ten Broeck got a draw, and that equalled John Heenan's achievement in the prize ring. Considering the complexity of what he had undertaken — the fact that he had to abandon his own customs and adapt to new ones; the fact that in horse racing there were more things which could go wrong than in perhaps any other sport; and the fact that he was challenging the British in the sport in which they most prided themselves on the uniqueness of their traditions — Richard Ten Broeck's achievement was a noteworthy one. He knew this and seems to have been content, but his countrymen were not very generous in their recognition, and subsequent sporting history has taken little notice of him. In 1867, after a decade abroad, with no acclaim to greet him, he returned to the United States.

*

From then on it was all anticlimactic. The South Ten Broeck had known was gone forever. Everywhere there were new faces in the jockey clubs, new horses on the tracks. Racing remained rough and disreputable, but the frontier openness was disappearing; it was slowly becoming more systematized, more standardized.

More important, enormously wealthy men like Leonard Jerome, Cornelius Vanderbilt, and James R. Keene had come into racing during his absence. There was less room for a lone wolf like himself. He had always matched his individual skill against that of the pack, and it was harder to do that now. The old planter aristocracy had not been nearly so formidable; he had not been bothered by their social pretensions, and he could just about match their money. These new tycoons had fewer pretensions but unlimited money; it was difficult to get into their games at all. Although his name was still well known — one of the leading thoroughbreds of the 1870s was named for him — his dominant matchmaking role was over.

All through Richard Ten Broeck's career, stories and speculation about his financial situation hung about him like a smokescreen, and he may well have encouraged such stories, to make it more difficult for his opponents to know when he was bluffing and when not. In these latter years the stories about him were less trustworthy than ever. He was said to have married while in England and to have come back to America with an enormous fortune, but this was probably one of the Croesus stories. On his return, his English wife having died, he married again, this time a wealthy widow much younger than he. She was said to be socially ambitious; at some point the two of them returned to England, where they supposedly spent most of their combined fortunes. Then they went back to America, where he became the racing adviser to James R. Keene.

The prototype of the new post-Civil War American sportsman plutocrat, James Keene was born in England, emigrated to the United States in 1852 as a boy of fourteen, and made a fortune as a speculator in California in the 1850s and 1860s. In the 1870s Keene came east, became involved in some big plunges on Wall Street, and went into racing in a big way; and to help himself in this unfamiliar territory he shrewdly took on Ten Broeck as consultant. Sometime later Keene shipped his horses to England, and Ten Broeck went with him. Keene, a pokerfaced gambler of a type familiar to Ten Broeck, won and lost vast sums with "motionless indifference." Once, upon seeing one of his horses, which was leading in a race, break down just short of the finish line, "he viewed the dire calamity with composure, not moving a muscle. He only remarked to friends: 'Owners must put up with such things.' " (The fact that he had just sold the horse previous to the race may have had something to do with the serenity of his disposition.)[34] There were similarities in the careers of the two men. Keene had seen every side of life in his California wanderings, as had Ten Broeck on the Mississippi, and both dealt with such wild extravagance by using cool calculation. Ten Broeck had found an heir.

But there were important differences between this relationship and the one Ten Broeck had formed forty years earlier with Colonel Johnson. This was not a partnership. Ten Broeck was an appendage. There were also important contrasts between the tone of this period and that of the Jacksonian era. Keene and his contemporaries were narrower, harder. These men could have almost anything they wanted, and they were arrogant in a way the Jacksonians never were. The chief reason for this was the amount of money they had and where they made it. Ten Broeck lived on what he made as a gamesman at the track. Keene's big killings didn't take place at racetracks at all, but in business offices, behind closed doors.

During these years, Richard Ten Broeck seemed resilient and imperturbable as ever, dressing still in the dandyish style of the 1850s. He and his wife moved to California, where they lived in growing disharmony. He became very difficult. His wife questioned his sanity and sought to have him committed to a mental institution. Ten Broeck contested the case, which attracted much newspaper publicity, and won. He then filed for divorce and was left to a life of increasing solitude. Old age was unpleasant for him.

He was almost certainly broke and made arrangements for a man to come to his house, a small white frame cottage in San Mateo, to value the racing trophies and mementos that he still had all around him and that were his last likely means of support. When the man arrived he found that sometime in the night or early morning of August 1, 1892, Richard Ten Broeck had died in his sleep, in bed, with his arms folded over his chest, composed and unflappable as always, "the most intrepid gambler that ever backed a race-horse, bucked the tiger, or bluffed on a pair of deuces."[35] The obituary stories in the San Francisco papers were a jumble of errors and tall tales. Ten Broeck would have laughed. People will believe anything.

When a man lives to a great age, his survivors are hard pressed to remember which part of the past he truly belonged to. This was especially so with Richard Ten Broeck, because much of his career pointed forward and not back. Yet he had grown up a Jacksonian sportsman, and remained one to the end. Even there, in his obscure home in California, many miles and many years distant from those fabulous days of the 1850s, which had echoed with the ringing triumphs of Lexington and the might-have-beens and victories of his challenge to Britain, half a century removed from his partnership with Colonel Johnson, and almost unbelievably remote from the United States of James Madison, into which he had been born eighty years before — even there, in San Mateo, the memory of the sporting world of the old general retained a little of its once-potent spell in the recollection of those simpler and more spacious Jacksonian days conjured up by the name Richard Ten Broeck had given the small and lonely cottage in which he died — the Hermitage.

Paul Morphy

7

Paul Morphy
Against the World

THROUGHOUT the nineteenth century Americans continued to seek some kind of moral justification for sport and play, an attitude that was as old as America itself. Benjamin Franklin had reflected the persistence of this view when, in his essay "The Morals of Chess," he urged his countrymen to take up chess because it was so wholesome a pastime.

> Those who have leisure for such diversions cannot find one that is more innocent; it may in its effects on the mind, be not merely innocent but advantageous.[1]

Franklin's countrymen, then and later, declined to follow his advice and become chess players in large numbers; and, when we think of the poker-playing, horse-racing Jacksonian sportsmen, men not notable for their innocence, Franklin's words strike us as wryly amusing. But they become tragically ironic if we apply them to the life and career of a greater chess player than Franklin ever dreamed of being, a young man who went on the most extraordinary sporting journey of the 1850s, and who is the one indisputable genius in the history of American games, Paul Morphy.

*

Paul Charles Morphy was born in New Orleans on June 22, 1837, the descendant of an Irish family that had emigrated to Spain in the eighteenth century, Morphy being a corruption of Murphy.[2] Paul's grandfather, Diego Morphy, eventually abandoned Spain for Santo Domingo, left there during the slave revolt of 1793 and went to Charleston, South Carolina, where he served for a time as Spanish consul, finally ending up in New Orleans. Paul's father, Alonzo Morphy, grew up and lived all his life in New Orleans; he had an exceptionally successful career as a lawyer, member of the Louisiana legislature, state's attorney general, and judge of the state supreme court. Paul's mother, Thelcide Louise Le Carpentier, was French, her family having moved to New Orleans from the West Indies. She was inordinately conscious of the superior social antecedents of both families, and family memoirs are replete with references to the gentility of the family stock. "No society," wrote Paul Morphy's niece many years later, "was ever more exclusively select than that of the Vieux Carré of New Orleans . . . based upon an aristocracy descended from noble families of Spain and France."[3] This note of snobbery sets the tone of the social traditions within which Paul Morphy grew up.

Creole society represented a cluster of anomalies. Older and more traditional than the dominant American culture engulfing it, narrow and provincial, its social arrangements were correspondingly dense and complex. A marginal culture in a region that was becoming increasingly conscious of its own peculiarity, Creole social behavior, with its powerful vein of snobbery, its mesmeric narcissism, and its pervasive claustrophobia, tended toward the fantastic and the exotic — qualities heightened in our minds because it is now most familiar to us through a literary genre that emphasized precisely those characteristics: the "local color" sketches of George Washington Cable and Kate Chopin and, later, the plays of Tennessee Williams. So it is no wonder Paul Morphy at times seems most comprehensible not in the company of Jefferson Davis and John C. Fremont, John Cox Stevens and Richard Ten Broeck, but in that of Madame Lalaurie, Mrs. Pontellier, and the "Gentleman Caller."

Paul Morphy went to school at the Jefferson Academy in New Orleans, where, like many another studious little boy who preferred reading and writing, he entirely avoided school sports and all other kinds of physical activity. Unlike most young boys, however, the most momentous event of his life occurred at age ten. His father taught him the moves of chess. He grew up in a chess-playing family; his maternal grandfather played it avidly; several members of the family on the Morphy side played it; and his Uncle Ernest, his father's brother, one of the best chess players in New Orleans, took him well beyond the basic moves and gave him insight into the game's theoretical intricacies. Paul learned so rapidly that by age twelve he was more than a match for any of his relatives. For a while he found adequate competition outside the family, because New Orleans, in the 1840s, was one of the liveliest chess centers in the United States.

At thirteen, Paul was sent to St. Joseph's College, a Jesuit institution in Spring Hill, Alabama, where, for the next three years, it seems that he gave up chess entirely. Abrupt discontinuities occurred throughout Paul Morphy's life. He didn't play chess, didn't keep a board or men with him, and wouldn't even mention the game. (He did, however, play chess at home during vacations.) The reason given for this in family memoirs was that Paul wished to concentrate entirely on his studies. Perhaps this was at his parents' prompting, perhaps it was his own desire, perhaps both. At least in retrospect, this episode suggests not only remarkable self-discipline or docility for a young boy but also indicates that chess was already something he identified with unserious activity. It also suggests that accommodating chess to "ordinary" life might be no easy matter for him. His studies went well at St. Joseph's, and in 1853 he took up the game again, although he played only with friends, in private. He got his M.A. in 1855, graduating with honors; he then returned home to New Orleans, studied law, and got his law degree in 1856, on condition that he not practice until he legally came of age.

All along, Paul Morphy's chess precocity had attracted attention. In 1849 Ernest Morphy sent an account of one of his nephew's games to L. Kieseritzky in Paris, a famous chess master and editor of the chess magazine *La Regence*. In May of 1850, in New Orleans, Paul Morphy played against Johann Jakob Lowenthal, a Hungarian who had taken up both chess and politics, had participated in the struggle for Hungarian independence, and had been compelled to flee the Austro-Hungarian empire. Lowenthal came to the United States, and, though he had yet to establish his reputation securely, he was without question a formidable player. The forty-year-old Hungarian and the thirteen-year-old boy played three games; Morphy won two, and the other was a draw. The Morphy family tradition held that Lowenthal embraced Paul and told him he was destined to be the greatest player ever known — a version of a familiar romantic episode, the genius/artist recognizing his heir apparent. Lowenthal's comments, as they have come down to us from other sources, were a good deal less flamboyant; but they reveal the generosity of a man who at this time was in ill health, depressed at living in a foreign country, and discouraged at his own uncertain prospects: "The achievement of the young Paul argues a degree of skill which it is wonderful that a child could have attained."[4] Lo-wenthal would show the same generosity in the future, by welcoming Paul Morphy to London, and by editing a book of his games. In the early 1850s some of Morphy's games were published in the United States. Lowenthal's comments were spread about, and word of Morphy's brilliance reached chess circles as far away as New York. Then, suddenly, two events changed Paul Morphy's life and his chess career: his father died very unexpectedly in November of 1856; and in 1857 he was invited to play chess in New York City.

*

In the spring of 1857 the New York Chess Club, eager to demonstrate the recent growth of chess in the United States, proposed a national chess congress, to be held in the fall. The chief aims of the congress were to bring together the best players in the country to compete for prizes, to form a national chess association, to agree on uniform rules, and to publish a book on the congress that would include a history of chess in the United States, thus contrasting the meager past with the flourishing present.

Of history there was certainly little enough. The game was played by individuals in the early eighteenth century, but it had no public existence. The prevailing anonymity was momentarily broken by the appearance, in 1732, of an essay on chess by Lewis Rou, a New York clergyman. Very little is known of Rou, and no more was heard of him after this. Much was subsequently heard of the most famous early American player, Benjamin Franklin. I have already noted his essay "The Morals of Chess," which was written in France and first published in the new United States in 1786. Not even Franklin's patronage and example could alter prevailing attitudes, however; when he returned to America from France, Franklin found so few players and so little interest that he abandoned chess and took up cards instead.[5]

In America during the 1790s there weren't enough resources to establish chess clubs or associations, the kind of institutional support then available in many European cities and an essential element in the spread of chess there. The few interested individuals in America were separated by vast distances and were often unknown to one another. There were few chess books, and all of the small number published in the United States were copies of English ones. Furthermore, chess shared in the general disapproval directed against sports and games: it was seen as frivolous and wasteful. In addition, it had special disadvantages peculiar to itself. The game seemed too difficult ever to be popular. It also seemed effete, too closely associated with the idleness of the aristocracy. Unlike other aristocratic games and sports — horse racing, for example — it seemed adaptable neither to the democratic simplicities of Jeffersonian America nor to the exuberant expansiveness of Jacksonian America. And it was foreign in another sense. It was played mostly by people of foreign birth and was identified, from city to city, with pockets of immigrant culture, German, English, French.

There were intermittent efforts to establish chess clubs, but these, like many other sporting ventures, clubs, and associations at this time in the United States, never lasted very long. As a result, the game spread only very gradually and sporadically in the first forty years of the nineteenth century. A very few details about the history of chess clubs in some of the larger American cities will indicate how shallow the American roots of chess were. The first club in New York City dated from at least 1802; that soon dissolved, and as late as the early 1850s its various successors were still moving, year after year, from one hotel or café to another, without enough members to establish a permanent home. And there was no unofficial home for chess like the one the offices of the *Spirit of the Times* provided for horse racing. In Boston, the chess club, set up in 1845 with twenty members, disbanded in 1848; and only eight or ten members remained to sell the club's few pieces of furniture at auction. Philadelphia prided itself on its chess tradition. There the first American chess book was published, and a chess club was established in 1826; yet there too nothing was permanent. Chess players didn't have their own club but met at the Athenaeum to play.

Chess flourished in New Orleans, the most foreign of American cities, if anywhere. A chess club was founded there in 1828, died out in two years and then was revived in 1844 by an émigré, Eugene Rousseau. That too soon disbanded and wasn't reestablished until Paul Morphy took it in hand in 1857. Still, there were fitful signs of vitality by the mid-1840s. In 1845 Charles Henry Stanley, an Englishman resident in New York City, played in the first important series of interregional matches, in New Orleans: he played thirty-one games (later published) against Eugene Rousseau. Stanley's victory established him as the leading American player. In 1846 he started the *American Chess Magazine*, the first American periodical devoted solely to chess. It lasted just one year, and by the late 1840s interest had waned again. "Our chess public was singularly apathetic," a later historian wrote. "It seems to have sunk into one of those periodical fits of inaction to which every art and pursuit are subject."[6]

Then, in the 1850s, the pendulum of interest swung the other way. The international chess tournament in London in 1851 was a powerful goad to Yankee pride. Improved cross-country travel, speedier communications with Europe, a sharp increase in the number of German immigrants — all these factors aided the chess revival. Numerous clubs sprung up nationally — in Chicago, in a cluster of Kentucky cities, in San Francisco, in Alabama, in upstate New York, and in Maine. Important too was the proposal for the national congress, the response to which was sufficiently encouraging to allow New Yorkers to push on. There were serious problems to be overcome. The main one was the vexatious question of location. As Daniel Willard Fiske, librarian, geographer, journalist, secretary of the New York club, and chief instigator of the congress, wrote: "In a country like ours, where the political, commerical and literary interests of the nation are not concentrated in a single metropolis, but diffused among a number of large cities, it is always difficult to select a point of meeting which shall suit all the members of any profession or every practitioner of any art." Nor was there a "special season of festivity, some national or general occasion of re-union."[7] And finally, there remained the ever-present difficulty of finding the resources to finance the congress. Fiske proposed that individual subscriptions be solicited nationally, but he also considered solving the two problems at one stroke by locating the congress in whichever city raised the most money. As William Porter could have told him, living in a federal union and a decentralized culture was a complex fate.

Eventually the other cities gave way to New York, which had after all initiated the idea and whose members had individually contributed the most money. Committees of correspondence and cooperation, from other cities, helped work out the details. A date in early October was agreed upon. Then, at the last moment, the severe financial panic of 1857 almost wrecked everything. Finally, $1,177.50 was subscribed, enough to cover publicity, arrangements, publication of the book of the congress, and prize money. Invitations were sent to the various leading cities. Paul Morphy was New Orleans's choice as representative. On October 6, 1857, against long odds, the first American Chess Congress opened.

*

New Yorkers were skeptical about Paul Morphy's chances. Precocity was one thing, actual competition another; and arrayed against Morphy were fifteen experienced players (seven of whom were European by birth). No doubt their first look at Morphy reenforced their skepticism. He was not a commanding figure, this young man of twenty years who seemed even smaller than his five feet four inches. He had a very large head, dark luminous eyes, and a well-proportioned body except for unusually small hands and feet. Everyone later testified to the delightfulness of the smile that occasionally crossed his face, the pleasantness of his manner, the invariable neatness of his dress, the modesty of his demeanor.

Once play began, he took complete command. He swept his first three matches, winning nine games, losing none, and drawing one. In the final round he met his most serious rival, Louis Paulsen, another precocious player, twenty-three years old, born in Europe but at the time living in Iowa. Famous for his exhibitions of blindfold play, a most formidable opponent, even Paulsen proved no match for Morphy, who won five, and drew twice. Paulsen did win one game, the only one Morphy lost. "All went down, almost without a struggle, before the conqueror from New Orleans," wrote J. J. Lowenthal in his report of the tournament in an English newspaper.[8]

American chess players were ecstatic at "the brilliance of the star which had risen in their midst."[9] Morphy was asked to edit *Chess Monthly*. And some players wanted the newly founded American Chess Association to challenge the European masters immediately. Others urged caution, pointing out that Morphy was still very inexperienced: "Were we to make this national challenge, we should appear ridiculous when our champion is defeated, which he certainly will be."[10] But such objections and doubts were overborne. Morphy lingered in New York City until December, then returned to New Orleans. From there he issued a challenge to all American chess players, giving odds of a piece. At this point the American Chess Association sent out a parallel challenge to Europeans, offering stakes of from $2,000 to $5,000 per side. Not surprisingly, no challenger came forward. Howard Staunton, regarded as the leading English player, took note of the American challenge in the chess column he edited in the *Illustrated London News*. He commented that such a match might be arranged in Paris or in London, but that no European master could be expected to drop everything and expend the time and energy necessary to journey to the United States. He then added, condescendingly, "The best players in Europe are not chess professionals but have other and more serious occupations." (This idea and these phrases, as we shall see, were to figure importantly in Paul Morphy's life.) However, Staunton did seem to promise he would play Morphy if he came to Europe "to win his spurs among the chess chivalry there."[11]

Despite his mildness of manner, Paul Morphy was aggressive and impetuous. The idea of challenging the European masters was much on his mind. At the conclusion of the New York tournament, when prizes were awarded, Morphy presented Paulsen with a gold medal in recognition of his blindfold play. Morphy, who had a considerable talent for public speaking in the florid style of the period, converted his praise into one of those manifestoes of American cultural independence so dear to Jacksonian audiences.

> Sir, I claim you for the United States. Although not a native of America, you have done more for the honor of American chess than her most gifted sons. Old Europe may boast of her Stauntons and Anderssens, her Harrwitzes and Lowenthals; it is the greater boast of America that the blindfold chess of Paulsen has not yet been equalled . . . We fling our proud defiance across the waters. Come one, come all! Let the super-human feats of our Paulsen be performed with equal success by the much-vaunted European chess knights! Let the much and deservedly extolled Harrwitz enter the lists! We challenge him — we challenge all the magnates of the Old World.[12]

Morphy made up his mind to carry that proud defiance across the waters himself. In New York he had befriended Frederick Milnes Edge, an Englishman then living in America. Edge agreed to serve as his secretary and went ahead to England, introducing himself to members of the various London chess clubs, preparing the way for Morphy's arrival. Edge, whose admiration for Morphy was limitless, served as confidant and counselor in addition to making practical arrangements. He was determined to spare no effort to reveal to Europeans the true brilliance of the young stranger from across the Atlantic. (When he and Morphy eventually returned to America, Edge wrote a small book, *The Exploits and Triumphs of Paul Morphy*, which is an indispensable contemporary source.) Morphy's visit was planned with care to accomplish two major objectives: to play in the annual British Chess Association meeting and to play the leading continental masters head-to-head.

Idealistic and unworldly, Paul Morphy overcame the reservations his family had about his youthfulness (he turned twenty-one the day after his landing in England in June of 1858). But no one could do anything about his naiveté. He set out on his pilgrimage a true American innocent, believing that a commonly shared passion for chess would remove all obstacles, overcome personal vanities, and mitigate national jealousies (if indeed he imagined such things existed). It seems that Edge spoke for both of them when he wrote:

> Chess is a bond of brotherhood amongst all lovers of the noble game, as perfect as free masonry. It is a leveller of rank — titles, wealth, nationality, politics, religion, all are forgotten across the board.[13]

Morphy's journey caught the imagination of the small but growing number of Americans who played chess, as well as that of many others who didn't but whose fancy was seized because they saw it as another of those cultural duels in which Americans pictured themselves as fighting the combined might of all of Europe. As a contemporary said, somewhat enigmatically, it was "Narcissus against the Titans."[14]

*

The growth of European chess afforded an illuminating contrast to the American situation.[15] Originating in India, gradually carried west by the Persians and Muslims, the game was now one thousand years old in Europe. It had been played increasingly throughout the Middle Ages, had surmounted the early opposition of the Church, and had finally attracted the interest and support of nobles, courts, and monarchs, until, by the time of the Renaissance, after countless changes, it had emerged as more or less the game we know today and was already embedded in a literary tradition, descriptive and poetic, in both manuscript and print. In the sixteenth century chess found its first serious analyst and theoretician in the Spanish writer Ruy Lopez, and the many noteworthy works of analysis that followed his reached a climax in the writings of a remarkable eighteenth-century French composer and chess player, Andrew Danican Philidor (1726–1795). Philidor's reputation and influence were based equally on his success as a player and on the lucidity of exposition of his ideas in his books. His were the first texts "to explain the principles of play and to accompany the moves with reasoned notes." Philidor, the wonder of his age at blindfold play, then (and later) regarded by many people as the archetypal example of cerebral brilliance, was the first player of the modern type, of which Paul Morphy was a supreme example — the player as mental phenomenon.

From 1700 to 1850 Paris and London became the chief centers of chess activity, as the earlier ones, in Spain and Italy, slipped into the background. The social context of the game changed. Although members of the nobility patronized the game and played it, chess in these years became much less of a courtly, aristocratic amusement and more of a middle-class game, especially in England, where the game ceased to be part of the fashionable aristocratic world. This change was symbolized by the opening, in the late seventeenth century, of coffee houses as places where chess was played. The Café de la Regence, for example, became the center of Parisian chess competition about 1750; it was a public place accessible to many and a magnet for players from all over the Continent. Eventually, the coffee houses and cafés were replaced by clubs intended solely for chess, often very opulent ones. And at the same time chess moved out of the private drawing room into the public chess club, it also began to be viewed as a profession and not solely an avocation. Chess games had long been the occasion for private wagers — the association with gambling was part of chess's aura of profligacy — but now stakes and prize money began to be put up by third parties. This money made it possible for notable players to journey across the continent for important matches, and, at a more humdrum level, it allowed the emergence of a new type of chess player, the chess professional, who supported himself by playing all comers for a few shillings or francs per game.

Chess became more cosmopolitan. Philidor moved easily across all of Europe, scoring triumphs in both London and in Berlin. The increased familiarity of players with one another stimulated rivalries and raised the level of competition. A few players became national celebrities, and their countrymen increasingly identified with their successes and failures. Masters trained and inspired their pupils, who in turn sought to excel the masters, notable players thus succeeding each other with accelerating rapidity. Deschapelles succeeded Philidor only to be soon eclipsed by his more brilliant pupil de la Bourdonnais. Schools of players and of playing had been identifiable since the advent of the Spanish style of Ruy Lopez and of the Modenese school, but now these subtraditions became more self-conscious and readily copied.

London, which rivaled and then surpassed Paris as the creative center for chess in the first half of the nineteenth century, became the center for the diffusion of chess information: sporting papers, chess columns in ordinary newspapers, and editions of chess games originated there. The most important British influence was that of William Lewis, not himself a powerful player, but whose writings are landmarks in the history of the modern game. In his *Progressive Lessons* of 1831 and 1832, Lewis began the synthesis of the prevailing schools of chess and the rationalization of chess theory. He also trained pupils who implemented his theoretical formulations in actual play. The most notable of these was an Irishman, Alexander McDonnell, who in 1834 played de la Bourdonnais in a celebrated match, won by the Frenchman, which inspired such interest that chess activity was given a great boost everywhere. McDonnell died suddenly, but in the 1840s Howard Staunton emerged as Britain's leading player, and in 1843 he secured a measure of revenge for Britain by defeating the then-leading French player, Charles Saint-Amant. This was the high point of Staunton's playing career. His most important role was as a writer and editor. His *Chess-Player's Handbook*, of 1847, long ranked as the leading British and American textbook; and his column in the *Illustrated London News* was highly respected.

William Lewis's chief influence was in Germany, the scene of the last important development in nineteenth-century chess that touched Paul Morphy's career. The game had always been widely played in Germany, but now, as the socially exclusive chess clubs began to admit a wider range of players, Jews in particular, and as good clubs grew up in Breslau and Hamburg, in addition to the one founded in Berlin in 1803, the level of play rose dramatically. The Lewis school of play was taken up by a group of younger players who eventually became known as the Seven Stars of Berlin, and the result was a series of publications that began the rich tradition of German chess analysis. Breslau was the home of two of the greatest players of this period, both of whom played Paul Morphy — Daniel Harrwitz (1823–1884), who spent most of his time in Paris, and Adolf Anderssen (1818–1879).

Sharing a common tradition of play, Europeans wished to test the abilities of their leading players. This took the form of international tournaments, a feature of chess life which was part of the larger movement in the nineteenth century that resulted in international congresses, fairs, expositions, and associations and that, in sport, reached a climax with the rebirth of the Olympic games in 1896. The Crystal Palace Exhibition of 1851 spawned the first chess tournament of this kind. The winner of this great affair was Adolf Anderssen, who thus deserves to be thought of as the world's first, though unofficial, chess champion. His return to Germany was a triumphal progress.

European chess in the 1850s was an activity of formidable complexity and sophistication. No wonder Frederick Edge found that British players were skeptical of Paul Morphy and his New York victory. "Chess requires many long years of attentive study, and frequent play with the best players," they all agreed, "and neither of these your friend has had. Depend upon it, he will find European amateurs very different opponents from those he has hitherto encountered."[16] Edge was slightly nettled but acknowledged that such sentiments were entirely reasonable. The culture within which chess flourished was a complex one. Chess traditions matured slowly over time. All great art took time. It was highly unlikely, therefore, that the flowers of chess would blossom in Louisiana's swamps.

It was into this European scene that Paul Morphy, a comet of unknown magnitude, blazed in the summer of 1858.

*

Morphy wasted no time. At various London chess clubs he was welcomed politely — Edge had done his work well — and he began playing. Once more he met Johann Lowenthal, now living permanently in England, editor of an important chess column and fully established as a player. The two played a match for £100 in July and August, with Morphy winning nine games, losing three, and drawing two. He also played and defeated John Owen and Samuel Boden, leading English players. The annual British chess meeting that took place in August had been one of Morphy's prime objectives, but he now decided not to enter it. Instead he gave a brilliant demonstration there of blindfold play, against eight opponents, a larger number than anyone had ever competed against before. The result of the British conference tournament added indirectly to his luster because it was won by Lowenthal, who defeated Howard Staunton in the second round. Morphy in these months played many other English players, including most of the important ones; but he didn't play against Howard Staunton. The two of them had met soon after his arrival, and Morphy, in his impetuous way, had suggested they immediately play some casual games. Staunton declined. However, in one match Staunton acted as consultant for one side and Morphy for the other. Morphy and his partner won. But Staunton refused to play Morphy straight on.

In the 1850s Howard Staunton remained an imposing figure. In an unusual way, he combined great skill in chess with scholarly interests. He was then engrossed in preparing an edition of Shakespeare's plays, work which undoubtedly took him more and more away from chess; but he continued to write copiously on chess, for newspapers, and this accounted for his persistent contemporary influence. His historical importance at that time rested on his defeat of Saint-Amant in 1843. He hadn't been able to sustain the position gained him by that victory and had been defeated in the two most important tournaments he had entered in the 1850s. There is no doubt that in Morphy's mind the importance of playing Staunton was out of proportion to Staunton's abilities or reputation as of 1858. But that, given the nature of the situation, was irrelevant to Morphy. Staunton had been the commanding figure ten years before, when Paul Morphy was learning chess; he had owned and studied at least one of Staunton's books, the book of the tournament of 1851. In addition, it is possible that Staunton was the target of Morphy's considerable ambition and combativeness. On the title page of the 1851 tournament book, Morphy, with the sarcastic superiority of youth (he was then fourteen) had scrawled: "By H. Staunton, Esq., author of the *Hand-book of Chess, Chess-Player's Companion,* etc. (and some devilish bad games)."[17]

For many reasons, then, Morphy wished badly to play Staunton. Apparently Staunton did not wish to play him. There were reasonable grounds for his refusal to do so, but surely Staunton should either have agreed to play or clearly indicated he would not do so. Instead there ensued a series of challenges by Morphy and a protracted number of delays, postponements, and excuses by Staunton. Eventually all this was aired in the press and exacerbated by the intervention of partisans on both sides. And Staunton conducted much of it in a tone of superiority and contempt that seemed to come easily to him. For all of his previous service to British chess, Staunton had become a deeply divisive figure. Morphy was surprised and pained. Finally, Staunton announced that he would never play Morphy.

The Continent remained to be invaded. Morphy went to Paris, and to the Café de la Regence, where Franklin had played eighty years before and perhaps seen Philidor. As Franklin had tamed the lightning so now Morphy, "less of a sage, perhaps, but infinitely more of a chess player,"[18] tamed the leading players there. He sought out and challenged Daniel Harrwitz, the "King of the Regence." Harrwitz accepted the challenge. Morphy began badly, as he often did, but soon asserted his superiority; and when their match stood in Morphy's favor, 5–2–2, Harrwitz refused to continue and withdrew in a sulk. The ideal of the brotherhood of chess players was taking a beating.

In a generous spirit, other players stepped forward. Morphy mastered them all. He once more performed his stupefying blindfold exhibition — in the ancestral home of Philidor — against eight able opponents at once; and he defeated them all in a ten-hour match, a remarkable exhibition of concentration and stamina. He received calls from the French nobility. The American consul wished to introduce him to the emperor. He was invited to share the box of the duke of Brunswick, a chess fanatic, at the Italian Opera — not to see the opera but to sit, with his back to *Norma,* and play chess against the duke and Count Isouard. He won everything with consummate ease. Paul Morphy's performances excited extraordinary enthusiasm; he was given ovations in the Regence and on the sidewalks outside it. He was petted and admired on all sides (except Harrwitz's). No doubt the adulation came more easily to the French because they attributed his brilliance to his half-Gallic ancestry! The sculptor Le Quesne did a bust of Morphy, which, at a testimonial celebration, was solemnly crowned with laurel.

The climax of Paul Morphy's chess-playing career came in Paris, in a match that meant more in chess terms than anything that had preceded it. Adolf Anderssen, still the leading player of the day, traveled from Germany to Paris to play Morphy, despite the fact that some of Anderssen's countrymen insisted it was demeaning for him to go to meet the upstart American youth. But Anderssen, forty years old and at the peak of his powers, an excitable, formidable presence, was as generous as Lowenthal had been. The contrast between the massive German and the diminutive American only added to the drama. True to form, Morphy began shakily, losing the first game and drawing the second. But then, inexorably, he gained command and eventually triumphed 7–2–2. Anderssen made no excuses. When friends suggested that his defeat was due to his not playing as well as usual, Anderssen replied: "No, he did not let me."[19] After that, although Morphy stayed on the Continent until spring, he played little chess. He didn't need to. The results spoke for themselves. Of the 315 games in Europe and England of which there is a record, Paul Morphy won 227, lost 42, and drew 46. In April of 1859 he returned to London, perhaps still hoping that Staunton would change his mind. After a month of adulation in London equal to that he had received in Paris, Paul Morphy sailed for the United States. The great journey was over.

*

Morphy was greeted as a returning hero. The doubts of the year before were forgotten, and writers and speakers let rip with rhetoric. It was said that Paul Morphy had gone

> to the great capitals of Europe, to the centers of old civilisations, and there throwing down the gauntlet . . . in mental conflict, [presented] a sublime picture of moral and intellectual power that has no parallel in history.[20]

As had been the case with John Stevens's victory at Cowes, it was sweet to defeat the Europeans at things in which they particularly prided themselves. It was sweeter still that Morphy's victory was a triumph of the American mind. This would inspire American youth in the future by making them realize that intellect could surmount any difficulty. "Did not Paul Morphy, by the power of his unaided genius, render easy what was considered impossible, and not rest content until he had the world at his feet?"[21]

His victory was celebrated with dinners, trophies, prizes, and speeches — many speeches. In Boston, at a dinner presided over by Oliver Wendell Holmes, toasts were offered by Chief Justice Shaw of the Massachusetts Supreme Court and by President Walker of Harvard. James Russell Lowell read a poem written for the occasion; and Morphy was presented with a gold wreath. In New York the Union Chess Club gave him a silver wreath, and a few days later a large group gathered at New York University to see him presented with a set of chessmen and a board. The chessmen were of gold and silver, with pedestals of polished carnelian. The board was of rosewood inlaid with silver, and each corner had a wreath of gold encircling the letters *P. M.* In the center of the board was a silver plate with the inscription: "To Paul Morphy — A recognition of his genius." There was of course yet another speech.

> Sir, yours is no common lot. There is no parallel to the present proud position occupied by you. Neither in this nor in any preceding age has there lived a man who could truly say, "I am first in my special walk or profession," and have the whole world respond amen. Who could ever say, "I am the greatest poet or author, painter or sculptor, orator or statesman"? Even the transcendent genius of Nature's great dramatist [Shakespeare] stands not altogether alone.[22]

Now Paul Morphy stood alone. We shall see the haunting implications of that phrase later; but at the moment he was haunted by nothing — and spoiled by nothing. The visiting English politician Richard Cobden, who met him at breakfast in New York, was struck by his "peculiarly modest bearing" and heard him "speaking modestly of his rare gift."[23] Robert Bonner, the sporting gent who published the New York *Ledger,* hired Morphy to do a series of chess columns at the unheard of salary of $3,000 per year, paid in advance. Morphy gave a series of exhibitions, showing his confidence in his own superiority by giving odds of a knight to anyone who played him. He knew he must return to New Orleans, but he lingered in New York, as though reluctant to break the spell.

*

Paul Morphy's claim to importance in the history of chess rests on the change he effected in the conception of the game's strategy. The slowly evolving type of play that had come to fruition in the nineteenth century had been combinational chess, a series of moves by combinations of pieces, worked out in advance, that would eventually give mastery to the player who could bring the most powerful combinations to bear. It was this kind of game Lewis championed and Anderssen played masterfully. In contrast to this, Morphy worked out a method of positional play, in which the chief object was to gain mastery of certain positions as play developed. The positional player was willing to sacrifice a good deal to assure these positions, because securing them ensured command of the game. The French called this audacious mode of play *à la Morphy.*

Historians of chess don't entirely agree about this interpretation, and even those who accept it don't agree about how long a time elapsed before Morphy's successors truly understood and assimilated his contribution; but on the whole they have seen considerable continuity in what followed Morphy's innovations. Wilhelm Steinitz, a great champion and theoretician, studied Morphy's games very carefully, took up where Morphy left off, and developed further the implications of positional play; his emphasis was on command of the center of the board. In 1866 Steinitz met and defeated Adolf Anderssen, and from then on he dominated the game for the next quarter century.

Morphy's countrymen, as we have noted, thought of him as representing the highest levels of their culture and made much of his accomplishments as proof of its intellectual maturity. They took for granted that there were distinctively American aspects of Morphy's play, and this view, however untenable, does afford an interesting insight into the American mind of the 1850s. One group of observers saw him primarily as a type of natural genius who depended on brilliant intuition for his success, a phenomenon owing more to nature than to science. In later years many stories embroidered this theme — "Chess was never taught him, but came to him quite naturally"; his genius wasn't the result of study but of "abnormal brain development in some special though unknown way."[24] Americans were by no means alone in being struck by the naturalness of Morphy's play. "He never seemed to exert himself, much less cudgel his brains," wrote the British chess master G. A. MacDonnell, who had seen Morphy play in London, "but played with consummate ease, as though his moves were the result of inspiration. I fancy he always discerned the right move at a glance."[25]

Some observers found an explanation in the fashionable science of phrenology, noting Morphy's massive brow and above it bumps that indicated the calculating faculty. The style of his game supposedly reflected this view. The "true Morphy manner" was that of forthright attack. "All pieces are at work. Not a move wasted, not a useful square unexploited." There was a Morphy maxim in this spirit: "Seize open lines."[26] He was the Farragut of the chessboard, which perhaps explained his occasional lapses and mistakes. He was certainly a kind of sportsman widely admired in America and elsewhere: bold, aggressive, innovative. Americans saw him as wholly freed from past traditions, a natural child of the New World.

Others thought this a superficial and misleading view. There was an erratic quality to Morphy's play. He often began badly, because he insisted on playing immediately upon arrival in a foreign place, even when he had had inadequate rest or was unwell. But temperamental recklessness should never be confused with his theoretical conception of the game itself. French observers in particular saw Morphy as analytical and cool, not impulsive at all; they believed that intense calculation most marked his play. Adolf Anderssen agreed with this estimate: "It is no use struggling against him; he is like a piece of machinery, which is sure to come to a certain conclusion."[27] And the English player Samuel Boden spoke of his diabolical steadiness.

Like any artist, Paul Morphy combined calculation and intuition in his art. He was taught chess methodically, read chess books, and bought them for his friends. But he apparently didn't spend much time in studying the classic games and believed that only one or two books on chess were of much value. Frederick Edge, trying to account for Morphy's mastery in conventional terms, was baffled: "I feel utterly at a loss to solve the problem of his skill." Edge decided that the most suitable epithet for Morphy was "the Newton of Chess, as though he had discovered the necessary, natural laws of the game."[28]

Morphy seems to have taken for granted that he had fundamentally altered the direction of chess; yet, so far as is known, he never examined the theoretical implications of his own play in print. In the 1860s he toyed with the idea of editing a book of his own games, which would have afforded him an opportunity to develop his ideas, but he never did this. He was in every way exceptionally modest but also supremely self-confident about his own gifts and historical role. In one of the few comments he ever made on these topics, he once confided to a friend that he didn't believe he had played very well in Europe, otherwise he would not have lost a single game.

Although his contemporaries didn't really know what to make of him — and who can blame them for that? — they realized clearly enough, most of them, that something momentous had happened. Said one: "Paul Morphy cannot be classed. He has revolutionized science. Paul Morphy is not only a dazzling player, he is a phenomenon."[29] In the words of an astute contemporary historian of chess, "all that can be said is that none of his rivals, from Anderssen downwards, was any sort of match for him."[30] In the century and a quarter that has followed Morphy's appearance, the theoretical aspects of chess have been so exhaustively explored that it is inconceivable that one player could upset the established order as Morphy did. This diminishes neither Morphy's stature nor what has been accomplished since. Wilhelm Steinitz summed this up by saying: "The progress of an age can no more be disputed than can Morphy's extraordinary genius."[31]

What about Paul Morphy's place in the history of American games and sports? Different as he was from his countrymen in many ways, he shared one aspect of their evolving sporting style: he was a remarkable example of the sporting poker face. He sat in complete control, with no show of nerves. During a match with Paulsen he waited two hours (this was before the days of chess clocks) for his opponent to make a move, with absolutely no sign of impatience on his part. When he played, he stared concentratedly at the board and only looked up when the problem had become clear and he could see his way through to a solution; or so it seemed.

On the other side of the board sat Morphy, looking, in his peculiar way, like a block of impassible, living marble, the very embodiment of penetration and decision. No hesitancy or excitement there, but all cool, calm action, knowing where it must end.[32]

Impassive in action, he was laconic in his comments. When the occasion required, he was capable of effective public speech; the prospect seemed to fill him neither with dread nor with elation. But left to his own inclinations, he said very little. Of blindfold chess, which people made so much of, he commented, "it proves nothing." When he first saw Simpson's Divan, the most opulent London chess club, he said only: "Very nice." As it turned out, that was a lot from "the most undemonstrative young man we ever met there." Morphy's example may have inspired young men who wished to play chess in the 1850s and 1860s, but after that period he had no direct influence. Chess historians have paid a good deal of attention to him, as have chess players, but outside of chess circles he has not been considered a figure of significance.

On the contrary, Morphy was a man of representative cultural importance. There are important parallels between his chess playing and the subsequent pattern of most American games and sports, as we shall see in chapter 11. As these games and sports have developed, positional play has come to dominate; indeed, those games that have become most popular owe much of their popularity to the fact that they allow positional domination. Morphy's chess style, for example, resembles American football, as it has evolved from rugby and soccer. Football is governed by the same impulse to gain mastery by means of command of territory from a set position on the field. It involves a series of combinational moves planned in advance that are intended to establish mastery and give victory. Whereas Morphy was considered by many of his contemporaries the epitome of the intuitive genius, others, as we have seen, viewed him as the supreme calculating genius — the representative type that became most important in American sport and in American culture in general. Paul Morphy had nothing to do with the trickster aspect of the American gamesman but everything to do with the Napoleonic, managerial side. He represented the gamesman as scientist, one who planned moves far ahead of his opponents. In this way Morphy was in the tradition of Colonel Johnson and Richard Ten Broeck. He represented a powerful American sporting ideal, the gamesman as mastermind.

*

At age twenty-two, on top of his world, with every reason to expect increasing maturity and fame in his art, Paul Morphy began to give up playing chess. After 1859 he never again played in a tournament. He played only a few games in public. He did not write about chess or observe other players. Even among his friends, in private, he devoted less and less time and attention to chess.

How to explain this? It is true that the Civil War exploded across Paul Morphy's life within a year and a half of his return to New Orleans. When Louisiana seceded Morphy volunteered his services for the Confederacy's diplomatic corps. (He spoke French, German, and Spanish fluently.) No place was found for him. He maintained a very detached view of the legitimacy of the war, neither sympathizing with Louisiana's secession nor offering any support for the Union cause when New Orleans was occupied by the Yankees in 1862. He opened an office and attempted to practice law but failed utterly, not attracting a single client. However much the Civil War interrupted the progress of Morphy's life and career, it cannot explain what happened. Horse racing was devastated, and yachting was rendered impossible, but chess playing could have continued had Morphy wished it; and it certainly could have been taken up again when the war was over.

But he didn't take it up again. In 1862 Morphy's mother and sister Helena fled to Havana and then to Paris, and he eventually followed them, playing a few games in Havana, as well as in Paris, but only with friends and never in public. He didn't go near the Regence. He returned to New Orleans in 1865, but there was nothing for him to do there, so he went back to Paris in 1867 and stayed with his sister and brother-in-law for eighteen months. While he was in Paris a great international chess tournament took place, but he would not even go near the site. In 1871, the Second American Chess Congress was held in Cleveland, and a concerted effort was made to induce him to play. He refused.

Paul Morphy had always said very little. Now he spoke almost not at all. Life in New Orleans became a pattern of unvarying routines. Sunday began with a morning paper in the lobby of the St. Louis Hotel, then mass at the cathedral, a walk about Jackson Square, and finally dinner with brother Edward and his family. If he found that a stranger had been invited he politely excused himself and went home to dine. His weekday movements never varied. Punctually at noon, dressed very dandyishly, with monocle, small walking stick, and gray kid gloves, he went for a walk. He visited the French market and selected a flower for his lapel, bought rice cakes to give to the small children in the neighborhood, sampled the "fromages a la crème," to decide which to take to his niece. He walked up Royal Street to Canal Street, about Canal Street and vicinity, and then back down Royal Street to his home. On this went, day after day, into the 1870s, while the transcontinental railroad was completed and tens of thousands of people surged across the plains, Steinitz defeated Anderssen, and Union troops remained in New Orleans, up Royal Street to Canal Street and then back down Royal Street, while the centennial was celebrated across the land, scandals ravaged the Grant administration, Union troops were withdrawn, and Reconstruction passed away, up Royal Street to Canal Street and then back down Royal Street, the rice cakes and the honey cakes and the hotel lobby and the mass and the cathedral, then back home to his room, scrupulously neat and tidy, his shoes arranged in perfect semicircular fashion in the middle of the floor.

On his promenades Morphy began to develop the habit of stopping and staring so intently at pretty faces that these walks became something of an embarrassment to his family and gave rise to the rumor that his oddness had an erotic element. His one remaining passion was music. His mother was very musical. She played the harp and piano, sang beautifully, developed a large musical library, and composed trios. For many years she worked on an opera, *Louise de Lorrain,* which remained unfinished at her death. There were weekly musical evenings at the Morphy home, and increasingly on these occasions Paul withdrew himself so that he could listen unobserved. Yet at the opera, where for years he rarely missed a performance, he enjoyed being seen, and liked walking about, during intermission, with friends of both sexes.

More disturbing symptoms appeared. He began to imagine that he was in danger of being poisoned and refused to eat anything not prepared or supervised by his mother or sister. He thought friends were trying to destroy his clothes, and he once attempted to attack one of these friends with his walking stick. This was the only violent act he ever committed, and he was subdued with pathetic ease. Worst of all, he conceived a great hatred for his brother-in-law, J. D. Sybrandt, a lawyer and the administrator of his father's estate. Paul Morphy came to believe that Sybrandt had defrauded him of his inheritance, and he spent years in preparing a legal case against him, much to the Morphy family's mortification. There was no evidence whatever to support his allegations.

Rumors about him circulated in chess circles, and some gossip appeared in print. In 1882 his family finally attempted to put him in a sanatorium, but he refused to go and, it is said, argued so rationally against this move that the family had to give up the idea. All that remained now of his fame as a chess player was the memory of the great journey a quarter of a century earlier. Outside New Orleans he was only a name, and even that was half-forgotten. His walks and the opera were all that occupied his interest. Or were they? Morphy once told a friend that he had a chessboard and pieces close at hand. And he apparently kept up with some aspects of contemporary chess. One wonders if he was aware, in 1874, of the death of Howard Staunton, on June 22, his own birthday?

In 1882 he recognized and spoke to a well-known visiting chess player whom he encountered on the street. In 1883 Wilhelm Steinitz came to New Orleans and asked to see him. When told this, Morphy replied enigmatically, "I know it. His gambit is not good."[33] An interview between the two men was finally arranged, on the express condition that chess not be mentioned. The result was a very awkward meeting of ten minutes. The board and pieces were close at hand, and who knows what games he played in his own mind; but during these last long years of his life, leading up to his death of an apparent stroke, at home, in the bathtub, on July 10, 1884 — just three weeks after his forty-seventh birthday — Paul Morphy was not known to have played a single game of chess. To a friend he once said: "I am no player."[34]

*

Why *did* Paul Morphy stop playing chess? His behavior seems so inexplicable in ordinary terms that it is difficult not to seek its cause in some psychic trauma. Few people would agree with H. J. R. Murray, the English historian of chess, who wrote that Paul Morphy "fell into a settled melancholy with which chess had nothing to do."[35] Surely chess had something to do with it. But what? And if not only chess, what else was involved?

In 1931 the eminent Freudian psychoanalyst Ernest Jones wrote an essay on Paul Morphy as a case study in paranoia.[36] Jones saw chess as a play substitute for the unconscious rivalry between son and father that culminated in symbolic father-murder. Such play has an especially anal-sadistic quality, because the mathematical nature of chess, unrelenting and merciless, produces a sense of overwhelming mastery on the one side and a sense of inescapable helplessness on the other. It is this characteristic that makes chess so gratifying but that also, in any serious match, places an exceptionally great strain on a player's emotional stability. Jones argued that Paul Morphy's prime characteristics as a player, boldness and confidence, demonstrated the extraordinary extent to which he had been able, as a youth, to sublimate the guilt attendant to the unconscious assault on the father. Such sublimation is always precarious. For Morphy it required that the dreadful symbolic parricide be met in a friendly manner, be ascribed to worthy motives, and be thought of as a grown-up and serious activity.

Jones further argued that with the death of Morphy's own father, Howard Staunton became a substitute father figure whom Morphy crossed the Atlantic to attack and overthrow. However, he failed to destroy the dreaded father, who then lashed back and for the first time revealed *his* hostility. Staunton's rebuff upset Morphy's delicate emotional equilibrium; by refusing to play him Staunton called into question Morphy's maturity and integrity. Morphy could not convert warfare into friendly exchange; he transferred his guilt about attacking the father into guilt about himself. Staunton's snub forced him to examine his motives for playing chess. Might they not be infantile and mercenary, as Staunton had intimated? So Morphy went back home to obey his father's wishes, which were powerful even from beyond the grave. He turned to the grown-up and indisputably serious profession of law and sought to placate the avenging spirits by sacrificing his chess-playing self. But it was too late. He couldn't establish his manhood; he could only retreat into his own private world. Neurosis eventually became psychosis and destroyed Paul Morphy's sanity.

This plausible and often eloquent analysis by Jones drew on most of the materials available three quarters of a century after the events themselves; little more of importance has come to light in the half-century since Jones wrote. Jones's explanation seems to me inadequate, but not because Jones was unaware of the essential points of the story. The limitations of his point of view are greater than that.

Jones's interpretation is severely limited by its own assumptions. When one reads about the lives of actual chess masters, as opposed to abstract "cases," one finds that while chess may well have been the emotional focus for the working out of deep libidinal conflicts, it was also often the means of resolving rather than exacerbating them. This is unsurprising to those who recognize the therapeutic power of art. Nor need one accept the dogmatic Freudian assumption that the very nature of chess is homosexual, that chess is only and inevitably a play substitute for unconscious father-murder.

What is the nature of this game when women play it, as they often do? The king-father is not the only object of sexual rivalry. The symbol of potency and force in chess is of course the queen; and it is striking that, as chess developed in Europe over the centuries, the single piece that gained most in mobility and power was the queen — which, in western European chess at least, is strongly identified as a woman. The game may thus be a play substitute for parricide, but the murder may be maternal instead of paternal. Or it may be both.

Furthermore, the working out of oedipal conflict through chess playing is immensely complicated, because the formidable queen operates as both supporter and opponent. When a player projects both hatred and love, this results in feelings of extraordinary ambiguity; for on one side of the board his chief tactical problem is to contain or destroy the queen, while on the other side he depends greatly on her power. Victory over one queen implies submission to another. In any event, Jones's explanation may satisfy those who accept its assumptions; but those who do not will have to do as we shall do and look outside the self-contained Freudian world to the particular social and family culture within which Paul Morphy actually lived.

Ernest Jones attempted to do this. He insisted that in seeking validation of the manliness and maturity of chess, Paul had the support of his mother, who in this respect opposed his father; given Jones's premise about rivalry of father and son, this was to be expected. But such bits of evidence as we have offer little support for this interpretation, which mistakes the nature of Thelcide Morphy's influence and vastly underrates it.

Where so much is speculation, one unarguable fact stands out: Paul Morphy's father and uncle were the ones who taught him to play chess and, having done so, fostered his talents and encouraged them. All the evidence points toward masculine support — from father, uncle, and brother, as well as from Lowenthal and others. Paul Morphy's trip to Europe was not necessarily made possible only by the unexpected death of his father. The trip grew out of his first visit to New York, and that in turn grew out of the training and nurture of the previous years. There is no conclusive evidence as to what Alonzo Morphy would have felt about the invitation Paul received from the New York Chess Club. But that Paul Morphy accepted it only a few months after his father's death reasonably suggests that it was something the family felt was in keeping with his father's wishes.

If indeed the European sojourn precipitated a crisis, it was perhaps the reverse of that described by Ernest Jones. Think of the trip as a challenge to Morphy's mother, an attempt to establish his personal independence, an effort to escape. It didn't succeed, but not because of the rebuff from Howard Staunton. After all, Adolf Anderssen (as well as many other leading players) competed against Morphy, and Anderssen was the dominant player of his day. There were snubs and disappointments in Europe for a naive young man, but the trauma didn't originate there. The problem wasn't a substitute father but an actual mother back home.

Paul Morphy was one of four children. Edward, the older brother, was also trained as a lawyer, and became a successful businessman; Malvina, the older sister, married a New Orleans lawyer and lived abroad much of the time with her husband, although they finally returned to New Orleans. Helena, the younger sister, never married and always lived at home. Edward and Malvina married and left home while their father was still alive. Paul and Helena did neither. Thelcide maintained the house on Royal Street all those long years after the death of her husband (she outlived him by twenty-eight years), keeping Helena and Paul very close beside her. In that spacious, rambling house, with its many rooms, she shared a bedroom with Helena, while Paul slept in a room immediately across the narrow hall. A later family member stated that on his return from Europe, Paul Morphy solemnly promised his mother that he would never again play chess for money or for any private stakes, that he would never play a public game, or a private game in a public place, and that he would not allow the publication of his name in connection with any aspect of chess.[37] Paul Morphy could neither escape from nor destroy the queen on his side of the board. Thelcide made her son ashamed of his playing, so he would give it up. It was chess and chess alone that could in some measure free him from the grasp of this imperious and possessive woman.

George Washington Cable's Creole stories, very often based on actual events and persons, brilliantly explore two aspects of that society's social decay. There is the theme of suffocation — families trapped within outworn conventions, turning back upon themselves within their crumbling houses, with doors locked, windows shuttered, and walls exhaling the fetid atmosphere of dissolution; or else turning to fantastic and eccentric behavior as a means of escape. There is also the theme, familiar to Creole society, of the possessive, domineering woman. Both of these themes are present in Cable's "The Haunted House on Royal Street," which takes place in a house Paul Morphy actually walked past each day, a house cursed by the presence of the terrifying Madame Lalaurie, who entertains with great elegance while presiding over a secret horror: slaves chained and tortured in the basement and attic. Eventually the secret becomes known, and a mob of infuriated citizens drives Madame Lalaurie away and ransacks the house. Occasionally, in Cable's sketches, someone escapes. But not often. Needless to say, no mob ever threatened the Morphy residence, but then neither was there any possible escape from the ghosts of this other haunted house on Royal Street.

*

Dreadful mothers. Substitute fathers. Runaway rhetoric? Let us look in a matter-of-fact way at the situation as Thelcide Morphy saw it at the time. For her, of course, there was no "problem" of Paul Morphy to be explained after the event. There was instead a precocious and unworldly boy, a source of both concern and pride for his loving parents. Their concern should not be exaggerated. It isn't likely that so practical a man as Alonzo Morphy indulged himself in dreams of international chess conquest by his son, or worried about the possible consequences of something so unlikely; nor did he feel that special arrangements for Paul's future were necessary, beyond the formal preparation for practicing law. Alonzo's legal practice and his substantial wealth provided enough security so that the boy with the phenomenal memory could go on playing his game while and until he established himself in his own right. No one could anticipate the disasters and triumphs that followed.

Step by step, after Alonzo Morphy's sudden death, things got out of control. The invitation from New York was impossible to refuse; it was a tentative effort at launching Paul into the world, and was strongly supported by everyone close at hand in New Orleans. But New York led to Europe, which was also impossible to refuse; and, astoundingly, Thelcide saw her son come into an inheritance glorious beyond anyone's imagining. After that, nothing could ever be as it had been planned, or as it had been before.

What kind of an inheritance was it? As Thelcide saw it, Paul came back crowned with chess glory but incapable of doing anything with his laurels. He came back not because his mother commanded him to do so but because he agreed that there was nothing else to do, no place else to go. The South in which Paul Morphy lived was, for all its veneer of gentility, a harsh and competitive place. The crown of Philidor was worse than useless in a society where masculine prowess was so prized, where the power to command was so nakedly based on force.

How could this tiny man/boy assert himself in the cotton exchange or in the law courts? "His fellow citizens looked upon him as a marvelous chess player and nothing more. His fame as a chess player was so over-shadowing that it seemed people were disinclined to regard him seriously in any other capacity."[38] Marriage? A family story tells us enough. Paul supposedly cared for a young Creole woman in New Orleans, but she rejected him because "he was only a chess-player." "Many women," his great-nephew later wrote, "would find an alliance with Paul Morphy, under the circumstances, impracticable."[39] It wasn't simply his small size, although that was probably not a negligible fact in a society besotted with physical prowess. Stephen A. Douglas, a northerner no bigger than Morphy, was a commanding figure known as "the little giant." No, it was not just smallness and the absence of masculine force; there was the *presence* of something else: the peculiar nature of his genius.

Paul Morphy's boyish charm and sweet disposition didn't entirely conceal the fact that he was something of a monster, a creature from a tale by Edgar Allan Poe come to life. A central theme of many of Poe's stories is that of a character who possesses extraordinary mental abilities, especially analytical ones. Poe's detective Dupin, for example, unraveled the puzzle of a crime by using his powers of logical reasoning, just as Paul Morphy unraveled, at a glance, the puzzle of a chessboard.[40] And Dupin, cool and imperturbably rational, was also Morphy-like in his deadpan aspect and his power of concentration. Even in his own lifetime, Morphy's gifts in this regard, in truth remarkable enough, had become legendary.

There were also similarities between Morphy and Edgar Poe himself.[41] Both had large, piercing eyes, which stared through to something behind the visible; both had a modest physical build that suggested sexual underdevelopment; and both had an abstracted manner, which hinted at unearthly qualities. For Morphy, blindfold play represented that which was ghostly. The 1850s were a time of feverish interest in popular manifestations of the occult — table-rapping, spiritualism, and phrenology. A Scottish newspaper account of an exhibition of blindfold play by Daniel Harrwitz, in Glasgow, in which he played two matches, communicates vividly this sense of wonder at being in the presence of something supernatural.

We can hardly attempt to convey to the minds of our readers the difficulties of such a marvellous performance . . . when the mechanical objects of the chessmen and chess boards are abstracted and no longer exist save in the powers of the mind; when the windows of the brain are closed down, and faculties of sight hermetically sealed; when all that is left of the chess board and men is in their vague and timid shadow, wandering spectre-like across the mental chamber.[42]

Harrwitz insisted that he seldom attempted this mode of play, "as he found it was attended with too much mental exertion." Behold the young Morphy, then, playing eight formidable opponents and beating them all! No wonder even Staunton remarked after one of these demonstrations, "marvellous, marvellous."[43]

In the ordinary world, however, the phenomenal is disquieting, even alarming. It was said that Morphy could recite almost all the civil code of Louisiana from memory, a wonder bordering on the grotesque. In regard to Poe and Morphy, exceptional mental powers were thought of as unhealthy, destructive. Overintellectualization must inevitably lead to some kind of torment or horror; to drink, drugs, or dementia. The demonic writer ended up raving in the gutter, the brilliant prodigy went mad, while prosaic souls thanked the heavens for talents denied them. The moral was clear. Mental development must never outstrip physical development. Even actors were susceptible to this weakness. William Macready, the English tragedian, suspected of being overly cerebral in his acting style, was accused of being "deficient in muscular power" in a paper called the *Patriot*.[44] In contrast to the sedentary thinker, there was the active outdoor sportsman. In Britain as in America this contrast was pervasive, with each extreme combining philistinism and puritanism: on the one hand there was the unchecked impulse and feverish unhealthiness of art; on the other, there was self-discipline and solid materialism. If only, as a boy at Jefferson Academy, Paul Morphy had been persuaded to take more exercise and cold showers.

From Thelcide's point of view, her son's triumphs must inevitably lead to a disastrous denouement. There remained nothing for her to do but take care of him and protect him, wondering all the while at the capriciousness of the gods who bestowed such gifts on this perennial child of hers, who was at once both a son and a puzzling stranger. A few days after Paul Morphy's death, Thelcide Morphy responded to the condolences sent her by the Manhattan Chess Club, expressing gratitude that "a few superior minds have not forgotten him, in this world where everything disappears so rapidly," and concluding with a touching reference to "that which was the glory of the son and the everlasting grief of the mother."[45]

*

There are still other ways to look at Paul Morphy's life. Morphy was an amateur in an increasingly professional society. As Richard Ten Broeck found when he encountered the Mississippi Valley cotton planters, southern sportsmen, more than their counterparts in other sections of the United States, still paid homage to the landed aristocracy's contempt for trade, especially as expressed in the idea that no gentleman supported himself by his games or sport. This view was shared by the numerically small but influential southern commercial and professional class to which the Morphys belonged. Paul Morphy's determination not to enrich himself by his chess playing was a class, not just a personal, attitude, antedating his trip to Europe and Howard Staunton's snide hints that he was only a penniless adventurer.

He refused to accept financial assistance for his trips to New York City and to Europe. Once abroad, where chess professionalism was well established, he most emphatically did not do as the Europeans did. He could not alter the convention of playing for money stakes, but he persisted in trying to circumvent it. He played Lowenthal for stakes of £100 and, upon winning, gave him a present for his new house worth £128. In Paris, after defeating Harrwitz, he refused to collect the stakes of 290 francs, until informed that not to do so would deprive those who had backed him of their winnings; so he took the money and used it to help defray Anderssen's expenses in coming from Germany.

Paul Morphy's one recorded public outburst had to do with this sensitive matter. Colonel Meade, chairman of the New York welcoming committee, in his speech of greeting on Morphy's return from abroad, alluded to chess as a profession and to Morphy as its most brilliant exponent, to which Morphy took such vehement exception that the poor man resigned from the committee. Nothing seems to have pleased him more than to be described as illustrating "at home and abroad, the character of an American gentleman."[46]

But even this took care of only half the problem. He was a gentleman, but was he a sportsman? Shooting, hunting, horse racing, card playing — all these forms of amusement were comprehensible to the southern sporting world. But not chess. Paul Morphy would have gained more respect among such men had he been some kind of sporting gamesman, instead of a games player. He found himself at a dead end: a professional chess career was impossible, yet an amateur career was unthinkable.

He might have evaded the disdain of both the sportsman and the bourgeoisie, had he been able to appeal to a tradition of patronage. In Europe chess took its place within the larger tradition of aristocratic patronage for the arts. Adolf Anderssen, a school teacher, was given an honorary doctorate by the University of Breslau, in recognition of his chess prowess. The small and privileged group who admired his talent commanded sufficient influence to give their wishes effect; they were not in the least perturbed because that talent was appreciated by only a minority of the populace. The supportive signals received by the players at a venerable institution like the Regence indicated unmistakably that they were not being judged by conventional standards of morality, masculinity, or popularity. As for chess professionals, honor wasn't in question. They were judged, as other professionals were, by their proficiency. Given this standard, it was likely that preferment and rewards of all kinds would be forthcoming.

Genius was an ultimate form of privilege, and its own justification. It consorted very uneasily with equalitarian ideals. Where recognized, as Morphy's clearly had been, it was likely to entitle one to gain entry into the world of larger affairs. On the eve of Morphy's return to America, the *Illustrated London News* commented that "we have a firm belief that a career of more than national usefulness is open to Paul Morphy."[47] But that was not the case. Paul Morphy instead encountered that prevailing dislike of the exceptional which made gifts such as his a disability rather than a privilege. When he opened his law office, upstairs at 12 Exchange Place, nothing happened. No doors opened. No deference was given. No clients came.

True, in a moment of nationalistic fervor Americans had made a fuss about Morphy, but in the uproarious jingoism of the 1850s, Holmes, Lowell, and all the rest toasted him mainly because he had trounced the foreigners. Paul Morphy's success, like that of the other sportsmen of this decade, was most interesting to Americans as an episode in cultural foreign relations.

Paul Morphy not only accepted this situation but approved of it. Although he apparently never took any interest in party politics, his own views, with a slight shift in terminology from the chessboard to the marketplace, reflected the spirit of Jacksonian laissez faire. Special talents should count for no more than anything else.[48] Men proved their worth in competition, at games and at business.

Morphy would surely have agreed with the Stevens family's hatred of the old steamboat monopoly. No special advantages, no special claims, for genius or for anything else. He told a New York audience:

> Chess never has been and never can be aught but a recreation. It should not be indulged in to the detriment of other and more serious avocations — should not absorb or engross the thoughts of those who worship at its shrine, but should be kept in the background, and restrained within its proper provinces. As a mere game, a relaxation from the severe pursuits of life, it is deserving of high commendation. It is not only the most delightful and scientific, but the most moral of amusements. Unlike other games in which lucre is the end and aim of the contestants, it recommends itself to the wise, by the fact that its mimic battles are fought for no prize but honour. It is eminently and emphatically the philosopher's game. Let the Chess board supersede the card table and a great improvement will be visible in the morals of the community. [Loud applause.] [49]

So much for the horse racing, cockfighting, gambling South, for the cavalier ideal of an imprudent but honor-bound aristocracy, and for such southern sportsmen as Colonel Johnson and Wade Hampton. Paul Morphy was a southern man with northern principles.

*

There remained one other possible escape for the artist — retreat to Bohemia. Let's compare Morphy with another small man, also left fatherless in his teens, who had a dominating mother and possessed a precocious artistic talent: James McNeill Whistler. Three years older than Paul Morphy, Whistler, at age twenty, at West Point, found himself at more of a dead end than Morphy did in New Orleans. Determined to be an artist, Whistler concluded by the mid-1850s that such a career was virtually impossible in the United States; so he escaped to Paris, where he was living in 1858 when Paul Morphy triumphantly arrived.

In Paris, Whistler found the personal style that suited him — dandyism. He also found a justification for his art, the idea of art for art's sake. And although his career was a stormy one and he often bitterly felt the absence of enlightened appreciation from a philistine public that derided his art, still he found in Europe what he needed most of all — a tradition of sufficient complexity and density against which he could define himself and his work, if only by opposition. In Europe there was no need to explain why one put daubs of paint upon a canvas.

Whistler too had a formidable mother, whose religious convictions he didn't share. He didn't return to her; she eventually followed him to Europe, where, by some mysterious process, he came to terms with her by converting her into a subject for his art. Many years before, in Paris, at the height of his Bohemian dissipation, while he was establishing his sexual identity by a series of liaisons that would have been exceedingly awkward back home, this process was already underway. "What, Jimmy, you have a mother?" a friend had mockingly asked. "Yes, and a very pretty bit of color she is too, I can assure you."[50]

Whistler found his way out of the trap by emigrating. So did Henry James and many others. So, most especially to the point, did Ernest Guiraud, an exact contemporary of Morphy's (born the day after Paul Morphy), who came from exactly the same background. The precocious son of a French musician, Ernest Guiraud grew up in a musical New Orleans culture that quickly recognized his gifts — he had a youthful opera produced there — but that could not sustain him professionally. He went to Paris to study at the Conservatory and remained there. Guiraud's life was not Bohemian. He was very respectable and successful, composing, teaching, and contributing to two masterpieces — he wrote recitatives for *Carmen* and finished the orchestration of *Tales of Hoffman*.

Imagine Paul Morphy born and raised just as he had been, in the same family, of the same class, with the same talent, but in Paris — a simple enough transformation given his own expressed preferences: "Oui, Oui," he would say of New Orleans, "mais ce n'est pas Paris." Imagine him blazing into prominence and then encountering the obstinacy of Staunton and the petulance of Harrwitz. Can one imagine that Paul Morphy, as the petted darling of the Regence, the conqueror of London, and the protégé of the aristocracy, would have felt what he did was not serious and manly? He had the bad luck to be born at the right time but in the wrong place. Why, then, didn't he stay in Paris, flowing with the tide of his self-interest, his personal inclination? Whistler and Guiraud broke free and flourished. Wasn't Paul Morphy free to save himself?

To such a question most readers would probably answer yes and no. All chess players, indeed all sportsmen, are subject to imperious psychological impulses they can only partly understand and control; yet many play chess seriously, or dedicate themselves to their chosen sport, and master the emotional implications in ways Paul Morphy couldn't manage. We are all defined to some extent by the pervasive dictates of social class, limited to some extent by material conditions, dominated in varying degrees by ideas and allegiances.

Yet many of us live within or rise above these categories and manage to avoid disaster. Most historians and biographers would stress that no one explanation can account for Paul Morphy, and that the answer to the riddle of his life, if there is an answer, is to be found in some combination of explanations. But what if the reply to that is that the explanations, even when taken together, still leave us in the dark?

*

Even as Paul Morphy was walking his obsessive rounds in New Orleans, Henry James, in London, was pondering the question of the relationship of tradition to individual talent that has run through so many of these pages. "The moral is that the flower of art blossoms only where the soil is deep, that it takes a great deal of history to produce a little literature," wrote James, with direct reference to American culture in the Age of Jackson.[51] He insisted on the seemingly common-sense view that great talents do not come from nowhere and that somehow the ground must be prepared for the appearance and achievements of genius. This was precisely what Ralph Waldo Emerson meant, in the middle of the tumultuous 1850s, in his letter to Walt Whitman about *Leaves of Grass:* "I greet you at the beginning of a great career, which yet must have had a long foreground somewhere, for such a start."[52]

A long foreground. A deep soil. In short, tradition. Although James and Emerson were writing about literature, their ideas may appropriately be applied to chess, "the art of the intellect," and of all games the one with the oldest written tradition. In a celebrated passage, Henry James elaborately enumerated the items of high civilization that had been absent from American life in the early years of the nineteenth century. "The natural remark, in the almost lurid light of such an indictment," James concluded, "would be that if these things are left out, everything is left out. The American knows that a good deal remains; what it is that remains — that is his secret, his joke, as one may say."[53]

So one may say that for a historian of American sporting culture, Paul Morphy is precisely such a joke, a tragic, enigmatic joke played on Henry James and Emerson and on the idea of tradition. The wrong culture produced Paul Morphy. The one with everything left out brought him in. Tradition — pardner, when you say that smile. Or rather, when you say that, don't let on that you see the joke. Do as Paul Morphy did and keep a straight face, even if it kills you.

THE GREAT FIGHT FOR THE CHAMPIONSHIP.

BETWEEN JOHN C. HEENAN THE BENICIA BOY, & TOM SAYERS "CHAMPION OF ENGLAND,"

Which took place April 17th 1860, at Farnborough, England.

THE BATTLE LASTED 2 HOURS 20 MINUTES 42 ROUNDS, WHEN THE MOB RUSHED IN & ENDED THE FIGHT.

HEENAN stands 6 ft 1½ in, fighting weight 190 lbs. Born May 2nd 1835.   SAYERS stands 5 ft 8 in, fighting wt. 150 lbs. Born 1826.

PUBLISHED BY CURRIER & IVES.

152 NASSAU ST NEW YORK.

HEENAN VERSUS SAYERS

8

John C. Heenan
and Adah Menken

AT THE END of a decade of sporting challenges, we come to the story of John Heenan's challenge to the English prize ring. A tempestuous story, a brutal sport. But it wasn't the brutality of the prize ring that gave this chapter of American sporting history a lurid quality. It was race and sex. And politics. The clamorous tone owed as much to the political passions of the time as it did to the fury of pugilism.

John Heenan's story is sporting and theatrical melodrama. The cast is large and varied: Bill Richmond and Tom Molineaux, two remarkable black fighters; Adah Menken, William Macready, and the sporting theatrical world of those days; Mose the fire laddie and the scandalous *Mazeppa*. The scenes are as varied and numerous as the cast of characters, and quickly changing: from the California gold fields to the theaters of London, from Tammany Hall to the opera house at Astor Place; and the curtain comes down in Paris as well as in Green River, Wyoming. But the end of the drama will come soon enough. We will take it up, now, at one of its earlier high points, at Farnborough, Hampshire, England.

*

Dawn, April 17, 1860, in a meadow near Windsor. A prize-fight crowd of several thousand people, typically English in its make-up: members of the peerage and the House of Commons, military officers, men of the church, poets and journalists, clerks, shopkeepers, and publicans, Newgate butchers and Billingsgate fish porters.[1] The fight was technically illegal and, as a precaution against interference by the police, had been scheduled for early morning; so two chartered trains had left London Bridge Station, supposedly in secret, at four o'clock that morning.

In two corners of the roped-off twenty-four-foot ring, the fighters' colors were brilliantly displayed in the early morning light. John Carmel Heenan, the American known as the "Benicia Boy," had an eagle with thirteen white stars on a blue background. Tom Sayers, the English champion, the royal standard of Great Britain, at each corner of which a lion roared defiance. The physical contrast between the two men was equally vivid. John Heenan had described himself, in the exaggerated talk of the frontier, which the English so much enjoyed hearing, as "half alligator, half horse, and a bit of snapping turtle."[2] If the reality was somewhat less bizarre than that, it was impressive enough. John Heenan was not quite twenty-six years of age, stood a bit over six feet, and weighed about 195 pounds, with long arms and "immense muscles" (in the Benicia, California, railroad shops, where he got his nickname, he had used a thirty-pound sledgehammer for twelve hours a day). Tom Sayers was less imposing, because smaller: he was thirty-three years old, five feet eight inches tall, about 160 pounds, with much shorter arms. But he was compactly strong, with powerful shoulders and wrists. The two men also made a sharp contrast in coloring: Sayers was "dark as a mulatto, Heenan as fair and white as marble." The American giant's only possible flaw, in the opinion of some fans, was his skin, which was "too delicate and would bruise too much."[3]

Whatever the disparity in size, the Englishman betrayed no unease; on the contrary, Sayers gazed at his "terrible antagonist" with perfect self-confidence. Heenan won the toss and selected the corner in the higher ground of the sloping meadow; this allowed him to sit, between rounds, with his back to the rising sun, which was constantly in Sayers's eyes.

Like their physical characteristics, the two men's lives contrasted. John Carmel Heenan was born in West Troy, New York, of Irish parents, in 1834. After a little schooling he was apprenticed to a machinist but gave that up to go to California, in 1852. He worked for a while in Benicia, then began prize fighting under the tutelage of a wandering English ex-fighter named Jim Cusick. Because of the turbulent conditions of the time, prize fighters were much in demand as bodyguards and strong-arm men, and this gained them many enemies. As a result, when the vigilante reformers of the mid-1850s gained control in northern California, many prize fighters were singled out as objects of revenge. One of the most famous, "Yankee" Sullivan, committed suicide rather than be lynched.

John Heenan prudently returned to the East, enlisted his muscles in support of Tammany Hall in New York City and got a job in the Customs House in return. Handsome and, in comparison to other prize fighters, easygoing, he might have been content with that; but his admirers egged him on to challenge John Morrissey, the leading American fighter of the 1850s. (In the unorganized state of prize fighting there was no recognized champion.) When the two men finally met, at Long Point, Canada, safely away from the American law, Heenan was entirely unready to fight, and Morrissey won easily. Heenan demanded a rematch, but Morrissey, as crafty a character as the Benicia Boy was a simple one, refused all challenges. In an effort to force Morrissey to give him a return fight, it was proposed (by Heenan's English trainer, Aaron Jones) that Heenan challenge the English champion, Tom Sayers. A victory in England would be splendid stuff, and it would surely force Morrissey to agree to a return match. Arrangements with Sayers were slow and complicated but were finally worked out by December, 1859. The fight was set for the following April.

Tom Sayer's path to that Farnborough meadow was less glamorous. Although the golden days of the English prize ring were over by the time he was born, in Brighton, in 1827, the prize-fighting traditions amid which he grew up remained powerful. He moved to London as a young man, worked as a bricklayer, and then took up prize fighting as a familiar, alternative form of work. Sayers took on and defeated men much bigger and stronger than he, and soon earned a reputation as a giant-killer. In 1857 he defeated the most prominent of the big men, William Perry, the "Tipton Slasher," and thus became the recognized English champion. Sayers's honesty and pluckiness, combined with his relatively small size, made him especially popular; during his prime English prize fighting underwent a temporary revival.

Perhaps because it seemed the climax of a decade of sporting rivalry, the Heenan–Sayers fight caught the fancy of people who had up to that time paid little attention to prize fighting. It also caught the fancy of newspapers on both sides of the Atlantic. "This challenge has led to an amount of attention being bestowed upon the prize ring which it has never received before," wrote the *Times* of London, which disapproved of the affair but concluded with an air of resigned finality that "as somebody was to be beaten, it might as well be the American."[4]

On his side of the ocean, John Heenan sounded the patriotic note, laying down his challenge in verse:

I'll wind our colors 'round my loins
The blue and crimson bars
And if Tom does not feel the stripes
I'll make him see the stars![5]

If most sporting journalists of the time couldn't rise to such poetic heights, they could at least keep up a constant din; and they did, finding national, even international, significance in the event. Both fighters managed to keep their heads and, like good professionals, approached the battle with no personal animosity. That, briefly, was the background of the two men who at 7:30 A.M. advanced to the center of the ring and began to fight.

*

A pattern was quickly established and maintained throughout the fight: strength versus agility, Heenan's reach and weight against Sayers's mobility and quick thinking. There was no shortage of endurance or courage on either side. The fighting style of the time was a great advantage to Heenan, because, as the bigger and stronger of the two, he could throw Sayers down and hurt him a good deal in doing so. Heenan dominated the early rounds. He put Sayers down in each of the first seven, but each time Sayers quickly came back up to scratch. Sometime in the fourth round a crucial injury changed the complexion of the fight. Sayers damaged his right arm, rendering it almost useless; from that point on he held it against his chest, only using it occasionally, with excruciating pain, in an effort to disguise the extent of his injury from Heenan. But ringsiders noticed it immediately. On the other side, Sayers soon brought blood from Heenan's nose and punished him around the eyes. By the eighth round Heenan's right eye was almost closed. So it went until the thirteenth round, when Heenan knocked Sayers down with a blow instead of throwing him down. From the thirteenth to the twenty-fifth rounds, most rounds ended with Sayers down. Odds at ringside shifted strongly to Heenan, but he too was in serious trouble. His hands were swollen and pained him terribly every time he landed a blow. His face was a red smear. From round twenty-five through round thirty-three, Heenan made desperate efforts to end the fight, but Sayers was too quick and avoided serious injury while hurting Heenan with his left.

They had fought for an hour and a half, and both were in a ghastly state. Neither gave any sign of quitting. At this point the police arrived and forced their way to ringside. But they didn't stop the fight. In the thirty-seventh round Heenan got Sayers's head under his left arm, as though to pull him down, and entangled it in the ring ropes. Sayers began to strangle. The umpires ordered the ring ropes cut, as provided by the rules, and both men fell to the ground. Confusion reigned. The police now attempted to intervene, but the crowd stopped them from effectively doing so. Both fighters regained their feet and were surrounded by spectators, who, while keeping the police at bay, pushed in on the fighters, leaving them little free space. They fought four more rounds under these conditions. The loss of space hampered Sayers most, and he took fearful punishment, but he showed astounding courage and wouldn't go down.

From this point on accounts of the fight differ sharply; not only were the passions of spectators aroused by the protracted fury but it was also very difficult for anyone actually to see what was happening. By the forty-first round, Heenan's eyes were both almost completely closed; it was said that at one point he hit one of his seconds "a tremendous blow" thinking he was Sayers. The forty-first round was the last. The crowd was pressing in too close. The referee stopped the fight and declared it a draw. It was now past 10:00 A.M. They had fought for well over two hours. Except for his injured arm, Sayers, astonishingly, didn't seem to be much damaged; but Heenan, virtually blinded, had to be helped away from the ring.

The outcome of the fight was as sensational as the fighting itself, and as hotly disputed. Americans in general insisted that the officials had favored Sayers and that the behavior of the crowd had cost Heenan a likely victory. The British replied that Heenan had repeatedly fouled Sayers and that, given Sayers's injury, a true result had been impossible from early on. Everyone agreed that the fight had lived up to, or surpassed, all expectations. "Something in the fight appealed to a very universal sympathy," wrote the poet Frederick Locker-Lampson, who had been present. "It was magnetic — and why should it not continue to move us?"[6] It was talked about by fight fans on both sides of the Atlantic for years. Long after, controversy continued to rage.

A draw was the best decision possible under the circumstances. Both men had been courageous beyond measure, and Englishmen took justifiable pride in the pluckiness of the smaller man, agreeing with the sentiments expressed in an anonymous article about the fight attributed to William Makepeace Thackeray:

England should ever have need of a few score thousand champions who laugh at danger; who cope with giants; who, stricken to the ground, jump up and gaily rally, and fall, and rise again, and strike, rather than yield.[7]

In those days the American press was rarely to be outdone by anyone in expressions of national pride. And even those Americans who felt cheated of victory took pride in the fact that the English champion had been challenged on his home turf and had been battled to a draw.

In America, interest in the fight, very great to begin with, was strained to the breaking point by the long delay in finding out the details of the outcome. When the first newspaper reports arrived three weeks later they were eagerly snatched up. On his return to the United States, Heenan was given a roaring greeting by a large crowd when his ship docked. A large sum of money was raised by public contribution and given him as a suitable reward for a national hero. William Russell, the famous English war correspondent, who was visiting the United States in the spring of 1861, was astonished, at a breakfast in New York City attended by serious-minded and otherwise sane editors and newspapermen, to find much more animated argument about the Heenan–Sayers fight, at that point over a year old, than about secession.[8] The firing on Fort Sumter restored some perspective.

*

Prize fighting was preeminently an English sport. Originating there in the late seventeenth century, by 1750 it had assumed a recognizable form that, for a long time, existed nowhere else in the world.[9] For the next hundred years it was conducted under the London Prize Ring rules, which strike us as excessively rough but which actually represented a softening of earlier brutality. Under these rules a twenty-foot-square ring, enclosed by a rope, was marked out; a referee or umpire kept order and someone marked time. A line was scratched across the middle of the ring; fighters, when knocked or thrown down, had to come back to the line, or be brought back by their seconds — "brought up to scratch" — within thirty seconds, or the fight was over. There was no fixed length for each round; the fighters fought until someone went down. And there was no fixed number of rounds; they fought until one of them could not continue. No distinction was made as to weight; it was taken for granted that bigger and stronger men had an advantage. Fighting was bare knuckle, without any cover or glove for the hands; hence the continuing use of the term *pugilism,* from the Latin word for fist.

At this stage in its development, prize fighting was still closely connected with wrestling. Fighters could use almost any tactic — shoving, tackling, tripping — to slam their opponent to the ground; damage was dealt out as much by these means as by striking blows with the fists. The rules stipulated that "no person is to hit his adversary when he is down, or seize him by the hair, the breeches, or any part below the waist; a man on his knees is to be reckoned down." Most fighters cut their hair short to prevent hair-pulling; they stripped to the waist and wore long breeches; and they had their own colors, which they wore at the waist or stuck to the corner ring post. Matches often took place out-of-doors, so most fighters wore spiked shoes to give them a firmer foothold for pushing and shoving.

The referee kept order and declared the winner. Fight crowds were notoriously turbulent and often interrupted the proceedings, as did the seconds, who hung about their man's corner, ostensibly to give him aid and advice but also to find some way of causing trouble for the opponent. The prize was usually money, a very modest amount. If bigger money was made, it came mainly from the wagering, of which there was a great deal. Prize fighting was as notorious as horse racing for its skullduggery, although its crookedness was less complex.

For Americans, prize fighting was one of the unexpected blessings of independence.[10] It had been introduced into the colonies by British sailors during the Revolutionary War. Unlike Great Britain, where it was legal or at least tolerated, in the United States it was illegal everywhere, and authorities for a long time made determined efforts to stamp it out. Because of its illegality, it was, of all the sports of these years, the one about which fewest public comments were made. It is certain, however, that the English traveler of 1817 who, finding little else to admire, commended the Americans because "prize boxing is unknown in the United States" was misled.[11] It was there, but took place furtively, sporadically, and surreptitiously.

Slowly prize fighting began to spread. Its history in America differed from that of most of the other inherited English games and sports, in that Americans made little effort to change its form. American prize-fight fans, although eager to establish national superiority, were traditional folk, and British traditions still powerfully held sway. Prize fighting's increasing popularity in America may also have been connected with a similarity in the harsh and brutal conditions of lower-class life in both countries. American law was not as savage as the British criminal code of the late eighteenth century, nor were American cities as squalid, even in their worst sections, as London; but American culture had a distinctive feature that more than made up for these deficiencies — the tradition of violence associated with the frontier.

Rough-and-tumble was one of the aspects of frontier life most frequently commented on by both foreign and native observers. This is how an English traveler described a Kentuckian getting ready to fight:

> The question is generally asked — "Will you fight fair, or take it rough and tumble? I can whip you either way, by God!" The English reader knows what fair fighting is, but can have little idea of rough and tumble; in the latter case, the combatants take advantage, pull, bite, and kick, and with hellish ferocity strive to gouge, or turn each other's eyes out of their sockets.[12]

No doubt there was as much folk art as accurate reporting in this; travelers often swallowed the tall tales Americans fed them. But rough-and-tumble was an important part of American life, from cockfighting and frontier dueling to the higher reaches of government, witness the comment heard in the Kentucky legislature at the outbreak of the war against England in 1812: "We must have war with Great Britain — war will ruin her commerce, commerce is the apple of Britain's eye — there we must gouge her!"[13]

Matter-of-factness was perhaps the most remarkable characteristic of this kind of fighting. Jim Jeroloman, a tough New York shipworker, fought the ubiquitous and much smaller "Yankee" Sullivan in the prize ring and was easily beaten. Jeroloman complained that he had been handicapped because eye-gouging, biting, kicking, and stomping were forbidden by prize-ring rules. He scathingly described prize fighting as a pastime for children. Prize fighting was certainly no more brutal than ordinary service in the army or navy of the time, and it may well be that the tenacious support for it, against vehement and powerful opposition, was based on the fact that it was actually a way of containing the ever-present ferocity of life all about. The prize ring was, like the magic rings created to protect the lawgiver and the priest in other primitive societies, a place of order amid prevailing chaos.

For many years prize fighting in America was too disreputable to merit public notice. We know little about it for another reason as well. Many of the early fighters in the United States were black men, some of them free blacks in the cities, some of them slaves who fought exhibitions for their masters. Such men were excluded from Anglo-Irish-American prize-fighting culture that was slowly taking hold in the cities. As a result, the first two important American prize fighters were black men who fought in England. The stories of their lives exist only in sketchy form, encrusted with later fictions and legends, but a few facts can be filled in. For the first chapter of American prize fighting, fifty years before Heenan met Sayers, we must turn once again to England.

*

The first of these black men was born in Richmond, Staten Island, New York, in 1763, and for this reason named Bill Richmond. His name suggests that he was a slave, but nothing is known of his life up to the time of the Revolution, when New York City was occupied by British troops.[14] At that point Bill Richmond somehow came to the attention of General Percy, later duke of Northumberland, who brought him under his protection as a servant and, in 1777, took him to England. An "intelligent youth of good capacity," Richmond was put in school in Yorkshire, then apprenticed as a cabinetmaker. The remainder of his story can be found in *Boxiana,* by Pierce Egan, a man-about-town, journalist, playwright, and wit of early nineteenth-century London, whose many volumes about the prize ring are irreplaceable sources of information.[15]

Richmond's pugilistic career began accidentally. While attending the races at York, he was insulted by a soldier named Cocky Moore, "the terror of Sheffield." A fight was arranged to settle the matter, and, although outweighed by forty pounds, Richmond astounded everyone by beating Moore easily. What followed was predictable. "Richmond's milling qualities rather getting abroad," wrote Egan; "a few of the lads who had a bit of fight in their composition, envied his success." Richmond fought two more soldiers and then a blacksmith, thrashing all three. A more remarkable encounter soon followed.

One evening, while Richmond walked the streets of York "with a female under his protection," a man named Myers, who, along with a woman named Shepherd, managed a brothel, called Richmond a "black devil" and "insulted the young woman for being in company with a man of colour." It was agreed to settle the matter with a fistfight. At the appointed time and place "a great concourse of people" showed up. Myers, who was accompanied to the site of the battle by "the shepherdess and her flock," had by then lost interest in the proceedings and attempted to back out; but the crowd forced him to fight. Egan described the scene in his inimitable style.

> The battle now commenced and raged with fury for some time, but upon Myers getting the worst of it, the above Covess, and her damsels rushed into the ring to prevent their *Bully* from being annihilated, and took him away; but the spectators interfering, persuaded Myers to return and finish the battle like a man, who being ashamed of his conduct, agreed to it, when Richmond soon taught him very properly to acknowledge, that it was wrong, and beneath the character of an Englishman, to abuse an individual for what he could not help — either on account of his *country* or his *colour*. Myers very properly, received a complete milling.

Richmond moved to London, where, in 1804, at age forty-one, "little known to the metropolitan boxers," he fought a man named George Maddox and was beaten in the third round. After this defeat he hit his stride, defeating "Youssup, a Jew," in six rounds, in a well-contested battle that earned him a purse of ten guineas and considerably increased his stature as a pugilist. In July of 1805 he fought Jack Holmes, the Coachman. Richmond leveled "Coachee," who was obliged to confess he had "arrived at the end of his journey" by the twenty-sixth round. He then took on a baker, weighing 238 pounds, "whose dough was well kneaded" in just two minutes. In October of 1805, for twenty-five guineas, Richmond was matched against Tom Cribb (who will reappear shortly in our story), then a young man just beginning his illustrious career. Cribb was much younger and more talented, but for the first half-hour of the fight Richmond was untouchable. Pierce Egan was astonished at Richmond's "singular movements," which most likely meant that he was backpedaling, dodging, and blocking Cribb's punches — new tactics at the time. It was a familiar sporting episode: the crafty veteran stalked remorselessly by youth. Richmond kept Cribb at bay for an hour and a half before losing.

Even by the standards of the time, when men often fought until well into middle age, Richmond's longevity was remarkable. "In the ring," Egan wrote, "in point of activity, he stands nearly unrivalled." As late as 1809 Richmond was defeating formidable opponents. He was still fresh enough at the end of one match to leap over the ropes and grab hold of a troublemaker named China-eyed Brown, who had shouted that Richmond "had got a white feather in his tail." He was still fighting at fifty; and it was said he looked no older than thirty-five. Richmond was the Archie Moore of his day and resembled that great fighter in his craftiness and worldly wisdom.

Pierce Egan, a generous but discriminating judge, thought Richmond was entitled to a niche "among the first-rate heroes, though his science was completely intuitive and he had never received formal lessons." Richmond had a very good left hand and excelled at hitting and getting away. He was a steady trainer, avoided the bottle, and was an excellent second. After he retired from the ring, he ran one of the more popular of the sporting pubs, the "Horse and Dolphin" at Leicester Square, and gave boxing lessons.

Richmond's character shines out over the distance of the years. He was extraordinarily good-natured yet not obsequious. His manner of responding to racial slurs was well known. Although aware of his lowly social station as a prize fighter and publican, he managed somehow to make others recognize his personal dignity. As Egan put it, "There are times when he has a different character to support and must not be intruded upon." In the United States a career like Richmond's was impossible for a black man. Even in England, where traditions of good sportsmanship overrode prejudice about color, life for a black demanded remarkable self-control and wariness. "There were few subjects upon which he suffered himself to be lulled to sleep," wrote Egan, and then added a comment that would have gained the wholehearted agreement of P. T. Barnum or any other gamesman: "His experience in life, has taught him to awake to the tricks of it."

Bill Richmond had by this time lived in Britain for forty years and had taken up the ways and games of his adopted homeland. "Notwithstanding the defect in one of his knees," it was written, "he excells as a cricketer." But his generous spirit was likely touched by the difficulties faced by other black men, and perhaps he remained sympathetic to Americans. At any rate, sometime around 1810 another black American, a man with a temperament very different from Richmond's, but who had greater natural fighting ability, appeared, "unknown, unnoticed, unprotected, and uninformed," at the Horse and Dolphin.

*

His name was Tom Molineaux. Who he was, where he came from, and how he got to London remain uncertain.[16] We know less about him than about Richmond, because Pierce Egan knew less. Molineaux came to London a "perfect stranger," a "rude, unsophisticated being." He never managed to make a place for himself there as had Richmond. There has been much speculation about Molineaux's background, but little factual information exists to go on. One early tradition was that Molineaux had been a Virginia slave and had gained his freedom as a reward for his ability as a fighter. It was said that he had worked in the markets in New York City and there had gained a reputation as a pugilist. If so, there would certainly have been no future for him in New York as a black prize fighter. Word of Bill Richmond's success may have got back to the small but lively black community in Manhattan. What we do know is that Tom Molineaux crossed the Atlantic.

Molineaux was about thirty when he arrived in London. A much bigger man than Richmond, he impressed everyone with the beauty of his physique: "all the requisites of a modern gladiator — unbounded strength, wind un-debauched, and a great agility; his frame was perfectly Herculean; his bust, by the best judges of anatomical beauty, considered a perfect picture. It was a model for statuary."

With Richmond's guidance, Molineaux established himself as a prize fighter. His first fight was in July of 1810, when he disposed of a man named Barrows in convincing style. A month later he fought Tom Blake, "Tom Tough! a boxer of great repute and practice," and overwhelmed him. It was a sensational performance for the newcomer.

No wonder other fighters viewed him "with jealousy, concern, and terror." An element of racial prejudice was present in insinuations that Molineaux lacked courage; but hostility toward him was probably as much due to his foreignness as to his color. It seemed unthinkable to English prize fighters that a foreigner could beat them on their native ground in a sport that was their own. Thus one English observer "who went into ecstasy in his admiration for this hero of Colour . . . has often been heard to exclaim that 'Molineaux only wanted an English heart' to place him at the top of the tree."

Whatever the views or prejudices of various individuals, the English prize ring gave Tom Molineaux a chance to challenge Tom Cribb, who, after his victory over Bill Richmond in 1807, had gone on to become champion and was now at the height of his power and fame. Anticipation and alarm, among the English prize-fight fancy, rose to great heights at the prospect of the fight. Arrangements were quickly made, and on December 18, 1810, at Copthall Common, near East Grinstead, the two men met in freezing weather, in a pouring rain. It was one of the half-dozen most celebrated fights in the history of the British prize ring. Only a few others, among them Sayers versus Heenan half a century later, rank with it for sustained excitement and drama. "Interest in all former contests was trifling when compared with this," Egan wrote, and all Englishmen "felt for the honor of their country."

The betting exceeded "any thing of the kind that had gone before." Molineaux was five feet eight and a quarter and weighed 198 pounds, while Cribb was five feet ten, 200 pounds. Cribb dominated the first nine rounds and dealt out great punishment, bloodying Molineaux's face and cutting him about the eyes; but Cribb too had taken a beating, and Molineaux, far from fading away, came on very strongly in the next half-dozen rounds. Cribb had to change his tactics, staying away from Molineaux as much as he could. The odds fluctuated back and forth as each fighter seemed to gain strength and then lose it, rally and then weaken, while the fans were in an uproar of excitement and apprehension. This went on through twenty rounds, by which time both men were in dreadful shape. Then Molineaux made his great bid, dominating the next eight rounds and battering Cribb. But the Englishman would not stay down.

In the twenty-ninth round Cribb closed one of Molineaux's eyes completely. Pierce Egan thought this the decisive moment of the fight, and Molineaux may have thought so too, for he made a supreme effort in round thirty, a furious onslaught, proving "what a resolute and determined hero" he was and fighting "in spite of every disadvantage, with courage and ferocity unequalled, rising superior to exhaustion and fatigue." Cribb came back for more, however, and hurt Molineaux badly in round thirty-one with a blow to the throat. From then on it was simply a matter of which man could stand longest on his feet. Round thirty-four was the last one "that might be termed fighting." After that both men were too bloody, battered, and exhausted to do anything but lean on each other. At the end of round thirty-nine Molineaux "complained for the first time that he could fight no more." His seconds urged him to try one more round, but he fell down from exhaustion.

Later accounts had it that Molineaux was cheated of victory by Cribb's seconds, who, it was alleged, created a diversion after round twenty-eight that gave Cribb extra time; otherwise, they main-

tained, he could not have come up to scratch. But that wasn't
Egan's view. He didn't minimize the partisan nature of the crowd,
but he insisted that, despite it, Molineaux had a fair chance. Like
many famous prize fights, controversy was almost an inextricable
part of the excitement of the event, especially with so much money
on the line.[17]

A rematch was inevitable, but in the meantime there were stories,
which may or may not have been true, about riotous living on Molineaux's part. There is no question that Cribb prepared himself
with utmost seriousness. He got a famous English long-distance
runner and fight fan, Captain Barclay, to help condition him — this
may mark the origin of the boxer's training camp in the modern-day
sense — and by the time of the second fight Cribb was rock hard,
weighing 185 pounds as contrasted with the 200 pounds of the first
fight. Cribb said ruefully that he would rather fight Molineaux
again than go through the ordeal of another such training period.

When the two men met again, at Thistleton Gap, near Grantham,
on September 28, 1811, Cribb won decisively, in eleven rounds that
lasted a total of less than twenty minutes. An enormous crowd
turned up for the fight and saw Cribb establish early dominance, although the fighting was again heated and even. In the ninth round
Molineaux's jaw was badly injured, perhaps broken. Somehow he
continued for two more rounds, which should have been enough to
dispose forever of doubts as to his courage.

After that, all was downhill for Tom Molineaux. Whatever he
made from the second fight — Cribb took up a collection for him —
didn't last long. We know from Pierce Egan that Molineaux was il-
literate, and he seems to have been less able than Bill Richmond to
deal with those "tricks of life" black men in a white world experienced at first hand. Sadly, one of the stories that comes down to us
is of a falling-out between Richmond and Molineaux. Pierce Egan
reported that for a long while before his death, Molineaux was ema-
ciated from some kind of wasting illness. He scraped together a living by traveling with a circus, teaching boxing, and giving exhibitions, so some remnants of the fame of his fights with Tom Cribb
still hung about him. He died in Galway, Ireland, in the quarters of
the band of the 77th Regiment of the British army, on August 4,
1818.

*

Bill Richmond and Tom Molineaux didn't belong to an American
prize-fighting tradition in which they could make professional ca-

reers for themselves, nor did their prize ring achievements have any discernible influence on the subsequent history of the sport.[18] For a very long time, in fact, American prize-ring lore virtually ignored them, and when the Molineaux–Cribb fights were referred to they seemed almost as distant as Homeric epics.

In the 1820s and 1830s the anonymity of prize fighting's early years gave way to a new stage, in which its opponents admitted its existence but bitterly lamented it. Fans were prepared to go a considerable distance to get away from the law: a favorite location for a fight was a barge or an island in the middle of a river or bay, where legal jurisdiction was unclear. Prize fighting remained a local activity, however, supported by a local hero's fans and their betting. Taverns and barbershops, the usual centers for indoor sports and gambling, were unadaptable to prize fighting. So it took place in lofts, obscure warehouses, and the back rooms of dance halls and brothels. Livery stables were also a common place for fights. A New Yorker, recalling his youth of the 1840s, remembered the livery stable as the spot where he and his friends, children of very respectable families, first sampled some of the forbidden amusements of the time: dog fights, cockfights, rat killing, and a boxing match between two women naked from the waist up.[19]

The prestige of the English prize ring remained immense. The skills of English managers and trainers, regarded as the most adept practitioners in the world, were much in demand in America. The boxing manuals and boxing instructors were English, and so too was the published literature. But American prize fighting was now firmly enough established to begin to attract fighters from Ireland and England, especially as the prize ring in England began to decline. "Deaf" Burke, a topflight English fighter, came over for fights in New Orleans and New York in 1837; and in 1841 Ben Caunt, the English champion, made a nonfighting visit. There was probably more continuous contact between the two nations in prize fighting than in any other sport, so that John Heenan's expedition was part of an established pattern of transatlantic crisscrossing; but of course intellectuals who called for the outward expansion of American culture didn't know about this or have it in mind as the sort of thing they wished to encourage.

The late 1840s mark prize fighting's visible emergence, its way blazed by increasing publicity. Notices of forthcoming fights appeared in newspapers and were openly posted. In 1849 the sport achieved its first event of national prominence, the fight between Tom Hyer and Yankee Sullivan. Tom Hyer, a New York butcher, was born into a prize-fighting family; his father Jacob had been a fighter. James Ambrose Sullivan, born of Irish parents in London, came to the United States as a young man, got into prize fighting, and became known for his hatred of England and his loyalty to his newly adopted land. He fought with the stars and stripes around his waist and took the name "Yankee." Despite this, he was still thought of as a foreigner, and some of Tom Hyer's popularity was due to the fact that he was native born. Hyer's trainer, George Thompson, an Englishman, was brought over specifically to prepare Hyer for the fight with Sullivan, and the *New York Herald,* much to the disgust of many citizens, sent a reporter named Joseph Elliott to report on both fighters and their training for the fight — the first time this had ever been done in America.

Improved transportation played a role in elevating this fight into a national event of a modest scale; and so did the protracted and very public negotiations about the purse and the site. "Those who wish to attend the great fight," a newspaper article ran, "should be in Baltimore next Tuesday. There will be no difficulty in ascertaining there where the stakes are to be pitched."[20] Arrangements for the fight were so open they boomeranged. The police made a determined effort to break it up and arrest the fighters, who narrowly evaded them. At the last minute a new location was found, and, on February 7, 1849, at Rock Point, Maryland, the fight finally went on. Hyer won decisively, after furious fighting, and Sullivan was carried away in a blanket. Hyer eventually retired from the ring, while Sullivan recovered from his injuries, went off to California, and there met the savage fate that awaited him. And so began the long series of American championship fights that stretches down to our own time.

*

Of all the sports of the Age of Jackson, prize fighting most clearly reflected class feelings. This is apparent in the distinction between prize fighting, a sport for the masses, and sparring, the art of individual self-defense. Prize fighting spread despite the opposition of respectable people of the upper classes; sparring, because of their support. In the turbulent state of American city life, sparring served a useful function for the young middle-class men who learned it; but they learned it for another reason: it was a "gentlemanly" activity, much as knowing how to handle a sword had once been a skill that distinguished members of the aristocracy.

Sparring was one of the first athletic skills to be taught in the schools and academies of the time. Behind this lay something important: the growing anxiety on the part of city dwellers that, cut off from the country and from rural sports, and thus from health-giving nature, their bodies were degenerating. As cities grew rapidly in size, people depended on vehicles to take them from place to place. Walking became the first un-American activity. An alarm was sounded that rang throughout the nineteenth century and down to our own day, when it has reached deafening levels.

> To do anything in the world, we don't want mental strength merely, but physical abilities also; an educated mind in a weak carcass is like a powerful engine on board a leaky steamboat.[21]

The metaphor was new, but the idea was as old as the Greek ideal of a sound mind in a sound body. This view contrasted with another image from the classical past, the urban nightmare of imperial Rome, with its mobs and its savage gladiatorial combats. On this subject Oliver Wendell Holmes wrote: "Boxing is rough play, but not too rough for hearty young fellows. Anything is better than this white-blooded degeneration to which we all tend."[22]

The first sparring teachers were William Fuller and George Kensett, Englishmen who came to the United States in the 1820s. Because gymnasiums were rare, they taught their pupils in private homes, in ballrooms, or on the stages of theaters. Kensett, "the scientific boxer from London," taught in Baltimore, Philadelphia, and Washington with considerable success. Fuller, a Norfolk farmer, stressed that he was teaching gentlemen "a useful, manly, and athletic exercise, at once conducive to health and furnishing the means of self-defense and prompt chastisement to the assaults of the ruffian."[23] He ended up in New York City, opening a gymnasium that catered to well-connected young men and was sufficiently pure in its amateurism to gain the support of Henry Herbert. Fuller's presence in America also had a tenuous connection with the careers of Richmond and Molineaux. Years before, Fuller had been a pupil of Richmond's and had fought, and lost to, Molineaux.

Unlike sparring, prize fighting was distinctly lower class.[24] Limited in extent to the cities of the middle states and the Northeast, it spread in the 1840s and 1850s into the new West and South. Its center was always New York City, to which fighters gravitated from inland and abroad. Though limited in extent, its appeal to its urban adherents was deep-rooted. Usually thought of as no more than the aggressive expression of certain individual attitudes, chief among which were male prowess and pugnacity, prize fighting was also a form of collective action. It was a form of social defiance. Its illegality added to its emotional power in this respect, because it made the defiance blatantly public. Flouting the laws of Yankee Boston and Knickerbocker New York was a way of thumbing one's nose at "them," a way to fight back. This was especially important to inarticulate people surrounded by people who were alien, articulate, and arrogant. Prize fighting was also an important adhesive element among those people, a bond that, for a few moments at least, held together drifters, artisans, laborers, shopkeepers, sailors, servants, young people, free blacks, prostitutes, and gamblers who otherwise had few things in common.

The gulf between the culture of the prize ring and that of the upper classes was greater in the democratic and equalitarian United States than it was in England. There too prize fighting was predominantly a lower-class sport, but its following extended upward through all classes. Most important, it was patronized by some members of the aristocracy, young "swells" and "bloods" who organized and attended fights, bet heavily on them, and occasionally befriended the fighters. It was this factor that, during the heyday of the English prize ring, from 1795 to 1820 — the days of the great champions like Jackson, Belcher, and Cribb, and even as late as the time of Heenan and Sayers — gave it a very special English flavor and style that was absent in America. The eventual withdrawal of aristocratic support was one of the main reasons for the English prize ring's decline after the 1820s.

The patronage of aristocratic dandies blunted the efforts of the prize ring's opponents and inhibited the zeal of the police. It did other things as well. It made it easier for young men to be patrons of sports as well as the arts; dandies might be thought foppish and self-indulgent but not necessarily unmanly. The dandy was often derided, but he could defy conventional opinion, and much of his energy went into doing just that. At the same time, his interest in prize fighting served as a bridge between social orders. Regency England's most famous group of pugilistic dandies clustered around "Gentleman" Jackson, champion of the prize ring from 1795 to 1800 and a friend of Byron's. Jackson entered respectable society, opened a boxing school in which he taught the sons of the aristocracy self-defense, and, at the coronation of George IV in 1820, organized a royal bodyguard of famous prize fighters. This was a sign of the regard in which Jackson was held personally, but it also made clear that however lowly prize fighters were, they too occupied a fixed place within the society of the realm.

The tendency in the United States was the opposite. Where class identities were fundamentally clear, as they were in England, social restrictions could occasionally be relaxed; but where they were fundamentally ambiguous, there was a continuing anxiety to clarify and separate. The American middle class, feeling much less secure, needed to exclude groups such as the prize fighters and their followers from respectable society. This was the same attitude that had made Andrew Jackson move so cautiously in respect to horse racing.

There was also a special emotional element associated with all this. The American middle class loathed the peculiar English tradition of aristocratic patronage as much as it did the brutality of the prize ring itself. Perhaps more. The dandy at the prize fight became one of those symbols, so vital to the Jacksonian mind, of the contrast between European corruption and American virtue. For Hezekiah Niles, a journalist of the 1820s, prize fighting represented English culture at its most hateful: a class-ridden social order and a way of life that allowed, indeed encouraged, men

> to beat and abuse and possibly kill one another, as has frequently happened, in the presence of nobles and divines in England. We are not yet fashionable enough for such things in the United States.[25]

Wicked Europe!

Given this, we can see why Americans were so reluctant to admit that prize fighting even existed in their country. To do so was in effect to admit that class feelings existed as well. And it also suggested something even more important: the possibility that America did not have a special destiny, that the new Republic would be condemned to move along the familiar blood-stained historical path of the Old World. Prize fighting was a badge of lost innocence.

A quarter of a century after Hezekiah Niles's comment, Philip Hone, the diary-keeping friend of John Cox Stevens, confided to his journal some thoughts on this subject, the passionate intensity of which contrasted strongly with the cool and urbane manner in which he usually faced the world. Hone was infuriated by an incident in which an American prize fighter named Lilly, having fought and killed his opponent, escaped American authorities by taking a ship to England. There, Hone reflected bitterly, he will be all the fashion in that refined country, whose sensitive tourists faint at the recollection of the tobacco chewing and spitting Yankees, and lose their delicate appetites at our vulgar substitution of the knife for the fork. The man who killed his man here will, by that heroic exploit have un-Yankeefied himself there. He will become an associate of the magnates of the land. His name will be enrolled in the Court calendar with the Belchers and Springs, the Cribbs and the Dutch Sams, and his portrait will adorn a page of the elegant literature of British science; the Yankee Lilly alongside the black champion in hot pressed volumes in superb bindings which occupy a place in the boudoirs of the British fair alongside of "Flowers of Fancy" and Mills's "Chivalry."[26]

Bloody old Europe!

In America, the sense of a yawning gulf between the upper and lower classes, combined with worries about physical degeneration, produced familiar anxieties about order. Philip Hone's anger about England was transformed into unease about prospects at home. "The amusement of prize fighting, the disgrace of which was formerly confined to England," he wrote, "has now become one of the abominations of our loafer-ridden city."[27] By 1860 a New York newspaper described "the pugilistic and sporting fraternity" as "the most riotous, unscrupulous and pestilential crew that ever a city was cursed with." A visiting Frenchman emphasized the dangers of a situation in which upper-class control was so surprisingly absent. Salomon de Rothschild commented on a boxing match he went to in 1859: "What interested me most was that the audience was composed of people from all the dangerous classes of New York."[28] Americans understood that sporting events in Britain, though often rowdy, functioned as a means of allowing the lower classes to let off excess steam. But in New York and in other eastern cities, people were increasingly inclined to fear that prize fights weren't a safety valve but a time bomb.

*

Prize fighting had ethnic, as well as class, aspects. The dandy was absent, but the Irishman was very much present. The Irish dominated American prize fighting throughout the nineteenth century. Ethnic identities are never a simple matter, and to be Irish in America had long involved more ambiguity than was apparent at first glance. It was, for one thing, a triangular ethnic and cultural consciousness — Anglo-Irish-American. It made a great deal of difference whether the fighter was an emigrant to America from Ireland or was a native-born American of Irish descent. And of course national feeling was often less important than religious affiliation.

The "Scotch-Irish," so ubiquitous in American culture in the eighteenth and nineteenth centuries (Andrew Jackson was one), were aggressively Protestant and often anti-English.

Ethnic and racial self-consciousness fed on hostility to the dominant culture, but it radiated down as well as up, cutting across the loyalties class feeling sometimes provided. The bitterest political rivals of the Tammany Democratic prize-fight gangs were gangs composed of members of the Native American party or the Whig party — gangs whose class identity was very like that of the Democrats but who organized themselves mainly to express anti-Irish and anti-Catholic feeling. So, too, from early on, Irish-American fighters were persistently hostile to black prize fighters, would not fight them, and tried to exclude them from the prize ring.

Prize fighting during the Jacksonian era was a mosaic of local situations. Unlike most American sporting fraternities, such as those of horse racing, trotting, sailing, and chess — groups who wished to move beyond their local or regional boundaries and become national — prize fighters and their fans were intensely local. Ethnic consciousness was one of the factors that accounted for this. Even decades later, after John L. Sullivan had become a national champion, the heart of prize fighting was still in the neighborhood, and the neighborhood in an American city was likely to be an ethnic one. When Tom Cribb died in 1848, the obituaries in English newspapers noted the death of a man who was to a considerable extent a national figure, if not exactly a national hero (he was that as well for many people). Although identified with his class, Cribb was also a representative of a larger culture that was homogeneous in a way American culture could never be. Cribb was described as the Wellington of his class: "All classes from peer to peasant recognized his courage, honor, honesty and withal, the kindliness of his heart."[29] Think how differently the obituary of Tom Molineaux would have read.

As if that weren't enough, another element in prize-fight culture added further to its complexity. Prize fighters were fervent jingoes. This was the reverse side of their intense ethnic consciousness. If their Irishness, for example, marked them off from the predominant culture, patriotism was a way of identifying them with it. They were especially moved by national symbols — flags, badges, colors, songs, and slogans. In their eyes, democracy was identical with the future of the Union; and they were ardent expansionists. The Mexican War of 1846–1848 was vehemently supported by all of New York's prize-fight groups, whatever their party label.

The story of Bill Poole is representative of many others. One night "Butcher Bill," prize fighter, street fighter, and stalwart in Captain Isaiah Rynders's Nativist gang, after a lifetime of mayhem and brawling, was cornered in a saloon and shot down by his enemies. For fourteen days he lived on, with a bullet near his heart; his fight for life gained him more attention than he had ever received in the streets or in the prize ring. When Poole finally died he was given a magnificent funeral, with brass bands and with five thousand people walking behind his hearse. A play was quickly written about his martyrdom, and, when performed, the dying words of the Butcher Boy were greeted with thunderous applause: "Goodbye, boys; I die a true American!"[30]

*

Anglo-American sporting rivalry in these years, however intense, usually ended with expressions of good will and fellowship among the participants. Its effect on fans, even (or perhaps especially) fans far from the action, was often very different. Appealing to a vast group of people, sport revealed some of the deeper animosities embedded in the populace as a whole; it revealed, and sometimes released, such passions. This is what gives sporting rivalries such significance as expressions of popular sentiment — sentiment of a kind not articulated in any other way, and certainly not articulated in essays or speeches. One of these traditionally popular American animosities, the hatred of England and English culture, was at the heart of an incident that, while not actually a sporting event, released the passions of a considerable number of the members of New York prize-fight culture. This was the Astor Place Opera House riot of 1849.

The background of the riot was theatrical. The two leading actors of the day, the Englishman W. C. Macready and the American Edwin Forrest, were rivals who shared a bitter mutual dislike. Their quarrel, originating in jealousy and accusations of slander, had become public knowledge by 1849, and the American press had as a matter of course converted it into a question of national honor and rivalry. In that year Macready toured the United States, concluding his visit in the spring with a series of performances in New York City. A haughty and difficult man, Macready made little secret of his contempt for his audiences, his fellow actors, and even his own profession; and he had an especially low opinion of American culture. ("Let me die in a ditch in England, rather than in the Fifth Avenue of New York," he confided to his diary.)[31]

Such views were sensed by Forest's vociferous New York partisans, who stirred up feeling against the arrogant Englishman, feeling that was heightened by the fact that, since Macready had announced this as his last visit to America, it was a final chance for revenge. When Macready finally appeared at the opera house at Astor Place on the night of May 7, in *Macbeth,* eggs, refuse, and even chairs were thrown down at him from the gallery. Macready abandoned his efforts to edify the barbarians and prepared to return to England. Leading citizens of the city rallied to his support, however. They published an appeal in the newspapers, urging him to try again, and to rely on the good sportsmanship of American audiences.

Meanwhile, what had begun as a theatrical vendetta assumed more threatening proportions and provoked wider feelings. Rumors somehow circulated throughout the city that British sailors were going to come ashore, from ships in New York harbor, to support their countryman. And it was also rumored that the mayor had already called out the militia. All this to protect a foreigner! Macready, with more courage than wisdom, acceded to the appeal of his friends (he had no illusions about the sportsmanship of his enemies) and agreed to appear once more at the opera house, on the evening of the tenth. The volatile nature of the affair should have been clear enough from posters that appeared on the morning of Macready's rescheduled appearance.

WORKING MEN
SHALL
AMERICANS
OR
ENGLISH RULE
IN THIS CITY?

THE CREW OF THE BRITISH STEAMSHIP HAVE
THREATENED ALL AMERICANS WHO SHALL DARE
TO EXPRESS THEIR OPINION THIS NIGHT AT THE
ENGLISH ARISTOCRATIC OPERA HOUSE!
WE ADVOCATE NO VIOLENCE, BUT A FREE EXPRESSION
OF OPINION TO ALL PUBLIC MEN.
WORKINGMEN! FREEMEN!

STAND BY YOUR
LAWFUL RIGHTS
American committee[32]

That night a large crowd gathered outside the opera house. The tension had been heightened by the news that the militia had indeed been called out and would soon be appearing at Astor Place. Inside, the house was packed; every seat taken, the aisles filled, and all the standing room long gone. It wasn't *Macbeth* that had brought these people, some of them sitting in their shirtsleeves, others with their hats on. In the opera house! According to a source sympathetic to Macready, "the ampitheatre and parquette were crowded with hard-looking men — a dense mass of bone and muscle."[33] Although restless, the audience inside and the crowd outside remained orderly. Tension mounted. A very long delay, then the curtain finally went up. The play began. Macready appeared.

He was greeted with an explosion of noise; within moments fighting erupted everywhere. Macready fled the stage and, by extraordinary good luck, escaped unharmed from the theater. Outside, the militia, after a good deal of marching and countermarching, indecision and confusion, with fighting swirling around it, found itself involved in a pitched battle with one of the local gangs, the Bowery B'hoys. They charged the troops, who then fired — whether at the Bowery B'hoys or into the crowd was not clear. Peace was finally restored after a few hours, although firing continued sporadically while the Bowery B'hoys erected barricades in some of the streets leading from the opera house. Twenty-two people were killed.

What had seemed a trivial matter ended in horrible violence, the cause of which remained obscure. As always, some people were quick to offer explanations. Respectable opinion, the opinion of Macready's supporters, showed little understanding and, with the European revolutions of the year before freshly in mind, lapsed into a semihysterical analysis of a since-familiar sort. Anxieties about a time bomb had proved all too justified. Wrote the *New York Herald:*

> The late fearful riot has opened up a new and alarming subject of investigation, and that is how far anarchical socialism . . . has operated in this community in unsettling the foundations of law and order and arraying the poor against the rich.[34]

The need for order! Equally revealing were the comments of Captain Rynders, a gang leader who yielded the palm to no one in his hatred for foreigners and his facility for demagogic claptrap. The firing by the militia was, in his opinion, part of a long-standing conspiracy by the authorities, whose intention from the first had been

> to please the aristocracy of the city at the expense of the lives of unoffending citizens — to please an aristocratic Englishman backed by a few

sycophantic Americans. It was more important to these aristocrats that Mr. Macready should play before them than that they should prevent a riot.[35]

The Battle of Astor Place was in many ways a typical incident in the protracted clash between new and old, native and foreign, traditions of culture. Had Andrew Jackson commanded the militia that night, he would have shown little mercy to the Bowery Boys. Even so, he would have sympathized with their desire to exalt the people above a hateful aristocratic tradition, and he would certainly have understood the feelings of rage and the desire to strike out at one's enemies. But New York City at midcentury was a long way from Clover Bottom and the Hermitage, and it was no longer clear who was foreign and who American. The prize-fight culture represented by the Bowery Boys was as foreign to many Americans as William Macready's culture was foreign to the Bowery Boys. What if the effort to create a native American sporting culture had been misconceived from the first? Would America have not one culture and one style, but many? As an example of how much American sporting groups already differed from each other, it is interesting that the night after the riot, neighborhood brawlers and sports with cheeky insolence darted out from their barricades and heaved paving stones at the militia.

*

The prize ring was one center of urban sporting culture. The firehouse was the other.[36] Sporting and political life in the neighborhoods were brought together by the volunteer fire companies. Until after the Civil War, when volunteer companies were disbanded and professional ones took their places, cities depended on the volunteers for their fire fighting. The work was hazardous and hard; fire fighting was done with hand-drawn, hand-pumped machines. Despite this, membership in a fire company carried prestige: John Jay, Aaron Burr, and Alexander Hamilton were among the notable members of fire-fighting companies, and George Washington was a great enthusiast.

New York City was divided into numerous small fire-fighting districts. Citizens of these districts organized their own fire companies to give them extra protection. Members of a company generally served from five to ten years. They received no pay but were exempt from jury and militia duty and got fancy certificates of membership. They slept at home, and so, when there was an alarm, they had to go first to the firehouse. This was often awkward, because members

The Life of the Fireman — The Night Alarm

didn't have to live in the fire district they served. Gradually, therefore, it became common for members to build bunkhouses at the firehouse, where they slept while on call. Membership became more closely identified with neighborhood residence, and the firehouses soon became social centers.

Firehouse social life developed its own traditons — chowder parties on Saturday night (chowder was the fireman's characteristic food) and occasional grand dinners. Companies often had a steward whose responsibilities included taking drink to the scene of a fire — with predictably disastrous results. The temperance movement of the 1840s and 1850s stopped much of this, but many companies stuck to their unregenerate ways. Firehouse social life had its notorious side — an all-male atmosphere of heavy drinking, prostitutes, and gambling; but the firemen became most famous for their more respectable social functions, such as the annual fireman's ball (first organized in New York City in 1829) and the fireman's fund, created to raise money for charity.

Membership in volunteer fire companies had to be approved by the city government and was restricted to a certain number of men. This made it a form of political patronage especially attractive to politicians, because it didn't cost the city any money. The actual size of a company was always larger than its formal membership. Attached to each station was a group of boys and men, called runners, who weren't admitted to formal membership because they were too young or because the rolls were filled. These runners dashed to the fires, aped the firemen in dress and manner, and worked voluntarily around the firehouse. Many famous firemen began as runners.

Fire companies were specifically forbidden to engage in political activity, but they continually and openly did so. Their political allegiances usually reflected those of the district. Although some companies were made up of wealthy and well-connected men, the ranks of the volunteers more and more represented the social composition of the immediate neighborhood. In the 1830s and 1840s, this meant immigrant, working-class, prize-fight people. The companies were filled with rowdies and roughs, or they could call on the services of rowdies when required. The period from 1830 to the Civil War was one of great turmoil, and in New York City, at the center of the riot-filled turbulence, were the famous gangs of the time —the Dead Rabbits, the Bowery B'hoys, the Forty Thieves, the Short Boys, the Chichesters, the Old Maid Boys, and many others.

At the forefront of the membership of companies and gangs were the prize fighters. They were there to swell the size of the companies in parades and rallies; they were strong-arm men and enforcers. When necessary, the prize fighters served as repeaters on election days; it was they who voted the dead rolls from the cemeteries. During this period there was an atmosphere of incessant fighting: between rival gangs and between rival fire companies; and in the streets, legislative chambers, taverns, and hotels. Opponents fought about abolitionism, temperance, religion, and ethnic origins. Fist-fighting pugnacity touched everything.

Black Joke Engine #33 was made up of street brawlers. Its captain from 1832 on was Malachi Fallon, who eventually became Warden of the Tombs and opened a popular saloon that was a gathering place of politicians. His fire company was an important political force. Tom Hyer was a member of this company in the 1840s. Fallon's power was also based on two independent military companies, the Baster Blues, named in honor of a man killed in the Mexican War, and the Black Joke Volunteers, numbering 1,000 men, who were fully armed and equipped with uniforms that included red shirts, black trousers, leggings, and glazed caps. The company marched in a great demonstration for Polk and Dallas, the Democratic presidential candidates in 1844, and for this flagrant violation of the rules was disbanded. Then Fallon, like many others, went to California. The company was re-formed in 1852, and in 1863 its members committed the first overt act that produced the terrible antidraft riots of that year.

Boss Tweed was foreman of the Americus Engine #6 (the Big Six). The company's engine had a tiger on it, later appropriated by Tammany Hall (when Tweed was boss) as its symbol. Tweed used the fire company as a political base in his rise to power. Members of the Red Rover Engine Company #34 included "Butcher Bill" Poole; Mike Walsh, saloon-keeper and sports journalist; and Ely Hazleton, the most famous street fighter of his day, about whom only meager information has survived. The foreman of this crew was David C. Broderick, a politician who also went to California, where he eventually became a United States senator. In 1859 he was killed in a duel. When New York City firemen heard of his death they held a parade and elaborate funeral ceremonies, accompanied by much eulogistic oratory. A specially written drama, *Three Eras in the Life of a New York Fireman,* based on incidents from Broderick's career, was performed at the Bowery Theater.

*

The theatrical and sporting elements of this culture were vividly combined. The dinners and the drinking, the rallies, parades, and balls, were efforts to make up for the pageantry and ritual so lacking in democratic Jacksonian public life. Many Americans wanted to erase every scrap of ritual associated with traditional European culture. This was more difficult to do than had at first seemed to be the case; but even if it were done, what communal ceremonies or pageantry would take its place? [37]

Formal public occasions in America were few and far between: the Fourth of July and an occasional inaugural parade. The pomp associated with an established church was also lacking. To fill the void, Americans created informal, unofficial public gatherings. The sporting events of the 1840s and 1850s were among the most important of these; very few other events brought together so many people. Often a modest amount of pageantry was directly associated with the sporting events themselves. Trotting races at county fairs were enlivened by parades and beauty contests; horse-racing promoters added other forms of entertainment and festivity between races; and prize fights had their own touches of ritual and color. But people were still limited by scarce resources and, even more important, were inhibited from breaking away from conventional restraints and altering the inherited sporting traditions. It took P. T. Barnum's genius to realize that entertainment could be the primary means of satisfying the need for communal ceremony and ritual. And as sports became a form of professional entertainment, sporting events stressed this aspect. Indeed, such elements were added to almost every public occasion, almost every form of play. The strength of this need in American culture is seen everywhere today: in halftime shows at football games; and when Americans throng the gates of Buckingham Palace to see the Changing of the Guard.

The race to the fire was both a game and a show. The firemen had gorgeous materials to play with, and they were uninhibited in their playing. They decorated their firehouses with lively exuberance and dressed with appropriate flamboyance at the firemen's balls. And then there were the parades! The first one in New York City, on the Fourth of July, 1825, marked the beginning of an annual event. There were also special occasions: Lafayette's visit in 1824; the opening of the Erie Canal in 1825; the completion of the Croton Aqueduct in 1842; and Jenny Lind's visit in 1851. The most famous of these special events was the visit of — think of it! — the Prince of Wales, in 1860. The firemen staged a tremendous march in all their massed splendor, with gaudy uniforms, gleaming equipment, and torches flaring in the night.

They lavished time and imagination on their uniforms. This was an outrageous form of exuberant play, like the tall tale. Firemen vigorously opposed every effort to standardize their clothing, although they all wore the large, broad-rimmed leather fire helmets. In the 1820s firemen wore white duck suits, with black belts. They became more unrestrained in the 1830s, when the basic uniform became kersey cloth with huge side pockets, enormous white bond buttons, black belts, and red woolen nightcaps. Some men carried canes. In the 1840s firemen really hit their stride: they sported red flannel shirts, high black boots, blue-black trousers, shiny leather belts, and blue coats. In hot weather they went coatless, wearing very wide, fancy suspenders of all colors, fastened with large elaborately ornamented clasps. In these guises did the American dandy appear.

The machines were more decorated than the men. Fire engines were covered with elaborate patterns, painted in the brightest colors, with brass shined until it gleamed. Specially constructed panels were mounted on the machines, front, back, and sides. Well-known painters, such as Inman, Quidor, and Quigg, painted scenes on these: the labors of Hercules and (of course) the burning of Troy. Patriotic themes abounded: Washington's camp at Valley Forge, and Jefferson's signing of the Declaration. There were also more common scenes and pictures: clipper ships and the *America*. The names of the machines and companies were equally colorful: the Hayseeds, the Blue Boys, the Rooster Boys, the Red Rover, Old Sal, Old Jeff, White Ghosts, Shad Billies, Dry Bones, Hay Wagon, Veto, Elephant, and Bean Soup, to name a few. One company named itself after the great trotter, Lady Suffolk; another was named after the famous thoroughbred, Fashion. Old Turk's men were famous singers; the Old Stags not only painted that animal on their side panels but also made a strange noise, supposedly the call of a stag, as they ran through the streets.

The firemen loved their machines, insisted they were almost human, kissed them, and addressed them by affectionate names. These brawny brawlers and stammering street fighters loved their machines unashamedly, in a way they could not always love their women. Frank Clark, who started as a runner for the Old Turk Company when he was eleven, rose to be foreman, and led the company in President Pierce's inaugural parade in Washington in 1853, was famous among his peers for his abashed but unwavering loyalty to his machine. There was a fire on Clark's wedding night. He dashed into action, still wearing his wedding suit, and didn't return for three days. Chided about this he replied: "What was a feller goin' to do? Let the old gal get passed?"[38]

In the game of fire fighting, losing the race to the fire — getting "passed" — was a crushing defeat. The race to arrive first at the fire was the most exciting part for many spectators, of all ages, who ran through the streets with and after the firemen. The firemen were often accused of caring much more about winning the race to the fire than about fighting it once they got there, and, considering the conditions and the equipment they had to use, who could blame them?

This game had distinct phases. First, the runners ran ahead to clear the way, or to obstruct the path of their rivals. Once at the scene, they captured the nearest hydrants or cisterns and defended them against the rival company. Finally, the climax, which signalled complete victory, "washing" a rival machine — that is, pumping so much water onto the other machine as to damage its paint and decorations. "Washing" contests became so popular that they were staged as special events on the Fourth. Having an engine washed was the greatest humiliation for any company. Its men wore mourning bands and flew streamers of crepe until they wiped away the disgrace, usually by washing some rival. One representative anecdote captures the mood. An old member of the Black Joke Company was dying:

"What's happened to the en-jine," he demanded of a fellow fire laddie.

"Jake, the en-jine got washed today!"

With a supreme effort, raising himself up: "then let me die: I envy not your hold on life."[39]

This culture produced one of the classic sporting types of the Age of Jackson. This man was an urban sportsman, one of the people. He belonged to no yacht club or turf club, read no newspapers, and wouldn't have known what a tradition was if asked. His games were played in the streets, and his home was the firehouse.

*

Onto the stage he swaggered, rolled-up trousers stuffed into high black boots, wearing a shiny stovepipe hat, a bright red shirt, and a pearl-buttoned pea jacket, his long hair soaped, puffing away at a big cigar, a "long nine." On February 15, 1848, when the audience in the Olympic Theater in New York City recognized him, there was a roar of applause and cheers. He was Mose, the Bowery B'Hoy — fire laddie, tough guy, alley fighter, the sport of the waterfront saloons and brothels — leaning against a fireplug, drawling out the slang of the city streets.[40]

Mose first appeared in Benjamin Baker's play, *A Glance at New York*. It was an enormous success, running for twelve weeks. Baker was a theatrical prompter who as a boy had been a runner with the Peterson Engine Company, carrying the signal lantern ahead of the engine and sleeping curled up under the engine's tongue. Mose was played with convincing authenticity by Francis S. Chanfrau, one of four brothers who were all members of the Old Maid Company, one of the toughest companies of brawlers, which included such leading prize fighters of the time as Country McCluskey, Sam Skinner, Johnny McCleester, and Sam Banta.

The play consisted of a series of fast-moving scenes of New York lowlife. It was set in a wharf hangout for thugs and a dance hall, where Mose triumphed over his opponents. There were plenty of special effects, including several brawls and a fire. The characters were minutely observed, for Baker had seen them all at first hand. Mose was modeled on a man whom both Baker and Chanfrau knew — Moses Humphries, leader of the Bowery B'Hoys, a fireman of the Lady Washington Company, which was the deadliest rival of Baker's and Chanfrau's Old Maid Company. A man of massive build and flaming red hair, he was one of the most ferocious street fighters in New York. Even while Moses Humphries lived, stories about him abounded. According to one story, Moses, his engine having been washed and the B'Hoys having deserted the company, shipped out for Hawaii, where he became an intimate of the King of the Sandwich Islands, opened a saloon and billiard parlor, married a native woman, and fathered forty children.

In the many versions of the play that followed its initial appearance, Mose appeared in various places — France, China, Arabia, San Francisco, and Philadelphia. The play was adapted to the circus and even turned into a dance. All through the 1850s and 1860s, and down into the 1870s, actors made reputations playing the lead. Mose appeared in humorous stories, pamphlets, and newspapers and made Frank Chanfrau famous in his day.

Mose was always fighting and competing. Strident and fiercely patriotic, he reflected the noisy Jacksonian democracy of his time.

Although rowdy, he was not especially tricky. He knew all the city's games, but he was too impulsive and too physical to be a gamesman. He spoke in a drawling, languid lingo, which he delivered in a totally impassive tone, and he specialized in bumptious, flippant repartee, fearing no one and respecting no one.

Mose had been around — dance halls, brothels, everywhere — and he knew what most women were for. He had a girl friend, Linda the cigar girl. Linda was a tart, but Mose treated her decorously and properly and defended her virtue from the lechers all about, because she would someday become his wife. And a wife wasn't like those other women. Like his engine, Mose's woman would eventually become his "old gal" and then his "old pal." Raucous and tough, Mose was rather prim about sex. The firehouse was a long way from the Cedars and the world of Frank Forester, but Mose was a Jacksonian sportsman through and through.

*

The fight against Tom Sayers was John Heenan's great moment. The years that followed were times of sad and steep decline for the Benicia Boy. Not wanting to fight in the Civil War, Heenan had returned to England in 1861. He and Sayers gave a series of exhibition matches, and when public interest waned, Heenan toured the country with a circus. In December of 1863 he was matched against the English champion, "Sailor" Tom King, and King won in twenty-five rounds. Heenan was hopelessly out of condition, and it was widely believed that he had been drugged. The ensuing scandal hastened the reforms that brought an end to bare-knuckle fighting in England.

After the Civil War Heenan returned to the United States and once again went to work for Tammany Hall. Still popular, he served mainly by being present at political rallies. He opened a gambling parlor but couldn't make a go of it. He fought as a sparring partner for the last notable English prize-ring champion, Jem Mace, who, with prize fighting virtually at an end in England, toured the United States and Australia. Finally, Heenan decided to return to California. But he never got back to the land of starting over. He died on the way, on October 25, 1873, in Green River, Wyoming.

Even those who disapproved of Heenan may have felt a touch of regret at the death of this generally likable soul. The pattern of his sporting career — the swift rise, the adulation, the rapid decline — was a familiar one. More surprising was how far Heenan got, and

Adah Menken

how well known he became, without a major victory to his credit. He lost or drew in all his most important fights. Good luck and publicity could already take a sporting figure far in America.

In the history of the prize ring, Heenan is important because his career marks one of the last high points of bare-knuckle pugilism, and the beginning of its end. In the history of American sport, he has a more unusual distinction. John Carmel Heenan was the first well-known American athlete to be associated with sexual scandal. His love wasn't for a fire engine, a boat, or a horse; it was for a woman, publicly and erotically so. Though we may remember him now for his indomitable fight against Sayers, his contemporaries were likely to associate him with a fight in which he was over-matched, the battle of Heenan versus Menken.

*

The story of Adah Menken's life is bold in outline, fuzzy in detail.[41] Born in 1835 near New Orleans, of Jewish parents, her father's last name was apparently Theodore, and her given name was Adah Bertha. Her father died while she was an infant; her mother remarried, a man named Josephs. Adah had some schooling, learned several languages, and became interested in the theater and in literature, especially poetry. Her stepfather died when she was eighteen.

Adah was thrown back on her own individual resources, which, as the world and especially the men in it would learn, were considerable, though unconventional. For the next two or three years she worked as a dancer, as a model for a sculptor, and as a circus performer. In 1856 she married Alexander Isaacs Menken, the son of a well-to-do Cincinnati dry-goods merchant. Menken lost whatever money he had in the panic of 1857, and Adah embarked on a theatrical career, touring the Southwest with very little success but tasting audience applause for the first time — a taste she forever craved. She also revealed her histrionic talents: "Her voice was good, her figure superb, her manner electric."[42]

In 1859 Adah Menken went to New York City, where she made an unsuccessful theatrical debut. She and Alexander Menken separated. She mingled with the crowd of writers and sporting types, now rather self-consciously Bohemian — Walt Whitman was among them — that met at Pfaff's beer cellar, the successor to the literary sporting hangouts of the time of William Porter and Henry Herbert. She also began her open defiance of conventional American sexual mores. She met John Heenan, who was just then preparing to go to

England to fight Tom Sayers, and very much in the public eye, and she had an affair with him. Adah said she believed Menken was divorcing her, and so she "married" John Heenan in September of 1859. While the Benicia Boy was in England she bore him a son, who died shortly after birth. In the scandal that followed, Alexander Menken denounced her and then *did* divorce her. Heenan, on his return from England, repudiated his marriage and, with sanctimonious hypocrisy, denounced her as well. And just at this point, Adah's mother died in New Orleans.

Adah Menken responded to the scandal with great spirit, writing to the newspapers to defend her own conduct and arraign Heenan's cravenness. The Benicia Boy got more than he had bargained for. But this period marked the lowest point in Adah's fortunes. She had no money, few friends, and no prospects. There was no reason to think her different from countless other women who had been similarly treated. But Adah Menken was different. She fought back. Having become embroiled in scandal, she meant to profit by it. She abandoned whatever ambition she may have had for a career as a serious dramatic actress and turned to theatrical melodrama, for which there was a voracious appetite in America. She had two great assets in this endeavor: her body and the fact that she was already something of a spectacle. She got financial backing and the advice and newspaper support of Robert H. Newell, who, under the name Orpheus C. Kerr, was one of America's best-known cracker-barrel folk humorists. His writing, dry and laconic but with a vein of wild frontier improbability about it, was much admired by Mark Twain. In June of 1861 Adah Menken opened in Albany, New York, in a dramatization based on Byron's poem *Mazeppa.* She was a scandalous sensation and awoke next day to find herself infamous.

The climax of *Mazeppa,* and the source of the scandal, was a scene in which she appeared naked — not actually so, for she wore very thin flesh-colored tights — and tied to the back of a horse that carried her round and round and up a mountainside. This was a very effective dramatic stroke and, making use as it did of a live horse, real ropes, and a series of rickety and precipitous platforms, it involved her in genuine physical danger. Men admired her pluckiness as well as her erotic charms. This trumpery, *Mazeppa,* established Adah Menken's name in the public's mind. She was advertised as "the naked lady" and "the most perfectly developed woman in the world."

Striking while the scandal was hot, Adah Menken went to San

Francisco in the fall of 1863 and repeated her success there, on the stage and at the box office. Newell went with her; they had been married the year before. He encouraged Adah's literary aspirations, but he and Adah were personally incompatible and had quarreled bitterly within a week of their marriage. Newell was shy, retiring, and, like many humorists, rather morose-natured. Menken's reputation as a poet had preceded her to San Francisco, and there she became the center of another literary circle, this one including Bret Harte, Joaquin Miller, and Mark Twain. While in San Francisco, Adah Menken wrote a short essay for the *Golden Era,* the California literary paper. We will return to this later in the chapter.

In 1864 she left for England, without Newell but with a new man, Captain James Berkley. A young American admirer, Edwin James, who served as Menken's secretary, confidant, and publicist, preceded her to England, preparing the way. She opened in *Mazeppa,* of course, and the publicity, the horse, and the flesh-colored tights did the rest. Success at the box office was again paralleled by success in befriending literary men, including Dickens, Charles Reade, Swinburne, and Dante Gabriel Rosetti.

Increasingly restless and extravagant, Adah Menken returned to the United States in 1865 and divorced Newell. She lived in New York City with Captain Berkley: more scandal, more publicity, many quarrels. She married Berkley in August of 1866, perhaps only to legitimize her expected child, for she was pregnant; then she abruptly left New York. Berkley returned to California. Adah Menken went to Paris.

Once again, in defiance of the odds, she triumphed. In a play called *The Pirates of the Savannah* she scored the greatest success achieved up to that time by an American actress in the French theater. Napoleon III came to see her. Admirers showered her with gifts and propositions, and she was taken up by yet another literary set, this one revolving around the elder Dumas and George Sand (the latter was godmother of the son born to Menken in Paris in November of 1867). Adah then repeated the same piece, with equal success, in Vienna. In the winter of 1868 she went back to London but found it difficult to recapture her earlier notoriety. She was "generally broken down," according to Edwin James, and was known to be losing her figure. She made a last appearance on the stage at her own benefit performance in London, in May of 1868, then returned to Paris to make one last try at the theater. It was too late. Alone and penniless, she died in Paris on August 10,

1868, attended by a rabbi, a Hebrew testament under her pillow. A stage horse, covered in black, preceded her coffin through the streets of Paris to Père la Chaise cemetery. There were fourteen people at the funeral.

Edwin James tried to raise money to have her remains moved to the then more fashionable Mont Parnasse cemetery and to have a marker erected. None of Adah's sporting and literary acquaintances, lovers and friends in three nations contributed anything. "Neither Dumas nor Swinburne nor any of the thousands of leeches who drank her champagne and reveled in her society and manifold charms knew her in death," James wrote bitterly. James contributed the bulk of the money, with the rest coming from the sporting Captain Berkley in California. In 1869 a stone marker was raised over a new grave in Mont Parnasse; on one side was her name and on the other the gnomic phrase "Thou knowest." James also saw to the publication of a volume of Adah Menken's poems, something she had always talked about and hoped to arrange. The week after her death the book appeared, dedicated to Charles Dickens and entitled *Infelicia*.

*

Adah Menken unquestionably belonged to the American theatrical sporting culture of the 1840s and 1850s, a culture in which she grew up and whose values she absorbed, although the exotic scandal of her life tended to obscure this. She continued the self-dramatizing and flamboyant romantic strain of Henry Herbert, with whose life her own had much in common: both lives were characterized by restlessness, expatriation, wild fluctuations of mood, a longing for death, and a chronic sense of unhappiness. In Adah Menken this merged with something else that was in the broadest sense a sporting style — the reckless life of the aristocrat contemptuous of conventional opinion. She explained her extravagance to Ed James: "Ed, when I get so that I have to borrow, I want to die."[43]

She combined this extravagance with a less obvious kind of sportiness — a cool and sophisticated understanding of herself and her position in the world. Her grand gestures often turned out to have been carefully calculated and rehearsed. She was a gamesman of the first order. Her career was a trick played on society, an illusion, like those flesh-colored tights, which, in the overheated imaginations of her male admirers, seemed not to be there. As audacious a gambler as Ten Broeck, she was almost P. T. Barnum's equal in using publicity. In fact, her entire life — a series of yarns and stories, a succession of improbable events that may have been true, and true happenings that seemed improbable — had the quality of a tall tale adapted to the urban theatrical world.

Unlike most romantics (and very unlike Henry Herbert in this respect) she had a considerable sense of humor about herself. She mingled passion and detachment to an extraordinary degree. She had a good time spending her money and enjoyed playing with the common symbols of success and culture. In England she referred to herself as the "Royal Bengal Tiger," hired a coach with liveried driver and footmen, and adopted a crest — a horse's head surmounting four aces. When she was in New York with Captain Berkley, they lived in a Seventh Avenue brownstone she called Bleak House, in honor of her friend Dickens but also hinting at her life with the captain. Like so many others who have been raved over by the public, she developed an enormous contempt for popular taste. Born and raised in the South, she went to dangerous lengths to make clear her sympathy with the Confederacy. In the North she decorated her rooms with Confederate flags.

From the time of Adah Menken's first production of *Mazeppa*, her courage and earthy high spirits appealed to men. She understood her limits as an actress; her line was liveliness and spontaneity. Americans continually described her as an "original," suggesting that some new kind of talent had been revealed, while Europeans could easily translate her into the familiar image of the New World child of nature.

Still, her primary appeal was sexual. Few things are more evanescent than the past's notion of charm or sexual appeal. Adah's plump roundness seems laughable today. Was this the figure that drove ten thousand horsemen frantic? Indeed it was. She was woman as temptress, the dark-haired Mediterranean symbol of sexual desire, contrasted with the blonde image of purity, who appeared throughout American culture, in the works of major writers like Fenimore Cooper and Nathaniel Hawthorne, and also in those of minor ones, like Henry William Herbert.

Adah Menken's sexual appeal had another quality as well. It had a sense of playfulness. She was erotic but not dangerous. From the first, her appeal lent itself to jokes: her line as an actress, it was said, was not a clothes line; or, she was a handful as well as an armful. The jokes were tributes to her spirited combativeness, and they no doubt betrayed a certain degree of male nervousness; but mainly they suggested that she didn't pose the threat of an uncontrollable sexual conflagration. Adah's sexuality, although exotic in its settings, was domestic in its tone. With her, it seemed, men could abandon their exhausting masculine role-playing and speak honestly, unaffectedly, man to man.[44] What American sportsmen wanted, despite all their leering, winking, and joking, was not a bedmate but a playmate — someone who understood their lingo, someone who could be a friend. Adah Menken had a quality that has reappeared frequently in American life since then: the quality not of a Bengal tiger but of a good guy, a pal. Adah, old sport!

*

Adah Menken developed the idea of women as the sporting companions of men in the essay she wrote in 1863 for the *San Francisco Golden Era*. The piece was entitled "Swimming Against the Current," and in it she tried to locate herself as an American writer of her time.[45] Very short and overwrought, it is nonetheless a moving personal statement and a serious challenge to the culture of democratic equality.

Adah Menken's basic theme was the irreconcilable conflict between a few special individuals, "God's children of inspiration," and the plodding masses. Her controlling metaphor was that of the person of superior talents, the athlete, who swims against the tide, braving the "roaring storm of anyone who challenges the majority." Such an individual could be explained by no tradition. His appearance, Adah insisted, was mysterious. Yet even such a hero suffered moments of weakness when he looked downstream and saw thousands of

> boats moving smoothly with the current, and rocking softly the rich, gay, happy, and successful passengers. He hesitates. "Shall I join them? Shall I blot out God's voice that calls me," he asks? No, he cannot resist that holy voice. Onward is his course — he must swim again.

Most people were not strong enough, and they perished, "poisoned with disappointment, insult or ridicule by an ungrateful people — poor Edgar A. Poe, for example."

One hero had swum against the current and survived, however — Walt Whitman, "the American philosopher who is centuries ahead of his contemporaries." Whitman survived but was ignored.

> He is too far ahead of his contemporaries; they cannot comprehend him yet; he swims against the stream, and finds no company. The passengers,

in their floating boats, call him a fanatic, a visionary, a demagogue, a good-natured fool, etc. Still, he heeds them not.

Someday, Adah Menken believed, marble markers would be erected over the graves of such heroes.

Adah Menken's detractors ridiculed her artistic pretensions and ignored her verse. Interest in her, then and later, concentrated on the scandalous aspects of her theatrical reputation. In fact, she was a woman of independent views who derived her ideas from her own experience and who held on to them in the face of the full weight of respectable disapproval. After all, she had the insight, unlike more balanced contemporaries, to respond to Walt Whitman's voice and to something else as well, something that marks her out as the most original of the sporting figures of Jacksonian America — Whitman's vision of a different kind of manliness.

One of Walt Whitman's most cherished images was that of a future in which America would be populated by a race of "freedom's athletes," individuals whose lives would be marked by a quality of "brave delight." Men and women would play and work together, unashamed of their bodies, unafraid of innovation, unconfined by convention and the past. Walt Whitman said this incomparably better than Adah Menken could ever say it:

> I am the teacher of athletes,
> He that by me spreads a wider breast than my own proves the
>   width of my own
> . . . .
> The boy I love, the same becomes a man not through derived
>   power, but in his own right,
> Wicked rather than virtuous out of conformity or fear,
> . . . .
> First-rate to ride, to fight, to hit the bull's eye, to sail a skiff, to
>   sing a song or play the banjo.[46]

But then Whitman said it incomparably better than anyone else could either. And Adah Menken did more than simply say it or write it — she tried to live it.

The athlete Adah Menken actually loved was hardly what Whitman had in mind: handsome but small-minded, he was shocked by Adah's shamelessness. So were most of her contemporaries. But no matter. Almost three quarters of the way through the nineteenth century, Adah Menken, in a roundabout way, testified to the continuing power of the old Jacksonian yearning for a new kind of sporting life. Her vision of true manliness as complete freedom from convention went back to Whitman; and beyond him to Emerson, who was Whitman's inspiration and who wished to sweep away all the inherited forms:

> Why need we copy the Doric or the Gothic model? Beauty, convenience, grandeur of thought and quaint expression are as near to us as to any, and if the American artist will study with hope and love the precise thing to be done by him, considering the climate, the soil, the length of the day, the wants of the people, he will create a house in which all these will find themselves fitted.[47]

Beyond Emerson, we return to that Jacksonian hope, naive but noble, that America would build a new house of culture in which ordinary people could become heroes, and heroes could find a home.

PART III

LOOKING BACK AND LOOKING FORWARD

Hiram Woodruff

9

Hiram Woodruff:
Wait and Win

JOHN GREENLEAF WHITTIER'S *Snow-Bound* was published in 1866. It was an instantaneous success, reached a vast popular audience, and established Whittier's reputation, for a time, as America's most beloved poet of everyday life. Once so widely familiar that it was unnecessary to summarize its story for the average reader, *Snow-Bound* has in the twentieth century somehow become a childhood classic that is unread by adults, ignored in university courses on American literature, or dismissed, when not ignored, as treacly sentiment. Yet it is not naive. It contains a shrewd analysis of America's cultural situation in the middle of the nineteenth century.

Snow-Bound is a poem about transformation. It begins with the furious "roar of Ocean on his wintry shore" and with the all-obliterating snowstorm that changes daylight into darkness,

> The gray day darkened into night,
> A night made hoary with the swarm
> And whirl-dance of the blinding storm . . .

a darkness finally giving way to an external world changed almost beyond recognition:

> We looked upon a world unknown,
> Or nothing we could call our own.
> No cloud above, no earth below —
> A universe of sky and snow!

Familiar, prosaic New England has been changed into a wonderland of poetic fantasy: corncribs turned into domes and towers, a bridle post transformed into an old man with a high cocked hat.

Of course the familiar world is still there, beneath the blanket of white. A semblance of the old order is restored by clearing a path, feeding the animals, and gathering firewood. Then night falls, the storm rages again. The focus of the poem shifts to the family sheltering safely within its farmhouse: a fire roars in the fireplace, cider simmers on the grate, and the dog and cat are curled up near the hearth. Whittier's poem is more than a description of a household enclosed and threatened from without; it is a celebration of the family sustained from within by the resources of its traditions: the family *as* the world.

As is the case with all poetry genuinely rooted in folk culture, there was no need for Whittier to make up his characters. The stories within the story of his poem present only familiar types: pioneer father and mother; spinster aunt; unmarried older sister, innocent younger one. There is also the uncle, a countryman of a most ancient type, the unlettered master of folkcraft and nature lore, who,

> . . . innocent of books
> Was rich in lore of fields and brooks,
> In moons and tides and weather wise,
> He reads the clouds as prophecies,
> And foul or fair could well divine,
> By many an occult hint and sign,
> Holding the cunning-worded keys
> To all the woodcraft mysteries.

Another person shared the family hearth those snow-bound nights. Though not a member of the family, he is the central figure of this Yankee tale:

> Brisk wielder of the birch and rule
> The master of the district school.

Unlike those dour, harsh masters the Porters and Ten Broeck writhed under, this schoolmaster exemplified the playful side of Yankee culture, while still retaining the celebrated Yankee versatility:

> Could doff at ease his scholar's gown
> To peddle wares from town to town
> Or through the long vacation's reach
> In lonely lowland districts teach . . .
> The moonlit skater's keen delight,

> The sleigh-drive through the frosty night,
> Happy the snow-locked homes wherein
> He tuned his merry violin,
> Or played the athlete in the barn
> Or held the good dame's winding-yarn.

A transmitter of traditional learning, which he had got in "classic Dartmouth's halls," he managed somehow to warm the chill foreignness of the classics so that the "mirth provoking legends" of Greece and Rome came to have "all the common-place of home." Even the darker side of the European tradition, represented by Puritan superstition and witchcraft and retold in Whittier's time in Nathaniel Hawthorne's tales, was brightened and its mystery drained away. With a kind of Emersonian magic, the schoolmaster managed to turn the European past into something natively American.

> Little seemed at best the odds
> Twixt Yankee pedlars and old gods . . .
> And dread Olympus at his will
> Became a huckleberry hill.

Whittier's poem reflects the countrified world into which he had been born on December 17, 1807, in Haverhill, Massachusetts; and most of his readers still identified themselves with this world in 1866. Theirs was a pious, native culture suspicious of all things foreign. Not surprising, then, that its favorite sport was the most American of the sports of Jacksonian America — trotting. The people who read Whittier's poem were the same people who watched Hiram Woodruff's trotters race.

*

Hiram Woodruff's *The Trotting Horse of America: How to Train and Drive Him; with Reminiscences of the Trotting Turf* appeared in 1868. As its author was not "a ready penman," *The Trotting Horse* was one of the first examples of a kind of sportswriting that would subsequently become quite popular, the ghostwritten life.[1] In this case, the "ghost" who edited the book and added a biographical sketch of Hiram Woodruff was Charles J. Foster, an important sporting figure of the time and the man who succeeded William T. Porter as editor of the *Spirit of the Times*. Foster thought up the idea of the book and persuaded Woodruff to tell his story. Initial chapters appeared in the *Spirit* and were so enthusiastically received that Woodruff went on with it, setting down a lifetime's experience and knowledge of horses. The book was both a handbook about trotting horses — how to train them, treat them, and drive them — and an unassuming history of trotting in America in the nineteenth century that concentrated on the celebrated trotting horses of the time, most of which Woodruff had ridden and driven.

Reticent about himself, Hiram Woodruff wrote almost nothing about his boyhood and his family, and, regrettable as this was in one way, it was entirely appropriate in another, for his ideas about horses were the most important things he had to talk about. These ideas are what make the book more than a curiosity now. Although Hiram Woodruff never saw *The Trotting Horse* in book form — he died before it was put in its final shape and sent to the printer — he had given Foster instructions about what to select from newspaper material. The result was a volume that reflects his personality as well as his ideas.

Hiram Washington Woodruff was born on February 22, 1817, in the hamlet of Birmingham, in Huntington County, New Jersey, one of the sporting counties where Frank Forester had roamed. He was the second of four children in a family of horsemen. His family had none of the social pretensions sometimes associated with the term *horseman*, however. Quite the contrary. Later on, when Hiram had become famous, the equalitarian conventions of Jacksonian democracy required that the humbleness of his origins be suitably exaggerated; so it was hinted that he had been born in a stable (although not a log stable). Actually, the Woodruffs were neither rich nor poor; they were solidly established farmers, horsemen, and businessmen. Hiram's father was a successful trainer, who had built up a stable of his own horses and was the proprietor of several racetracks. His Uncle George was a notable rider and driver of trotters. Two of his brothers were also associated with horses. Hiram had almost no formal education; the stable and track were his schools. For a while it was intended that he learn a trade, perhaps become a hatter, but nothing came of that. From the time he was a little boy all he cared about was horses.

Hiram was precocious. Taught by Uncle George, the diminutive lad started handling horses in trial heats by the time he was ten. In 1831, at fourteen, he rode in his first race for money, and won. At sixteen, he rode in an important match race before a large crowd at the Union Course, and won again. In those days trotters ran long distances and, if they ran in harness, pulled heavy wagons. Riding and driving, but especially driving, demanded strength and stamina, and Hiram, although small, was remarkably lithe and strong, with the "constancy and courage of a bull-dog of true English breed."[2] For all his precocity, however, he wasn't pushed too quickly but was allowed patiently to learn the necessary skills of his craft and to gain experience in all phases of trotting, so that when he eventually established himself as the leading driver in the country, his reputation was solidly built and he maintained his predominance, although often challenged, throughout more than thirty years of active racing life. Hiram lived his motto, "wait and win."

In the history of American sport few performers have ever dominated their rivals to the extent that Hiram Woodruff dominated his. He raced throughout the East, in New England and the Middle Atlantic states, and also in the newer trotting states of the West. But he was not only a rider and driver. He bred and trained horses and for five years struggled, in Massachusetts and in New York, at the difficult job of racetrack proprietor. Only once did he try work unconnected with racing, living briefly in New York City, where he was a partner in a Broadway saloon. But he didn't like the work, and city life wasn't at all to his taste. He eventually settled on Long Island in 1851 and lived there the rest of his life, dying in March, 1867, just three weeks after his fiftieth birthday.

An uneventful life, except for the trotting. Yet that was enough to make him famous and admired by millions. *The Trotting Horse* went through at least nineteen editions after his death and was translated into German. His editor wasn't exaggerating when he wrote that "all over the country there was not a man in America, except perhaps General Grant, esteemed by a greater number of people."[3] This indicates the affection in which Hiram Woodruff was held and also the extent to which trotting had entrenched itself in the interest and loyalty of the people. To understand how that came about we must turn back to a period earlier than any discussed in the pages of Hiram Woodruff's book, and explore the origins of trotting as an American sport.

*

In colonial America, saddle horses were numerous and readily available. The trotting horse, a specialized version of the saddle horse, was as common and widespread as the saddle horse. No one bothered about bloodlines when it came to saddle horses; performance alone counted, not pedigree. England had long bred a fine stock of saddle horses, and for many decades these were shipped to North America. Any enterprising American horseman wanted to breed his horses to them, but such breeding was haphazard and indiscriminate. No one section of the country could claim to be the birthplace of the saddle horse, nor could any claim a monopoly on quality. From time to time, however, one area might achieve a higher reputation for its stock. Early on, Rhode Island developed a breed of large strong horses commonly acknowledged as the best in America for saddle work and for riding — the once-famous Narraganset pacers. Southerners and northerners alike prized them for their dependability.

Most work with horses was done in the saddle. America was not yet a culture of wheeled vehicles. Roads and paths were too rough and too few and far between. Men carried what they could in saddlebags, and horses were often very heavily and ingeniously loaded. Heavier and more cumbersome goods were sent by boat, or hauled by oxen or by teams of lumbering dray horses. Thus, although the horse remained, as it had through the ages, the symbol of speed and mobility, qualities summed up in the racer, people also associated it with labor. Though lyric poetry hovered about the thoroughbred, the trotter was entirely prosaic. In America in the early nineteenth century, such an association elicited great respect. The trotter was a regular fellow.

The standard gait for the saddle horse was the "pace" (or "amble," as it was called in Britain), right and left pairs of legs moving together in a series of alternating, parallel movements. For a rider in the saddle this was a comfortable glide that didn't tire either horse or rider too much. The contrary gait, the "trot," was a crosswise motion, with the foreleg on one side and the hind leg on the other moving together. For the rider, this vertical motion was vigorous and jerky. Saddle horses seemed to fall naturally into both types of gait, and most could be trained to do either, although some resisted any change in their original, natural pace. Through most of the eighteenth century, natural pacers were everywhere most highly valued.

In Great Britain in the late eighteenth century, however, the role of the saddle horse changed decisively. Roads were improved, and an irresistible movement from the saddle to wheeled vehicles resulted. The horse was put in harness, and British riders became drivers. Vehicular speed became the main objective, and the highways of Britain were soon dotted with speed maniacs. Vehicles were made much lighter. The British built a whole series of wagons and carriages — curricles, phaetons, and coaches — designed to go faster and faster. The end result was the light and graceful gig, which, with a fast horse to pull it, "has been the best friend to doctors and undertakers they ever found."[4]

When pulling a vehicle in harness, the saddle horse not only lost its saddle but also had to change its gait. On harder manmade or improved surfaces, the ambling pace, pulling from side to side, gave a rough rocking motion that made the occupants of a vehicle feel in danger of being pulled to pieces. The rhythmic, pistonlike trotting motion, it turned out, was much better for driving, smoother for the passengers, and more endurable for the horses as well. By the end of the eighteenth century, few pacers remained on British roads.

Trotting also lent itself to racing, whether the rider was on horseback or rode in a vehicle. This kind of racing enjoyed only modest popularity in Britain. Perhaps it didn't gain more favor because, although it was a venerable sport and various forms of it were popular on the Continent, it had not been practiced in Britain for a long time. More important, trotting could never rival the established position of thoroughbred racing as the sport of the aristocracy and therefore the sport emulated by the British middle class. By contrast, trotting enjoyed many advantages as an American sport. Americans didn't have to start from scratch, since there was a British tradition, but this wasn't an imperious tradition demanding that it be copied whole. There was no spell to be broken. In America it was the thoroughbred that seemed a bit exotic and, because of its aristocratic pretensions, troublesome to assimilate.

The Revolutionary War stimulated the use of wheeled vehicles in America and, by interrupting the importation of English breeding stock, forced American horsemen to concentrate on improving what they already had on hand. The war also had subtler long-range effects. The growing interest in the sporting possibilities of saddle horses coincided with the beginnings of national independence. Like so many other activities in this early period of fervent cultural nationalism, trotting gained much of its flavor and favor from the feeling that it was independently American. Trotting was marked by unassuming self-confidence among its adherents. The absence of strident jingoism in trotting circles is the most impressive evidence of how thoroughly it had grown up with the country. By the 1820s it was widely acknowledged, in the United States and Britain, that American trotters were equal to any in the world, probably superior, and still improving. As a result, there was relatively little transatlantic rivalry.

Material conditions fostered its growth. The saddle horse was everyman's horse. Wealthy persons could indulge themselves with fancy stables and equipment if they wished, but ordinary trotters and their simple wagons and carts could compete on equal terms. And in these early years trotting didn't require special racetracks of its own. Its tracks were everyone's — a street or lane in any village or town, or in the countryside. It took place everywhere and went on throughout the year. In winter, horses were sharp-shod and sleighs took the place of wagons. Then main streets and country roads were the setting for one of the most delightful forms of sporting amusement, and the countryside echoed to that memorable sound of pleasure, the music of sleigh bells. Trotting appealed to women, for many of them were expert drivers and could care for, train, and drive horses as well as any man. Racing arrangements were simple: trotting didn't distinguish between owner, trainer, and rider. The more formal occasions for racing were not yet separate events but were part of everyday life: county fairs, militia days, election days, camp meetings.

"The harness horse is the democratic horse," ran the trotting adage, and the atmosphere surrounding the sport confirmed it. Possessed of none of the high-strung overrefinement of the thoroughbred, the trotting horse was a no-nonsense animal, strong, not at all neurotic. And its morals were pure. Not associated with formal meetings and matches, it was less publicly connected with gambling. When the revulsion against the corruption of thoroughbred racing swept the northern and middle states in the first decade of the nineteenth century, resulting in the prohibition of thoroughbred racing in many states, trotting neatly filled the vacuum. It didn't interest aristocrats, but it suited gentlemen very well, and in the 1830s Henry Herbert was already proclaiming it as the ideal amusement for urban gents. "There is scarce a gentleman in New York who does not own one or two fast horses," he wrote.[5] Virtuous and hard-working, the trotter was the middle-class sporting animal incarnate, a perfect symbol for the simplicity of the early Republic.

*

Trotting as a sport expanded greatly in the 1820s. Frontier conditions gave way to a more settled society. Roads were improved and cut through new areas, and wheeled traffic increased enormously in volume. Training devices were invented to turn pacers into trotters. The growing network of canals absorbed more of the business of hauling goods, releasing horses for lighter work in harness. Throughout the land there was a greater sense of lightness, of release of energy, of shaking off the past, and the perfect symbolic expression of this was the breakdown of the old-fashioned vehicle in Oliver Wendell Holmes's enormously popular poem, "The One-Hoss Shay," which suggested that cumbersome creeds and customs would not withstand the challenge of this new age of speed.

Knowledge of wheeled locomotion was rather rudimentary, but Americans learned by trial and error. Greater speed resulted from improved equipment. Trotters pulled two kinds of vehicles, four-wheeled wagons and two-wheeled carts. Experiments showed that, however ungainly it looked, a large-circumference wheel and a high-placed load lessened the strain on the vehicle and minimized vibration. In 1804 a design for hanging the carriage body on elliptical springs was developed; and this made riding over cobblestones much gentler. Although these developments could be applied to both two-wheeled and four-wheeled vehicles, the two-wheeled carts had greater maneuverability and speed for racing, and it was on these that designers concentrated their efforts. At the beginning of the nineteenth century such a cart might well weigh two hundred pounds. Every effort was bent toward making these carts — sulkies as they came to be called — lighter. Heavier woods and iron were replaced by American ash and hickory, tough-fibered but light. All extraneous decoration was removed. By the late 1820s Americans had developed a stripped-down sulky, weighing 108 pounds, that was not elegant by conventional standards but was so delicately balanced that it could be set going by the slightest touch.

In 1829 the American trotter Tom Thumb was taken to England and dazzled everyone with his speed and endurance, trotting one hundred miles on Sudbury Common before a large crowd. The English were as interested in what he pulled as in how quickly he pulled it. Stimulated by increasing racing competition, Americans proceeded to push their ideas further. In the 1830s sulkies were made that weighed ninety-five pounds. Soon weight was reduced to eighty-two and, by the end of the decade, to sixty-eight pounds. In these vehicles, as in their nobler contemporaries, the clipper ships, form was strictly adapted to function. We have already seen that Horatio Greenough admired the *America* and the trotter equally as examples of functional design. His praise might well have been provoked by the sight of the trotter Ripton and its new sulky in 1844 — "the lightest, strongest, and handsomest ever." He would surely have delighted in the words of an anonymous observer:

> Though light as a feather, it is made of such excellent materials as to be capable of carrying two persons without straining. Its spokes are so thin, long and numerous, and its body so fragile and light, that it looks for all the world like an over-grown Daddy Long Legs, or a gigantic spider.[6]

Speed became the standard by which trotting horses were measured. Trotting races were usually of three to five miles in length, with three to five heats in each race, and remarkable feats of endurance were much admired. But very early on, the mile was established as the standard length for trotting races. And for the mile, three minutes was the index of speed.

In 1810 a New England horse known only as The Boston Horse trotted a mile, pulling a sulky, in 2:48½. This seemed so remarkable that many horsemen refused to believe it. In 1818 a group of skeptical New Yorkers arranged a race in which another New England speedster, Boston Blue, trotted a mile in under three minutes (the record of the exact time has been lost). This horse was thought to be so sensational that he was later sent to England, where, as "the slate-colored American," he was matched against the best trotters there. By the end of the 1820s, 2:30 had become the insurmountable barrier, and it resisted all assaults throughout the 1830s. In 1839, Dutchman, with Hiram Woodruff driving, ran three miles, against the clock, in 7:32½, doing the middle mile in 2:28; so Dutchman was the first under-2:30 trotter. But no horse had yet done a single mile in under two-and-a-half minutes, and some observers insisted that such speed was beyond the physical capacity of any trotting horse. Then, in 1843, Lady Suffolk, just beginning her splendid career, smashed the record to smithereens with a 2:28½ clocking. Once the barrier was broken, new records were continually established: Lady Suffolk moved it down to 2:26 in 1849, Tacony lowered it in 1853, and other horses reduced it still further, until, in 1866, still in Hiram Woodruff's lifetime, Dexter, the fastest trotter of his day, lowered the record to 2:18.

Trotting became a popular spectator sport. Tracks had to be built to accommodate the city people who wished to watch their favorites run. In 1823 trotting was introduced at the Union Course on Long Island; and after that many tracks were built throughout the country. These had the same shape as tracks for thoroughbred racers, but had rounded corners and smoother turns for the sulkies to get around. There was also a rapid improvement in training and handling, and in equipment. Famous trotters attracted fans who knew little about horses. More money began to be given for purses, and this produced gambling and trickery. The informal innocence of its early years passed away as trotting came of age. Hiram Woodruff grew up with, and dominated, this golden age of expansion. And so we return to him, his book, and his story.

*

Square-faced, firm-jawed, blunt-talking, "intolerant of quackery in any shape," Hiram Woodruff reminds one of his almost exact contemporary, Henry David Thoreau (1817–1864). The best of the writing in *The Trotting Horse* conveys a little of Thoreau's country terseness. On Lady Suffolk: "She hung on to the last stride, like a dog to a root"; on longevity in horses: "I don't mean vegetating about, half dead at the root and rotten at the trunk"; and on men's passion for horses: "so strong as almost to pass into insanity."[7]

The practical wisdom in Woodruff's pages was based on empirical observation. He described his book as "a guide and fingerpost, showing the way to practical experience, rather than a substitute for experience itself." And he insisted, on the basis of a lifetime's observation, that there could be no one general rule about horses: "Any man who pretends to lay down fixed rules . . . is either a fool or an impostor, and very likely both." Woodruff's personal judgments were firm but undogmatic: "If I had had less to do with [horses] for nearly forty years, I might be more positive in my assertions."[8] The life of the horseman was based on experience and not on logic.

That experience was as wide-ranging as anyone's. Hiram Woodruff had become a major figure in the trotting world when a decade still remained in Colonel Johnson's Napoleonic career. Hiram's career almost exactly overlapped Richard Ten Broeck's greatest days. Yet there were important differences between his style and values and theirs. In Woodruff's career there was nothing of the gamesmanship and gambling strategies of those two great thoroughbred entrepreneurs. They moved in the great world, while his world was parochial: "He was open and frank as a child: he could not even think a rascality: and rascals as well as honest men knew it."[9] Hiram Woodruff struck his contemporaries as being naturally good. This was not something they were used to, which may account for the air of surprise apparent in most references to him. He was not the least bit sanctimonious; he understood the roughness of the people he worked with, the stable and saloon atmosphere of their lives. And he was no prude: he was affable and liked a drink after a day's racing. Ordinary people liked his tolerance of others, but it was his uncomplicated ideas about sporting honesty that earned him their deepest admiration.

Between the lines of Hiram Woodruff's matter-of-fact book there is a tone of deep despondency. The frequency of cheating and trickery in racing is revealed in the offhand way Woodruff noted that simple honesty had become unusual. It was apparent in his dead-panned praise of the driver Horace Jones, who, according to Woodruff, "never threw a race, in my judgment." Ordinary honesty shone out like a beacon in a time when owners bet against themselves, trainers disguised the condition of their horses, and drivers "pulled" their nags. Trickery in regard to racing time was a province all its own. And if the clocks were not fixed, the timers bribed, or the records faked, there were other things that could be done. Prudent buyers of trotters, who often paid fancy prices based on time trials they watched and clocked themselves, were well advised to carry their own surveyor's chains in order to measure the length of the track, because that might well have been altered. Even P. T. Barnum would have been impressed by such audacity.

Hiram Woodruff understood all this, and he understood the underlying problem: good men didn't take any responsibility. He spoke from the point of view of a proprietor who had to struggle with the problem:

> The best way to discourage rioting and roguery upon our race-courses is to take care that the guilty shall never secure their sole object, the plunder. As long as they are permitted to get and hold the money, they will care but little for what people say to them in the newspapers or otherwise.[10]

Woodruff knew intuitively what Barnum converted into a principle of behavior: that being notorious could pay off. There was no point in lecturing the rascals, as William Porter was apt to do in his newspaper. Hold up the purses! Declare a no-contest! Keep the rascals from the plunder!

This rarely happened. Too much money was involved. Crookedness and weakness were not limited to the lower classes of horsemen, or to the marginal racing establishments. At the Suffolk Park Course in New York, one of the best, a famous series of contests between Flora Temple and George M. Patchen, Jr., held before enormous crowds, resulted in rowdiness and scandal. George Patchen was the underdog in the betting. In one heat, just as he was about to overtake Flora Temple, a crowd of men rushed out onto the track and, waving hats and clubs, distracted Patchen, in order to protect their bets. Nonetheless, Flora Temple was declared the winner.

The rowdiness and the outright cheating weren't the only problems. Trotting's growing popularity brought with it difficulties and temptations of other kinds. In the last dozen years of Hiram Woodruff's life, there developed a popular form of trotting called "hippodroming." Two or more trotters traveled together from track to track, running in what were advertised as races. Were they races? There was nothing at stake to encourage one or the other to try to win: the drivers and owners simply divided the profits, whoever won. But these events were promoted as races and not simply exhibitions. This was that happy hunting ground for gamesmen that lay somewhere between conventional sport and outright deceit. Hippodroming was popular at small-time exhibitions and county fairs, but famous trotters, owned by supposedly reputable men, were also involved. Many people maintained that these exhibitions were only what they seemed to be; and as for that, spectator beware.

*

If Hiram Woodruff represented the older idea of the sportsman, James Eoff represented the newer gamesman. Woodruff described Eoff as "a very able trainer and driver," adding bluntly that Eoff was "generally thought to be as hardy and unscrupulous as any man in our profession." Eoff was "a great master of humbug," of enveloping a horse with so much mystery and speculation that people were prepared to believe anything he said about it.[11]

Eoff's handling of Princess was a classic example of his techniques. In California he picked up a mare called Topsy, a horse of unusual beauty but of undetermined racing quality, who up to that time had had little success. Eoff renamed her Princess, trained her brilliantly, and won matches for large sums of money. He then brought her east in a blaze of publicity and dollar signs. Eoff was a shrewd judge of horses, and Princess did have great potential. Woodruff always thought her slightly overrated, but it was difficult to say how good Princess was, or could have been, because she was rarely run in a straightforward way. Eoff, her owner, trainer, and driver, was free to do as he wished; and he was always up to something with her.

Princess, the new wonder horse, attracted enormous attention; so much so that the owner of Flora Temple grew unnecessarily apprehensive and agreed to a match on the basis of a private deal, agreed to ahead of time, for the division of the gate money. So an element of ambiguity, of hippodroming, was present from the very start. The publicity about Princess's fabulous California performances (and winnings) was effective. A huge crowd showed up for the race against Flora Temple, and surprisingly large amounts of money were bet on what was, after all, an unproven horse.

The actual results of the race were less noteworthy than the atmosphere of gamesmanship surrounding every aspect of it. Flora Temple won the first heat, but it was insinuated around the track, probably by Eoff himself, that Eoff would not let Princess win. This satisfied the spectators' desire to pretend they had inside information denied others. It also credited Eoff with power he didn't in fact have. Even a defeat didn't mean what it seemed to mean. The focus of concern shifted from the horses to the men involved. In the second heat Flora Temple "broke" and ran badly but still won. Many people maintained, with considerable plausibility, that Eoff had pulled his horse, but no one came forward to substantiate this charge. And this only fueled the opinion that Princess was unbeatable when allowed to be.

A week later the two horses met again, and the result caused a sensation. Princess won both heats handily. Hiram Woodruff insisted that the explanation was obvious: Flora had been overraced and was tired. But by this time few people cared for such a simple analysis. One race, in Woodruff's view, wasn't enough evidence upon which to decide anything. Wait and see.

The wisdom of this view was borne out when the inevitable rematch took place. Flora Temple was rested and ready. In a smashing performance, she won in straight heats, in terrific time, and clearly established her superiority. Or did she? A curious situation had been created by James Eoff's manipulation of mood and publicity. Victories by Flora Temple didn't convince the public of Princess's inferiority. "Many people yet believed that Eoff could win any race if he liked to do so," Woodruff wrote. He attempted to explain the irrationality of the betting public.

> It is often the case that when a trotter wins with great ease, especially if the one defeated is a famous one, a calculation is forthwith made in

which it is assumed, not that the loser was "off," but that the winner is greatly superior. This assumption is commonly erroneous.[12]

The difference between good horses, Hiram knew, was always slight. Superiority was established only in the long run of time, in the results of an entire career.

People didn't understand this because they wished to believe something else, something personified by James Eoff, who was tricky to the point of dishonesty, inscrutable and manipulative. James Eoff represented power — the power to control events. Human calculation was what determined things, not chance. Behind the façade of apparent surprises and upsets, the managerial master was firmly in control. However shabby Eoff's objectives, American sporting fans admired his manipulative skill, perhaps because of the hope it gave them that the disorder in their society was an illusion and that behind it lay some kind of deeper order.

Hiram Woodruff despised the James Eoffs of the sporting world, and his views on hippodroming were equally forthright. He didn't like it, never had anything to do with it, and criticized it in his book. The nature of his criticism was muted, however, by his live-and-let-live Jacksonian principles. He was too much one of the people to do more than register an individual protest.

> The people have sanctioned the system; and these exhibitions draw immense crowds all over the country from Maine to Missouri . . . If the people who pay for it, knowing what it is, are satisfied, I have neither the right nor the inclination to interfere.[13]

Barnum would have winked. Hiram Woodruff shrugged his shoulders. He was no reformer, but he was an honest man. Wasn't that enough?

*

The names of famous trotters became household words in homes where the names of poets or politicians were unknown. The horses' racing lives were turned into archetypal stories. There were a number of these: the rags-to-riches story; the story of the nation's sweetheart; and the story of the shooting meteor. Sporting heroes were usually young and vigorous, but every once in a while a hero appeared whose great achievement was to defy time. The story of such a hero is the Old Veteran's story, and in such a tale, talent, character, and beauty mattered less than longevity. In the Jacksonian years one story of this kind touched such profound springs of emotion that it became enshrined in American folklore and folksong.

LADY SUFFOLK

Once upon a time she was a young gray mare. In 1835 Dave Bryant saw her in a small Long Island town. She was a two-year-old, pulling an oyster wagon. He liked what he saw, so he bought her for $112.50 from the butcher who owned her, and rented her out to patrons of his stable. Someone, impressed by her gait, advised Bryant to race her, and he did, with fantastic results, results out of a fairy tale — which of course this was.

She started her racing career without any fuss. At five she ran against a bay gelding named Sam Patch, for a purse of eleven dollars, and won handily. Hiram Woodruff was the rider: "I liked the looks of the wiry little gray mare and knew she could trot a little." Gradually, she built a reputation. In the next five years she trotted against the best, winning and losing in equal proportion. People began to notice her remarkable endurance. She shirked no job, scamped no task, dodged no opponent. She had speed and she had character, but even more she had an unbendable spirit. When beaten she needed only a brief rest before she tried again. And she usually won the return matches.

The years rolled on. She got better as she got older. She ran in famous races against Beppo. In her lifetime she raced in 138 recorded match races, many of them four or five heats. She may have run in five hundred heats, all told. It wasn't until she was fifteen and had been racing ten years that she really hit her stride. She became the indomitable trotter of her time: "Hard as steel and tough as whalebone," said Hiram Woodruff. Up and down the land campaigned "the old gray mare."

Lady Suffolk was no hero to Dave Bryant; she was a money-making machine. Dave Bryant was hard and grasping. Only a fairly good driver, he was often clumsy and reckless. He raced the gray mare far too much, but she didn't seem to mind. In the days before railroads were common, the two of them traveled together over country roads, from track to track, the gray mare pulling her racing equipment behind her. She'd arrive at a track and race that same afternoon, then trot on in the evening to the site of the next race. Bryant's idea of training was simple: "he fed her and gave her plenty of work." And she thrived on it. The years rolled by and her rivals came up, were beaten and left behind, and then disappeared. But not the old gray mare.

In 1849 Lady Suffolk was sixteen. She trotted in twenty races that year and scored some of her greatest victories. She lowered the world's record for the mile to 2:26. When challenged by a new and formidable rival, Lady Moscow, Lady Suffolk took her on in a series of sensational races. Moscow fell. In 1850 people suddenly realized that there wasn't any horse like her — never had been and probably never would be. Her fame was at its peak. All America wanted to see her. Bryant took her on a tour of some of the newer cities — Buffalo, Cincinnati, St. Louis — then down the fabulous Mississippi to Mobile and New Orleans. It was the progress of a queen. At every stopping place crowds gathered. At seventeen, she was the wonder horse of endurance, as much a wonder as Jenny Lind, or as any of Barnum's curiosities. But now, for the first time, she began to falter. ("The old gray mare she ain't what she used to be . . .")

She was nineteen. Her speed was slackening. She was being beaten a bit more often, and soon a bit more often than that. As always, new horses — Mac, Pelham, Jack Rossiter, and Trustee — came at her, relentlessly challenging the champion. There can only be one champion. She was finding it harder. She was twenty and though she defied time, she couldn't defeat it. No one can. The glamour was going, the supremacy had gone. Out of the field a challenger came up much as the old lady had come up — Flora Temple:

a little rough-coated bay mare with black mane and legs and a black bobbed tail. She was the very devil to train — flighty, willfull; several owners tried and gave up. Her well-set neck, firm shoulders, fine head always tempted the unwary. And they always had to give up. Once, she sold for $13.00. A man saw her ambling along at the end of a cattle drove, bought her, and two weeks later sold her to George Perrin of New York City. He called in Hiram Woodruff as her rider. And miraculously she began to be trained: stopped mixing her gaits, stopped jumping in the air, changed her rippety-clippety stroke for one which came to be her trademark: clean, even, long, low, a locomotive stroke. And then she came with a rush and by '55 was at the top. She stirred the crowds, tough and cynical, in a special way; for at heart they were desperately sentimental. She was archly feminine, petite. Set off against the huge wagons and the larger, sturdier horses she seemed a cricket, a hummingbird. Men wept. The crowds went wild. *Flora!* No chance against that matchless piston-like, all conquering stroke. *Flora Temple!* The new Queen of the track.

LADY SUFFOLK AND LADY MOSCOW

And what were they saying about Lady Suffolk now?

> *The old gray mare she ain't what she used to be*
> *ain't what she used to be*
> *ain't what she used to be . . .*

The old lady was losing regularly. Very sad. In 1853 she raced only twice. She had stayed too long. The old gray mare had turned completely white. She should have quit while she was ahead. But you can't quit if you're not a quitter. She was twenty and had raced for fifteen years. Sporting crowds are sentimental. But they're also cruel and fickle. Now she was no longer a wonder of endurance: she was used up, worn out, a has-been. She retired in 1854. About time. The end of our story: "Thus is passed away from the turf to a resting place beneath it, an old familiar."

> *The old gray mare is dead.*

Folklore is one of the surest preservers of fame. But what was preserved here? Not the memory of the great champion. She was immortalized by song and remembered for her decline. Very few who sing *The Old Gray Mare* know that it refers to Lady Suffolk, the old gray mare of Long Island. So she's spared something. What *we* gain from this story is a piece of harsh folk wisdom: there's no fool like an old fool (and I don't mean Dave Bryant). Still, it's something. After all, who sings about Flora Temple?

*

As a driver, Hiram Woodruff was renowned for his superb sense of pace, his coolness under pressure, and his consistency. The fans put their money on Hiram, not on the horse. He was the first American rider to achieve that ultimate degree of eminence. "It's twenty to thirty percent in favor of any horse that Hiram Woodruff drives. I don't care who drives the other horse." So wrote Nathaniel Parker Willis, journalist, poet, editor, and one-time collaborator with Henry Herbert. Willis summed up what Hiram represented to his time in one brilliant sentence: "He is as fine a specimen of the open air man, born to a field open to all comers, as I have met in all my life."[14]

In bridging the gap between the 2:40 trotter, the best when he began racing, and Dexter's 2:18 at the end of his racing career, Hiram Woodruff personified change and progress. And, as he always insisted, there was still more change and more speed to come in the future. His racing records would be remorselessly obliterated, and he was content that this should be so. Admiration for the past could become stifling if carried too far. Much as he admired Dutchman's achievements, he felt that "it will not do to let it become a superstition with us."[15] No superstition in Hiram Woodruff, the open-air man. But was all change progress? About that Hiram Woodruff had his doubts.

In *The Trotting Horse* he put forward two ideas that challenged some of the most powerful assumptions of his culture. He counseled patience to an impatient people, attempting to cultivate in his readers an understanding of the slowness of true growth: "Nothing in nature comes to maturity early and lasts long."[16] He vehemently opposed the overtraining he saw all around. "Much speed without much work" was one of his adages, at a time when people made a fetish of hard work. Even worse, Woodruff believed, was the greedy eagerness to get results too quickly; for instance, to take two- and three-year-old horses, "in the sap and green of youth," and, with the aid of force-feeding and harsh discipline, to race them too soon and too often. Hiram Woodruff disagreed sharply with the toughness of methods like Andrew Jackson's. These might gain an individual a reputation for sternness, but they were bad for the horses and for everyone else. Given enough time, nature would perfect the "hardy enduring frame in her own cunning way."[17]

At this point we come to a remarkable flight of Hiram Woodruff's moral imagination: a questioning of the value of speed, the very thing that had brought about his own fame. Too much might be lost by overemphasizing speed, Hiram wrote. This applied to more than racing and horses: "I can remember when it took three times as long to tan a hide of sole-leather as it now does. The increased rapidity of the process is no doubt a gain to the tanner and shoemaker; but how is it with the people who wear out the boots?" Slow maturity was giving way to haste and waste. All around him, in the 1860s, he saw cheapness and shoddiness driving out quality, and he opposed this as eloquently as he could. Men should build and nurture slowly, "so that in the course of time — time that tries all — we shall earn a solid and enduring reputation — wait and win."[18]

Woodruff's second main idea put forth in *The Trotting Horse* came into even more conflict with a dominant value of the traditional American sporting style, then and today. Hiram Woodruff stressed the power of love. Of course he could be firm when necessary: "It don't answer to go to coddling with such a one," he wrote of an especially obstinate animal. And of another, he remarked: "He had to have something to wake him up, and let him know that real business was to be transacted." But Hiram was firm only when really necessary, and only as appropriate for the individual creature involved. He never used force to show how tough *he* was, and never beat animals as an indirect way of instilling fear in other human beings. Firmness, yes: but not the firmness of the whip. "The whip does more harm than good in a head-to-head struggle," he wrote. "Natural emulation incites the horse to do all he knows in such circumstances." And he concluded: "The business of the driver is to aid [the horse's] efforts and assist him, not by lathering away at him with the whip; which is no aid at all."[19]

Love the horse. Make it understand what you want. Hiram was one of those men who could talk to horses. As a boy he had loved horses, and he remained all his life a boy who loved them. They greeted him with whinnies of welcome when he walked through the stables. Between Hiram and his horses there was a mysterious feeling, "a kind of magnetic touch which the horse no sooner feels than he seems inspirited and animated with new life." He had a loving touch. People remembered the moments of speed but didn't understand that these had been prepared for by countless moments of gentle restraint and patient love.

The intimate association of horse and driver was the work of a lifetime. True judgment could not be called up out of nowhere, nor could it be "applied" as if it were an external device. It could only come from an inner discipline. As Hiram Woodruff wrote in praise of another driver, "His judgment is good at times when judgment is absolutely required, which is just when some people lose it." And then he added, slyly, "and, besides all that, he knows enough to wait until his time has come." Everything depended on the driver's mastery of himself: "Some men that have hold of horses don't know themselves, and therefore it is not to be wondered at that the horses don't."[20] Thoreau would surely have agreed, and, for that matter, so would Socrates.

*

Like Henry William Herbert's many volumes, Hiram Woodruff's one book has long been forgotten. Few people today would have the patience to read through its close-packed pages, and if they had, they wouldn't find colorful description or the pictorial re-creation of the trotting world of that day. Yet of all the vanished worlds of the

American sporting past, Hiram Woodruff's is most familiar to us. His world is familiar in a way that owes nothing at all to the printed word. We know the world of county fairs and races at the crossroads, famous trotters and their spiderlike sulkies, villages and farms, summer sport and winter sleighing, because it was recorded by a group of largely anonymous craftsmen: the salesmen and printers, artisans and painters who worked for

CURRIER & IVES
"COLORED ENGRAVINGS FOR THE PEOPLE"

If American sport was popular, like American politics and religion, why shouldn't American art be popular too? The motto of Currier & Ives was "art for the millions," and the firm sent prints directly into the places where Americans lived and worked.[21] They were used up, worn out, thrown away because they were so plentiful, so unpretentious. The prints were household art. They weren't intended for the connoisseur, museum, or collector. According to conventional notions, they weren't art at all but entertainment, amusement. Currier & Ives didn't care.

Currier & Ives was in the business of producing art; it wasn't a patron of the arts or of artists. Currier & Ives: the name of the firm sold prints, not the names of individual artists. (Few of the firm's artists were even known.) The firm was as utilitarian in spirit as the trotters and sulkies it portrayed, employing the best artists and lithographers available to it because the most interesting subjects and the best artistic treatment sold best. But appeal to the market, not to intrinsic artistic quality, determined if a print was kept in stock. Currier & Ives: people understood, trusted, and bought. That name meant everything. There has been only one phenomenon like it since — Walt Disney.

If art was to be popular, it was necessary to find out what the people wanted. Currier & Ives didn't dictate taste; they satisfied it. Art had to be put in people's hands quickly and cheaply. Currier & Ives: their genius was in selling. People bought prints at the store office in New York. Peddlers sold prints off their carts in the big cities. Traveling salesmen roamed the countryside. But most of the selling was done by mail. The firm issued catalogues that listed prints in stock, and these were available to any customer on request. Currier & Ives also opened a sales office in London, from which prints were sold throughout Europe. The French preferred clipper ships, the

English went for Western scenes. (Maybe they'd had enough of the clippers.) Prints came in many sizes, many prices. All sales final — cash only. A more famous phenomenon followed in their footsteps — Sears, Roebuck and Company.

If art was to be popular then it had to be mass produced, or reproduced. Currier & Ives streamlined production. Sales were in one building, the store, while production was in another building, the factory. In the factory one floor was reserved for storing the many lithographic stones, which were sorted into many different bins — the best sellers in one place, the failures (to be used again) in another. Nothing was wasted. Artists, lithographers, and letterers were on another floor, and colorists were on still another. The printing presses were separate. The heart of production was the coloring line. A dozen young women worked at long tables, in the middle of each of which was an example of the color effect desired. Each colorist applied only one color and then passed the print on to the next colorist. A "finisher" touched things up where necessary.

The muse of the clipper ship and the trotting sulky spoke American. Like other immigrants, lithography learned to do so too, but it took some time. Lithography originated in Bavaria at the end of the eighteenth century, and then was taken up in France and England. About 1820, a pupil of the painter Gilbert Stuart introduced it in the United States. Artisans and craftsmen had to be imported to teach its techniques and adapt it to commercial purposes. The first American lithographic firm was J. and W. Pendleton of Boston. In the early 1820s Pendleton brought the first lithographic pressman to America, a Frenchman named Dubois. By 1828 Dubois needed an apprentice assistant; the firm selected a fifteen-year-old New Englander named Nathaniel Currier. After five years with the Pendleton brothers, Currier moved to Philadelphia. In 1834 he joined the swelling tide of young artists and journalists moving to New York City. He set up a firm there with a partner, broke that up, and went into business on his own in 1835.

In those years lithography was primarily a branch of journalism, and was used to illustrate the news for the rapidly growing newspaper press. Portraits and the depiction of special events were much in demand. Nathaniel Currier's first successes were drawings of fires — city fires in New Orleans and New York City and, most sensationally, a print of the burning of the steamboat *Lexington* on Long Island Sound in January, 1840. The firm prospered. In 1852 Currier employed a bookkeeper named James Merrit Ives, who was also a skilled lithographer and did some lithographic work for the firm. Within five years Ives showed that his talents effectively complemented Currier's. In 1857 he became a partner, and the firm adopted the name by which it became famous.

Currier and Ives: art for all tastes — railroad prints, portraits of celebrities, a series on Mississippi River life. They also explored a new art: advertising. P. T. Barnum, a good friend of Nathaniel Currier's, had suggested this line of work, to serve railroads, insurance companies, circuses, steamboat companies, and sports promoters. Currier & Ives did a series promoting the oddities on display at Barnum's Museum. They also did sheet music and campaign banners for political parties: razzmatazz for the masses.

More than anything else, Currier & Ives did sporting prints: clipper ships, pugilists, iceboats, sailing races, steamboats, and even a print of the new game, baseball, which was played in Hoboken at the Elysian Fields. And horses, horses, horses: thoroughbreds and trotters, standing and running; famous match races and anonymous gallops. Both partners were intensely interested in horses. James Ives was keen on trotters, made frequent expeditions to racetracks to sketch them, and kept a couple of fast trotters for his own use in New York City. One of the firm's most popular prints, "The Road — Winter," was of one of Nathaniel Currier's trotters. It shows Currier with his wife. This print was a present to Currier from his employees, who produced it especially for him. He was delighted with it. Thriftily, he added it to the firm's stock.

Up-to-date in production, innovative in selling, Currier & Ives served as a model for the way entertainment came to be produced and sold for a mass audience in the decades ahead. But in other ways the firm was old-fashioned and paternalistic. By the 1890s, when Currier was dead and Ives retired, the firm had rapidly declined. It declined because the new technology had been ignored. Not until too late did Currier & Ives explore chromolithography. Perhaps even more damaging, their vision of America was backward looking, a vision of an individualistic and small-scale past — a couple or a family or a very small group doing things together. And the style was perfectly suited to the simplicity of this picture: bright colors, child-like innocence, stiff and jerky movements of unsophisticated country folk aware that their portraits were being painted.

Ordinary moments, familiar scenes. The winter scenes were the most familiar and memorable of all. Winter sports in the United States had a special flavor and beauty. Ice-yachting was especially beautiful, with white sails against the green pines of the mountains, boats gliding swiftly across the ice-blue whiteness. Sleighing scenes: the blanket of innocent white after the blizzard. Currier & Ives: we think most often of the clear brisk world of winter white, and this evokes for us, even when we don't at first realize it, the world and scenes with which we began this chapter: the world of John Greenleaf Whittier.

*

Let's return now to that once-familiar picture, *Snow-Bound*. The last part of the poem makes it clear that the story we have been reading is a memory of a long-vanished world: the mother and father, the aunt and the sisters are dead; and the schoolmaster has gone on to other things. Only the poet-narrator remains to repeal the passage of time by opening the book of memory.

But *Snow-Bound* is not only, or even primarily, about the past. It is also a poem about change and the future. Time is not the only element that has transformed the country world of years before. Whittier saw clearly by midcentury that science and technology had become the great transformers and obliterators of the old family world. And in a brilliant stroke he showed this, by bringing back the schoolmaster: but the schoolmaster transformed. He had first appeared in the conventional guise of the inheritor and transmitter of the traditional European culture of arts and letters. But it becomes clear that he had also inherited what Emerson and the others had always ignored — the European scientific tradition. The diffusion of scientific information by means of new technology, "the quick wires of intelligence," would change everything beyond recognition. No huckleberry parties anymore, no bothering with the classics. Greece and Rome were superseded by the newspaper, telegraph, and railroad; and no family could shelter safely away from their effects.

Whittier understood that the struggle between a tradition-bound culture and the unbound culture of the future was likely to involve the loss of things that were precious to him. Raised in a tradition of Quaker frugality and simple living, he realized that the price exacted by progress would involve, among many other things, the loss of simplicity and ancestral piety. Whittier was prepared to pay that price. "Wise-handed skill" must take the place of "blind routine." In this respect he looked forward while Hiram Woodruff looked back. In order to move forward, the seductive spell of history, the "spectral past," the "monograph of outlived years," must be resisted:

> Clasp Angel of the backward look
> The brazen covers of thy book . . .
> Shut down and clasp the heavy lids.

The seduction of poetry itself also had to be resisted. Poetry was a spell, another kind of enchantment. Why is it that "the dreamer leaves his dream midway"?

> For larger hopes and graver fears:
> Life greatens in these later years,
> The century's aloe flowers to-day.

No waiting for gradual change or development. Yankee know-how will have the aloe flower today!

Of course Whittier knew that the need to create poetry, or any other art, was an imperious one, a need not entirely controllable by human will. A poem might be wrenched into existence against one's will. Memory was involuntary, and history was perhaps inescapable. "In some lull of life," Whittier wrote, "in a throngful city the worldly man will dream again of the innocent joys of boyhood."[22] Like Henry Herbert, who saw the essence of sportiveness as a moment of contemplation, Whittier imagined the dream-moment as a foil against the turmoil of present-day action. This moment contains the poised tension between past and future, between pointless playfulness and controlled will.

Hence the importance of snow scenes and winter memories in the American imagination. Snow is a metaphor for memory, for the dream-moment. For the poet, the painter, and the sportsman, the storm doesn't threaten; it preserves. An earlier world of childhood and innocence is protected by the blanket of white. For a moment, change is forgotten and our minds, in reverie, wander playfully back to the past. For a moment art convinces us of its finality. Time is frozen, and the poet and his audience, the dreamer and his dream, are one. Then the whiteness fades, the moment passes, and the crystalline spell is shattered.

*

Near the end of his book — that is to say, near the end of his life — Hiram Woodruff recalled a wintry memory of sleigh riding, "when the air is keen and frosty, the sky clear, the snow deep and crisp and you can dash along" behind a high-stepping trotter like the marvelous

Ripton, the King of the Sleighers! What a peal his bells would ring as he dashed down Yorkville Hill, pounding away with those white legs of his as if he would strike down to the ground, no matter how well packed and deep the snow might be. Here would be a group at this house, and another at that, taking their hot toddy to keep the cold out; and as they heard the swift shaking of the bells, and the fast stroke of *Ripton*'s feet like a charge beat upon the drum, they would run to the door and windows and crowd the stoop, and cry "Hallo! here comes Hiram and the white-legged pony!"[23]

Hiram Woodruff looked back and saw all that slipping away: "It's more than twenty years ago since those times." City railways, traffic, and heat had made that impossible: "There is no jingling of the sleigh-bells there now, no matter how good and deep the snow may be."[24] Where now were those people crowding on the stoop and crying, "Hallo! here comes Hiram!"? William Porter, Dutchman, and the Union Course were gone, and the rhythmic beat of the hooves was silenced. Hiram Woodruff was dying.

He was a country man. His brief stay in New York City had shown him where he belonged. Much of the wildness had gone from the country. Something was lost by that, and much, very much, was gained. Hiram Woodruff never sentimentalized the harshness of the country life of earlier years. But near the end of his life, his spirit was moved by the memory of those wilder days, and he felt most at home in the still, empty stretches of Long Island, where country and ocean met, where "with hand upon the shoulder of his horse, he could hear the booming of the wild waves on the beach."[25]

Maybe Hiram's worldly concern with speed seemed ironic as he contemplated that one's end comes quickly enough. But his temperament was not agitated by such musings, and his spirit remained tranquil. He picked out the place where he wished to be buried — a hillside, overlooking the ocean. (Whittier had already described it in *Snow-Bound:* "Green Hills of life that slope to death.") Many friends gathered round in the winter of 1866–67, as his health failed rapidly. Hiram Woodruff died at midday on March 15, 1867, "without a groan or a pain, as a baby falls asleep." And the last clearly articulated word he spoke was "horse."[26]

*

On the day of Hiram Woodruff's funeral, the people of the farms and villages came from everywhere to pay him tribute. The day dawned bleak and threatening. Although it was mid-March and spring was near, snow began to fall; lightly at first, then more and more heavily. Soon all the wagons and carriages came to a complete stop. They were left behind while the mourners struggled on foot to the top of the hill. Snow fell throughout the service, and one of those present later wrote, in Whittier-like language, "white-bearded Winter had come back to shiver over the grave of this great, honest man." Then the service was over. People straggled down the hill and scattered into the thickening gloom, hurrying off to the warmth of their firesides. Behind them nothing moved. Everywhere the snow lay thick and deep.

P. T. Barnum

10

P. T. Barnum:
Games and Hoaxing

THE NAME of Phineas Taylor Barnum, if it is remembered at all today, is associated with the circus or with the statement "a sucker is born every minute," a saying that reflects a good deal of his philosophy but doesn't wholly exhaust his significance. P. T. Barnum was the greatest showman of the nineteenth century, the first master of hokum and ballyhoo, what we now term public relations. He was proud to be acclaimed the Prince of Humbugs. That he was one of the central figures in the history of American popular culture is an estimate long ago accepted, from the time of his often scandalized but also admiring contemporaries down to the present. All the same, it may seem odd to find him included among American sportsmen, especially since he personally loathed organized sports. How does the Prince of Humbugs fit in among the sportsmen and gamesmen of Jacksonian America?

Barnum was the first great master of urban amusements. His mastery was not of the content of any of the forms of entertainment but of their style. His genius was seeing that their style *was* their content. Barnum anticipated the rhythms of American games, rhythms of surprise reflecting a culture of quick change. He adapted country games to the city and then enticed country folk to come and be introduced to something new and urban. He expanded the notion of spectacle far beyond the limits of the enclosed spaces of theater and circus, museum and arena. He identified spectators' hunger for participation. He understood the uses of publicity. And he joined the company of those who challenged the culture of the Old World. But more than anything else, P. T. Barnum was the archetypal manipulator and manager, who took the odd and aimless forms of play and converted them into complex games. The frontier trickster, the pokerfaced gambler, the Yankee con man — all these elements Barnum absorbed and shaped into his own vision of sportive amusement, a vision entitling him to be called the greatest of nineteenth-century gamesmen.

*

He was born, with uncharacteristic sloppy timing, on the 5th of July, 1810, in Bethel, Connecticut. His parents on both sides were descended from a long line of New Englanders. His father, Philo, was a tailor, a farmer, a tavernkeeper, an innkeeper, and a livery-stable operator. "With greater opportunities and a larger field for his efforts and energies he might have been a man of mark and means."[1] But he had no means and he made no mark. Phineas was named for his maternal grandfather, Phineas Taylor, who gave his infant grandson an inheritance at his christening, a gift-deed to five acres of land, the whole of nearby Ivy Island. As the boy grew up he was constantly reminded of this stake in a dazzling future. Finally, when he was ten, he was allowed, in a state of intense excitement, to go see his property for himself. He found that it was a worthless piece of nettle-covered swampland, inaccessible and uninhabitable, with only snakes for tenants. "The truth flashed upon me. I had been the laughing stock of the family and neighborhood for years."[2] But his grandfather, "a great wag in his way," *had* in fact given Phineas a priceless gift, a birthright of hoaxing.

Phineas grew into a clever, rebellious young man who defied his elders and betters in many ways. He was a Jacksonian in the heart of Federalist/Whig territory, and a freethinking anti-Puritan in the inner sanctum of Calvinism. His father died when he was fifteen, and Phineas went out on his own. At nineteen he married a young seamstress named Charity Hallett. Never one to hide his views (or himself) from the public eye, he became consistently associated with disreputable activities and entertainments: lotteries, a beer saloon, the theater. He ran a country store for a while. There he learned principally that "sharp trades, tricks, dishonesty and deception are by no means confined to the city."[3]

In 1831 Barnum edited the *Herald of Freedom,* a newspaper in Danbury, Connecticut, setting himself up as spokesman for the people against the established order, to such effect that he was sued for libel, lost, and served sixty days in jail. His release from prison was the first of his great public triumphs. Having developed a profound aversion to manual labor and country life, and having determined to live by his wits and to associate himself somehow with the growing love of public amusements in cities, he moved to New York City in 1834.

His training in the general store was to prove invaluable. He had absorbed the fundamental elements of his craft, the Yankee traditions of joke-playing and storytelling. ("There is no country, perhaps, in which the habit . . . of what is termed hoaxing is so common," wrote a visitor to America in 1838.)[4] Even more, he had imbibed the vinegar of Yankee business practice, in which deception was the rule, anything went, and tit always called forth tat. Consider this typical anecdote. A Connecticut grocer, who was also a church deacon, was heard to call downstairs to his young clerk:

> John, have you watered the rum? Yes, sir! And sanded the sugar? Yes, sir! And dusted the pepper? Yes, sir! And chicoried the coffee? Yes, sir! Then come up to prayers.[5]

Barnum took these tricks and applied them rigorously to the raw material of popular entertainment.

The 1830s were precarious years for Barnum. He ran a boardinghouse and a grocery. Always on the edge of respectability, he became interested in the circus and toured with Aaron Turner, one of the first impresarios in the United States. He then left Turner and started his own circus, which had horse-drawn wagons and a tent and featured jugglers, musicians, singers, and dancers. But he had little luck, and in Nashville in 1837 "Barnum's Grand Scientific and Musical Theater" was disbanded. Barnum demonstrated his incapacity for conventional business by becoming one of the very few American entrepreneurs ever to lose money selling patent medicines. He groped in the dark, trying to find his way: "The business for which I was destined had not yet come to me."[6] He hired the Vauxhall Garden in New York City for a variety show but had no success. He went on another circus tour; nothing came of that either. Gradually he realized that "to appear before the public in the character of a showman" was the business for which he was destined. But where? How? As the decade came to an end he returned to New York City, where he supported himself by writing newspaper articles and advertisements.

Then, in 1841, Barnum saw his big chance, and he seized it. Scudder's American Museum, located in a commanding position on Broadway, was up for sale. Like many of the other institutions of this time, American museums were not yet differentiated by specialization of function. They were combinations of natural history museum, historical archive, and art gallery; and essentially, despite their chaotic jumble of curios, relics, and oddities, they were places of learning. Peale's Museum in Philadelphia was the most famous example of the prevailing American type.[7] Nor were museums clearly marked off from other public places. James Russell Lowell's reminiscences of the barbershop of the time show that it too was a kind of museum: on the walls were prints of curious birds and animals, and of historical heroes; over the fireplace were Indian bows and arrows, or fantastically carved whales' teeth; in the corners were New Zealand paddles and war clubs. And the cigar store and tavern were very like the barbershop and museum.

The curiosities and artifacts that came into the town and city from the outlying world — a world of increasing literacy and expanding travel and communication, a world of newspapers, the telegraph, and fast clipper ships — gravitated to the walls of such places with little sense of order or arrangement. But out of this jumble came the concept of the museum as we know it — a place where space and time were rearranged, items were detached from their historical contexts, and a self-contained world was set up within walls. Barnum, needless to say, never articulated his ideas in these terms, but he saw that there was very much that could be done, and he put ideas similar to these into practice. He had often visited Scudder's Museum and now wished to buy it and do something with it, something different. "What do you intend to buy it with?" asked a friend. "Brass," replied Barnum.[8] And, after a complicated series of not overscrupulous maneuvers, he succeeded in doing so. Barnum's American Museum opened in 1842. He never looked back.

*

In his operation of the museum, Barnum moved partially along the old lines. He augmented its collection of natural curiosities, purchasing live as well as stuffed animals of every description and relics of all sorts. But his real emphasis lay elsewhere. His museum was no longer really concerned with education; it became primarily a place of entertainment. Barnum emphasized experience, not learning. He wished to amuse, not edify. He didn't look to Europe, that great living museum of the past; instead he looked outward to the contemporary world all around him. He wanted to reproduce within his museum's walls a kind of amusement based on the common culture that had up to then been kept firmly outside.

So Barnum added the entertainments of the country people among whom he had grown up: the first Punch and Judy show; a family of fleas; ventriloquists; gypsies; a waxworks; jugglers; rope dancers; automatons; albinos; knitting machines; educated dogs. Of course this produced furious criticism. A burlesque opened in New York entitled "Where's Barnum?" — a satire directed against "those mongrel, nondescript collections" he had assembled. It poked fun at Barnum's temerity in applying "the classic word 'museum' to designate an exhibition of broken down jugglers and nigger minstrels."[9] Barnum was delighted. It gave him free publicity. And his critics missed his point anyway. His museum was a place to meet and talk, a place to see and be seen. It was a home for strangers.

He altered the emphasis of the museum in another way. His name ran across the front of the building in huge letters. Barnum was always at the museum, walking about, chatting with the customers. *He* was one of the exhibits. He wished his museum to reflect his personality and intended that personality to be the talk of the town. To achieve this he employed all the publicity devices he had learned earlier, but on a gigantic scale: lights, huge posters, and an endless stream of newspaper notices. "Sir," he said, "advertising is like learning — 'a little is a dangerous thing.' "[10] He knew the effectiveness of shocking. He promoted a long series of exhibitions of freaks, monstrosities, and curiosities; but these were not simply examples of a vulgarized interest in Gothic romanticism, watered-down Brockden Brown and Edgar Poe. The distinguishing thing about Barnum's freaks and monstrosities was that they were fakes, and widely known to be such. To Barnum, even the horrible was a kind of joke. He had actually made his start in this line several years before, when he first came to New York City. He had discovered a black woman named Joice Heth, unbelievably shriveled and aged in appearance, and he publicized her as being the 161-year-old ex-slave who had been George Washington's nurse. Barnum made a good deal of money from this stunt and, more important, proved to his own satisfaction that there was no limit to the credulity of the simple citizens of the Republic.

Barnum hadn't been able to follow up on that. Now, with a proper showplace for displaying the fruits of his ingenuity, the showman went to work and dazzled the country with his gumption. There was the Feejee Mermaid, who had the body of a fish and the head of a monkey, and whose authenticity was vouched for by Dr. Griffin, a noted British scientist (who was in reality Levi Lyman, a Barnum employee who later reformed and became an influential Mormon); there was the Woolly Horse, part horse and part sheep, discovered by Captain John C. Fremont, the Pathfinder, in his western explorations (Captain Fremont of course had done no such thing, but he was thousands of miles away and his denial took months to reach New York); and the Swiss Bell Ringers, who sported Swiss costumes and Swiss mustaches (they were really the Lancashire, England, Bell Ringers; Barnum was sure Americans would think their Lancashire accents were Swiss-talk). It didn't matter that these frauds would eventually be exposed. That was part of the joke. Barnum got people to go to his museum in enormous numbers; some went there to *be* tricked. That was the game. And the museum was the place where all the games were perfected.

In other ways as well Barnum broadened the appeal of his museum. He presented a series of regular dramatic performances, at a time when the theater was still anathema to many people, especially the less-educated evangelicalized masses he needed to attract. Faced with that massive body of conservative opinion, he moved cautiously. But he moved. He sensed that these Americans would stand for almost anything, provided they thought it respectable; and he had a brilliant insight: he realized that respectability in American culture was more nominal than substantive. The name of the thing was what mattered; a thing was what it was called. Had he heard of it, he would have understood and appreciated an incident that involved William Macready and that goes some way toward explaining why that actor had such a low opinion of American culture, even before the debacle at Astor Place. This incident involved an entirely fictitious story of Macready's thrilling rescue of a child from danger. Macready continually denied the story, but people persisted in believing and repeating it. Invited to perform in Charleston, Macready encountered a Dr. Irving, who told him that he wished to use "the child" to publicize Macready's appearance in that city. Macready vehemently told Irving that the story was not true. Irving was surprised but unfazed: "Never mind, it will do for our religious people."[11]

The task of the promoter, or the publicist, was to make things seem what they were not; a task made easier for Barnum because he realized he was dealing with people who insisted on seeing themselves as realists and who doggedly believed they knew precisely what reality was. Such a temperament and such a philosophy are made to order for gamesmen (as Adah Menken also understood). Following up his insight, Barnum had the happy inspiration of taking the oral tradition he found flourishing all about him — this was the age of lecturers such as Emerson and preachers such as Charles Grandison Finney, of stump speeches and campaign songs — and converting it to his own purposes. Barnum called his theater the Public Lecture Room. What could be more respectable, more reassuring, than that? There he showed only the most moral dramas: *Moses, Joseph and His Brethren,* and the phenomenally popular temperance tract, *The Drunkard.*

Many of the visitors to Barnum's museum were country bumpkins who regarded the city with wonder and suspicion. Barnum made it impossible to miss his place. Said one of these Yankee yokels in a contemporary play:

> What tarnal comical creturs these towns are. I'll be darned but I guess I've lost my way, though I chalked the corners of the streets as I went along.[12]

The museum was made accessible to ordinary people in other ways as well. There were no complicated procedures, no mysterious rules of conduct known only to the initiate, no tone of rapturous hush in the presence of Great Art. At Barnum's, common people felt at home, just as horsemen felt at home at the racetracks. They frequented it the way sportsmen from out of town had frequented the offices of the *Spirit of the Times* when William Porter presided there. The historian of the volunteer fire companies spoke for the fire laddies when he wrote of Barnum's: "No stranger went to New York and came away without seeing it; for many, it comprised in a nutshell all that was worth seeing in the city."[13] Imagine Mose at any other kind of museum.

Barnum invented the continuous performance, an enduring tradition in American vaudeville and the cinema. It was a conveyor belt of amusement. There was a show every hour, every day, including holidays. People could come almost any time that suited them; they brought their lunches and their families and stayed all day. And all at twenty-five cents per person, children half price. The museum opened every morning at sunrise, a time country folks could understand. You had to get up very early to beat Mr. Barnum.

*

Barnum made popular entertainment respectable by turning it into a business, a very successful business and one that had a divine sanction:

> Men, women and children, who cannot live on gravity alone, need something to satisfy their gayer, lighter moods and hours, and he who ministers to this want is in a business established by the Author of our nature.[14]

How was that for turning the tables on the puritans! His countrymen admired his success. "He can well afford to have jokes cracked on his broad brow," wrote one, "for he is now the wealthiest 'showman' in all creation, and can buy out half a dozen of the leading shows in Europe or America."[15]

The business was organized and made systematic. Barnum sent out scouts to spot raw material, which was then brought to one central location and prepared for public consumption. He was the emergent middleman who came between the creator and the consumer. He packaged, promoted, publicized. He was like his mercantile contemporaries A. T. Stewart and Jordan Marsh, and even more like his friends Currier and Ives. When, after the Civil War, he realized his heart's desire by touring with a circus, he organized the enterprise with greater care than any military expedition had been planned up to that time. A regular circuit was established, the dates were set well in advance, and, with lots of blaring publicity, a need was created, stimulated, and then satisfied. Barnum transported his circus by rail, going only to towns large enough to guarantee receipts above a fixed sum. So efficient was the operation that the entire show could be taken one hundred miles, unpacked, taken through a morning parade and afternoon and evening performances, and then packed up and sent off to the next stop, all within twenty-four hours. His circus was a model, like Currier & Ives, that American spectator sports would follow as they expanded into national businesses.

Barnum's talents extended well beyond his organizational skill. In the years ahead sports promoters would have many lessons to learn from the master. Barnum lavished on his business the artist's interest in technique and style. His own imagination had an odd and playful strain that popped out in ways surprising even to him. A part of him always mocked physical perfection and athletic prowess. It was the gamesman's hostility to the strong but simple-minded sportsman. Barnum went in for freaks, not perfect specimens. Even his semisporting enterprises showed this. When he organized a Great Buffalo Hunt at the racetrack in Hoboken, he made sure that it turned into a joke, a mockery of the real thing. His mixture of the bizarre and freakish was ridiculous, not frightening. It was designed to produce amusement, not a thrill of terror. The playful side of his imagination revealed itself in the element of childlike wonder and childlike expectation that marked everything he did. Children or childlike dwarfs played very large roles in his humbugs.

But the dominant element in Barnum's imagination was the rhythm of surprise, of sudden changes and shifts, of discontinuities. And discontinuity is the fundamental rhythm of American games, as we shall see in the last chapter of this book. Back in Andrew Jackson's day, Alexis de Tocqueville had suggested why this sense of disjunction was so common in America:

> The woof of time is every instant broken, and the track of generations is effaced. Those who went before are soon forgotten; of those who will come after no one has any idea.[16]

In 1833 Chicago was a small village of seventeen houses riding crazily upon lots of shifting sand; in the near vicinity the howling of wolves could be heard at night. By 1860 it contained over 100,000 people, and within another decade or so (fire and all) it came to be the second largest city in the nation, the epitome of lusty industrialism; and all this, from sandlots to Sandburg, within half of Barnum's lifetime.

The reverse was equally familiar although less frequently recalled by historians. Take an example from the same region and time. New Salem, Illinois, to which Abraham Lincoln came in the early 1830s, promised to become an important, certainly a permanent, place; yet it soon went into rapid decline, and by the early 1840s, in the words of Lincoln's law partner, William Herndon, it had vanished "like a mist in the morning." And think of all those racetracks, begun so bravely and with such grand expectations of permanence and fame, now also gone without a trace.[17]

The connections between such discontinuities and the rhythms of a culture's amusements are difficult to untangle. One of them may be the obsession with speed that we have so often encountered. Another may be the pervasive power of the sense of newness.[18] It was at about this time that *old-fashioned* came to be a common term of disapproval and disparagement among all classes, conservatives and democrats alike. The declining sense of local attachment and the erosion of a sense of place were also reflected in American amusements. And still another connection may be found in the early awareness of a sense of impersonality in American life. The combination of all of these things had a tremendous impact on American sporting life and on the form and rhythm of its games. Americans turned their backs on the idea of wisdom, on deference to anything venerable, on slow growth and patient maturation: wait — and lose! Instead, they wanted information, quickness, immediate results: fast foods, speed reading, short cuts, and the fast buck. They consequently looked away from cricket, long-distance running, the idea of amateurism, and anything natural. They wanted, and they got, the T-formation and the hundred-yard dash.

Barnum understood. There was always a fresh bill of fare at the museum. He always aimed at the sudden change, the odd twist, the surprise ending. He savored most of all "the jolts and surprises, the air of public excitement and pulling off unaccountable feats" that he had first tasted when running the lottery in Bethel. After Barnum, O. Henry.

Side by side in American culture ran the contradictory impulses of competition and cooperation. Barnum played on both and with both. His tricks were one way of competing. One of his stunts was to introduce an act and then introduce a rival to it. Both acts often prospered. He would begin a show and, when interest flagged, take space in the newspapers to attack it. He was fighting a duel with his audience, but he somehow contrived to persuade them that they were on his side. He felt the enormous force of his audiences' wish for mutual participation, for the sharing of a common experience; for example, waiting together for the unpredictable surprise.

There was nothing new in Barnum's recognition that people competed for power, money, and fame; but he saw that they would also compete in appearing ridiculous, which perhaps was new. They paid *him* so they could compete with each other. The showman let them show off. Maybe they were absurd, but at least they felt they mattered. They brought dogs, poultry, flowers, and babies, and he organized the competitions. He saw to it that everyone was rewarded in some way, with medals, diplomas, or prizes. Everyone won something, and the old and venerable emblems of privilege and superior achievement — honors, titles, and rewards — were also mocked.

The audience shared something else: confidence in Barnum's skill at manipulating them. They knew they were safe in the hands of a master gamesman. P. T. Barnum took up where Colonel Johnson left off. He had vastly more complex and manipulable materials to work with. This was his most important role in the history of American sporting culture. Barnum saw the game as countless Americans would come to see it. The world was manmade. Nothing need be left to chance or history: "There is no such thing in the world as luck."[19] Every detail could be considered, every factor allowed for, every contingency anticipated, every problem solved. Barnum was the Napoleon of amusement: after him came a legion of managing masterminds. American fans fervently wish to believe that some great intelligence presides over everything, that some superbrain is in charge. In a pinch it is even reassuring to believe in conspiracy theories. More terrible if *no one* were in control.

*

Barnum made popular entertainment more respectable, but he was also determined to prove that he could make even the highest and most refined culture popular. From early on he looked across the Atlantic, and it was there, in the home of high culture, that he found his greatest challenge and the means to achieve his greatest triumph — Jenny Lind.

Jenny Lind was one of the performing wonders of her age. Although Barnum had never heard her sing, the Swedish Nightingale represented to him the highest level of musical taste. He wished to show, by bringing her to America, that his own taste ranged beyond Feejee Mermaids. She drove a hard bargain: all traveling and boarding expenses would be paid by Barnum, who would also furnish her with a maid, a male servant, a carriage and horses, a conductor and a baritone of her choice, plus $1,000 per concert, for up to 150 concerts over an eighteen-month period. Jenny Lind wished to come to the United States for two reasons. She wanted to make money so she could endow her favorite charity, a hospital for poor children in Stockholm; and she wished to free herself from the immoral atmosphere of grand opera (especially in France and Russia, where she had determined never again to sing). She therefore looked with great favor upon a tour of the simple and virtuous American republic.

Barnum risked everything in bringing her. He revealed his dominant business trait — taking a chance. Bankers scoffed at the notion that Americans would pay steep prices to hear operatic arias. How realistic was that? Barnum had to mortgage his museum and borrow from friends to raise the money he needed. He was jolted when, having signed the contract with her, he mentioned to a railroad-conductor friend that he had signed Jenny Lind. "Jenny Lind?" the trainman asked. "Is she a dancer?" Barnum accepted the challenge, the first great transatlantic challenge of the 1850s. "Here was an opportunity to turn all doubts into hard cash." He promoted her for all he was worth: "She was effectually introduced to the public before they had seen or heard her."[20] They found out who she was. They found out what she did. And they were never allowed to forget her name.

Jenny Lind supplied a crucial hint and Barnum snapped it up. He saw that she was the perfect heroine for the cultural drama he was producing. The way to make her high art popular was to make it common; and the way to make it common was to sell it not as art but as ordinary morality. Her tour was the Public Lecture Room all over again. It reflected the Jacksonian hatred of exclusiveness. In his publicity Barnum stressed the purity of Jenny Lind's character. Virtually nothing was said about Jenny Lind the artist. This pleased her very much. Barnum also stressed her admiration for the United States, organizing a competition (for $200) for a song, written by an American, that would be sung by Jenny Lind as a "Welcome to America." As it turned out, there were 753 entries, all dreadful; but she went along with the stunt like a good sport and managed two verses of the winning entry.

In September of 1850, only a few days before California entered the Union, and with only slightly less commotion, Jenny Lind arrived in America. Her welcome was a tumultuous one, whistles and foghorns from the ships in New York harbor, a crowd of thousands shouting to her from the pier, flags, archways of flowers. The whole event could not have gone better had it been carefully rehearsed. (And of course in a way it had been.) Jenny Lind went into raptures about the view, then blew a kiss to an American flag, saying "There is the beautiful standard of freedom; the oppressed of all nations worship it." (Barnum had unaccountably neglected to have a Swedish flag displayed, so at the last minute a flag of one of the German states was run up in its place.) Her accompanying baritone, Signor Giovanni Battista Belleti, added a suitable ethnic note: "Here is the grand New World at last, first seen by my fellow countryman Columbus."[21] With that for a start, with crowds swarming around her hotel, and with a midnight serenade by the musicians of the New York Musical Fund Society, accompanied by 300 firemen in red shirts, could there be much doubt that the tour would be a triumphant success?

Barnum was careful to keep "society" from monopolizing Jenny Lind and thus antagonizing the masses, upon whose support the venture depended. The masses responded by showering her with every possible sign of their admiration: freedom of the city, clothes and furniture named for her, water carafes with her name and face on them, songs and poems in her honor, even a cigar named after her. Later, a theater in San Francisco and a fine trotter were given her name, and a clipper ship was called *Nightingale*. Barnum's last lingering anxiety was wiped away when tickets for the first two concerts at Castle Garden had to be auctioned off, so great was the demand, bringing $17,864.05, an average of $6.38 for each ticket. Various hotels and firms bought blocks of tickets for their own purposes, thus launching an enduring American business venture — ticket scalping.

Jenny Lind was apprehensive about living up to all this acclaim, and she showed her nervousness at the beginning of her first aria, the "Casta Diva" from Bellini's *Norma*. But she conquered her nerves and then her audience, which nearly swooned when, near the end of the concert, she produced a guitar and accompanied herself, singing folk songs from her native land — a common touch that matched the homeliness of Barnum's message to her in flowers over the stage: "Welcome Sweet Warbler."

*

What did American culture mean to Jenny Lind? When they were touring the west, Barnum took her to see the Hermitage. (In 1837 Barnum had gone there to pay his personal respects to his hero.) Jackson had been dead five years, but Jenny Lind found the appropriate symbol for what his home represented to her. She was delighted by the singing of the mockingbirds. In Europe she had heard them sing, but only in wirebound cages; here, in the trees, they sang wildly and freely.

The tour was a long one, and before its end the enthusiasm of even American audiences had somewhat subsided. Not everyone had succumbed unreservedly to the "Lindomania" anyway. Walt Whitman heard her and was distinctly cool. He thought her singing lacked conviction and passion. But his opinion, in this as in so many things, was that of a minority. What did Jenny Lind represent to her almost delirious audiences?

Jenny Lind personified European high culture at its most brilliant. Barnum, insofar as he cared about such things, believed that
Jenny Lind was indisputably the real thing. His gamble was
whether so aristocratic an art could be made palatable for so democratic a people as his fellow citizens. And certainly the tour gave an
enormous boost to the popular American awareness of operatic
music.

But this time the joke was on Barnum. He didn't get what he
bargained for. His audacity was less remarkable than it seemed at
the time. The fact was that the aristocratic operatic tradition was already a thing of the past. In Europe, opera was changing, and so
was its audience. It was being transformed from an art patronized
by the aristocracy to one cultivated by the bourgeoisie, and Jenny
Lind was only one element of this transformation. Mendelssohn,
who met Jenny Lind in Berlin and who admired her extravagantly,
was puzzled by her. "She is as great an artist as ever lived; and the
greatest I have known," he said. But then he added: "She sings bad
music the best."[22] What Jenny Lind actually represented was thus
open to question.

None of this was Barnum's primary concern, however. He had
defied the bankers, and it had paid off. He had made the high and
mighty of New York society come to him for tickets, on his terms.
As for the questions of culture involved in all of this, his feelings
were a mixture of smugness and disdain. Jenny Lind was his greatest business speculation, and nothing more: "I risked much, but I
made more." In his autobiography he wrote that he "pulled at [the
public's] heart-strings to get at their purse-strings."[23] In a way the
entire tour was only another kind of hoaxing.

He had a chance to play some delightful jokes on the people.
Jenny Lind insisted on secrecy about her arrival at any place where
she was to sing, so that she would not be disturbed. Barnum fostered this element of surprise whenever possible. In Philadelphia,
however, this proved impossible to arrange. Crowds gathered outside the hotel where Lind was sleeping. So Barnum placed her
shawl and bonnet on a friend, who impersonated the Nightingale,
appearing at a balcony and waving, while the crowd roared its de-
luded welcome. When the tour arrived in New Orleans by steamer,
they found an enormous crowd awaiting them. Surprise was impossible. "I am sure I can never get through that crowd," wailed the
Nightingale. "Leave that to me," said Barnum. Barnum's daughter,
wearing a veil over her face, impersonated Jenny Lind, and, as the

two of them descended the gangplank, a man, at Barnum's instigation, shouted "Open the way for Mr. Barnum and Miss Lind"; and the entire crowd followed them to their hotel. A few minutes later, Jenny Lind left the ship entirely unnoticed.

Barnum loved it. The hoax was of course publicized. They went on to Cincinnati, where another crowd awaited them at the steamboat landing. The old ruse would never work again. Or would it? When people are overconfident and certain they know what's what, the gamesman is in his element. Barnum took Jenny Lind's arm and they descended the gangplank. A man Barnum had once again planted in the crowd called out: "That's no go, Mr. Barnum; you can't pass your daughter off for Jenny Lind this time!" And then other Ohioans took up the cry: "That won't do, Barnum! You may fool the New Orleans folks, but you can't come it over the Buckeyes." And so Barnum and his "daughter" passed by while they stayed and hollered for Jenny Lind.[24]

The Prince of Humbugs! Barnum had already enjoyed great coups that made him internationally notorious well before Jenny Lind's tour. There was his first tour of Britain and the Continent — with Tom Thumb. Barnum took the tiny general there against the advice of friends, who told him the British would never fall for it. But of course they *had* fallen, like a ton of nutmegs. The nobility showered invitations and presents on Tom Thumb, and thrust money into Barnum's hands; and thousands packed the theater where the general was on display. Even Queen Victoria allowed Tom Thumb and his friend to call on her — three times. In Paris, where King Louis Philippe carried on like all the rest, it was just as bad — or good.

So much for aristocratic good taste. But that wasn't all. Confronted with the splendor of the great tradition of European culture, Barnum responded by making crassly outrageous offers to do with it what he knew best — to buy it up. He attempted to take Madame Tussaud's waxworks back to the United States (it was, after all, his line of work); to haul away a tree on which Byron had carved his name; and to purchase Shakespeare's house. What he couldn't offer to buy, he mocked. In his own museum he exhibited a frightful wax figure of Queen Victoria and advertised it as "an exact likeness"; and he named an orangutan after Fanny Elssler, the celebrated dancer.

Then came one of his craftiest ideas. He would build a home appropriate for an American gamesman. And in what style would it be? Anything Barnum pleased. In England his eye had been caught by the Royal Pavilion at Brighton. He commissioned architects to furnish him with plans and drawings for the site he had selected, outside Bridgeport, Connecticut, and so close to the New Haven Railroad that everyone could see it from the train.

The result was Iranistan, a combination of Byzantine, Moorish, and Turkish, "the only building in its peculiar style of architecture of any pretension in America." Peculiar it was. And lavish. Elegant furniture was made especially to suit each room; the stables, conservatories, and outbuildings were "perfect in their kind." There was a profusion of trees, and expensive waterworks supplied the fountains that splashed in the grounds where Rocky Mountain elk and reindeer roamed. The whole thing, Barnum said with a perfectly straight face, was not only a "tasteful residence" but also especially "adapted to the spot of ground selected for my homestead." Adapted indeed. That was another joke, because Iranistan meant "Eastern Country Place."

Jenny Lind visited Barnum there and said that but for Iranistan, she never would have come to America. How so? One of his letters to her had been written on stationery engraved with a picture of Iranistan. Jenny was impressed: "I said to myself, a gentleman who has been so successful in his business as to be able to build and reside in such a palace cannot be a mere adventurer." Another joke? Did she actually mean what she said? And did Barnum believe what he wrote? What a pair![25]

"There sits the old master, over in Europe, like a parent." So wrote D. H. Lawrence. "Somewhere deep in every American heart lies a rebellion against the old parenthood of Europe," and this expresses itself in both "corrosive obedience" and "unremitting opposition."[26] Lawrence failed to mention Barnum, who had quite a different way of dealing with Europe. Barnum exorcised the spirits that haunted the Hermitage. He broke the spell. All that fuss about culture — what was it but another kind of game? He could play it, make it amusing, and win some money too. The old gamesman winked at European culture behind its back. The man who built Iranistan didn't think all that history, all that tradition, was in the least threatening — only ridiculous.

*

This has become a familiar theme: Mark Twain dealing with it in *Innocents Abroad;* and General Grant remarking how attractive Venice would be if only the canals were drained. To exorcise

Europe by buying it up is the "sacred rage" of Waymarsh in Henry James's *The Ambassadors*. Closer to Barnum's time, William Randolph Hearst bought up much of European culture, kept it packed in shipping cases, and never looked at it again; perhaps he bought it so that *no one* would have to look at it again.

Yet Barnum mocked not only the respectable and traditional. The same treatment was accorded to the masses. Inside Barnum the Jacksonian democrat, there was a vestigial Calvinist, a southwestern storyteller, or a caustic Whig who popped out every once in a while and said that the masses were the biggest humbugs of all. On an outside balcony of the museum, a brass band played for the public's enjoyment: "Music for the Millions," it was called. But Barnum said of it, "I took pains to select and maintain the poorest band I could find."[27] As he walked about the museum, smiling at the folk, he carefully collected — like H. L. Mencken and the *New Yorker* magazine of later decades — all the remarks he and his employees overheard that illustrated the imbecility of common opinion. Many of his jokes partially revealed his contempt. On the Fourth of July he stretched American flags from his museum across the street to the church opposite, and when the church wardens protested, Barnum went out into the street and played on the bellicose jingoism of the crowd, members of which said to the church wardens: "Well, I should just like to see you dare to cut down the American flag on the 4th of July; you must be a Britisher to make such a threat as that."[28] Barnum could have explained even Astor Place.

He advertised a "cherry colored cat," which people in the museum had to pay extra to see; when they jammed the room to view this phenomenon, they found only a very ordinary black street cat and a laconic Yankee custodian who said, "some cherries are black." The people loved it. Barnum knew better than anyone how snobbish Americans could be about European things; but he never failed to deceive them into thinking something was European when it was not. And he enjoyed a double joke by saying in his autobiography that he only did it to check "our disgraceful preference for foreigners." He put up a sign that read "To the Egress." The people rushed to see this creature, only to find themselves outside, having to pay again to get back inside.[29] They loved that as well. "Stung again! By gosh! If that don't beat everything!" Then, still slapping their thighs with much mirth, they rushed away to persuade others to fall for it too.

*

The private Barnum can be searched for in his labyrinthine autobiography, *The Life of P. T. Barnum Told by Himself* (1855), which, in the thirty-six years following its publication, appeared and reappeared in seven editions, all different, some bearing different titles, all rewritten by Barnum. He used to give it away at the museum, but the book gives away very little about its author. It is a classic of concealment. Perhaps there was no private Barnum. Somewhere along the line the public figure swallowed the private one — a familiar occurrence in American history. It happened to Walt Whitman, who also knew something about self-publicity and whose *Leaves of Grass* shares a birthday with Barnum's *Life;* it happened to Mark Twain, an old friend of Barnum's who immensely admired the *Life* and who perhaps learned some of his own masterful deadpan timing from it and its author; and of course it happened to many others later on — Jack London, Ernest Hemingway, and Norman Mailer. Whitman and Twain left behind them works of genius as well as the memory of a public personality. What did Barnum leave behind?

He left behind the one thing he perhaps felt more unambiguous affection for than anything else — the circus. He created the three-ring circus as it came to be known in America. Yet he had no affection whatever for animals; perhaps the manager of a circus cannot. In the last thirty or so years of his life, Barnum insisted that he was a country man. But he had none of the country man's interest in animals and field sports. When many animals on exhibition at the museum were destroyed in the several terrible fires that ravaged that building, Barnum was coldly indifferent to their fate. The circus was a means by which he could place humans and other animals on the same level, as objects for dispassionate observation and display. What else did he leave behind him?

His name. He attached all value to his name, none to his character. "Mention my name," the Prince of Publicity would say when he dropped into newspaper offices, and it didn't matter much whether he was praised or blamed. Half a century later Franklin Roosevelt grasped the significance of that point and applied it to mass democratic politics. Madame Tussaud's once asked Barnum's permission to do him in wax. Was he willing? "Willing? — Anxious! What's a show without notoriety!"[30] Traditional opinion was shocked by Barnum's attitude. For many people, his name was synonymous with dishonesty. Writing to a friend in 1866 about troubles her husband was having producing one of his operas in France, Giuseppina

Verdi, who had no exalted opinion of French morals, made an interesting comparison.

> It doesn't surprise me that charlatanism and imposture are greater in America than in France, since the Barnums were born, or were invented, in America. The French are the charlatans par excellence of Europe, though one must agree that they have much wit and, I would dare to say, good nature in their charlatanism. Perhaps they will perfect themselves by the example of the Americans, but for the present they are slightly less dishonest.[31]

Millions of Americans wouldn't have agreed with this, or cared. For them, it was typical European snobbery. Where values and standards were wholly relative, character was relative too; where traditions and customs were so uncertain, who could stick to one code of conduct or sportsmanship? But a name — a name was a thing in itself; it had an existence of its own. A "good" name took decades to establish. But why couldn't a better one be made overnight? "Better" because in an impersonal world, character can't compete with notoriety, and the test of something is whether it works or not. If we're only names to each other, what are we if our names are unknown?

Barnum helped create the face with which to gaze upon such a world — impassive, imperturbable, deadpan, the great American sporting face, the gamesman's face, the poker face. Barnum's contribution was to adapt this face to city life, to realize how it could be used by the countryman in the city, and, on a broader level, to see it as a mask for new men in a new country. A traveler spoke of "those impassive and frozen American faces," and at the same time noted that in groups these people were easy, turbulent, and vivacious.[32] The nineteenth-century actor George H. Hill told of playing a farce in an upstate New York town without getting a single laugh from the audience during the entire evening. Imagine Hill's surprise when told by one of the yokels, later that evening, that he and the entire audience had in fact been enormously amused. Why, then, asked Hill, hadn't they laughed?

> I tell you what it is, now; my mouth won't be straight for the next month, straining to keep from larfing. If it hadn't been for the women, I should a snorted right out in the meetin'.[33]

In those traditional formal public spaces and places inherited from Europe, Americans felt very ill at ease. What was more stilted, European visitors always remarked, than American politicians in the U.S. Senate, ponderously playing at being noble Romans? What could be more forced and unnatural than those southern planter-adventurers, when required to create social roles to match the classical columns of their houses? Surely it was clear by now that the American sportsman could never find a home in the Hermitage? He must do as Barnum did and not play *at* that old sporting style but play *with* it.

In their own spaces and places, however — at religious revivals, barn raisings, and sporting events — Americans felt freer, more boisterous, more relaxed. These were *their* places, imagined and built by them and not forced on them by history. The legacy of the past. Refuse the legacy! Americans created new kinds of public occasion to suit themselves: parades and chowder parties, potlucks, barbecues, and firemen's balls. Oscar Wilde understood this in a flash, and was witty about it:

> There are no trappings, no pageants, and no gorgeous ceremonies. I saw only two processions: one was the Fire Brigade preceded by the Police, the other was the Police preceded by the Fire Brigade.[34]

Barnum felt in his bones that old forms, protocols, and manners had already been modified in practice. When he and Jenny Lind were in Washington, President Fillmore called, and left his card, Jenny Lind being out. When she returned and found this, she was in a flurry to call on the president immediately. "Why so?" Barnum inquired. "Because he has called on me and of course that is equivalent to a command."

> I assured her that she might make her mind at ease, for whatever might be the custom with crowned heads, our Presidents were not wont to "command" the movements of strangers, and that she would be quite in time if she returned his call the next day.[35]

Nowhere were Americans more at ease than at their own sporting events: they were boisterous, as Andrew Jackson had been at his cockfights; and they were noisy and rowdy, especially at racetracks. They called out, shouted, commented, and vocally made their presence known, because they felt their presence somehow mattered. Philip Hone had found a very different atmosphere at the races at the Champs de Mars course near Paris: "There was no shouting, no triumph amongst the men."[36]

Even as Americans laughed, however, they had to be wary. A laugh was all right, but a last laugh, a winning laugh, was best of all. Imagine sportsmen believing that losers could be in a good humor! The poker face was a game face in a land where all life was treated as a game, and it was never abandoned because the game never ended. Those who play by the rules perish by the rules. Remember General Braddock, who marched through the forest according to the European rules. Remember the British at New Orleans. The Indians didn't invent the ambush, but they perfected it. Americans could never make up their minds about that. Were the Indians sportsmen or gamesmen?

T. S. Eliot and P. T. Barnum. Worlds apart. Two very different views of tradition. But perhaps they weren't as different as they seemed. Eliot too had tried to unite high culture and popular culture. He too had taken on Europe. Perhaps taken it in a bit? Eliot may not have read Barnum, but he had certainly assimilated him. Think of that deadpan voice:

> there will be time
> To prepare a face to meet the faces that you meet.

And wasn't there a lot of humbug in those all-too-solemn notes to *The Waste Land?*

*

American culture was a world of surfaces, where very little was permanent or what it seemed. In public Americans said something quite different, and said it at the tops of their voices: that it was a world of love and sporting fellowship, of working together, of teamwork and brotherhood. In the long run at least. But, as John Maynard Keynes pointed out, "in the long run we are all dead." As Barnum said, however, Americans really must check "our disgraceful preference for foreigners." So let's turn instead to Josh Billings, one of Lincoln's favorite folk humorists: "Honesty is the best policy in the long run, but for short distances Humbug has made pretty good time." Believers might find consolation in the hope of heaven, but the world Barnum looked out on was the world of that neglected Jacksonian, Herman Melville. It was the world of Melville's *Confidence Man,* the world of a Mississippi River steamboat on April Fool's Day, where there could be no confidence because there was no trust, and no trust because life had been turned into a con game played by con men. P. T. Barnum, trust buster.

What made *Barnum* laugh? Practical jokes with a strain of brutal coarseness. He once arranged to have a thief, who had been apprehended by the police, exhibited at the museum (admission one quarter) under the notice, "live pick-pocket." On April Fool's Day he sent a fake dispatch to an employee, informing him that his house and all his possessions had burned to the ground. Some fun! Uncle Phineas would have liked it. Barnum once bribed an Indian interpreter to bring ten Indian chiefs — who had come east to visit President Lincoln — to the museum, where, without their knowledge, they were exhibited as part of the show, in such a way as to make them seem ridiculous. More fun! But since everyone was always being tricked, everyone had to be constantly wary. Observers noted on the faces of most of the visitors to the museum "the impassive look of the pioneer in the face of danger."[37] The visitors whooped and hollered at the skill of the wizard in charge, but they never forgot that the laughter was always at someone's expense. Eternal vigilance was the price of permanent anxiety. After Barnum, Buster Keaton.

The efforts Jacksonian Americans made to create and sustain a democratic society and to understand the implications of what they had done are analyzed incomparably in Alexis de Tocqueville's *Democracy in America*. That work contains a haunting prophetic passage about the likely results when traditional ways give way to equalitarian ones. As social classes become more equal, said Tocqueville, their members become more indifferent to, and estranged from, one another:

> Aristocracy had made a chain of all members of the community, from the peasant to the king; democracy breaks that chain, and severs every link of it.

In such a situation, Tocqueville continued, people feel that

> they owe nothing to any man, they expect nothing from any man; they acquire the habit of always considering themselves as standing alone, and they are apt to imagine that their whole destiny is in their own hands.
>
> Thus not only does democracy make every man forget his ancestors, but it hides his descendants, and separates his contemporaries, from him; it throws him back for ever upon himself alone, and threatens in the end to confine him entirely within the solitude of his own heart.[38]

Phineas Barnum's genius — the entertainment of strangers. The American sportsman had many houses but no home. How could he, in a country obsessed by the desire to move, move, move, as an end in itself? We are pieces on a chessboard, and no more to each other than a name. Yet this vision of Barnum's was in no way an anguished one. There was no Calvinist self-torment. Jonathan Edwards's mankind, dangling like a spider over the fiery pit, had been left behind in Bethel, with all the rest of the soul-destroying relics of the past. The legacy of the past. Of tradition. Grandfather Phineas Taylor's legacy of swampland. Renounce the legacy!

P. T. Barnum's tone was matter-of-fact, commonplace. Why all the fuss? Barnum had thought and said that entertainment was a business established by the author of our nature, and he humbly took that nature as he found it. In doing so, he shared the prosaic, accepting attitude of those racetrack people and prize-fight fans who also took human nature as something given. Shortly before he died peacefully in bed, at home in Connecticut, on April 7, 1891, Barnum calculated that in his long lifetime he had entertained over eighty million people — probably more than any other person in all history had entertained up to then. Americans counting numbers again. He had dominated his time as Andrew Jackson had dominated an earlier age. He died content. He had done what he could, and, whatever that was, people got what they had coming to them.

It might seem farfetched, then, to suggest that Barnum belongs in the company of those, like Henry William Herbert and Paul Morphy, who have known the darkness of despair and madness, or of those, like Herman Melville and Nathaniel Hawthorne, whose vision pierced beneath this playful human surface, penetrated to the core of human nature and found — nothing? Hawthorne died with the thunder muffled. Melville, we know, drew back and lapsed into silence. After a boring day at the New York customs house, did he amuse himself by going uptown to laugh at the show at the museum? Was Barnum the gamesman the Clown Prince of Nihilism? Of course not. What a joke.

Phineas Taylor Barnum was no nihilist. For one thing, the word itself is un-American, and he was nothing if not American — American to the mysterious core. Besides, there *was* something at the center — pure technique. "As a manager, I worked by setting others to work."[39] Old Humbug knew the gamesman's creed: You can do something to everyone all of the time, and everything to someone some of the time; but friends, that little green light calling to us from beyond the harbor, winking at us from across the fresh green breast of the New World — that little green light is the faith that we can do everything to everyone all of the time. The name of the game is Yankee know-how. And *that's* no joke.

R. C. Schenck

R. C. Schenck:
From Draw Poker to
the Twentieth Century

AFTER BARNUM and the sportsmen of the 1850s, the tide of popular culture flowed with increasing force from West to East. European interest in the more popular forms of American literature continued, and the tall tales and gold-rush stories of Mark Twain and Bret Harte found a wide audience; but the emphasis shifted, and American cultural influence increasingly came to be exerted through other vernacular forms: industrial and commercial products, publicity and sales methods, forms of business organization, and, above all, Yankee technology of all kinds. This went so far and so fast that by the end of the nineteenth century an Englishman was driven to write a book entitled *The Americanization of England,* sounding an alarm that would swell in volume and importance in the twentieth century. After England, the world: movies, cars, and television, Mickey Mouse and Coca-Cola. And along with these, baseball in Japan and the Caribbean, and basketball all around the globe.

One final footnote to this transatlantic theme. It involves a little-known incident in the history of American games, and it allows us to look forward into that Americanizing future and see how the sporting traditions of Andrew Jackson's day have reached their full flowering. This footnote is in the person of an affable, middle-aged American, whose life united games and diplomacy, politics and poker.

*

Robert Cumming Schenck was born in Ohio on October 4, 1809.[1] He was orphaned at age twelve, but a generous stepfather helped him get an education. He went to the state university in Miami, Ohio, took a degree and then practiced law. He was much more interested in the game of democratic politics than in the law, however, and he soon revealed an extraordinary capacity for political survival. Skeptical about Jacksonian Democracy, he became a Whig, was elected to Congress in 1843, and served there until 1851, when the Whig party began to disintegrate and he was defeated for reelection. He then managed to get himself appointed minister to Brazil. Impressed by the economic potential of the Amazon basin, he promptly attempted to open it up for development by means of a commercial treaty, but he was unsuccessful in that venture and eventually returned to America and to Ohio politics. He became an abolitionist and shrewdly identified himself with Abraham Lincoln and the Republican party, which was then arising out of the Whig wreckage.

When the Civil War broke out he was rewarded with an appointment as brigadier general in the Union army. He was wounded in the first battle of Bull Run. Soon after that he relinquished his commission, returned to Ohio, and eventually found himself back in Congress, emerging there as a vehement exponent of radical Republican reconstruction of the South. He failed to be reelected in 1870. But his luck held. His old friend Ulysses Grant, then in the White House, stepped in and dealt him a surprising hand, appointing him minister to England. When, in June of 1871, Robert Schenck boarded ship to cross the Atlantic and present his credentials at the Court of St. James, he was making his first visit to Europe.

Schenck arrived in London at a momentous time in the history of transatlantic diplomatic relations. The Treaty of Washington, recently signed by the two nations, had established an arbitration commission to settle various bitterly contested issues arising out of the Civil War and to resolve other long-festering scores. The lengthy period of intense Anglo–American antagonism was drawing to a close. All through 1871 and 1872 Schenck busily aided the arbitration commission's work. When that was finished, his diplomatic labors eased considerably. Grant's reelection in 1872 meant that Schenck could continue in London if he wished to do so. And he did. He was a popular figure and an amusing character, well-received in London drawing rooms and in the great country houses; his oratorical humor and breezy informality gave the English what they took to be a whiff of the colorfulness of the Wild West.

But these happy times came to an abrupt end. The American West was characterized by other things besides breeziness and tall tales; it was a land of reckless speculation and shady dealings. A few months after his arrival in England, Robert Schenck had become involved in one of those speculative ventures: he had allowed his name to be listed as a member of the board of directors of a Utah silver mine, the "Emma" Mine. He said he had to do this because he was a poor man and the expenses of his post were considerable. London was no place for a poor republican. There was criticism of a minister's taking part in a company that was selling shares in the country to which he was accredited. Schenck, alarmed at the criticism, telegraphed U. S. Grant for advice. Grant, no stickler on such points, replied that Schenck "had a right to invest his money in anything he chose, if it were honest"; he also advised that withdrawal from the board was prudent. That apparently was the end of that. Public criticism died down, and British investors silently beguiled themselves with dreams of fabulous profits.

In 1876 the Emma Mine Company collapsed. Investors lost everything. The land of golden promise had once again turned into the land of stacked decks and con men. Stung again! The British victims, who never seemed to learn, were furious, and far from silent. Tempers weren't improved when an article was published in the *New York Tribune* reproducing a letter from Minister Schenck to a shady character who was among Emma's promoters.[2] In February of 1876 the House of Representatives passed a resolution instructing its Foreign Relations Committee to ascertain what action President Grant might take in regard to General Schenck's connection with the Emma Mine Company. When this was announced in the *Times,* it became clear to all that Schenck would not be able to continue in his post, especially since further embarrassing evidence was published in other London newspapers. He had to go — and he did. He didn't resign, make a statement, or formally withdraw, but simply boarded ship and sailed for home on March 4. On the whole, it wasn't an inspiring way to mark the centennial year of American independence.

*

The Emma Mine scandal and Robert Schenck's minuscule diplomatic achievements were soon forgotten. But the notoriety associated with his name lingered. That notoriety was based on something else. In 1872 he published a small book entitled *Draw: Rules for Playing Poker.* It was later said that he wrote the book in order to teach the game to Queen Victoria and the royal family. Actually, he wrote it at the request of an English friend, at whose country house he had spent a weekend, and to whose guests he had explained the rules of this exotic Yankee game, "of which some of them already knew a little."[3] As a compliment to Schenck, his handwritten rules were privately published: "It was very prettily done," Schenck wrote. Other editions soon followed in the United States.

Schenck's book, really just a pamphlet of fourteen pages, was the first effort to set down the rules of draw poker, which was at that time still a new version of the game. His summary of the rules has proved to be a standard one, with the exception of his opening statement: "The deal is of no special value and anyone may begin." The explanation of the rules was accompanied by occasional additional comments, in which the author went beyond mere rules and identified certain aspects of the essential character of the game. Schenck's phlegmatic little book brought down on him "the wrath and reprehension of many good people in America" — outrage and scandal that were attributable not just to the gamesman's precepts in the book, but even more to the unsavory reputation of the game at that time. To explain this attitude, we must briefly look at the history of poker in America.

Although they have been inveterate gamblers in all aspects of their culture, Americans have not invented any important card or dice games.[4] The most popular of their gambling games — faro, poker, and craps — are all of foreign origin. They were adopted by, and adapted to, American culture in the early nineteenth century; and all three games entered the country by way of New Orleans. Of these three, the most widely popular and long-lasting has been poker.

Poker's leading features were assumed in the process of its Americanization. As first played in New Orleans, at the beginning of the nineteenth century, it was the old Persian game *As Nas,* to which had been added elements of other Italian and Spanish card games of the seventeenth and eighteenth centuries. The first and most important change in poker was the increase in the number of cards used, from the original twenty or so to fifty-two. The most important contemporary influence on the evolving game was Brag, a popular English game of the eighteenth century, from which poker borrowed two crucial elements — wild cards and the idea of bluffing. For a number of years poker was also known as a "brag game." For its name, the game is indebted to the French *poque* and to the frontiersmen traveling down the Mississippi to New Orleans, who learned the game but never mastered French spelling or pronunciation; they turned *poque* into poke and finally into poker, a process more or less completed by 1825.

After that date the game spread quickly from the coffee houses and taverns of Louisiana and back up the Mississippi. At first it was thought of as exclusively a western and southern game. A New Yorker described it as "for all time the favorite game with the southerners, who never feel so happy as when they can succeed in 'bluffing' somebody off."[5] Until the 1840s poker was little known in the Northeast; and as late as 1848 the *Spirit of the Times* felt compelled to explain its rules to its readers. But poker spread phenomenally quickly in the 1850s, and by the time of the Civil War it was firmly established everywhere.

Poker gained a special hold on the American imagination, figuring countless times in drama and melodrama, and, later, in the movies. Few Western dime novels or films failed to include a climactic poker-playing scene. Poker also enriched the colloquial language. For example, the phrase "passing the buck" originated in poker. The practice of passing the deal to the left after each hand developed soon after the introduction of draw poker, and this led to the custom, originated on the frontier, of using a "buck" — an object, commonly a knife (with a buckhorn handle) — to mark who had the deal. A player who didn't want to deal was allowed to ante and pass the buck, a custom that has withered away in poker playing but remains firmly embedded in other walks of American life.

How can we account for the game's enormous and perhaps unprecedented popularity in America? The structure of poker encourages risk taking. It has also been a flexible and changeable game, not just in the sense that for a long time it was without clear and fixed rules — for Schenck's pamphlet marks the end of that period of its history — but also because the use of wild cards makes it seem permanently changeable. It has spawned many variations, and its continuing vitality was shown by the fact that two new forms, draw and stud poker, were not introduced until the mid-nineteenth century. Poker has proved equally attractive to country and city culture. It remained disreputable for a long time, because it was seemingly so dangerous, exciting, and risky; but it never had strong class or ethnic associations. Nor did it have sexual ones, although proper women were not supposed to play cards at all. In the West, at least, women cardplayers and women gamblers were not uncommon. Still, its tone has always been decidedly masculine, as much a symbol of masculine power as the board room, political caucus, and locker room. Betting has always been a supremely important aspect of poker, and the moment of climax, the jackpot (an early nineteenth-century addition), is also an essential part of its appeal.

Undoubtedly, poker's popularity has also been intimately connected with its pervasive atmosphere of deception and dishonesty, which was the source of much of its reputation for dangerousness. In the nineteenth century, a few professional poker players were known for their honesty, but cheating was a widely accepted aspect of play. American poker players were prolific inventors of new methods of cheating. Cardsharpers used marked and stripped cards; they stacked and milked the pack; they dealt from the bottom or surreptitiously exchanged one pack for another.

When all else failed, they invented the necessary devices for cheating, such as special spectacles and glass reflectors that were hidden among the chips. They developed vest, leg, knee, belt, and sleeve holders for cards, some of which were complicated gadgets operated by wires, springs, and clamps. Bottom dealing was brought to perfection in the Mississippi Valley in the 1830s and had a tremendous vogue for twenty years, falling into slight disfavor after that, not only on moral grounds but also because it was so difficult and so often bungled by the inept. When properly done, bottom dealing was a certain winner. "Almost any person, with a little practice, can deal from the bottom," wrote an experienced cardplayer in 1873; "but to perform the feat while several pairs of keen eyes are concentrating their gaze on your fingers and the pack held by them, requires an amount of coolness and nerve which is possessed perhaps by not one man in a million."[6] That of course didn't stop many from trying.

The pervasive atmosphere of cheating and deception may well be what has made poker seem to be such an accurate reflection of "real" life. Schenck's few personal comments seem to reflect this view.

> In the game every player is for himself and against all others, and to that end will not let any of his cards be seen, nor betray the value of his hand by drawing or playing out of his turn, or by change of countenance, or

any other sign. It is a great object to mystify your adversaries . . . To this end it is permitted to chaff or talk nonsense, with a view of misleading your adversaries as to the value of your hand. A skillful player will watch and observe what each player draws, the expression of the face, the circumstances and manner of betting, and judge, or try to judge, of the value of each hand opposed to him.

Bluffing had to be carried out boldly, or else "nobody will be likely to believe in his pretended strong hand."

Schenck's personal style, in his poker playing and in his political career, downplayed bluffing and emphasized cool prudence. He ended his book, and his observations on the game, with a succinct summary emphasizing chance and warning against the gamesman's intoxicating temptation to think he can surmount any odds. The main elements of success in the game, according to Schenck, were: "(1) good luck; (2) good cards; (3) plenty of cheek; and (4) good temper."[7]

*

Poker and chess exemplify American game playing in its two major aspects: psychological manipulation of the players and tactical mastery of space. For Americans, the complexities of poker reside primarily in the states-of-mind of the players, not in the combinations of the cards. Poker is essentially a test of nerve, not intelligence. It is psychological warfare, and so are most other things in life — diplomacy and love, politics and business. Chess was as foreign a game as poker was a native American one; yet chess has also had a remarkable cultural resonance for Americans. They came to see it as the image of their national expansion, since it involved occupying territory and outmaneuvering opponents. The frontiers of the American sporting mind are frontiers of space. But while chess has to do with the power of the mind over a horizontal plane that is the site of immensely intricate maneuvers, it also involves mental competition against an opponent — feint and thrust, anticipation and counterthrust. Chess symbolizes forethought and planning — the planning of order to be imposed upon indeterminacy — but it also involves the imposition of one's will upon an opponent. Like poker, it is psychological warfare. This aspect of the game was summed up brilliantly by Charles Francis Adams, Jr., who, at the end of a career of public service and business success, reflected on how much better chess was suited to the American temperament than was conventional academic education.

What would for me have been the most valuable of [courses] for purposes
of mental training has never been proposed — a course in chess! Gravely
to suggest it even would give rise to a look of surprise — probably a smile.
Yet what is it but the German *Kriegspiel* adapted to civil life? In playing
chess, you must have a defined plan of campaign and follow it up in-
telligently and consecutively; you must watch your opponent and understand and meet his play. You must measure yourself against him. All this
I have been doing after a fashion throughout my life; yet I never went
through any special training and preparation for it. A course in chess
would have been for me — *Kriegspiel*. So, also, for others. Why not sometimes educate through amusement? [8]

Poker and chess reflect the deepest aspiration of the American
sporting mind: the desire to make play scientific. Science for the
American gamesman means analysis: the identification of certain
means that produce certain results, the effort to systematize those
means, and then the attempt to create a plan of action based upon
this analysis. The sportsman of Harry Archer's type, who ultimately
concerns himself with cause and effect even more than with action,
dominates the sporting imagination of Americans. Nothing should
be taken for granted or accepted merely because it is customary;
every aspect of a game or sport, whether an individual or a team
sport, should be isolated and studied so that it can be shaped and
made over. Games need not simply be part of an unquestioned historical or traditional inheritance.

This way of thinking shaped the development of distinctively
American games and sports, a predictable result of the old Jacksonian search for an indigenous culture. But it also shaped the way
in which traditional games and sports were adapted to American
sporting life. In both cases, what had been rudimentary in Jackson's
time became more self-conscious and elaborate in the twentieth
century. Games became or were American by being scientific.

What happened was this. The flow of freely moving play was
stopped and broken into pieces. Barnum understood this sense of
discontinuity perfectly. Stopping and starting replaced continuous
movement. This meant that each segment of a game could be dealt
with individually and could be planned ahead of time. This process
was applied to time as well as to space and movement. Time was
stopped, divided up, and taken out. And the interrelationship of all
these segments was made infinitely stronger by the fact that parts
could be substituted for each other continuously.

The playing field, especially the practice field, is the laboratory where all these pieces — time, players, and sequence of moves — are studied. The coach or manager is the scientist in charge of the laboratory, which has many specialists at work, each dealing with certain aspects of the problem. From the practice field, the gym, the chalk session, the scouting reports, and the film room, the data is transmitted to the coach/manager, who is administrator as well as scientist. (When games become very complex businesses, a general manager or athletic director often assumes control over everything and everyone, including the field manager.) All of this data is incorporated in the master plan for the next game. Given enough study and patience, enough will power and skill, every contingency can be anticipated, and a perfect play or game is the result. Such a view is based on the assumption that habits can be corrected, custom altered, and human nature disciplined. Practice makes perfect. Accidents needn't happen. Thus the opposing team isn't the ultimate opponent: the real opponent is chance.

American football is the classic example. Created in the 1870s and 1880s, it grew out of the desire to invent something distinctively American that could be played at American colleges. Made up of elements of the English games of rugby and soccer, the original football game was a fluid game, despite the fact that it involved massed groups of men wedging themselves together, and depended on brute force. What subsequently distinguished it from rugby was the development of the idea that the controlling team must achieve a specified distance within a fixed number of plays (the number varied for quite a while) in order to make a first down, and thus begin another cycle of plays for the purpose of getting another first down. This allowed a team to control the ball for long periods of time and to use plays called ahead of time. Football differentiated itself from soccer by subordinating the foot to the hand and by limiting and defining the moves that could be made with the hand-passed ball; over a period of time, free passing backward and forward came to be sharply restricted. Movement was directed forward.

Baseball's popularity owed a great deal to many social and cultural factors, but it also owed much to the sport's evolved structure — its fixed number of innings and outs, and its specified number of balls and strikes (though here again a period of trial and error was needed before the number was settled on). Every pitch or movement was discrete and conceived of as part of a larger sequence. And changes in baseball over the first three quarters of the twentieth century have all been along the lines described above: there is greater specialization of function, and more players are manipulated; and the game is now controlled more from the dugout than from the field.

Basketball, a natively invented game dating from the 1890s, fits squarely within this pattern, with its endlessly repeated sequence of movements up and down the court, forward movement always being aimed at the point of focus, the basket. It is true that the original game was actually more static. There was a center jump for control of the ball after every score. In that sense modern basketball is a more fluid game. But the prevailing tendency has been to restrict fluidity, by the introduction of sequences of planned plays; by the use of set patterns on offense and defense; and, most notably, by the introduction, in professional basketball, of the twenty-four-second rule, which forces a team to give up the ball and prevents the unlimited passing back and forth that threatens to make the game fluid and less controllable.

This same pattern of interrupted movement is found in individual games as well, despite the fact that, given the structure of the game, one would not think it relevant. Take tennis. From the 1920s on, the direction of American tennis has been steadily away from long baseline rallies, protracted and indeterminable, and toward a forward forcing game that emphasizes the serve and control of the net, so as to end a rally before it can begin. The game has become a series of staccato bursts of power, defined sequences within the overall pattern of stroke and return.

The Jacksonian passion for speed is still present. It can be detected in this pattern of controlled sequence. For decades Americans cared more for sprints and dashes, in every kind of race, than for longer distances, and they still do; but this preference is now subordinated to the larger general concern for record keeping, which provides raw material for scientific analysis. William Porter, that rudimentary statistician of the 1840s, would be astounded at the volume of statistics, tables, records, and charts pored over by millions of sporting fans today. This concern with measurement is a reflection of the desire to establish an absolute standard of human achievement. In a world where so much is shifting and changing, where even history is revised regularly every generation, the record book is perhaps a source of certainty. There some final answer may at last be found. Yet balanced against that is the equally widespread belief that all records are provisional because human achievement is infinite. After all, we're not governed by the past, however splendid or sentimentally remembered: Babe Ruth gives way to Roger Maris and Henry Aaron. Record keeping is a roundabout way of asserting the belief that progress is undeniable.

Science, speed, space, and sequence: American team games present another aspect of these phenomena in relation to each other. Americans insist that they desire speed, or action, in their team games; but it is a mechanistic ideal, teamwork as clockwork. This supposedly explains why baseball supplanted cricket in popular favor, and why it has been supplanted (if it has been) by football. And fans do value movement, sudden bursts of movement — a long pass, a home run, a fast break, or a slam dunk — just as they relish rugged physical contact. But in fact they aren't much interested in the amount of movement in a game in proportion to its duration. Again, football is the prime example. The ball is in play only some seven or eight minutes out of sixty. And in baseball, too, not much happens in terms of continuous action. Americans really don't mind this, because they don't want action, they want analysis. Or rather, for them, analysis *is* action. It's the time between the plays that they value, the time they can use to fit what's just happened into the context of their strategy, adjust their plans for the next move, and guess and predict. There is as much interest in the game plan as in the game.

As good gamesmen, fans believe that they shouldn't accept the evidence perceived by their eyes. Con men and gamblers have taught them that the hand is quicker than the eye, and debunking historians have shown that things are rarely what they seem to be. Therefore, in the mind of the fan, the obvious action, the game on the field, is continually transformed into speculation about another game — the one that had been planned or is still being evolved in the mind of the manager or coach. The attempt to impose control is the real drama. This is what accounts for the fascination with sporting events on television and with TV's most celebrated technological achievement, the instant replay. By means of this device, television promises to allow ordinary people to perceive the reality behind appearances. As the coach says, "Don't ask me what happened until I look at the films." As Henry Herbert insisted, the essence of sport is reflection, not action.

*

And not nature. American sports began in the country as part of the unbroken flow of time. One season's sport gave way naturally to another, with no schedule needed. Admirers of the functional,

American sportsmen believed they were working along natural lines in developing their games; stripping down and paring away so as to achieve the functional simplicity and beauty of a blade of grass or a clipper ship.

Interest in functionalism can easily become something more, something else, however. It becomes an interest in equipment. The technology of American sport is one of its most fascinating aspects. Sportsmen of Jackson's day were already very interested in equipment: the poker player's equipment, for example, was part of a larger interest. Frank Forester's stories are packed with inside information about equipment, and that interest was found in field sports and sportsmen everywhere. In America, the interest in equipment quickly transferred itself to other sports of every imaginable kind; and in all cases equipment was in some way used to modify nature. By contrast, field sports have remained relatively traditional. In trotting, and thoroughbred racing, sailing, and running, and, later, in the new team sports of the late nineteenth century, American inventiveness, and investment, in sports equipment has been remarkable: uniforms, shoes, poles, hurdles, and pits; starting blocks for sprinters, and starting gates for horses; electronic devices. And more inventions will come in the future, as this interest in technique and equipment turns inward and becomes the scientific study of diet and drugs, and the effect they have on performance.

Much of this concentration on art and science, as opposed to nature, has had to do with surfaces. As Barnum saw, but in a different sense, American life was peculiarly a life of surfaces. The wholly manmade racetracks of Jacksonian days pointed directly toward the future. Great ingenuity was subsequently devoted to improving surfaces of all kinds; but however refined and smoothed, natural surfaces remained natural. The field was still uneven; and games were decided by bad hops and odd bounces. Even worse, the weather was bad; the light failed; the wind was too strong. All that study, strategy, and practice wasted — just because of a clump of grass, a gust of wind, or the sun's glare! Nature was careless. Nature equalled chance. And so nature must not be yielded to but conquered: as the Rockies and the plains had been conquered, as space has been conquered. One major breakthrough was the replacement of natural surfaces with artificial ones. But even more changes were to come.

The logical result of a century and a half of American sporting life was the Astrodome. In it, nature gives way to the marvels of engineering technology; it is the proper place for games that are themselves examples of engineering. Now *everything* can be controlled. It doesn't rain there, it's never too hot, too cold, too windy, or too dark. With nature and time subdued, everyone is free to concentrate on the business at hand. No more chance (almost), and no more alibis. Inside the dome, there's no excuse for not winning.

The sportsman was uprooted from his natural locale and depended on publicity, so it was inevitable that his private life would shrink and disappear, engulfed by his public one. And as he lost his private identity, his private residence ceased to distinguish him. Today the player becomes identical with the public architecture within which he performs. And that architecture is finally free from the past and able to evolve a form of its own. The classical tradition continued until the building, in the 1920s and 1930s, of Soldier Field, Yankee Stadium, and the Los Angeles Coliseum; they were virtually the last connecting links with the Hermitage and Newmarket. The international style that replaced them is largely an American invention; and it is a gamesman's style — detached, cool, imperturbable, and functional. One new baseball stadium is now interchangeable with another; and different sports are interchangeable within each stadium. The Astrodome has suites of rooms; one could virtually move in and live there. Why not? The gamesman is right to feel at ease. For him, the Astrodome is home.

*

The futuristic dome is the ideal place for the genius on the sidelines, in the dugout, or on the bench — the great American manager. Control and planning presuppose someone in control, who does the planning, plots the moves, moves the pieces, and fools the opposition. The descendants of Colonel Johnson, Richard Ten Broeck, and P. T. Barnum dot the domescape. American culture is rich with manipulative geniuses for heroes: Morgan, Mellon, and Rockefeller managed men and money with dazzling skill; Eisenhower, more organizer than warrior, supervised the most complex operation of all time, D-day.

Control has shifted to the sidelines, where the pokerfaced Napoleon stands, sending in the plays. The sporting version of Napoleon encompasses a wide range of temperaments and styles. One kind of manager generates heat: he is belligerent and fiery. John J. McGraw, the "little Napoleon" of the baseball Giants, was the most famous of this type, and Leo Durocher later followed in his footsteps. Football has produced many representatives, ranging from Knute Rockne to Vince Lombardi and Woody Hayes. Pep talks, locker-room histrionics, and psychological inspiration and intimidation are some of the techniques used, and the power of will sometimes explodes as violence. These leaders sometimes lose control of themselves. But they usually aren't out of control: firing up the troops is an age-old tactic. Their anger and despair are manipulative; emotion is simply one more weapon to be used.

The style of the major tradition of American managing is different. It is the straightforward poker face: Connie Mack, not even in uniform, sitting out of sight in the dugout, wigwagging his scorecard; Joe McCarthy, directing the General Motors Yankees of the 1930s, coolly pushing buttons; and John Wooden, of UCLA, the unobtrusive manager of temperamental stars, whose genius was not in a style of play but in the ability to organize material. The most famous exponents of the poker face are found in football, because there the contrast between the unleashed passion and violence on the field and the almost disdainful mastery of emotion on the sidelines is most dramatic: Jock Sutherland, Bernie Bierman, Bud Grant, and Tom Landry are prime examples.

Two figures, the greatest managers of the middle third of the twentieth century, tower above all the rest: Paul Brown and Casey Stengel. Brown epitomizes the classic tradition in its most comprehensive form: he is distant, impersonal, and a brilliant coach and general manager as well. Brown combined technical innovation, a speculative mind, and an iron will. Everything was subordinated to a system. The chief emotion he communicated was impatience with error. American football owes more to him than to anyone since its inception. Casey Stengel, at first glance, seems not to belong. Casey Stengel, comic and clown, defied the odds and played hunches, always going against the book. But not really. He was Napoleonic in taking the wider view. He saw baseball not as a series of separate games but as an entire season, and he marshaled all his resources and, with perfect timing, threw them into the battle. He made baseball more conscious than ever of its interchangeable parts, using every bit of material, wasting nothing. Far from being outside the tradition, Stengel belongs at its center. Casey Stengel, the arch gamesman, was cold as ice inside. Casey Stengel, from K.C., played the country bumpkin when he was in fact a sly garrulous old fox. Ole Case: a Barnum of our time.

*

P. T. Barnum meant business. And so has American sports. Play is play, but sport is all business, big business, and it has been for a long time. Richard Croker, boss of Tammany Hall at the end of the nineteenth century, knew the score if anybody did:

> Ever heard that business is business? Well, so is politics business, and reporting — journalism, doctoring — all professions, arts, sports — everything is business.[9]

The patterns of American games may be ones of discontinuity, but the history of American sport is continuous. Many Jacksonian traditions have come forward to our time.

The continuous pressure to make sport popular has reached unprecedented proportions. Sport is entertainment and can pay stupendous returns, but to do so it must be publicized and must draw the people and their money. Everything that stands in the way must be removed. In the Jacksonian Era, means to achieve this were limited; but in the years that followed, national newspapers, then radio, and finally television allowed sports promoters to bypass old barriers of local and regional feeling and reach a national market. And the Jacksonian battle against exclusiveness has also continued. Class barriers haven't lasted long. But at the same time there have been few Astor Place riots. Sporting fans today are very conservative, as they always have been. What blew class barriers down wasn't the proletariat storming the gates of the jockey club, country club, or opera house. Barriers were broken not by guns and trumpets but by the cash register, the dissolving power of money.

And the Jacksonian ambivalence about exclusiveness has also remained. Who wants to belong to a club everyone can belong to? College football as an embodiment of English tone and ideas of sportsmanship lasted until World War I; then the Ivy League gave way, attention shifted, and the Middle West became big time. Although country clubs stemmed the equalitarian tide, their exclusive sports were taken away from them. Golf courses became public links; and as golf began to attract money, golfers began to come from all social strata. The Master's Tournament is a pretentious self-parody and shows how completely the battle has been lost. In no sport of today does money play a more unabashed role. The ranking of players is based almost entirely on how much money they have won on the tour.

It took longer for tennis to break away from its English tradition of gentility and restraint, on-court sportsmanship and white-suited decorum. Even in the 1930s and 1940s, clay courts and concrete courts attested to the encroaching power of popular interest, but from Tilden to Budge the spirit that prevailed was watered-down Wimbledon, and its Americanized version was Forest Hills. Then Pancho Gonzales, in the 1950s, and Arthur Ashe, in the 1960s, broke the spell of ethnic and racial exclusiveness. But the really radical figures were comparative insiders — Jack Kramer and Bobby Riggs, that Barnumesque con man. They were the ones who established the tennis tour, going out and creating a market. They showed that tennis was worth promoting. Amateurism was quickly blown off the court, and touring companies of players have now established competitions that convey the same ambiguous quality, somewhere between actual competition and show-business rivalry, that Hiram Woodruff hated in hippodroming. The change in the behavior of tennis crowds is most startling of all. But raucous and combative as they have now become, tennis crowds are after all very much like Jacksonian crowds at horse races or cockfights, hoping to influence, perhaps even determine, the outcome of the match.

*

What about those older Jacksonian sports, the subjects of this book? Trotting was the first of these to become businesslike and systematically organized. By the 1870s a Grand National Circuit of a dozen cities, from Buffalo to Chicago, was established, with race dates and programs scheduled in advance. This was a golden age of trotting. Even Dexter's records were surpassed, and one great trotter after another came on the scene. New York became the undisputed center of harness racing and breeding, and there the sport's great national race, the Hambletonian, was established. But the golden glow presaged decline. Trotting lost its hold in the cities. The advent of electrified public transportation, and, following that, the motor car, drove the trotter off the streets. Trotting couldn't achieve the large-scale urban orientation of thoroughbred racing. It remained tenaciously close in atmosphere to Hiram Woodruff's time and to its country origins. John Greenleaf Whittier's vigorous evocation of country life gave way to the hazy sentimentality of James Whitcomb Riley. Trotting remained popular but not big time. It remained local, the sport of the county fair and the small town.

Baseball expanded its hold on city populations, and much of its success in supplanting cricket as the national game, after the Civil War, was attributable to this. Baseball succeeded by retaining something of both cultures — rural playfulness and urban knowingness, an atmosphere of country pastures in the middle of the big city. Baseball's development into a big business, while initially less rapid and systematic than trotting's, was finally much more widespread and comprehensive. By the end of the nineteenth century two major leagues had developed, with teams in large cities where attendance and resources were greatest. A loosely linked chain of lesser teams connected the city centers with the sport's raw material, the boys on the farms and in the towns who aspired to sporting fame. In the 1930s, this system was perfected into a precisely graded hierarchical production and distribution system, a conveyer belt that carried every piece to its appropriate destination, from Class D to Class AAA and the majors. This was Branch Rickey's "farm system," a charming tribute to the country origins of the sport. Colonel Stevens would have been appalled at the way competition was ruthlessly squelched in the process, but this is actually one of baseball's most important claims to its place as the national game, for it mirrors the transformation of Jacksonian laissez faire into the monopoly capitalism of our day.

Prize fighting's national development after John Heenan's day had its own distinctive elements. The old prize ring was reformed, with change coming from England in the form of padded gloves and new rules forever associated with one of the sport's aristocratic patrons, the marquis of Queensbury. American prize fighters truculently resisted such sissified changes, but there was no stopping the new style of the 1880s. John L. Sullivan personified the transformation of prize fighting into boxing. He was the last of the great pugilists, a product of the local ethnic culture emerging from New York and Boston that had always been the breeding ground of brawlers. But he also represented the future and was a national and international figure. By the time the Great John L., overweight and overage but still thought of as invincible, fell before the stylish Gentleman Jim Corbett in 1892, the systematic organization of boxing was well under way, though it never became neatly ordered.

Boxing was organized; it was divided into various weight divisions, with agreement as to the champion in each division. The numerous local fight clubs gradually became informally connected; the smaller ones fed their raw material into the larger, and so on up to the center of the web, the fight clubs of New York City. Madison Square Garden became the Barnum's Museum of the boxing world, and, in the early twentieth century, Tex Rickard emerged as the sport's first flamboyant showman. Boxing began to regulate and supervise itself to a modest degree and thus became legal in most states; and as it became legal and prospered, it became semi-respectable, attracting a wider social following. In the 1920s, Rickard presided over the full emergence of boxing as a fashionable sport. The two enormously publicized fights between Jack Dempsey and Gene Tunney were national events, and they matched two men who harkened back to two very old traditions of the prize ring: Dempsey fought in the brawling tradition of rough-and-tumble, that of the firehouse street fighter, while Tunney represented, in a prim and proper way, the old style of the dandy, which went back to Gentleman Jackson.

At least these fighters represented a white man's version of those traditions. Racial and ethnic conflict remained ever present. Irish-American fighters deeply resented the presence of black fighters and did their best to keep them out of organized big-time boxing. John L. Sullivan wouldn't fight blacks. He represented the prevailing attitude. The 1890s and the first decade of the twentieth century were the most savage years of segregation and racial violence in American history. Yet even though black boxers were denied a chance at most prizes, they gradually managed to gain partial acceptance in the lower weight levels. And most fans agreed, in private anyway, that such fighters as Peter Jackson, Joe Dixon, Joe Gans, and Joe Walcott were as good as, or better than, the white champions of the time. Black boxing history is filled with uncrowned champions at all levels, but it was the heavyweight championship that mattered most and was farthest out of reach.

On July 4, 1910, exactly one hundred years after Tom Molineaux had had his first chance in England, a black man seized the crown and changed boxing forever. This was Jack Johnson, the most important heavyweight champion in the history of American boxing. By knocking out Jim Jeffries, Johnson not only won the title, but introduced the modern era of multiracial sporting life in America; for other sports were also exclusively white at that time. It was too much for most whites to bear. The proud and defiant Johnson was eventually stripped of his title and driven from the ring. But it was he, and the New Deal, that only a quarter of a century later made possible the triumphant career of Joe Louis, the only heavyweight champion who ranks with Johnson in historical significance. The Brown Bomber was the symbol of the slowly awakening vision of racial harmony in the United States, and he inaugurated the present period of boxing history, in which the ring is dominated by black fighters.

Horse racing long remained too mixed and chaotic to be systematically organized on a national scale. A national pattern finally emerged, however, three quarters of a century after William Porter's abortive efforts. Mighty plutocrats like August Belmont, Peter Widener, and William C. Whitney eventually gained control of New York racing, and from that dominating vantage point — in terms of crowds and money — exerted the kind of financial and social authority previously identified only with the British aristocracy. And so, although the early twentieth century, like the early nineteenth, was in many ways a low point in racing history — inveterate corruption made racing illegal in New York for a decade — a more businesslike and systematic organization finally came into being. The power and prestige of a few jockey clubs and a few large tracks — in New York, Maryland, and Illinois — set the tone. These clubs were able to enforce their rules. They offered large purses and attracted many spectators, and they overawed smaller jockey clubs and independent promoters. As Progressive reformers determinedly cleaned up vice in the cities, gambling was driven to the racetracks, the only places it was legal; and the tracks capitalized on this by policing themselves and their sport. National standards and procedures gradually developed.

Racing has become a machine for moneymaking, its operations as efficient as its modernistic grandstands are antiseptic, its tone perfectly adapted to the mechanical ring of the parimutuel machines and to the finish-line cameras and automatic starting gates. Success depended upon the attendance of the city millions. Racing came to have a year-long season, with winter racing in Florida and California, the meetings lasting several weeks at each track, the operation involving many races, many horses, and short distances. The purses grow larger each year, the racing form's records become more detailed, and the jockeys are wealthy and celebrated. Yet the sport is unpredictable as ever, the lure of inside information is as tempting, and the running of the horses is as beautiful to watch.

Over the years, wholly unplanned, three races, the Kentucky Derby, the Preakness, and the Belmont — which were only randomly related and were to a great extent the creations of modern publicity — came to constitute preeminent national racing events, known as the triple crown. Such interplay of chance and randomness is entirely fitting in the history of American horse racing. And modern horse racing has another point of connection with its Jacksonian past. The oldest of these races, the Kentucky Derby, emerged from obscurity very slowly. It is now over a century old. Such longevity amid great change serves, despite the bogus mint-julep-and-colonels atmosphere surrounding the race, to remind a few, at least, of the days of Lexington and Richard Ten Broeck, of the early days of the blue-grass country, and, before that, of Tennessee and the simpler sport at Clover Bottom.

*

Let us return briefly, then, to Jacksonian associations. Robert Schenck had already reached university age when Andrew Jackson went to the White House; and he had reached Congress before the old hero died. Schenck's identification with poker in some ways marks him, in popular terms, as more typically Jacksonian than Old Hickory himself. It isn't clear whether Andrew Jackson played poker or not, but one of the most famous "honest" poker players of the 1830s and 1840s, John Powell, was a friend of Jackson's and supposedly spent a good deal of time at the Hermitage. So it's highly likely that Jackson knew the game even if he didn't play it. In any event, Jackson played poker of other kinds all his life, and played it very close to the vest. Henry Clay and John C. Calhoun, in regard to the Bank of the United States and to nullification, had both called Jackson's bluff, only to find that he wasn't bluffing. Jackson didn't need Robert Schenck's book to learn how to play his cards to win.

In nineteenth-century America, poker and politics were closely associated. Washington, D.C., was for decades the greatest poker-playing town in the country. And the White House, from the administration of U. S. Grant through that of Grover Cleveland and down to that of Warren Harding, was notoriously identified with poker and its accompanying atmosphere of whiskey, cigars, and inside deals — an atmosphere that gave credence to Josh Billings's comment: "Although you find me here in Washington, I come of good family." Robert Schenck was once thought of as the most skillful of these political players. He had played in memorable games against Daniel Webster and Henry Clay, and he lived on to play in other celebrated games in the years after the Civil War, after his return from London.

Schenck had come back to America in 1876 in what would have conventionally been thought of as a state of disgrace. But he seems not to have felt this or to have been in the least bothered by his dismissal, keeping throughout the good temper that he had identified as one of the poker player's most necessary attributes. And by the standards of his time, and later times, his indiscretion was a penny-ante one. Schenck was cleared of any actual complicity in the Emma fraud and thereafter lived in Washington, benign and imperturbable, practicing law, playing poker, and observing the interminable political games that went on all around him. He had seen much and done much, and had survived it all. Blameless or not, the gray-haired old fellow died on March 24, 1890, full of years and guile. Sportsmen often come to melancholy, even tragic, ends. Gamesmen die peacefully in bed.

*

Time runs out for everyone. There's no stopping *that* clock. Until the end we move back and forth between polarities: tradition and innovation, gamesmanship and sportsmanship. The tendency to organize play was immensely strengthened in American culture because sport was a widely available means of controlling the looseness and limitlessness of life all about. The need for a native tradition, however, soon became the need to reject tradition. Deception became a form of freedom from the past. Once play became sport, Americans played a double game: the game within the rules and the game against the rules. One ordinary American gamesman put it simply. Having studied the rule book in spring training, Buck Ewing said to his players: "Boys, you've heard the new rules read. Now the question is: what can we do to beat them?"[10]

This tension between control and anarchy is very intense. The view that individuals possess the power to control events was memorably expressed by an American poet who loved sports: "Chance is a regrettable impurity," wrote Marianne Moore.[11] That view finds its nemesis in the ever-lurking suspicion that the world is chance, and nothing more. Most people move between such extremes, just as they move forward and backward in time, just as they travel to and fro from where they began to where they'll end. For countless centuries people have lived in cities and in the country, and have moved ceaselessly from one to the other, searching for excitement in cities, only to return to seek renewal in country ways and country games.

NOTES & INDEX

Notes

1. The Sportsman and the Hermitage (*pages 3–21*)

A primary source for Andrew Jackson's sporting career is his correspondence, James Spencer Bassett, ed., *The Correspondence of Andrew Jackson,* 7 vols. (Washington, D.C., 1926). The most useful biography is James Parton, *The Life of Andrew Jackson,* 3 vols. (New York, 1860). Parton, an English immigrant, became the most popular biographer of the mid-nineteenth century. Jackson had been dead only ten years when Parton began his research; so he could return to the scenes of Jackson's youth and talk to people who had known him, including a few who remembered him as a very young man. The result was one of the great biographies in our language. Parton's chief failing, in the eyes of later, more skeptical historians — that he didn't sufficiently distinguish between verifiable fact and contemporary legends and tales — is one of the most interesting features of his work for us now, because we can see the process of mythmaking at a popular level taking place in the pages of his book. Augustus C. Buell, *History of Andrew Jackson,* 2 vols. (New York, 1904) is also helpful on Jackson's youth and sporting activities; and so is Marquis James, *Andrew Jackson,* 2 vols. (New York, 1937). There are many other biographies of Jackson, but they concentrate on his political and military careers. Among these, the most helpful for the early days in Tennessee is Thomas Perkins Abernethy, *From Frontier to Plantation in Tennessee: A Study in Frontier Democracy* (Chapel Hill, 1932).

1. E. T. Clark, ed., *The Journal and Letters of Francis Asbury,* 3 vols. (London and Nashville, 1958), especially volume II, *The Journal, 1794–1816,* 4–6, 10, 41.
2. This quotation is attributed to Edward Bulwer-Lytton, the nineteenth-century English novelist.
3. Michel Chevalier, *Society, Manners and Politics in the United States* (Ithaca, 1969), 305. This excellent modern edition is by a notable Jacksonian scholar, Professor John William Ward. Change had been present from the start. The records of Plymouth Colony of 1627 reveal that it was agreed in a full meeting of the court "that fowling, fishing and hunting be free." C. E. Goodspeed, *Angling in America* (Boston, 1939), 2.

4. Parton, *Life of Jackson*, I, 109.
5. Frederick Marryat, *A Diary in America* (1839), ed. S. Jackman (New York, 1962), 11; and Chevalier, *Society, Manners and Politics*, 87.
6. Jackson, *Correspondence*, I, 42.
7. Buell, *History of Jackson*, I, 108–109. For Jackson's hatred of England, see Buell, *History of Jackson*, I, 117. Jackson said of Alexander Hamilton: "Personally, no gentleman could help liking Hamilton. But his views were all English; not in the least American." Buell, *History of Jackson*, I, 172.
8. *American Turf Register and Sporting Magazine*, Sept., 1829.
9. Jackson, *Correspondence*, VI, 425.
10. Jackson, *Correspondence*, VI, 172–173. See also, *American Turf Register*, April 1831: "I ask, what possible connection is there, or can there be, between the worth of the man and the blood of his horse?"
11. My sense of the broad extent of what we mean by the Jacksonian Age owes most to the book that remains the most brilliant overall treatment of Jacksonian culture, Arthur M. Schlesinger's *The Age of Jackson* (Boston, 1945). On Jackson's symbolic importance, see John W. Ward, *Andrew Jackson, Symbol of an Age* (New York, 1955).
12. Parton, *Life of Jackson*, I, 106.
13. Parton, *Life of Jackson*, I, 104–105.
14. See C. A. Finsterbusch, *Cockfighting All Over the World* (New York, 1929); Tim Pridgen, *Courage: The Story of Modern Cockfighting* (Boston, 1938); George W. Means, *The Game Cock from Shell to Pit* (New York, 1922); Archibald Ruport, *The Art of Cockfighting* (New York, 1949).
15. Jackson, *Correspondence*, I, 2.
16. Parton, *Life of Jackson*, I, 253.
17. Parton, *Life of Jackson*, I, 166. Jackson's admiration for Napoleon was lifelong. In 1807 he wrote: "Bonaparte has destroyed the Prussian army. We ought to have a little of the emperor's energy." *Correspondence*, I, 161. In 1818 Jackson was given a bronze bust of Bonaparte by citizens of New Orleans, and he noted this "display of gratitude paid to the fallen Napoleon by his countrymen" with approval. *Correspondence*, VI, 467. And as late as October, 1842, Francis Blair sent Jackson a willow cut from Napoleon's tomb at St. Helena, to be planted at the Hermitage. *Correspondence*, VI, 173–174.
18. *American Turf Register*, April, 1831.
19. As quoted in Clinton Rossiter, *The American Presidency*, 2d. ed. (New York, 1960), 150.
20. As quoted in T. H. Bird, *Admiral Rous and the English Turf, 1795–1877* (London, 1939), 83.
21. Jackson, *Correspondence*, I, 205. Jackson on prudence: "By always knowing your means, and living within them, you will get thro' life. This has been my rule and I recommend it to you." *Correspondence*, IV, 433.
22. Hugh Jones, *The Present State of Virginia* (London, 1724), 48. Jones went on to say: "The common planters, leading easy lives, don't much admire labor or any manly exercise except horse-racing, nor diversion except cock-fighting."

The best primary source for the organization of American jockey clubs is John Beaufrain Irving, *The South Carolina Jockey Club* (Charleston, 1857); also see the *American Turf Register* and the *Spirit of the Times*. John Irving was an English immigrant who served for many years as secretary of the South Carolina Jockey Club, whose history he wrote. There was never any doubt in his mind that American horse racing must approximate English racing as closely as possible, if it was to pretend to be the sport of the turf.

This view has been shared by most of the standard works on American horse racing that have followed Irving's. These include: Charles Trevathan, *The American Thoroughbred* (New York, 1905); F. B. Culver, *Blooded Horses of Colonial Days* (Baltimore, 1922); Frank Griswold, *Race Horses and Racing* (New York, 1926); John Hervey et. al., *Racing and Breeding in America and the Colonies* (New York, 1931); Fairfax Harrison, *The Roanoke Stud, 1795–1833* (Richmond, 1930); Fairfax Harrison, *The John's Stud, 1750–1788* (Richmond, 1931); and James Douglas Anderson, *Making the American Thoroughbred* (Norwood, Mass., 1916). I wish to emphasize that while I don't accept the general point of view of these books, they are indispensable for studying the subject.

John H. Wallace, *The Horse of America, in His Derivation, History and Development* (New York, 1897) deserves special note. A member of a distinguished Iowa farming, journalistic, and political family, Wallace's work carries on the family tradition of maverick independence. This book is odd, prolix, and packed with information and independent views. I have depended on it in many ways.

There are several fine general sporting histories that have material on horse racing: Jennie Holliman, *American Sports, 1785–1835* (Durham, 1931); Herbert Manchester, *Four Centuries of Sport in America, 1490–1890* (New York, 1931); John Allen Krout, *Annals of American Sport*, vol. XV of *The Pageant of America* (New Haven, 1929); Robert B. Weaver, *Amusements and Sports in American Life* (Chicago, 1939); and Foster R. Dulles, *America Learns to Play: A History of Popular Recreation, 1607–1940* (New York, 1940).

23. An example: "In the early days of racing in South Carolina, the gentlemen of the Turf . . . never ran their horses for the pecuniary value of the prize to be won, but solely for the honor that horses of their own breeding and training should distinguish themselves." Trevathan, *The American Thoroughbred*, 21.

24. Alexander Bruce, *Social Life of Virginia in the 17th Century* (Lynchburg, 1927), 199. The following books, although general historical works, contain a good deal of sporting information, mostly having to do with the South: Gaillard Hunt, *Life in America One Hundred Years Ago* (New York, 1914); James Truslow Adams, *Provincial Society, 1690–1763* (New York, 1927); Thomas J. Wertenbaker, *The First Americans, 1607–1690* (New York, 1927); Arthur M. Schlesinger, Sr., *The Birth of the Nation* (New York, 1969); Ulrich B. Phillips, *Life and Labor in the Old South* (Boston, 1937).

25. *American Turf Register*, June 1830. On the same subject: "After the close of the Revolution a perfect avalanche of race horses was poured

upon us, some of which were good, but a great majority of them were never heard of after their arrival, on the race course or elsewhere." Wallace, *The Horse of America,* 117.

26. Wallace, *The Horse of America,* 94.

2. The General and the Colonel (*pages 23–44*)

For this chapter I've used many of the same books as for chapter 1.

1. Buell, *History of Jackson,* I, 68–69.
2. Jackson, *Correspondence,* I, 111.
3. Parton, *Life of Jackson,* I, 64.
4. Jackson, *Correspondence,* V, 263.
5. Jackson, *Correspondence,* IV, 475.
6. Jackson, *Correspondence,* IV, 475.
7. Jackson, *Correspondence,* IV, 431.
8. Parton, *Life of Jackson,* I, 112.
9. George Templeton Strong, *The Diary of George Templeton Strong,* 4 vols., ed. A. Nevins and M. Thomas (New York, 1952), I, 263.
10. Parton, *Life of Jackson,* I, 228–229. This story is a good example of Parton as legend collector and storyteller. The account of the incident was often repeated, in many different versions. Parton's version best captures the flavor of popular admiration for Jackson.
11. Jackson, *Correspondence,* IV, 442. For the image of Jackson as both Hercules and Hamlet I am indebted to Louis Hartz's remarkable book, *The Liberal Tradition in America* (New York, 1955). Hartz's comment deserves fuller quotation:

> Imagine Andrew Jackson in the England of the eighteen thirties or forties . . . Where would he have stood? The fact is, he would not have known where to stand. He would have wandered homelessly over the face of Europe, a lost giant from another world finding parts of his personality in various places but the whole of it nowhere . . . The American democrat, for all of his giant size and his complex virtue, was a strangely pathetic figure even at home . . . It was not easy all at once to be a landed "aristocrat," a farmer, a laborer. Psychic tensions appeared. It reminds one that when the New World began to cross strains with the Old what emerged was not quite a Hercules but a Hercules with the brain of a Hamlet [pp. 117–119].

12. Jackson, *Correspondence,* IV, 442.
13. As quoted in Bird, *Admiral Rous and the English Turf,* 12.
14. Benjamin Franklin, *Autobiography.* James Parton put this wonderfully: "Jackson was . . . solvent by nature; a fact which goes far to justify the immovable confidence which the masses of the people came to have in their unlettered, and, in some respects, unlovely hero; while they could never be brought to love or trust some of his contemporaries, whose debts were as magnificent as their endowments." Parton, *Life of Jackson,* I, 114.
15. Anne Hollingsworth Wharton, *Social Life in the Early Republic* (Philadelphia, 1902), 211–212. On Washington, D.C., see Constance

McLaughlin Green, *Washington, Village and Capital, 1800–1878* (Princeton, 1962).

16. Greville is quoted in Bird, *Admiral Rous*, 143–144.
17. There is a good deal still to be understood about dueling in America. I found three contemporary nineteenth-century sources useful: Walter Colton, *Remarks on Duelling* (New York and Boston, 1828); James Sega, *An Essay on the Practice of Duelling, As It Exists in Modern Society* (Philadelphia, 1830); Lyman Beecher, *The Remedy for Duelling: A Sermon Delivered Before the Presbytery of Long Island* (New York, 1809). The one systematic treatment I know of by a recent writer is: William O. Stevens, *Pistols at Ten Paces: The Story of the Code of Honor in America* (Cambridge, Mass., 1940). See also Guy A. Cardwell, "The Duel in the Old South: Crux of a Concept," *South Atlantic Quarterly* vol. LXVI, no. 1 (1967), 50–69. There are many references to dueling in the sporting newspapers of the time.
18. D. H. Lawrence, *Studies in Classic American Literature* (Phoenix Edition, London, 1964), 56, 60.
19. My sketch of Colonel Johnson's career is based mainly on references to him in the *Spirit of the Times*. The entry on him in the *Dictionary of American Biography*, "William Ransom Johnson," is very helpful. There are some manuscript papers of his at Duke University that I have not seen, which deal primarily with his business affairs. A study of the economic basis of his horse racing would be instructive. That he is an important symptomatic figure in the development of American sports I have no doubt; nor did his contemporaries.
20. Josiah Quincy, *Figures of the Past* (Boston, 1926), 82–85. Eclipse vs. Henry is probably the most written-about horse race in American sporting history; there are many references to it in contemporary sporting papers and memoirs.
21. Trevathan, *The American Thoroughbred*, 138–145.
22. Jenny Holliman, *American Sports*, 121. Another estimate of the extent of sectional feeling is the following, written many years later, on the occasion of Eclipse's death:

> No one who ever witnessed the race will ever forget the clear and distinct manifestation of a feeling known before to exist, but called forth and embodied in that contest — in a manner quite as unmistakable as unprecedented — of North and South . . . It may seem trivial to say so, but it is nevertheless in our judgment entirely true, that the moral influence on the question of North and South . . . of the Eclipse and Henry race, was both decided and permanent — and that a leaven was set in motion which has been working ever since and finally that between that contest and the feeling aroused by the Wilmott Proviso a connection might be traced. [*Spirit of the Times*, July 31, 1847]

23. "In the old days professional turfmen were unknown. Now they dominate the turf. The Napoleon of the Turf, although respectable as a merchant, a planter, and a politician, is generally regarded as of the latter class." *Spirit of the Times*, Jan. 10, 1857.
24. See the recent book by Mark Girouard, *Life in the English Country House* (New Haven, 1978).

25. *Spirit of the Times,* Dec. 27, 1890.

26. *American Turf Register,* Jan. 1838.

27. The gamesman is closely related to the trickster but not identical with him. The exploration of the figure of the trickster owes most to the work of Carl Jung. The best explication of Jung's ideas that I know of is in Paul Radin, *The Trickster* (London, 1956). The trickster and con man have recently been provocatively studied by a number of students of American literature. See Richard Boyd Hauck, *A Cheerful Nihilism: Confidence and the Absurd in American Humorous Fiction* (Bloomington, 1971); Susan Kuhlmann, *Knave, Fool and Genius: The Confidence Man As He Appears in Nineteenth Century American Fiction* (Chapel Hill, 1973); and Warwick Waddington, *The Confidence Game in American Literature* (Princeton, 1975). See also the path-breaking study by Walter Dubler, "Theme and Structure in Melville's *The Confidence Man,*" *American Literature,* vol. 33, no. 3 (Nov. 1961).

28. *Spirit of the Times,* April 14, 1849.

29. "Sorry we are to record — what all must have noticed in these more degenerate times — that the sole object of the present race of Turfmen seems to be, to win the purses — no matter how." *Spirit of the Times,* Apr. 7, 1849.

30. Parton, *Life of Jackson,* I, 113.

31. *American Turf Register,* Jan. 1838.

32. On Talleyrand and English jockeys see *American Turf Register,* Sept. 1842. On Sam Bugg: Henry Watterson, *"Marse Henry": An Autobiography,* 2 vols. (New York, 1919), II, 213. Also see Thomas D. Clark, *Bluegrass Cavalcade* (Lexington, Ky., 1956).

33. *Spirit of the Times,* Dec. 27, 1890.

34. Ralph Waldo Emerson, *The Complete Works of Ralph Waldo Emerson,* vol. 4, *Representative Men* (Boston and New York, 1904), 224.

3. William T. Porter and the *Spirit of the Times* (47–65)

There are two indispensable sources for the study of William Porter's life and career. The first is the *Spirit of the Times.* I have looked at every issue from the years when Porter was associated with the paper but have of course used only a tiny fraction of the vast amount of sporting material in its pages. The second is the biography of Porter written soon after his death by his brother-in-law: Francis Brinley, *Life of William T. Porter* (New York, 1860). Much of the material for this chapter is taken from Brinley's book. There are also a few letters from Porter to Carey and Hart, the publishers of his two sporting anthologies, at the New York Historical Society. The biography of Henry Herbert, which Porter was working on at the time of his death, has apparently disappeared. There is a first-rate scholarly study of Porter, his newspaper, and their relation to American literature: Norris W. Yates, *William T. Porter and the "Spirit of the Times": A Study of the Big Bear School of Humor* (Baton Rouge, 1957).

1. Francis Baily, *Journal of a Tour in Unsettled Parts of North America, in 1796 and 1797* (London, 1856), 197.

2. Daniel Webster, who studied law in Salisbury, Vermont, with Benjamin

Porter's brother-in-law, and who was often in the Porter house, said that Benjamin Porter was the most attractive social companion he had ever known. But the surviving Webster–Porter letters are all about business matters. See Charles M. Wiltse, ed., *The Papers of Daniel Webster,* volume I, *Correspondence, 1798–1824* (Hanover, N.H., 1974), 73, 74, 83.

3. Brinley, *Porter,* 16.
4. Of course this had been happening for a long time. See Richard Bushman, *From Puritan to Yankee* (Cambridge, Mass., 1967).
5. Brinley, *Porter,* 22, 32.
6. *New York Mirror,* Nov. 15, 1829. For information on New York journalism I have depended on the standard works: Frank Luther Mott, *American Journalism: A History, 1690–1960* (New York, 1962); and Frank Luther Mott, *History of American Magazines,* 4 vols. (New York, 1938), especially volumes I and II. Also see James Playsted Wood, *Magazines in the United States* (New York, 1956), particularly for its circulation statistics, pp. 51, 55.
7. Details about the first issue of the *Spirit* can be found in: Carvel Collins, "The Spirit of the Times," *Papers of the Bibliographical Society of America* 40 (1946), 164–168; Richard Boyd Hauck, "Predicting a Native Literature: William T. Porter's First Issue of the *Spirit of the Times,*" *Mississippi Quarterly* 22 (1968/69); Clarence S. Bingham, "Letter to the Editor," *Papers of the Bibliographical Society of America* 48 (1954), 300–301.
8. Considerations of space prevent me from discussing here the work and career of a most interesting and important sporting journalist and editor, John Stuart Skinner, creator of the first American journal primarily devoted to sporting life — the *American Turf Register and Sporting Magazine,* which I have drawn on many times in these pages. Skinner's life and work can be studied in Benjamin Perley Poore, *Biographical Sketch of John Stuart Skinner* (1854). A third important figure, who ranks with Porter and Skinner as historian and editor, was Cadwallader R. Colden. Colden spent his life collecting materials on horse racing and edited two publications, the *New York Sporting Magazine* and its successor, the *United States Sporting Magazine,* from 1833 to 1836.
9. Brinley, *Porter,* 45.
10. Brinley, *Porter,* 37–41.
11. Brinley, *Porter,* 45.
12. Brinley, *Porter,* 43.
13. Brinley, *Porter,* 55.
14. For information on this period in British racing, and on this issue, I have depended primarily on Roger Mortimer, *The Jockey Club* (London, 1958) and on Bird, *Admiral Rous and the English Turf.*
15. An Argentine visitor noted: "The sentiment of unity, centralization, and organization struggles at a disadvantage against local and individual energy which is the basis of the political organization of the country and the product of the protestant spirit." Domingo Sarmiento, *Sarmiento's Travels in the United States in 1847,* introduced by M. A. Rockland (Princeton, 1970), 277.
16. Brinley, *Porter,* 269.

17. *Spirit of the Times,* May 22, 1847.
18. Brinley, *Porter,* 271.
19. Brinley, *Porter,* 69.
20. J. Frank Kernan, *Reminiscences of the Old Fire Laddies and Volunteer Fire Departments of New York and Brooklyn* (New York, 1885), 14–15. William Ellery Channing, in his "Remarks on National Literature," had been forthright: "We cannot admit the thought that this country is to be only a repetition of the old world." On the other side of the Atlantic, Thomas Carlyle, far from an uncritical admirer of American democratic culture, had at the same time seen things in it that were remarkable. He told Theodore Parker, in reference to James Bowie: "By Hercules! the man was greater than Caesar or Cromwell — nay nearly equal to Odin or Thor. The Texans ought to build him an altar." *Spirit of the Times,* July 13, 1850.
21. Brinley, *Porter,* 69.
22. There is a very large body of literature on Southwestern humor: F. J. Meine, *Tall Tales of the Southwest* (New York, 1930); Constance Rourke, *American Humor* (New York, 1931); Walter Blair, *Native American Humor* (New York, 1937); Kenneth Lynn, *Mark Twain and Southwestern Humor* (Boston, 1959). Especially useful for me was W. S. Hoole, *Alias Simon Suggs: The Life and Times of Johnson Jones Hooper* (Tuscaloosa, Ala., 1952). An excellent anthology is Hennig Cohen and William B. Dillingham, eds., *Humor of the Old Southwest* (Athens, Ga., 1975). Of particular importance is Norris Yates's book mentioned at the beginning of these notes for chapter 3, and the following articles: Eugene Current-Garcia, " 'York's Tall Son' and his Southern Correspondents," *American Quarterly* 7 (1955), 371–384, and the same author's "Mr. Spirit and the Big Bear of Arkansas," *American Literature* 27 (1955). But I wish to emphasize that I have only touched on a few of the aspects of the relationship between this kind of literature and American sporting culture.
23. Brinley, *Porter,* 66.
24. Brinley, *Porter,* 273.
25. Brinley, *Porter,* 79.
26. *Porter's Spirit of the Times,* Oct. 4, 1856.
27. William T. Porter, letter of Feb. 14, 1845, to Carey and Hart, *Miscellaneous Manuscripts,* #2284, New York Historical Society.
28. Brinley, *Porter,* 265.
29. Hoole, *Alias Simon Suggs,* 119.
30. Brinley, *Porter,* 268.

4. Henry William Herbert and Frank Forester (*pages 67–87*)

Henry William Herbert's voluminous writings are the primary sources for any study of him. A full bibliography of his work exists: William Mitchell Van Winkle, *Henry William Herbert: A Bibliography of His Writings, 1832–1858* (Portland, Maine, 1936). The most important essay on Herbert, on which I have drawn a good deal, as have all others who have written about him, is Thomas Picton's "The Story of His Life," an introduction to D.

W. Judd, ed., *The Life and Writings of Frank Forester* (New York, 1882), 2 vols. Also by Picton is "Reminiscences of a Sporting Journalist," *Spirit of the Times,* April 1, 1882. There are scattered letters by Herbert at the New Jersey Historical Society, New York Public Library, American Antiquarian Society, and the Library of Congress.

The 1930s marked the beginning of a revival of interest in Herbert, sparked by William Southworth Hunt, *Frank Forester: A Tragedy in Exile* (Newark, 1933); and Luke M. White, Jr., *Henry William Herbert and the American Publishing Scene, 1831–1858* (Newark, 1943). Two books that touch on aspects of Herbert's life are: Charles Hemstreet, *Literary New York, Its Landmarks and Associations* (New York, 1903) and Mrs. E. B. Hornby, *Under Old Roof-Trees* (Newark, 1908).

The intellectual and literary world of New York of this time is masterfully portrayed in Van Wyck Brooks, *The World of Washington Irving* (New York, 1944). Herbert's life as an immigrant can be studied in the context set by Rowland T. Berthoff, *British Immigrants in Industrial America, 1790–1950* (Cambridge, Mass., 1953).

1. William Hunt, *Frank Forester,* 24–27.
2. Judd, *Life and Writings,* I, 12–13.
3. The best general treatment of American social history remains Dixon Wecter, *The Saga of American Society* (New York, 1937). The conventional hatred of the theater is summed up by the words of Horace Greeley, whose views on many other things were far from conventional: "Each theatre contains within its walls a grog-shop and a place of assignation"; "a large proportion of those connected with the Stage are libertines and courtezans." Mott, *American Journalism: A History, 1690–1960,* 5th ed. (New York, 1966), 271.
4. Henry James, *The American Scene* (London, 1907), 23–24. There was a reason for moving to New Jersey rather than somewhere in upstate New York. Joseph Bonaparte lived in New Jersey, and for his benefit the New Jersey legislature had passed a law allowing aliens to own land. See Judd, *Life and Writings,* I, 88.
5. Judd, *Life and Writings,* I, 24–25. *The Magnolia* of 1836 contained five items by Herbert, and that of 1837 contained six. For a vivid account of the New York magazine and publishing scene in these years see Perry Miller, *The Raven and the Whale* (New York, 1956) and M. A. De Wolfe Howe, *American Bookmen* (New York, 1898).
6. Frank Forester, *The Deerstalkers,* 19–20.
7. Frank Forester, *The Warwick Woodlands,* 148. On the question of dandyism, note the following about the writer N. P. Willis: "An essential element of dandyism in Willis and everything he did was probably the cause of what might be called his personal unpopularity in print." Howe, *American Bookmen,* 112.
8. Frank Forester, *The Deerstalkers,* 163.
9. Frank Forester, *The Warwick Woodlands,* 134.
10. Frank Forester, *The Deerstalkers,* 149–150.
11. Henry David Thoreau, *Cape Cod,* 82.
12. Frank Forester, *The Warwick Woodlands,* 87.

Notes

13. Frank Forester, *My Shooting Box*, 123. Women as the enemies of the sportsman's freedom are a familiar theme. For example: "It is the woman who wants to deprive the man of his powder, shot, and whiskey, his guns and grog." *American Turf Register*, March 1831.
14. Henry Herbert letter, dated Dec. 5, 1857, in Herbert, *Miscellaneous Manuscripts*, #2665, New York Historical Society.

5. John Cox Stevens and America (*pages 91–120*)

1. Philip Hone, *The Diary of Philip Hone, 1828–1851*, 2 vols., ed. Allan Nevins (New York, 1927), II, 709–710.
2. The primary materials on the life of John Cox Stevens are the Stevens family papers at the New Jersey State Historical Society in Newark. These papers, available now on microfilm, contain no special sporting collection, but references to the family's sporting activities are to be found scattered throughout. Colonel Basil M. Stevens, in the early twentieth century, collected many notes and clippings in preparation for writing a book on the family. This was never completed, but the notes are in roll #45 of the microfilm edition. I refer to it throughout this chapter. An authorized biography of Colonel John Stevens, which contains a good deal of material on John Cox and his sailing brothers, was written by Archibald Douglas Turnbull: *John Stevens: An American Record* (New York and London, 1928). This is especially good on the family's business interests and affairs.
3. On the evolution of American sailing ships, see: Arthur P. Middleton, *Tobacco Coast: A Maritime History of Chesapeake Bay in the Colonial Era* (Newport News, Va., 1953); Howard Chapelle, *The History of American Sailing Ships* (New York, 1936); Frank Bowen, *A Century of Atlantic Travel, 1830–1930* (London, 1932); Frank Bowen, *The Golden Age of Sail, Indiamen, Packets and Clipper Ships* (London, 1925); Thomas J. Wertenbaker, *Norfolk, Historic Southern Port* (Durham, 1931); Henry Adams, *History of the United States During the Administrations of Thomas Jefferson and James Madison*, 9 vols. (New York, 1889–1891), especially vol. 7; and Louis J. Hennessey, *One Hundred Years of Yachting* (New York, 1949).
4. Henry Adams, *History of the United States*, vol. 7, 311–318.
5. Jasper Ridley, *Lord Palmerston* (New York, 1970), 156.
6. Turnbull, *John Stevens*, 185.
7. Turnbull, *John Stevens*, 354.
8. Robert Hale Newton, *Town and Davis, Architects* (New York, 1942), 297–298.
9. Philip Hone, *Diary*, 511–512.
10. *Stevens Family Papers*, microfilm roll #45, New Jersey Historical Society.
11. Turnbull, *John Stevens*, 454, 459.
12. For this section on clipper ships and the gold rush, I have used the previously cited books by Bowen and Chapelle, as well as: Basil Lubbock, *The China Clippers* (Glasgow, 1914); Edward Keble Chatterton, *Fore and Aft* (London, 1912); the same author's *Sailing Ships: The Story of Their Development from the Earliest Times to the Present Day*

(London, 1909); and Richard McKay, *Some Famous Sailing Ships and Their Builder, Donald McKay* (New York, 1928).

13. George Templeton Strong, *The Diary of George Templeton Strong,* 4 vols., ed. A Nevins and M. Thomas (New York, 1952), I, 86.
14. Domingo Sarmiento, *Sarmiento's Travels in the United States in 1847,* introduced by M. A. Rockland (Princeton, 1970), 219–220.
15. *Spirit of the Times,* Sept. 11, 1847.
16. Mark Twain, *Life on the Mississippi.*
17. Philip Hone, *Diary,* II, 767–768.
18. *Spirit of the Times,* Aug. 29, 1846.
19. *Spirit of the Times,* June 28, 1851.
20. *Spirit of the Times,* Sept. 13, 1851.
21. *Times* (London), Aug. 25, 1851.
22. *Spirit of the Times,* July 26, 1851.
23. *Stevens Family Papers,* roll #45.
24. *Stevens Family Papers,* roll #45.
25. *Spirit of the Times,* Sept. 13, 1851.
26. *Spirit of the Times,* Sept. 6, 1851.
27. *Spirit of the Times,* Sept. 6, 1851.
28. There are numerous accounts of the race. In the section that follows I have mostly used the lively account that appeared in several issues of the *Spirit of the Times,* which was based on on-the-spot observation by the paper's correspondent. See also: Thomas Lawson, *History of America's Cup* (Boston, 1902).
29. *Spirit of the Times,* Sept. 13, 1851.
30. Strong, *Diary,* II, 65–66.
31. Turnbull, *John Stevens,* 516.
32. Oliver Wendell Holmes, *The Autocrat at the Breakfast Table* (Cambridge, Mass., 1858), 171.
33. *American Turf Register,* Nov. 1830.
34. Horatio Greenough's essays appeared as *The Travels: Observations and Experiences of a Yankee Stonecutter* (New York, 1852). They were long out of print and now are available in an excellent edition that appears under the title *Form and Function, Remarks on Art,* ed. H. A. Small (Berkeley, 1947).
35. *Stevens Family Papers,* roll #45.

6. Richard Ten Broeck and the American Invasion
(pages 123–157)

1. For information on American horse racing in the nineteenth century, I have depended on many of the same sources indicated in chapters 1 and 2. In addition, I have leaned heavily on contemporary sporting journals — the *American Farmer,* the *American Turf Register,* and the *Spirit of the Times.*
2. *Spirit of the Times,* Oct. 16, 1847.
3. *American Turf Register,* Sept. 1837.
4. Bird, *Admiral Rous and the Spirit of the English Turf,* 208. There are many references to all these aspects of American horse racing in the *Turf Register* and the *Spirit of the Times,* and in travelers' accounts.

See also: Bruce, *Social Life of Virginia,* 199–215, and Trevathan, *American Thoroughbred,* 15–36.

5. For English racing and its contrast with American racing I depended most on Bird, *Admiral Rous;* T. A. Cook, *A History of the English Turf,* 3 vols. (London, 1901); A. D. Luckman, *Sharps, Flats, Gamblers and Race Horses* (London, 1914); William Day, *Turf Celebrities I Have Known* (London, 1891); Stephen Fiske, *English Photographs, by an American* (London, 1869); and, for the later period, T. H. Browne, *History of the English Turf, 1904–1930* (London, 1931). On Newmarket there is the excellent book by Roger Mortimer, *The Jockey Club,* previously noted; also Bird, *Admiral Rous;* and Eric Rickman, *Come Racing with Me* (London, 1951). The figures about jockey-club membership were taken from the *Spirit of the Times,* and are slightly inaccurate.

6. References to general disorder are so common in the sporting newspapers that it would be inconvenient to list them separately. It was their pervasiveness that eventually made me suspect that the picture of American racing given in Irving and his followers, Trevathan, Hervey, and others, was misleading. This subject deserves fuller study than I have been able to give it. On drunkenness, which, along with spitting, foreign travelers never tired of mentioning, see Charles Dickens, *American Notes and Martin Chuzzlewit.* The heavy drinking went far back. See the despairing comment made in 1815 by Bishop Asbury, whom I quoted at the beginning of chapter 1: "there was a dance — such fiddling and drinking! . . . We were greatly annoyed by a brigade of Kentuckians; can fiends be more wicked? The drunkards kept the house in an uproar." *The Journal of Francis Asbury,* 795.

7. *Spirit of the Times,* May 1, 1847.

8. *American Turf Register,* Feb. 1834.

9. Irving's *History of the South Carolina Jockey Club* is the source to start with for a study of the organization of American racetracks; but the jockey club in Charleston was not in some important respects typical of most American clubs.

10. Dale A. Somers, *The Rise of Sports in New Orleans, 1850–1900* (Baton Rouge, 1972), 29–30. This book is a model of the kind of local study that would put the history of American sports in a proper historical perspective. The greater part of it deals with the period after that of this book, but I have gained much from reading it. I should also add that Professor Somers's interpretation of some aspects of social history runs counter to the ideas I have expressed.

11. *Spirit of the Times,* Aug. 29, 1846.

12. *American Turf Register,* Oct. 1836.

13. *American Turf Register,* Nov. 1829.

14. *Porter's Spirit of the Times,* Dec. 20, 1856.

15. Oliver Wendell Holmes, *The Autocrat of the Breakfast Table* (Cambridge, Mass., 1858), 34–35.

16. A multitude of books and pamphlets put the case against gambling with uninhibited passion but doubtful effect. Two representative examples from the nineteenth century: Henry Ward Beecher, *Lectures to Young Men on Various Important Subjects* (New York, 1860) and Mason

Locke Weems, *God's Revenge Against Gambling, Exemplified in the Miserable Lives and Untimely Deaths of a Number of Persons of Both Sexes* (New York, 1816). A more recent study is Henry Chafetz, *Play the Devil: A History of Gambling in the United States* (New York, 1960).

17. Sources about the life and career of Richard Ten Broeck are scanty and scattered. I have depended on his autobiographical article, "Some Personal Reminiscences, Incidents and Anecdotes" in the *Spirit of the Times* of Dec. 27, 1890, published when he was 78 years old. Also see the sketch in the *Dictionary of American Biography*, volume XVIII. Emma Ten Broeck Runk's *The Ten Broeck Genealogy* (New York, 1897) is no help. There are occasional references to Ten Broeck in the *Spirit of the Times*, where he was always mentioned favorably, and in most of the books about American horse racing, the fullest appearing in Dale Somers's *Rise of Sports in New Orleans*. The books by Day and Bird touch on his English visit. There are no personal letters that I know of.

18. *Dictionary of American Biography*, XVIII.

19. *Spirit of the Times*, Dec. 27, 1890.

20. *Spirit of the Times*, Dec. 27, 1890.

21. *Spirit of the Times*, March 18, 1848; and *Spirit of the Times*, Dec. 27, 1890.

22. *Spirit of the Times*, Dec. 27, 1890.

23. Somers, *Rise of Sports in New Orleans*, 26–32; Gerald M. Capers, *The Biography of a River Town: Memphis, Its Heroic Age* (Chapel Hill, 1939); also the *Spirit of the Times*, March 25, 1848.

24. M. C. F. Houstoun, *Hesperos; or, Travels in the West*, 2 vols. (London, 1850), II, 70. See also Salomon de Rothschild, *A Casual View of America, 1859–1861* (New York, 1962), 111.

25. *Spirit of the Times*, Dec. 27, 1890.

26. Trevathan, *American Thoroughbred*, 305.

27. *Spirit of the Times*, Aug. 22, 1846.

28. *American Turf Register*, Dec. 1831.

29. *Spirit of the Times*, Aug. 22, 1846.

30. *Spirit of the Times*, Dec. 13, 1856.

31. For the story of Ten Broeck's fortunes in England, I have depended almost entirely on his own words in "Personal Reminiscences" in the *Spirit of the Times*, Dec. 27, 1890.

32. William Day, *Turf Celebrities*, 220–290.

33. Bird, *Admiral Rous*, 199–202.

34. The most interesting descriptions of Keene I know of appear in Stephen Fiske, *Off Hand Portraits of Prominent New Yorkers* (New York, 1884) and in Day, *Turf Celebrities*.

35. *Dictionary of American Biography*, XVIII; also, obituaries in San Francisco's *Bulletin, Chronicle* and *Examiner* for Aug. 6, 1892.

7. Paul Morphy Against the World (*pages 159–191*)

1. Benjamin Franklin, "The Morals of Chess," reprinted in Ralph K. Hagedorn, *Benjamin Franklin and Chess in Early America* (Philadelphia, 1958), 15–20.

2. There are two indispensable sources dealing with the life and chess career of Paul Morphy. One is Daniel Willard Fiske, *The Book of the First American Chess Congress: Containing the Proceedings of That Celebrated Assemblage, Held in New York in the Year 1857, with the Papers Read in Its Sessions, the Games Played in the Grand Tournament, and with Sketches of the History of Chess in the Old and New Worlds* (New York, 1859). The title is misleading. Although it is primarily about the Chess Congress of 1857 and was written to commemorate that event, it actually includes a great deal of very valuable material, which is to be found nowhere else, about the history of chess in the United States. In fact, so extensive did Fiske's researches become that the book grew to twice the size initially intended and was not completed until two years after the congress. As a result, the book's compilers were able to include an account of Morphy's trip to Europe. Fiske took pains to be accurate, giving Morphy the final version of the material for his approval.

The second important source is Frederick Milnes Edge, *The Exploits and Triumphs, in Europe, of Paul Morphy, the Chess Champion: Including an Historical Account of Clubs, Biographical Sketches of Famous Players, and Various Information and Anecdote Relating to the Noble Game of Chess* (New York, 1859). Edge's book is lively and, while wholly admiring, does not go in for exaggeration, on the sensible principle that the unvarnished truth about Paul Morphy was remarkable enough. Its chief limitation is one of scope; it is almost entirely about events in Europe and concludes with Morphy's return to the United States, which coincided with the publication of the book.

There are three books that deal primarily with Morphy's personal life, especially the years after his chess triumphs. All are difficult to get hold of. The most dependable and least eccentric in tone is a small volume by C. A. Buck, entitled *Paul Morphy: His Later Life* (Newport, Ky., 1902). Buck was an admirer who devoted himself to gathering information about Morphy. Buck's publisher said that much of that information came from "authentic sources" in New Orleans, with "Morphy's relatives and friends giving him great assistance." The accuracy of this claim is difficult to estimate, but Buck's views are sober and sensible. The other two books are more problematic. Louis Albert Morphy, *Poems and Prose Sketches, with a Biographical Memoir* (New Orleans, 1921) was privately published. The author was a great-nephew, and his book is both odd and interesting, devoting most of its attention to Morphy's illness and last years, and seeking to understand Morphy's life by means of some kind of doctrine of philosophical inevitability. Though pretentious and sometimes unintelligible, there are bits of information in it that appear nowhere else. Regina Morphy-Voitier, *Life of Paul Morphy in the Vieux Carré of New Orleans and Abroad* (New Orleans, 1926) is perfectly intelligible but unrelentingly snobbish in its main purpose, which was to establish the superiority of the Morphy family's social position. But it is of special value, for Mrs. Morphy-Voitier, a great-niece, quotes family letters and stories. It may well be that it was written as a sort of reply to Louis Albert's earlier account, an effort to set the record straight in a respectable fashion. But that record, like Morphy's life, is anything but straight.

There are a great number of books of chess analysis that refer to Paul Morphy. Very few of these contain any biographical material. J. J. Lowenthal's *Morphy's Games of Chess* (London, 1860), the first book about his games, contained a preface of a few words by Morphy himself. Philip Sergeant, the leading student of Morphy's chess playing, re-edited this book in an expanded form as *Morphy's Games of Chess* (London, 1916); there is material of interest in this and in Sergeant's *Morphy Gleanings* (London, 1932).

3. Regina Morphy-Voitier, *Life of Paul Morphy,* 28.
4. Philip W. Sergeant, *Morphy's Games of Chess,* 1–36.
5. See Ralph K. Hagedorn, *Benjamin Franklin and Chess in Early America* (Berkeley, 1958).
6. D. W. Fiske, *Book of the Chess Congress,* 50.
7. Fiske, *Book of the Chess Congress,* 55–56. Domingo Sarmiento, the Argentinian visitor, noted the same thing, describing Washington, D.C., as "a town which is the center of nothing, neither of the country's geography, nor of its intelligence, nor of its wealth, nor of its culture, nor its communications system." Domingo Sarmiento, *Sarmiento's Travels in the United States in 1847,* introduced by M. A. Rockland (Princeton, 1970), 257.
8. Sergeant, *Morphy's Games of Chess,* 1–36.
9. Sergeant, *Morphy's Games of Chess,* 1–36.
10. Frederick Edge, *Exploits and Triumphs,* 15–16.
11. Sergeant, *Morphy's Games of Chess,* 1–36.
12. Fiske, *Book of the Chess Congress,* 94.
13. Edge, *Exploits and Triumphs,* 12.
14. Sergeant, *Morphy's Games of Chess,* 1–36.
15. I have used H. J. R. Murray, *A Short History of Chess* (Oxford, 1963), for much of the historical background; this is an abridgment of Murray's classic that was published in 1913. A newer work that will take its place alongside Murray is H. R. Golombek, *A History of Chess* (London, 1976).
16. Edge, *Exploits and Triumphs,* 13.
17. C. A. Buck, *Paul Morphy,* 8–9.
18. Morphy-Voitier, *Life of Paul Morphy,* 19.
19. Edge, *Exploits and Triumphs,* 194.
20. Morphy-Voitier, *Life of Paul Morphy,* 24. For a description of the fuss made on Morphy's return to the United States, see the *New York Tribune,* May 26, 1859.
21. Morphy-Voitier, *Life of Paul Morphy,* 24.
22. Morphy-Voitier, *Life of Paul Morphy,* 23–24.
23. Elizabeth H. Cawley, ed., *The American Diaries of Richard Cobden* (Princeton, 1952), 201–202.
24. J. J. Lowenthal early on noted a distinctive aspect of American play: "One attribute of American play struck me forcibly, quickness. Here in Europe a match game occupies a whole day; but in America I have played three and four at the same sitting." Fiske, *Book of the Chess Congress,* 395–396.
25. G. A. MacDonnell, *Chess Life Pictures* (London, 1883), 79.
26. S. Tartakower, *A Breviary of Chess,* 119–121, 135.

27. Edge, *Exploits and Triumphs,* 194.
28. Edge, *Exploits and Triumphs,* 13–15.
29. Morphy-Voitier, *Life of Paul Morphy,* 20.
30. Edge, *Exploits and Triumphs,* 13–15.
31. Imre Konig, *Chess from Morphy to Botwinnik* (New York, 1977), 202.
32. Edge, *Exploits and Triumphs,* 158.
33. Sergeant, *Morphy's Games of Chess,* 1–36.
34. Sergeant, *Morphy's Games of Chess,* 1–36.
35. H. J. R. Murray, *Short History of Chess,* 88. C. A. Buck, *Paul Morphy,* p. 23, says the same thing.
36. Ernest Jones, "The Problem of Paul Morphy: A Contribution to the Psycho-Analysis of Chess," *The International Journal of Psycho-Analysis* XII, January 1931. A writer who has carried on this line of analysis, while refining and modifying Jones's position, is the player and analyst Reuben Fine. He has written a number of interesting books, among them *The Psychology of the Chess Player* (New York, 1967) and *Psychoanalytic Psychology* (New York, 1975).
37. Sergeant, *Morphy Gleanings,* 25–26.
38. Louis Albert Morphy, *Poems and Prose Sketches,* 99.
39. Buck, *Paul Morphy,* 21; and Louis Albert Morphy, *Poems and Prose Sketches,* 99–100.
40. Poe's M. Dupin spoke scathingly about chess: "The game of chess, in its effects upon mental character, is great misunderstood . . . The higher powers of the reflective intellect are more decidedly and more usefully tasked by the unostentatious game of draughts than by all the elaborate frivolity of chess. In this latter, where the pieces have different and bizarre motions, with various and variable values, what is only complex, is mistaken (a not unusual error) for what is profound." Poe, "The Murders in the Rue Morgue."
41. I am indebted to Professor Maurice Natanson of Yale University for initially pointing out to me that Poe and Morphy may be compared in various ways; those put forward here, however, are my responsibility. Another of these comparisons is to be found in T. S. Eliot's description of Poe as a writer whose prose seems neither English nor American: "There is a certain flavour of provinciality about [Poe's] work . . . ; it is the provinciality of the person who is not at home where he belongs, but cannot get to anywhere else. Poe is a kind of displaced European; he is attracted to Paris, to Italy and to Spain, to places which he could endow with romantic gloom and grandeur . . . He seems a wanderer with no fixed abode." Eliot, "From Poe to Valery," *The Hudson Review* vol. II, no. 3 (Autumn 1948), 327–342.
42. *Spirit of the Times,* Oct. 27, 1849.
43. Morphy-Voitier, *Life of Paul Morphy,* 16.
44. William Macready, *The Diaries of William Charles Macready, 1833–1851,* 2 vols., ed. William Toynbee (London, 1912), II, 249.
45. Morphy-Voitier, *Life of Paul Morphy,* 51.
46. Morphy-Voitier, *Life of Paul Morphy,* 22.
47. *Illustrated London News,* Apr. 30, 1859.
48. Many people in New Orleans believed that Morphy's "peculiar faculty"

was a positive disadvantage. Whitelaw Reid, a visitor to New Orleans, went to a dinner where, among the guests, "was a modest-looking little gentleman, of retiring manners, and with apparently very little to say; though the keen eyes and well shaped head sufficiently showed the silence to be no mask for poverty of intellect. It was Mr. Paul Morphy, the foremost chess-player of the world, now a lawyer, but, alas! by no means the foremost young lawyer of this his native city. 'If he were only as good in his profession as he is at chess playing!' said one of the legal gentlemen, with a shrug of his shoulders, as he spoke in an undertone of the abilities of the elder Morphy, and the hopes that had long been cherished of the son. They evidently looked upon the young chess player as a prosperous banker does upon his only boy, who persists in neglecting his desk in the bank and becoming a vagabond artist." Whitelaw Reid, *After the War, A Tour of the Southern States,* ed. C. Vann Woodward (New York, 1973), 261.

49. Sergeant, *Morphy Gleanings,* 24.
50. Stanley Weintraub, *Whistler: A biography* (New York, 1974), 47.
51. Henry James, *Hawthorne* (London, 1879), 3.
52. Emerson to Whitman, July 25, 1855, as quoted in *Selections from Ralph Waldo Emerson,* ed. S. Whicher (Cambridge, Mass., 1960), 362.
53. James, *Hawthorne,* 44.

8. John C. Heenan and Adah Menken (*pages 193–234*)

1. Almost every book on the history of the prize ring, English or American, contains some account of the Heenan–Sayers fight. The best account I know of, by someone actually present, is Frederick Locker-Lampson, *My Confidences* (London, 1896). All previous secondhand treatments are now superseded by the recent book by Alan Lloyd, *The Great Prize Fight* (New York, 1978), which should be considered the standard source. Mr. Lloyd is especially good on the network of transatlantic prize-ring contacts that formed the immediate background of the fight.
2. Trevor Wignall, *The Story of Boxing* (London, 1923), 170.
3. Wignall, *Story of Boxing,* 171.
4. The *Times* quoted in Wignall, *Story of Boxing,* 169.
5. Foster R. Dulles, *America Learns to Play: A History of Popular Recreation, 1607–1940* (New York, 1940), 146.
6. Frederick Locker-Lampson, *My Confidences,* 223–229.
7. Wignall, *Story of Boxing,* 175.
8. William H. Russell, *My Diary, North and South,* ed. F. Pratt (New York, 1954), 14.
9. The classic source for most of what we know about the English prize ring is Pierce Egan, *Boxiana; or Sketches of Ancient and Modern Pugilism; From the Days of the Renowned Boughton and Slack to the Heroes of the Present Milling Era, by One of the Fancy* (London, 1812). Egan was a journalist and man-about-town who had an acute historical sense and an insatiable interest in prize fighting and in life. His accounts, which appeared in the papers of the day and were published in book

form over a number of years, are witty and vigorously phrased. A cheap and readily available American edition would be of great benefit to all American students of prize fighting. Of the many other English books about the prize ring, I have depended most on Trevor Wignall, *The Story of Boxing* (London, 1923); and on *The Lonsdale Library*, volume XI, *Boxing* (London, 1931).

10. The American prize ring of course had no one remotely like Pierce Egan as contemporary observer and preserver. But there are some interesting contemporary sources, all of which are difficult to obtain: *Life and Battles of Yankee Sullivan, Embracing Full and Accurate Reports of His Fights with Hammer Lane, Bob Caunt, Tom Secor, Tom Hyer, Harry Bell, John Morrisey, Together with a Synopsis of His Minor Battles from His First Appearance in the Prize Ring Until His Retirement* (Philadelphia, 1854); and *The American Fistiana, Showing the Progress of Pugilism in the United States, from 1816 to 1873* (New York, 1873). Among the many more recent works, I have used Alexander Johnson, *Ten — and Out! The Complete Story of the Prize Ring in America* (New York, 1928).

11. Wignall, *Story of Boxing*, 209.

12. Pierce Egan, *Boxiana*, III, 566–567.

13. James Parton, *The Life of Andrew Jackson*, 3 vols. (New York, 1860), I, 261.

14. Pierce Egan's accounts are indispensable for an understanding of Richmond's career; but there are two pioneering works that appeared well before the current awareness of the importance of black athletes in American sporting history: Nat Fleischer, *Black Dynamite, the Story of the Negro in the Prize Ring from 1782 to 1938*, 5 vols. (New York, 1938) and Edwin B. Henderson, *The Negro in Sports* (Washington, D.C., 1939).

15. This and all quotations in this section are taken from Egan, *Boxiana*, 440–449.

16. Molineaux's career has lent itself to fantasy and exaggeration, for example in Louis Golding's *The Bare Knuckle Breed* (London, 1952); and even when the accounts are not so fictional as this, many comments are mainly conjecture. It is thought that Tom Molineaux's father, Zachary, was a prize fighter; and others have said that his grandfather was also. My account, in this section, is based on Egan, *Boxiana*, 360–371, 401–421.

17. It was subsequently charged that Cribb beat Molineaux because of interference by Cribb's seconds and because of the influence of the crowd. Egan said nothing about cheating by the seconds, and this was not the kind of thing he would have ignored. As to the sentiments of the crowd — "the crowd was in perpetual state of alarm lest the black should win" (*Lonsdale Library, Boxing*, 31) — there is no evidence that this made any real difference in the outcome.

18. The fight was not totally ignored; there are very occasional references to Molineaux in the sporting papers of the mid-nineteenth century, but no sense that Molineaux and Richmond belonged to a common prize-fight heritage.

19. Frederick Van Wyck, *Recollections of an Old New Yorker* (New York, 1932), 114.
20. *Spirit of the Times,* Feb. 3, 1849.
21. George Templeton Strong, *The Diary of George Templeton Strong,* 4 vols., ed. A. Nevins and M. Thomas (New York, 1952), I, 51. In the New York Public Library there are quite a few manuscript and type-script materials, as well as many pamphlets of the time, that deal with the question of physical fitness. For example: Charles Cardwell, *Thoughts on Physical Education: Being a Discourse Delivered to a Convention of Teachers in Lexington, Kentucky on the 6th and 7th of November 1833* (Boston, 1834).
22. Oliver Wendell Holmes, *The Autocrat of the Breakfast Table* (Cambridge, Mass., 1858), 146.
23. Wignall, *Story of Boxing,* 210. There is an excellent unpublished source for the study of early nineteenth-century sports and amusements in New York and vicinity that deserves full publication (parts of it have appeared in the *New York Historical Society Quarterly,* volumes 21, 22, and 23). This is Gabriel Furman, "The Customs, Amusements, Style of Living and Manners of the People of the United States from the First Settlement to the Present Time." Furman (1800–1854) was a lawyer and historian of New York City and Brooklyn, and this work, written about 1844, covers a wide range of amusements and sports in an unusually fresh and perceptive fashion. There is an interesting passage about boxing in his history: "In the City of New York, at the present day, boxing in its most refined state, together with other Gymnastic Exercises, as they are termed, is taught. It was introduced a few years since by Mr. William Fuller, a noted pugilist, at the 'New York Gymnasium.' There are no public exhibitions of pugilistic skill, all is conducted privately — so much so, that the windows of the exhibition room do not open to the public street." Furman, "Customs," 303–305, New York Historical Society, manuscript #2673.
24. For an example, see Robert Waln, Jr., *The Hermit in Philadelphia* (Philadelphia, 1821). This pamphlet contains a good deal of incidental information about the contemporary sporting scene, but it is mainly of interest for its furious attack on democracy and for its view that public prize fighting would have terrible consequences. This "foreign folly" would elevate "the coal heaver, the publican, the porter or the negro — who happen to possess muscular strength, large bones and a thick skull — into the rank of society and fashion."
25. *Niles Register,* Oct. 18, 1817.
26. Philip Hone, *The Diary of Philip Hone, 1828–1851,* 2 vols., ed. Allan Nevins (New York, 1927), II, 636–637.
27. Salomon de Rothschild, *A Casual View of America, 1859–1861* (New York, 1962), 30–31.
28. Rothschild, *A Casual View of America,* 30–31.
29. *Spirit of the Times,* June 17, 1848.
30. The loyalties of American prize fighters were often political in a directly personal sense, as suggested by the account of a fight between Lee Sims, a black blacksmith, and Elias Grimsley, a bully and loafer. Sims

thrashed Grimsley, saying at the end of the fight: "I'll let you know I am a Jackson man you damned Adams son of a bitch." *American Turf Register*, Sept., 1830.

31. William Macready, *The Diaries of William Charles Macready, 1833–1851*, 2 vols., ed. William Toynbee (London, 1912), II, 419.

32. Meade Minnigerode, *Fabulous Forties, 1840–1850: A Presentation of Private Life* (New York, 1924), 187–203. I have also used J. T. Headley, *The Great Riots of New York, 1712–1873* (New York, 1873) and Michael Feldberg's excellent *The Philadelphia Riots of 1844: A Study in Ethnic Conflict* (Westport, Conn., 1975).

33. Headley, *Riots of New York*, 114.

34. Minnigerode, *Fabulous Forties*, 208.

35. Minnigerode, *Fabulous Forties*, 205.

36. On firehouse culture I have most frequently consulted two books. One is J. Frank Kernan, *Reminiscences of the Old Fire Laddies and Volunteer Fire Departments of New York and Brooklyn* (New York, 1885) and the other is by that much-neglected historian of American popular culture, Herbert Asbury — *Ye Old Fire Laddies* (New York, 1930). See also Herbert Asbury, *The Gangs of New York* (New York, 1928).

37. The number of holidays or festive days had declined sharply. Gabriel Furman listed some twenty-seven such occasions in the late eighteenth century; by the Jacksonian period only a handful remained. Furman, "Customs," 45–47.

38. Asbury, *Fire Laddies*, 164.

39. Asbury, *Fire Laddies*, 170.

40. Many years ago Richard Dorson identified Mose as an important figure in the history of American folklore and popular drama. See *American Folklore* (Chicago, 1959), 68–69, and "Mose the Far-Famed and World-Renowned," *American Literature* XV (1943), 288–300. In these years — 1847 to 1849 — a play was performed in New York called "The Confidence Man," which was apparently filled with the joke-playing spirit of the New York B'hoys.

41. There are several books on Adah Menken. The best original source is the sketch of her appended to an edition of her poems edited by Edwin James, her secretary and publicist: *Biography of Adah Isaacs Menken* (New York, 1881). I have drawn on a recent and helpful biographical sketch by Thurman Wilkins in E. T. James, ed., *Notable American Women, 1607–1950*, volume II (Cambridge, Mass., 1971). Constance Rourke devoted attention to her in *Troupers of the Gold Coast* (New York, 1928).

42. *Notable American Women*, II, "Adah Isaacs Menken."

43. Edwin James, *Biography of Adah Menken*, 11.

44. Constance Rourke quotes her as saying: "No, I never lived with Sam Houston; it was General Jackson and Methuselah and other big men." Rourke, *Troupers of the Gold Coast*, 175.

45. Adah Menken, "Swimming Against the Current," *Golden Era*, Nov. 1863. All the quotations in this section are taken from this article. Adah Menken also wrote an interesting piece on women: "Women of the World," *New York Sunday Mercury*, Oct. 7, 1860.

46. Walt Whitman, "Song of Myself," *Leaves of Grass,* ed. S. Bradley and H. Blodgett (New York, 1973), 84–86.
47. Ralph Waldo Emerson, *Selections from Ralph Waldo Emerson,* ed. S. Whicher (Cambridge, Mass., 1960), 164.

9. Hiram Woodruff: Wait and Win (*pages 237–264*)

1. Hiram Woodruff, *The Trotting Horse of America; How to Train and Drive Him; with Reminiscences of the Trotting Turf,* ed. Charles J. Foster, with a biographical sketch of Woodruff by George Wilkes (Philadelphia, 1868). Throughout this chapter I have used my own copy of this book — the nineteenth edition, dated 1874, which gives some idea of its popularity. Along with Woodruff's book, Frank Forester's *Horses and Horsemanship,* referred to in chapter 4, is also a primary source. I have also found much in the *Spirit of the Times.* Fortunately, there is an excellent recent history of harness racing that is witty and perceptive: Dwight Akers, *Drivers Up! The Story of American Harness Racing* (New York, 1938; 2d ed., 1947). Akers is especially good on the period after Woodruff's death. See also: Jack D. Rittenhouse, *American Horse-Drawn Vehicles* (New York, 1948).
   A brief note on the two men who contributed to Woodruff's book. Charles James Foster, 1820–1883, was born in England, came to the U.S. in 1848, and wrote for *Porter's Spirit of the Times,* which he edited between 1860 and 1874 with intelligence and fair-mindedness, carrying on the Porter tradition of sports journalism. George Wilkes, 1817–1885, was a gamesman of a different sort. He was early on a writer for various underground sporting and political journals, served a term in jail for libel, and is most important for starting the *National Police Gazette* in 1845. He later gained control of the *Spirit,* which he continued as *Wilkes's Spirit of the Times.* Whatever one's judgment of him, he is one of the two or three most important and interesting figures in the history of American sporting journalism.
2. Hiram Woodruff, *The Trotting Horse of America,* xxv.
3. Woodruff, *The Trotting Horse,* xxxv.
4. Akers, *Drivers Up!,* 23.
5. Frank Forester as quoted in Akers, *Drivers Up!,* 41.
6. *Spirit of the Times* quoted in Akers, *Drivers Up!,* 62.
7. Woodruff, *The Trotting Horse,* vii, 128, 177.
8. Woodruff, *The Trotting Horse,* 42.
9. Woodruff, *The Trotting Horse,* xxx.
10. Woodruff, *The Trotting Horse,* 321. On dishonesty see also Akers, *Drivers Up!,* chapter 11, "Sharps and Flats."
11. Woodruff, *The Trotting Horse,* 296–302.
12. Woodruff, *The Trotting Horse,* 300.
13. Woodruff, *The Trotting Horse,* 288, 291.
14. N. P. Willis as quoted in Akers, *Drivers Up!,* 66.
15. Woodruff, *The Trotting Horse,* 165.
16. Woodruff, *The Trotting Horse,* 47.
17. Woodruff, *The Trotting Horse,* 167.

18. Woodruff, *The Trotting Horse,* 168, 169.
19. Woodruff, *The Trotting Horse,* 177.
20. Woodruff, *The Trotting Horse,* 46.
21. There are a considerable number of books on Currier & Ives, of which the most useful to me were: Harry T. Peters, *Currier and Ives: Printmakers to the American People* (New York, 1942) (Mr. Peters had a very large personal collection of Currier & Ives prints and published a full catalogue of them); Russell Crouse, *Mr. Currier and Mr. Ives* (New York, 1930); W. S. Hall, *The Spirit of America* (London, 1930); and the very beautiful *Currier and Ives' America,* ed. Colin Simkin (New York, 1952), based on plates owned by the Travelers Insurance Companies.
22. Whittier has begun to get more serious critical attention. See G. W. Arms, *The Fields Were Green: A New View of Bryant, Whittier, Holmes, Lowell and Longfellow* (Stanford, 1953); Edward Wagenknecht, *John Greenleaf Whittier* (New York, 1967); and J. B. Pickard, ed., *The Letters of John Greenleaf Whittier,* 3 vols. (Cambridge, Mass., 1975).
23. Woodruff, *The Trotting Horse,* 186.
24. Woodruff, *The Trotting Horse,* 186.
25. Woodruff, *The Trotting Horse,* xxvii.
26. Woodruff, *The Trotting Horse,* xxxv.

10. P. T. Barnum: Games and Hoaxing (*pages 267–289*)

1. P. T. Barnum, *Struggles and Triumphs, or Sixty Years' Recollections* (Buffalo, 1889), 23. Barnum has always interested biographers. There are a number of good books about him, as well as essays and chapters of books, to all of which I am much indebted. Most interesting of all is his autobiography, which, for all its polymorphous ambiguity, is the place to begin. Throughout this chapter I have used the edition noted above. M. R. Werner, *P. T. Barnum* (New York, 1923) is detailed and dependable. Constance Rourke has a chapter on Barnum in *Trumpets of Jubilee* (New York, 1927), as does Gamaliel Bradford in *Damaged Souls* (Boston, 1923). See also Charles J. Finger, *Life of Barnum* (New York, 1924); Harvey W. Root, *The Unknown Barnum* (New York, 1928); and Irving Wallace, *Fabulous Showman* (New York, 1959). Neil Harris's recent and perceptive *Humbug: The Art of P. T. Barnum* (Boston, 1973) is primarily a study of Barnum's contribution to popular American culture, not a biography. His evaluation of Barnum is different from mine in several important respects.
2. P. T. Barnum, *Struggles and Triumphs,* 20.
3. Barnum, *Struggles and Triumphs,* 20.
4. Frederick Marryat, *A Diary in America* (1839), ed. S. Jackman (New York, 1962), 6.
5. M. R. Werner, *Barnum,* 8.
6. Barnum, *Struggles and Triumphs,* 37.
7. Richardson Wright, *American Wags and Eccentrics* (New York, 1940), 79–81. James Russell Lowell's reminiscences are in his essay "Cambridge Thirty Years Ago," 61–63. Neil Harris's *The Artist in America,*

the Formative Years, 1790–1860 (New York, 1966), is an indispensable book. Also see Calvin Tomkins, *Merchants and Masterpieces: The Story of the Metropolitan Museum of Art* (New York, 1970).

8. Barnum, *Struggles and Triumphs,* 52.
9. *Spirit of the Times,* Dec. 16, 1848.
10. Barnum, *Struggles and Triumphs,* 185.
11. William Macready, *The Diaries of William Charles Macready, 1833–1851,* 2 vols., ed. William Toynbee (London, 1912), II, 245–247. As a small boy, Henry James remembered "gaping at the old rickety billboard in Fifth Avenue . . . sharply aware as ever of the main source of its spell, the fact that it most often blazed with the rich appeal of Mr. Barnum, whose 'lecture room,' attached to the Great American Museum overflowed into posters of all the theatrical bravery disavowed by its title." Henry James, *A Small Boy and Others* (New York, 1913), 154.
12. Richard Dorson, "The Yankee on the Stage — a Folk Hero of American Drama," *New England Quarterly* XIII (1940), 196–203.
13. J. Frank Kernan, *Reminiscences of the Old Fire Laddies,* 196–203.
14. Barnum, *Struggles and Triumphs,* 37.
15. *Spirit of the Times,* Dec. 12, 1846.
16. Alexis de Tocqueville, *Democracy in America,* volume II, 119–120.
17. James Parton noted this when he went to Salisbury, North Carolina, to trace Jackson's youth. Parton, *The Life of Andrew Jackson,* 3 vols. (New York, 1860), I, 102–109.
18. Bessie Pierce, *As Others See Chicago* (Chicago, 1933); John T. Farris, *The Romance of Forgotten Towns* (New York, 1924); William Herndon, *Abraham Lincoln* (New York, 1893). Another aspect is the preoccupation with size: "Our worthy citizens have a perfect mania for gigantic performances, musical festivals, monster concerts and that sort of thing, and the success of an entertainment depends more upon the size and wording of a bill than in the intrinsic merit of the performers." *Spirit of the Times,* Feb. 10, 1849.
19. Barnum, *Struggles and Triumphs,* 179.
20. Barnum, *Struggles and Triumphs,* 103, 111, 213.
21. Werner, *Barnum,* 148.
22. Werner, *Barnum,* 130–131.
23. Barnum, *Struggles and Triumphs,* 100.
24. Barnum, *Struggles and Triumphs,* 113–114, 120–121, 127–128.
25. Barnum, *Struggles and Triumphs,* 113.
26. D. H. Lawrence, *Studies in Classic American Literature,* 4.
27. Barnum, *Struggles and Triumphs,* 61.
28. Barnum, *Struggles and Triumphs,* 64.
29. Barnum, *Struggles and Triumphs,* 65.
30. *Dictionary of American Biography,* I, "P. T. Barnum."
31. Frank Walker, *The Man Verdi* (New York, 1962), 267.
32. Domingo Sarmiento, *Sarmiento's Travels in the United States in 1847,* introduced by M. A. Rockland (Princeton, 1970), 22.
33. Richard Dorson, *American Folklore* (Chicago, 1959), 66. Another story told by Hill makes the same general point. His theater company played in Stafford, New York, and was the first group of actors ever to play

there. The theater was a converted ballroom, and the audience sat as in a church, men on one side, women on the other. Hill realized that "the solemn behavior of the audience was in obedience to their conventional notions of public conduct, instead of the want of comic merit in his efforts." See W. K. Northall, *The Life and Recollections of the Late Yankee Hill: Together with Anecdotes and Incidents of His Travels* (New York, 1850), 13–15.

34. Hesketh Pearson, *Oscar Wilde, His Life and Wit* (New York, 1946), 53.
35. Barnum, *Struggles and Triumphs*, 114.
36. Philip Hone, *The Diary of Philip Hone, 1828–1851*, 2 vols., ed. Allan Nevins (New York, 1927), I, 222.
37. Constance Rourke, *Trumpets of Jubilee* (New York, 1927), 300.
38. Alexis de Tocqueville, *Democracy in America*, II, 120.
39. Barnum, *Struggles and Triumphs,* 111.

11. R. C. Schenck: From Draw Poker to the Twentieth Century
(*pages 291–311*)

1. There are scattered sources of information on the life of Robert Schenck. The *Dictionary of American Biography,* VIII, contains the basic information. Beckles Willson, *America's Ambassadors to England (1785–1928), a Narrative of Anglo-American Diplomatic Relations* (London, 1928) is informative about his service in London. Also see his obituary, *New York Times,* Mar. 24, 1890.
2. There is a study of the scandal: L. E. Chittenden, *The Emma Mine* (New York, 1876), goes into great detail. This pamphlet was based on testimony presented to the U.S. Senate Committee on Foreign Affairs.
3. Robert C. Schenck, *Draw: Rules for Playing Poker* (Brooklyn, 1880), i–ii.
4. George H. Devol, *Forty Years a Gambler on the Mississippi,* 2d ed. (New York, 1892) is a fascinating work. Herbert Asbury, *Sucker's Progress: An Informal History of Gambling in America from the Colonies to Canfield* (New York, 1938), 20–39, is very useful. Also very helpful is David Spanier, *Total Poker* (New York, 1977).
5. Asbury, *Sucker's Progress,* 23. References to poker as still being unfamiliar are found in the *Spirit of the Times* for Oct. 15, 1846, and Mar. 6, 1847.
6. Asbury, *Sucker's Progress,* 36.
7. Schenck, *Draw,* 5–17.
8. Charles Francis Adams, Jr., *Autobiography, 1835–1915* (New York, paperback edition, 1968), 34.
9. Lincoln Steffens, *The Autobiography of Lincoln Steffens,* 2 vols. (New York, 1931), I, 237.
10. "The greater part of the sharp practices and seemingly 'unsportsmanlike' plays [in baseball] really are the result of weaknesses in the rules and the refusal of the players to handicap the smart and speedy players down to the level of the mediocre brains and bodies . . . One may regret that the morality of the game is not higher — but if, for in-

stance, the ethics of cricket prevailed in baseball, the game would lose much." Hugh Fullerton, "The Right and Wrong of Baseball," *The American Magazine,* Oct. 1911, 724–732.
11. Marianne Moore, "Tom Fool at Jamaica."

Index